W9-BLP-598

Please remember that this is a library book,
and that it belongs only temporarily to each
person who uses it. Be considerate. Do
not write in this, or any, library book.

The Literature *of Adult* Education

WITHDRAWN

WITHDRAWN

WITHDRAWN

CYRIL O. HOULE

159706
VC Grad

The Literature of Adult Education

A Bibliographic Essay

Jossey-Bass Publishers • San Francisco

Copyright © 1992 by Jossey-Bass Inc., Publishers, 350 Sansome Street, San Francisco, California 94104. Copyright under International, Pan American, and Universal Copyright Conventions. All rights reserved. No part of this book may be reproduced in any form—except for brief quotation (not to exceed 1,000 words) in a review or professional work—without permission in writing from the publishers.

For sales outside the United States, contact Maxwell Macmillan International Publishing Group, 866 Third Avenue, New York, New York 10022.

Manufactured in the United States of America

The paper used in this book is acid-free and meets the State of California requirements for recycled paper (50 percent recycled waste, including 10 percent postconsumer waste), which are the strictest guidelines for recycled paper currently in use in the United States.

Library of Congress Cataloging-in-Publication Data

Houle, Cyril O., date.
    The literature of adult education : a bibliographic essay / Cyril O. Houle.
        p.   cm.—(The Jossey-Bass higher and adult education series)
    Includes bibliographical references and indexes.
    ISBN 1-55542-470-8
    1. Adult education—United States—Bibliography.   I. Title
II. Series.
Z5814.A24H68   1992
[LC5251]
016.374′973—dc20   92-12659
                                                                    CIP

FIRST EDITION
HB Printing   10 9 8 7 6 5 4 3 2 1   *Code 9267*

The Jossey-Bass
Higher and Adult Education Series

Consulting Editor
Adult and Continuing Education

Alan B. Knox
University of Wisconsin, Madison

Contents

Preface

When I first began to examine the literature on Adult Education expertly recommended to me I had much the same feeling of suffocating helplessness which a parachutist may experience when he has dropped from the skies above and landed in an impenetrable jungle. . . . It is all so truly a jungle that there are venomous snakes in it as well as birds of paradise.

—*James Truslow Adams, 1944, pp. 128-130*

If adult education is to achieve full stature in the service of human-kind, it must, like every other advanced practical field, base its art upon science. The accomplishments of a teacher, mentor, or facilitator result from interactions with learners, each educational program being adapted to the distinctive circumstances in which it is undertaken. But a substantial body of disciplined knowledge is now available in the literature for those who want to strengthen the skills gained from experience. Some of this knowledge is immediately useful to anyone who undertakes such tasks as teaching literacy classes, running residential conferences, or counseling troubled men and women. Some has relevance to such career roles as county agricultural agent, museum curator, or librarian. Some is related to the work of such institutions as community colleges, industrial or governmental human resource development programs, or churches. Some centers on such themes as continuing professional education, community development, or high school equivalency studies. Some focuses on lines of research followed by scholars. No matter what specific tasks a worker may undertake, he or she is very likely to find valuable help somewhere in the literature.

The growth of specialized bodies of knowledge can, of course, lead to fragmentation and keep workers from an awareness of adult education as a whole, thereby restricting their practice or the advancement of their careers. In such circumstances, the parallels between various kinds of practice and the synthesizing conceptions of the field disappear; as Yeats famously said, "Things fall apart; the centre cannot hold." Fortunately, however, those who want to profit from a broad understanding of the field or to learn from other kinds of practice than their own have access to a rich literature on its history, its philosophy, its principles, and its fundamental processes of operation.

Background

Adult education first assumed a fully rounded form in the literature in 1919. Long before that time, institutions designed to provide enlightenment for men and women had been established, and the term *adult education* had occasionally been used, though only to describe limited endeavors. For example, Hudson's *The History of Adult Education,* first published in 1851, is concerned almost entirely with the work of institutes set up in the early part of the nineteenth century to train young working men. In the late nineteenth and early twentieth centuries, so many programs aiming to educate men and women had been created in so many countries that a sense of shared identity began to grow among their sponsors or operators. At the turn of the century, Herbert Baxter Adams (1901) described a number of ventures but did not make explicit what they had in common. Almost two decades later, at the end of World War I, a committee of distinguished British leaders sought to understand that mutual interest and its manifestations. The powerful document that resulted is usually referred to as the *1919 report* because of its year of publication. It will be mentioned many times in the pages to come.

The sense of community identified or symbolized in that great document defines what is here called the "field" of adult education. This community includes all people who share the aware-

ness that the countless efforts of men and women to develop their
potentialities through learning have an essential similarity. Some
people feel that awareness profoundly; it may even be a fundamental component of their lives. Others hold the belief less strongly. By
small gradations, they are less and less involved until finally they
merge into the general population. The ideas on which the sense
of community are based are seriously discussed in what has now
become a vast literature. In 1980, Giere and Maehira tried to find
out how many people considered themselves to be writers on lifelong learning. Inquiries were sent to 750 persons identified by the
Unesco Institute of Education in Hamburg; 387 affirmative responses were received from persons in 47 countries. The distribution of authors by region was Europe, 201; North and South
America, 110; Asia, 44; Africa, 15; and Australia and Oceania, 17.

Organization and Scope of the Book

This book explores the nature and dimensions of the literature that
these and other authors have produced. The word *literature* sometimes carries a connotation of quality but is used here merely to
signify a body of writings. The references consist of an alphabetical
listing of 1,241 books. As noted at the beginning of that list, a
modest effort has been made to indicate the relative recognition that
the works have received. The three parts of *The Literature of Adult
Education* describe as succinctly as possible each author's purpose
and accomplishment. My opinions about the excellent qualities of
some books may be deduced from their description or placement,
but no attempt is made to provide a balanced assessment of their
successes or failures. I have tried to be objective about all works
mentioned, including those for which I have little respect. Each
book is placed where it seems to fit best within the overall framework, which was not imposed as part of a logical system or theory
but which evolved from consideration of the books themselves. It
represents my effort to portray the nature of the literature as it has
developed to the present time.

The quest for patterns has influenced the way in which this
book was prepared. Comprehensive bibliographies can best be compiled by teams of collaborators, beginning with systematic reference

searches and following or elaborating already-established categories and descriptors. But mine was a process of exploration, an effort to discern inductively a pattern in the literature. I have been steadily reading and rereading books about adult education since 1934, so I did not come fresh to the work of preparing this bibliography when I began it in 1978. Since then, I have read or scanned every work included here. To avoid too heavy a reliance on previous categorizations, it seemed best to go at random to the books themselves, annotating each one as I considered it. During most of the fifteen years spent at this task, I lived in cities with no research libraries; and because of other commitments, data gathering for *The Literature of Adult Education* could seldom be my primary occupation. The annotations had to be compiled in interstitial time, as access was available to university, governmental, public, and personal libraries in the United States and England; I also made substantial use of interlibrary loan arrangements, particularly those of the University of Chicago.

The final list of works included does not fully represent the literature of adult education for several reasons. (1) There was space and time to include only books, though that category includes both compendious volumes and slim monographs. Journal articles, pamphlets, chapters from symposia, and other, similar writings abound. The decision to exclude all nonbooks (except for a few special cases) was a wrenching one, since many are valuable and often point to new directions of scholarly inquiry. Their inclusion would have resulted in an unwieldy volume, though, or required a process of selection beyond my capacity to undertake. (2) Works were included only when their authors intended to make a contribution to the literature of adult education or of one of its component institutions or concerns. The field has benefited greatly from books prepared with other themes in mind, and every previous general bibliography has included some of them. Nevertheless, the number of possible sources seems infinite, and it is hard to know how to choose among them. It was not difficult in most cases to determine from internal evidence that an author was directly concerned with adult learning, but occasionally an arbitrary decision had to be made. (3) The limitations of time and linguistic ability restricted this listing to works available in English. (4) A few works seemed too esoteric, insubstantial, or ephemeral to include. (5) Some books could not be located, and others probably escaped notice because their real nature was hidden behind unfamiliar terms or formats. Books on adult education are included in many of the classifications and subclassifications used in comprehensive or specialized libraries; they can be found only by one who knows all the required terminologies and is prepared to search—often to crawl— along the shelves in many parts of the stacks, invade collections set up for special purposes, and learn how to use unfamiliar information-retrieval systems. The random approaches of the early years of my inquiry were gradually replaced by more systematic searches for as-yet-unexamined works, and as many of them as possible were tracked down. However, at press time, a number of items still could not be located.

The problem of inclusion was complicated at every point by the bewilderingly large number of books on adult education. Those who use its many descriptors to consult specialized data bases are flooded with references. For example, more than fourteen thousand items on adult education were added to the ERIC data base between 1966 and 1991. They are all in the public domain and do not include references protected by copyright, which are also legion. Even nonspecialized sources will furnish formidable lists of items. For example, one general university library consulted in 1990 recorded fifty-four entries by and about Paulo Freire. In the same library, patient education (a subspecialty of health education) was the subject of thirty-four entries, one of them a 1980 bibliography with 330 closely printed pages. These relatively specific topics suggest how huge the total literature has become. My task was to achieve breadth and comprehensiveness, to try to include all aspects of the field but not to plumb the depths of the more widely discussed ones. Some eminently qualified works have almost certainly escaped my attention. I shall appreciate hearing from readers who wish to nominate books for inclusion in any subsequent edition of this work.

As the books were read and annotated over the years, the need to put them in meaningful order created a constantly shifting pattern whose current version appears in this book. But beyond classification is interpretation. It seemed important to give meaning and sequence to what otherwise would have been only lists of related items. Thus, introductory, transitional, and summative materials were added to knit the items together and present them to the reader in what is properly seen not as a definitive work but as an essay—an early effort to define, describe, and interpret a meaningful whole. Insofar as *The Literature of Adult Education* is a bibliography, I hope it will achieve all the purposes common to such works, from the satisfaction of immediate reference needs to the initiation and support of lines of inquiry. But I also hope that its essay format will cause it to be a bibliography that is read.

Overview of the Contents

Part One includes four chapters that deal with the emergence and growth of the field of adult education as a whole: its history, its general description and analysis, the chief concerns of its leaders, and the nature of adult learners.

Chapter One identifies books that deal with the history of the field itself and of its precursor institutions.

Chapter Two includes works in which single authors, teams of authors, groups of essayists, or other constellations of writers examine adult education as a whole. The specific topics mentioned in later chapters are all touched on here.

Chapter Three focuses on the concerns of people who either provide or study the provision of adult education, those known (for want of a better term) as adult educators. What are the philosophical underpinnings of the field? How are its leaders trained? How are its results evaluated? How can it be shaped into an academic field? The exploration of these and other questions has created the bodies of writing identified in this chapter.

Chapter Four is concerned with the nature of adult learners. Who are they? How able are they? What are their needs and desires? Where are they located, both geographically and on various social scales? Why do they learn?

Part Two includes five chapters about the providers and goals of adult education. Chapter Five considers the institutions—schools, colleges and universities, and community colleges—first created for the formal schooling of children and youth; those institutions' assumption of the role of educating mature people has often not been easy. Chapter Six includes institutions created for lifelong learning, most of them long before the clarification of that concept in modern times. Among them are public libraries, museums, and the Cooperative Extension Service. Chapter Seven is given over to discussion of institutions and programs intended from the start to serve an adult clientele. Some are separate and autonomous, such as independent and proprietary schools, voluntary associations, and programs operated by government. Others are special services undertaken by institutions with other dominant functions, including labor unions, health care institutions, prisons, and the armed services. Chapters Eight and Nine examine the purposes that have given emphasis and weight to the field and define such significant sectors of service as adult basic education, continuing professional education, human resource development, and sensitivity training to foster human interaction.

Part Three treats the practice of adult education. Chapter Ten is concerned with broad approaches to program design and its component parts, while Chapter Eleven examines the major formats and settings in which learning occurs. The analytical part of the book concludes with a brief summation, which broadly assesses the current state of the literature.

Usually each book is cited by author and date in the place where its topic fits best, but some works have pertinence to two or more sections and therefore have multiple citations. (Sources not part of the literature of adult education are identified separately, as are some citations for the epigraphs.) Since much interweaving of themes exists, a topic that has a sharp focus in one section may also emerge directly or indirectly in others. To give but one example, leadership training is the direct concern of Chapter Three; however, it is also present or implicit in each sponsoring institution, is required for the pursuit of every goal, is part of the art of program design, and is considered in some fashion in virtually every general work in Chapter Two. That such interrelationships are to be found so frequently seems the surest evidence that adult education is indeed a field, not merely an assemblage of somewhat similar activities.

Acknowledgments

My greatest debt is to the W. K. Kellogg Foundation for encouraging me to develop and write the book. Russell G. Mawby and Norman A. Brown showed particular interest in it at all stages. The tedious task of typing various versions was coordinated by Pamela D. Hurley and carried out splendidly by Deborah J. Miller and her colleagues at the foundation's Information Processing Center.

Jane Faux Ratner somehow found time in her busy life to provide invaluable help on bibliographical and editorial matters.

Throughout the later stages of the manuscript's development, Alan B. Knox, consulting editor for Jossey-Bass, provided help and encouragement. When the references were about 90 percent complete, he and three consultants commissioned by Jossey-Bass examined them to see what additional books they could recommend for inclusion. The people asked to help in this undertaking were Jerold W. Apps of the University of Wisconsin, Sharan Merriam of the University of Georgia, and Thomas J. Sork of the University of British Columbia. Their selections were helpful in rounding out the bibliography. Three persons unknown to me were also commissioned by Jossey-Bass to read and comment on the manuscript; they will recognize the responses made to their profuse suggestions. As always, the editorial staff at Jossey-Bass has been exacting and helpful throughout the editorial process. I first gained a sense of the ultimate reality of the book during discussions long ago with Lynn Luckow of Jossey-Bass.

I am grateful to everyone named and to other people who helped locate books and take care of many other necessary tasks.

August 1992   Cyril O. Houle
                                                          Professor emeritus,
                                                       University of Chicago

                                                    Senior program consultant,
                                                       W. K. Kellogg Foundation

The Author

Cyril O. Houle is senior program consultant at the W. K. Kellogg Foundation and professor emeritus of education at the University of Chicago. He received his B.A. and M.A. degrees (both in 1934) from the University of Florida and his Ph.D. degree (1940) from the University of Chicago; all three degrees were in education. He holds honorary doctorates from Rutgers University, Florida State University, Syracuse University, DePaul University, New York University, Roosevelt University, Suffolk University, the State University of New York, Northern Illinois University, and the University of Wisconsin, Milwaukee.

From 1939 to 1978, Houle was at the University of Chicago. There he served on the faculty and also in numerous other capacities, notably as dean of University College, the university's extension division. During his time at the University of Chicago, he was engaged in research and teaching at the graduate level in the fields of adult and higher education. From 1938 onward, he had occasional contacts with the W. K. Kellogg Foundation; in 1976, his association with it became his central interest. He has also been a visiting faculty member at other universities, including the University of California, Berkeley; Leeds University; the University of Washington; the University of Wisconsin, Milwaukee; and Oxford University. He has been heavily engaged in community service at all levels of government and has worked in thirty-five foreign countries. His many honors and awards include the Tolley medal and membership in the National Academy of Education.

Houle has been contributing to the literature of adult education since the mid 1930s and has published books in every decade from that one to the present. He is also a specialist on the operation of nonprofit and governmental boards and has written a book on the subject, *Governing Boards* (1989).

The Literature of Adult Education

PART ONE

Emergence and Growth
of the Field
and the Literature

For a hundred and fifty years—some would say longer—books have been written about adult education. Now, near the end of the twentieth century, many new ones are produced each year. The first part of this bibliographic essay includes works that examine the field as a whole. The history of adult education is considered in Chapter One, and a general description of the field is included in Chapter Two. As the number of people involved in organized adult learning has greatly increased, two other clusters of the comprehensive literature have emerged. One centers on the ideas of the people who plan, provide, direct, and study educational activities; Chapter Three identifies works dealing with their underlying concerns about the essential characteristics of the field. The other cluster has to do with adult learners; Chapter Four identifies works dealing with their nature and needs.

ONE

The History
of Adult Education

The life of adult education evaporates from even the most competent record and leaves behind it only a powder of dates, names and events. . . . Which of us will ever forget, which of us could ever get into cold print, the anxieties, the hopes, the surprises, the triumphs, the frustrations, the companionship both anxious and hopeful of those long war years, when we hardly ever stopped working, when the always inexhaustible human interest of adult educational work reached out into altogether new areas of oddity and inspiration?

—*Ross D. Waller in Kelly, 1950, p. 91*

The broad outline of the history of adult education in English-speaking countries is fairly well accepted. Three periods can be discerned: the eighteenth, nineteenth, and early twentieth centuries, when precursor institutions flourished; the mid-twentieth century, when the field of adult education itself was established; and the later twentieth century, when that field came to be seen in the perspective of life-span learning, a conception not even yet viewed in its full scope and complexity. In this chapter, the general histories of the field will first be considered. Attention will then be focused on each of the three periods.

General Histories

The most substantial and fully realized history of adult education, centering on Great Britain, is provided by Kelly (1970). Taking up his theme in medieval times and carrying it forward to the present, Kelly deals with the various aspirations and motives for adult learning and the ways they found expression in both personal endeavors and organized forms of instruction. This second edition of his work has the advantage of including older sources newly come to light and of bringing the author's account through the major changes that occurred in the period immediately after World War II, a crucial time in the development of organized adult education. By using a broad definition of his subject, Kelly is able to describe many activities not often considered an integral part of the field.

Two English works cover much of the span of the social history of adult education in that country. Dobbs (1919) presents a pioneering study of how working men educated themselves during the period from 1700 to 1950. Special attention is given to mechanics' institutes, to public libraries, and to *education by collision*—the author's term for the enlightenment that comes from the debates and clashes of opinion inherent in a democratic society. Harrison (1961) provides a richly textured social history of adult education as it arose from the beliefs expressed in British life from 1790 to 1860. The author agrees with G. M. Young that "the essential matter of history is not so much what happened as what people felt about it as it was happening" (pp. xi-xii). Harrison is intimately familiar with the ideas and institutions of modern adult education in all their range and depth; when he looks to the past, he can trace the beginnings of organizations and movements, identify those that once flourished but no longer exist, and show the swelling growth of the field while still putting it in the context of each period of development.

The histories of American adult education are not so comprehensive as those of Great Britain. Adams's book (1944) shows how a distinguished modern American historian looks at the full sweep of adult education and how its major institutions emerged from the actions and thoughts of American society; however, the book is not itself a history. Grattan (1955) describes his work as a modest essay, but it has had a substantial impact on later writings. It begins with a consideration of early European cultures and continues with a description of British and American programs until the middle of the twentieth century. Knowles (1977) presents the most comprehensive history of adult education in the United States. His book is centrally concerned with the growth of adult education as a movement in which many goals, institutions, and programs are flowing together and will gradually mesh into a diverse but harmoniously synthesized accord. This second edition also highlights the changes that occurred after the book's first publication in 1962.

Several other works, though broad in scope, have a general historical orientation. Adler and Mayer (1958) examine the grand course of education from early Greek times to the present to make the case for a lifetime of learning. Goldman (1975) explores the Jewish tradition of lifelong study of religion; the book illustrates, with many quotations, how profoundly based the modern study of adult education can be. Ulich (1965) includes four essays describing the history of adult education in Denmark, England, Germany, and the United States.

Institutional Precursors of the Field

In the last half of the nineteenth century, an increasing number of institutions for the education of adults began to appear in both the United States and Great Britain. Many of these were fueled by a sense of social injustice and, particularly, by the desire to improve the quality of life of young working people, especially men. But learning opportunities were also created for and eagerly patronized by the middle class, which flocked to lecture series, created discussion groups, and read systematically and purposefully. Some of the institutions that would later become basic components of adult education were developed at this time—among them public libraries, museums, evening schools, and university extension. The histories of such ventures will be described later when each is considered separately. Some institutions crucial to the development of the field have disappeared or moved into new phases of existence; the major books describing them will be identified here.

The Adult School Movement

The adult schools were English institutions created by local churches, often those of the Quaker faith, to provide education in the Bible, religious principles, and literacy. The first such school opened in Nottingham in 1789. In 1814, Thomas Pole wrote an account of these schools that was reissued in facsimile in 1967. In an editorial introduction to this modern edition, Coolie Verner called Pole's work the first book on adult education ever published and offered an interpretive essay that outlines its relevance to a modern reader.

Three later books complete the history of the adult school movement to the present time. Rowntree and Binns (1903) describe these institutions from their earliest days until the start of the twentieth century, when they had thirty thousand members—their largest enrollment ever. Martin (1924) provides a full-scale, serious, and well-illustrated treatment of the adult school movement: history, goals, scope, and accomplishments. He concludes with a sober account of the possible future courses of development that the movement might take. Hall (1985) begins where Rowntree and Binns leave off, though he includes some retrospective information on the nineteenth-century movement. He makes clear that though the original pattern of instruction was a Sunday morning class, later programming broadened to include full-scale instructional centers, short-term residential programs, tours, publications, and many other forms of educational endeavor. The number of schools reached its maximum (1,955) in 1914, and the enrollment (113,789) peaked in 1910. By 1970, the number of schools had dropped to 234, and the membership had declined to 3,260. Hall's book ends on a decidedly elegiac note.

Mechanics' Institutes

The mechanics' institutes, designed to offer basic education and vocational skills to young workmen, flourished in Great Britain and the United States during the first three-quarters of the nineteenth century. Godard (1884) presents a biography of the founder of these institutes, George Birkbeck (1776–1841), who was a physician and lecturer on science. When the workmen who made scientific instruments under his direction showed keen interest in their nature and usage, he perceived the need for a kind of popular education not then available. At that time, there was widespread hostility to the idea that working-class people could learn or that it would be advisable to help them do so, as they could only pick up a smattering of information. Throughout Birkbeck's later life, he served as a sponsor of both these institutes and other adult educational ventures, either alone or with such leading intellectuals as Lord Brougham, Francis Place, and Jeremy Bentham. More than a true biography, Godard's work is a celebration of Birkbeck and of the institutions that he inspired. Kelly (1957) fills this gap by offering not only a full account of the life of Birkbeck, but also a description of the international movement developed from his efforts. In 1852, a prize was offered in England for the best essay on the history and management of mechanics' institutes. It was won by Hole (1853), whose book was republished in 1970. The work, an important source for those seriously interested in early adult education, is sufficiently anecdotal and lively to hold a modern reader's attention.

Hudson's *History of Adult Education* (1969), first published in 1851, is also chiefly devoted to the mechanics' institutes, though he includes other, similar enterprises. His focus is on the work in Great Britain, but he gives brief notes on educational efforts elsewhere, including the United States and India. By *adult education,* a term he was apparently the first to use, Hudson means the organized and institutional provision of learning opportunities, principally for "the lower classes of the community" (p. v). He complains, however, that such endeavors are almost always invaded by the middle class (an observation not uncommon in the history of educational institutions). Meanwhile, Hudson is all but overcome by the wonderful condescension of the upper classes in aiding the lower ones: "The beloved sovereign of these realms lends her fair and royal name" to worthy causes, and "the lawned Divine and the ermined Duke feel a pleasure in presiding over the festivals of the artizan and the day labourer. The press, the civic magistrates, the agriculturist, and the manufacturer all share in the benign impulse." As a whole, he saw this period as "the age of philanthropy and good-will to all men" (p. v). Maurice (1855) presents a series of six ponderous Victorian essays on the nature of adult education, particularly as it contrasts with the schooling of children. These lectures were delivered at the London Working Men's College, an organization sponsored by John Ruskin and other notables.

Lyceums

In 1864, Henry Barnard, major architect of the American educational system, indicated the circumstances out of which the lyceum emerged:

> The first quarter of the present century was marked by a constantly increasing energy in the working of the leaven of educational improvement. Toward the end of that period and during the succeeding decade the ferment wrought so actively as to generate a numerous, heterogeneous brood of systems, plans and institutions—many crude and rudely organized; many that never reached an organization; many that did their work quickly and well; few that have survived to the present time. Of all these, whether under the names of school systems (infant, free, monitorial, manual labor, agricultural, etc.) or of mechanics' institutes, lyceums, societies for the diffusion of useful knowledge, mercantile associations, teachers' seminaries, school agents' societies, library associations, book clubs, reading associations, educational journals, etc., none created so immediate and general interest, or excited for a time an influence so great or beneficent, as the American Lyceum.[1]

This movement (named for the grove where Aristotle taught) was created in New England in 1826 and spread rapidly throughout the country. Though Josiah Holbrook, its founder, envisioned the units as entirely local lecture and discussion groups, they soon began to form federations and came together in the American Lyceum in 1830. Hayes (1932) wrote the first major modern study of the

[1] Henry Barnard, "The American Lyceum." *American Journal of Education* (new series), Sept. 1864, no. 36, p. 535.

Lyceum, one that influenced all later ones. His monograph is a brief but clear and well-researched study of the origins and development of the movement, with particular attention to its contributions to the education of both children and adults.

Bode (1956) presents a scholarly but readable account of the lyceum. His narrative flow is swift and enlivened with many anecdotes and brief characterizations. The book is organized around the idea that the movement went through two phases. The first, which lasted until about 1846, was centered on local initiative and self-education. In the second, essentially completed by the time of the Civil War, the local lyceums became the bases of a national system of lecturers and other performers, who added inspiration, entertainment, and aesthetic experience to education. Throughout Bode's book, the lyceum is considered in light of its origins and its responses and contributions to the major currents of thought of the time. Noffsinger (1926) provides a somewhat sketchier account of the lyceums and relates them to the later traveling chautauquas.

The Chautauqua Institution

The Chautauqua Institution, founded in 1864 as a summer program to train Sunday school teachers, quickly expanded to become a major American organization. It was imitated nationally; it established a pattern for university extension, including scholarly publication; and it stimulated libraries, correspondence teaching, and local discussion groups. The institution still maintains a successful program at its encampment in upstate New York.

Providing an account by a founder of the Chautauqua Institution of its growth and development during the first ten years, Vincent (1886) reports an astonishing record of accomplishment. The book strongly expresses the spirit that suffused Chautauqua: a fervently religious and transcendental expression of an ideal of learning. Morrison (1974) presents a beautifully written, designed, and illustrated book, perhaps the best single volume on Chautauqua and its offshoots. Graceful and urbane in style, the book is based on primary sources and thus has scholarly roots. It also includes the fullest available bibliography on the subject.

Three other modern works also deal with Chautauqua. Hurlbut (1921) offers a richly illustrated chronicle with a roster of significant speakers and visitors. Like most other books on the subject, Richmond's clear and straightforward account (1943) stresses the golden age that occurred in the last quarter of the nineteenth century, when Chautauqua was an intellectual resource for the country's comfortable middle class. Gould (1972) encompasses the sweep of the whole "movement" but emphasizes the influence of the institution on the creation of other programs of adult learning, including the countless encampments throughout the country that borrowed the name of the original organization.

Traveling Chautauquas

The traveling Chautauquas, which took the name of the Chautauqua Institution but had no direct relationship with it, carried enlightenment and entertainment throughout the rural America of the latter nineteenth and early twentieth centuries. These programs varied, but a typical one unfolded like this: five auditorium-sized tents would be set up simultaneously in population centers close to one another. During the course of a week, lecturers, musical performers, plays, and other cultural "acts" would circulate among the towns; they would perform at matinee and evening shows at one place and then go on to the next. The following week, the cycle would start over again at another cluster of centers. Thus, entertainment and enlightenment were brought to the towns, villages, and countryside of America at a time before radio and television existed and when transportation was often tedious or harrowing.

The traveling chautauqua was a colorful part of the pageant of American life for half a century. It has not yet had a modern chronicler who could depict it as powerfully as Edna Ferber did the showboat in *Old Man River* or Meredith Willson did the roving entertainer in *Music Man*. But in its own day and afterward, popular accounts have been written by those who had worked on the "circuits," appearing day after day in the big tents. Case and Case (1948) offer a skillful and interesting account of what the traveling chautauqua was like and the experiences that it provided to its participants at various stages in its growth. The book points out that "during the peak year, 1924, an estimated 30,000,000 Americans sat in the brown tents pitched nearby some 12,000 Main Streets and enjoyed the lectures, music, drama, and other cultural items making up the typical Chautauqua week offering" (p. v). Scott (1939) provides a highly personal and entertaining account of the life of a performer from 1916 to the end of the era. MacLaren (1938) presents an evocative account of the various manifestations of Chautauqua, particularly the tent circuits and the independent ventures that existed alongside the original institution. The author was a performer at all three, and her brightly anecdotal account and pictures portray vividly the kind of life led by the "talent." As her title (*Morally We Roll Along*) suggests, she was mainly concerned with the spirit of religious uplift that pervaded the activities of Chautauqua and often led them to be referred to collectively as a crusade or movement. Horner (1954) describes the traveling circuits from the managerial side, the author having served in this capacity during the entire period of their existence.

Social Settlements

The fundamental idea of a social settlement, as first modeled by Toynbee Hall in London in the 1880s, was of a group of well-educated and socially sensitive men and women who lived together at a commodious house in the slums, trying to be of help to the poor people of the neighborhood. The first and most notable such institution in the United States was Hull-House, founded by Jane Addams in 1886 and described by her in 1910 and in many subsequent works. In her first major book, she records how a sense of outrage at the demeaning aspect of poverty led her to adapt the British model of the settlement to American life. Her aim was to study and ameliorate the living conditions of the poor by any means possible, but chiefly through adult education, which proved to be a key to the achievement of other goals. The ever-changing groups of people who came to live with her and her successors later emerged as key leaders in the reform of various aspects of American life. Miss Addams herself became a world celebrity, particularly after she won the Nobel Peace Prize. Another early pioneer in the movement was Graham Taylor, who created Chicago Commons in the slums of that city. Wade (1964) presents a full-scale account of his life and personality and gives particular attention to his contribution to the settlement-house movement.

Such centers grew in strength and influence during the early years of the twentieth century. In 1937, Hawkins focused on the adult educational activities that they carried out. At that time, the settlements had reached the full extent of their services, especially because of their influence during the Great Depression. Hawkins defines such an institution as "a privately supported agency that has as its operative base a particular neighborhood and that concerns itself with the social, economic, cultural, artistic, and intellectual interest of the restricted area and the community at large on which those interests impinge" (pp. xiv–xv). Hawkins recognizes that, in one sense, everything that the settlement house does is educational, both for the community and for the people who live in the house; she illustrates the depth and variety of such services. Most of her book, however, is devoted to activities that are directly and purposefully intended to be educative; she describes and analyzes typical illustrations of such services at a number of the country's leading settlements.

Danish Folk High Schools

The Danish folk high schools and others modeled on them have had a worldwide influence and produced an enormous literature in many languages. Throughout the twentieth century, people have visited Scandinavia and brought back to their home countries accounts of what they saw there. Livingstone (1944), for example, wrote a brief but powerful statement of the meaning of liberal education, the ways that its provision for adults has worked in Denmark, and the means by which it might be translated into British practice. His work has had substantial influence in both the United States and Great Britain, where it has helped give rise to a number of short-term residential centers for adults. Holm-Jensen (1939), describing the transplantation of the Danish folk high schools to other countries, shows the adaptation of institutional form made necessary by such transfer.

The Danish folk schools have had a continuing influence on American thought and practice, particularly in the 1930s. The basic work by Begtrup, Lund, and Manniche (1936) was first published in 1926 and went through a number of editions. The authors came from three different schools. Lund provided the historical and cultural background, whereas the other two authors described the operations of the schools, both generally and with extended specific examples. In reviewing the book for the *New Republic*, Eduard Lindeman said, "Americans will still have difficulty in understanding the Danish movement, but this volume provides an admirable approach; at least, no one need now be satisfied with second-hand interpretations."[2] Another influential book on the subject was written by Campbell in 1928. Hers is an intensely personal account of her experiences with the Danish schools and is both well written and well illustrated. A more recent discoverer of the schools, Davis (1971) brought to his study a thorough grounding in modern American humanistic social psychology. His book is not so much a description of the schools (though a great deal of information is provided) as it is the reaction of a modern American to the life of the folk high school today. Nielsen (1968) describes a kind of apotheosis of the institution in a Danish experimental model in which personal interaction is emphasized and learning is suffused with emotion; his title, *Lust for Learning*, suggests the central theme of the program. Paulston (1980), in a broadly based and solidly researched study, analyzes the Scandinavian origins of folk schools and their creation elsewhere around the world, particularly in the United States. Each manifestation of the form is viewed in terms of the primary social forces and movements that brought it into being and maintained it. Thus, one chapter deals with the folk schools designed to preserve Danish culture in the United States, and another describes how the Highlander Folk School in Tennessee changed in order to meet emerging social needs in the South.

Other Institutions

The focus on the foregoing kinds of institutions perhaps creates the impression that they were isolated examples. Actually, throughout the country's history, many programs designed to provide for adult

[2]*New Republic*, 1925, *49*(627), 85.

learning have been part of a rich context of social life. This breadth of provision has been described by many authors. Using as his resources the diaries, biographies, and newspapers of that period, Long (1976) has studied the continuing education of adults in colonial America. Inkster (1985) offers a collection of essays about vocational adult education by volunteer societies during the period ranging from 1820 until about 1914. The primary reference of the author is to practice in England, but chapters are also included on the work in the United States, Australia, Germany, Japan, and British India. Edwards (1961) deals with a familiar form of instruction: the special center for adult education. Their classes usually (but not always) conducted in the evening, these organizations use many generic names, including institute, evening school, and night school. Some are public, some cooperative, some proprietarial, and some philanthropic. The author treats the long history of such institutions, though devoting greatest attention to the later ones. His center of reference is Britain, but most of his general observations are universal in nature. Jones (1907) presents an account of the continuing learning available to young blue-collar workers at the start of the twentieth century. Stewart (1922) describes in affecting detail one of many efforts to provide literacy education, this time for mountain folk in Kentucky who came to what the author calls moonlight schools. Hill (1938) provides an account of men's literary and cultural clubs as they grew up in the British tradition and were adapted to American life. These autonomous groups usually arose spontaneously out of special local circumstances, flourished for a time, and died. Others found the secret of apparent immortality; sometimes, as with the YMCA, they proliferated into multicelled associations. Weeks (1966) furnishes a description of the origin and ongoing redevelopment of a pioneering adult educational institution, the Lowell Institute, which began in 1839 and has exercised a powerful presence in Boston. He depicts the social context of the institute and shows how its programs have changed over a 125-year period. The Lowell Institute started by providing public lectures to large audiences of adults but over the years has developed other forms of popular education, including the recent fostering of public radio and television.

The Establishment of the Field

"Before the month of June, 1924, the term 'adult education' was not in use in the United States of America." This orotund pronouncement (p. 3) is the first sentence of Cartwright's book *Ten Years of Adult Education*. Published in 1935, it is a description of the initial decade of the American Association for Adult Education (AAAE), from whose preliminary conference the author dates the first major American use of the term. But, as he and everyone else knew, the idea that adults can and should continue to learn throughout their lives had not only been manifested in the institutions already described, but was visibly present in many other organizations, associations, and movements.

The first full American expression of the belief that all these various efforts had a common theme is to be found in a government report published by Herbert Baxter Adams. Adams, then the premier historian and historiographer in the United States, interested himself deeply in various forms of organized adult learning in Europe and the United States and wrote about them in several monographs. In this final work (1901), written not long before his death, he describes adult education as it was undertaken not only by the universities, on which he had previously reported (Adams, 1900), but also by museums, libraries, clubs, and other cultural institutions. A modern reader will probably be surprised to see how widely his mind ranged over the whole field of the transmission of popular and high culture and how acutely he perceived the possibilities of intellectual and aesthetic growth. His work is close in coverage to the *1919 Report* (shortly to be described) but did not penetrate to the essence of the field. His bibliographies demonstrate how extensive the literature of what would later be called adult education had become by the beginning of the twentieth century. This point is reinforced by Grattan (1959), who includes excerpts of various works from 1710 onward, the aim being "to illustrate characteristic thinking by Americans about adult education over a period of two and a half centuries" (p. 7).

It was in Great Britain that the movement that was to create the field of adult education developed and gained momentum. Beginning in the 1870s, the two old universities, Oxford and Cambridge, had provided programs to extend liberal studies to working-class people. However, the most significant single event that was to create the new era was the founding of the Workers' Educational Association (WEA) in 1903 by Albert Mansbridge. Four years later, he brought a delegation of working-class people to a conference at Oxford, where they discussed with a group of its socially conscious scholars how that institution might most fruitfully reach the men and women who had not earlier been able to take advantage of the higher learning provided more fortunate young people. The report of the committee appointed to follow up this conference was published in 1909 as *Oxford and Working-Class Education*. It describes the history of the relationship of working-class people with Oxford from its earliest days and identifies the policies and patterns that should govern the arrangements that the conference and its follow-up committee thought essential. Mansbridge (1920) cites early antecedents and describes the strands from which the new movement was woven, chief among them university extension, the labor unions, and the cooperatives. The WEA's basic members were blue-collar workers; however, it was fortunate in enlisting the attention and support of young scholars, churchmen, and politicians, many of whom would later become eminent and a few of whom gained worldwide renown. Mansbridge's firsthand account describes the period in which the WEA established itself and the ideas that it sponsored. Stocks (1953) carries the story forward, recounting the first fifty years of the WEA in a clear and vivid fashion. She treats the WEA as a special-interest group that eventually achieved considerable power, partly through the strength of its ideas and partly through the leadership that it was able to attract and develop. Social forces also played a major part, and she concludes that "it is difficult, looking back on this formative period, to determine how much of the ship's progress was due to wind and tide—how much to skillful navigation" (p. 29).

Among many other activities, the WEA issued a series of annual yearbooks. One of these, the *WEA Education Yearbook* (1918), has often been cited and was reprinted in 1981. Many of its chapters are inherently interesting, but in retrospect the chief value of the book is that it provides a sense of the kinds of people and ideas about educational reform being considered near the end of

World War I. When the government felt that it could begin the task of planning for a peaceful future after that war, the Ministry of Reconstruction created for that purpose was persuaded to establish an Adult Education Committee composed of distinguished citizens who had been drawn into the support of that field. It was the final report of that committee whose breadth of vision and earnest—sometimes impassioned—advocacy gave rise to adult education as it has been known ever since.

The original report is a long and densely printed government document bound in a dark brown cover. It is cited in the references as having been issued under the sponsorship of the Ministry of Reconstruction (1919), but copies of the original edition are now rare. In 1956, the American, British, and Canadian national associations of adult education published three editions of the same book, *A Design for Democracy*, which contains essential portions of the great report along with a brilliant retrospective review by Ross D. Waller. In 1980, the entire report was reprinted in a volume (designated in the references as the *1919 Report*) that also contains preliminary documents issued by the original committee, as well as three summary papers by Harold Wiltshire, John Taylor, and Bernard Jennings. It is this 1980 volume that is most likely to be available and useful to a modern reader as it includes everything printed earlier (except the 1956 essay by Waller) and adds the three essays by modern authors.

The paper by Jennings concludes with the comment that the *1919 Report* became an instant classic without ever becoming news. But though newspapers did not give much space to the issuance of the document, its basic message had already been received by academic, political, artistic, and economic leaders. A number of papers and addresses were stimulated by its appearance, and substantial books on its theme began to appear. The Adult Education Committee had been chaired by the Master of Balliol College at Oxford. Parry (1920) edited a collection of essays, written by scholars at Cambridge in celebration of the report and amplifying various parts of it, dedicated to the Master of Balliol. They declared that the *1919 Report* "is so far unique in the history of education in Great Britain that it forms a definite, and to a large extent, exhaustive account of the vast amount of voluntary enthusiasm and effort which has been devoted to the cause of adult education, and asserts principles and makes proposals which, if whole-heartedly adopted and consistently acted upon, will undoubtedly transform the whole character of the national life" (p. 1). Thus, very visibly, the two ancient and prestigious universities joined to support the new movement, especially the parts of it that called for university leadership.

In 1923, Stanley presented a collection of eloquent and stately essays entitled *The Way Out* because the writers viewed adult education as the way to solve various social ills. Among the writers were Viscount Haldane, Harold Laski, Sir Eustace Percy, and other distinguished leaders. Yeaxlee (1925), a member of the original committee, wrote a massive two-volume work on the report entitled *Spiritual Values in Adult Education*. In 1929, Yeaxlee also published a book-length essay on the nature, accomplishments, and problems of adult education, particularly in England, ten years after the issuance of the *1919 Report*. In subsequent years, other interpretations were issued, not all of them wholly favorable. Marriott (1984), for example, argued that the report "was in fact a brilliant exercise in special pleading" (p. 92).

The British influence was quickly reflected in the United States. In particular, Frederick Keppel developed a deep interest in adult education, building upon a previous encounter with education in the American military forces in World War I. In 1926, he published a collection of essays (reprinted in 1968) showing the excitement of a mature scholar and senior university administrator (at Columbia) as he discerns a major new social movement. As president of the Carnegie Corporation, he was able to aid the new field financially, particularly by the creation and continuing support of the AAAE, which was a major influence in the field for about fifteen years.

Cartwright (1935) reports on this period in great detail, and other works were commissioned or supported (many of which will be described elsewhere in this book). A few general volumes will be given brief mention here. Kallen (1925) picks up the theme of workers' education prominent in the British movement and gives it an American interpretation. Evans (1926) also deals with this theme, though in a more concrete way. Peffer (1926) provides brief descriptions of many kinds of programs, including the open forum, the institute, individual schools, national associations, corporation educational programs, museums of art and science, and workers' education. Dorothy Canfield Fisher, at that time a celebrated novelist and social commentator, wrote in 1927 a popular interpretation of adult education called *Why Stop Learning?*—a personal interpretation of correspondence schools, parent education, university extension, and other forms and themes of adult learning. In 1930, Fisher published *Learn or Perish,* which reports on the influence of adult education in her own life. The book is the second of a distinguished new series on important educational themes, the first having been written by John Dewey. Bryson (1934) developed a plan for education in California, though the Depression prevented its implementation. *Adult Education and Democracy,* published in 1936, is a companion volume to Cartwright (1935). It contains three of the addresses and a panel discussion delivered at a tenth anniversary celebration of the AAAE and a recapitulation by Cartwright of its history.

The theories and practices of that decade (1925–1935) have had their articulate critics. A powerful and well-reasoned argument criticizing the new American movement was presented by Kotinsky in 1933; her principal point was that theorists and leaders needed to be much bolder in trying to understand the nature of adulthood and in building programs that did not suffer from the deficiencies and errors characterizing the education of children. Stubblefield (1988) has provided the corrective of history in dealing with adult education from 1920 to 1980. He broadened the scope of his inquiry beyond the endeavors of the AAAE and examined a number of people and topics, each of them both closely and broadly observed.

The British and American efforts to create an adult educational movement were paralleled to some degree elsewhere, most especially in European countries and their overseas dominions. An *International Handbook of Adult Education,* published in 1929, assembled brief descriptions of the programs in twenty-six nations and provided an international benchmark against which later developments could be measured. Though many countries were omitted (among them Russia and all the nations of Africa and South America), enough were included to demonstrate that a worldwide community of people interested in adult education was beginning to form by 1929. The Depression and World War II kept this community from growing further, but in the postwar years the threads of association would be picked up again, particularly by the United Nations and its affiliated organizations.

During World War II, Livingstone (1944) published his lucid and powerful book on liberal adult education. As already noted, this work had a substantial impact in Great Britain, aided by Livingstone's eminence as a scholar and the fact that he was the administrative head of Oxford University. The book quickly gained a group of devoted followers in the United States, particularly among the presidents of liberal arts colleges and their board members.

In Britain, the entire educational system was reorganized by the Education Act of 1944; among many other provisions, this act established a new field called further education. It includes instruction provided by various public and private bodies for full-time and part-time students beyond the compulsory school age, mostly in vocational, technical, cultural, and recreational subjects. This act set in motion an elaborate and vast system of offerings. Twenty years later, Peters (1967) described and evaluated the accomplishments of further education in a detailed and fully documented book.

The example of the *1919 Report* remained so vivid in British life that, as World War II drew to a close, another commission was appointed to map out a plan to carry forward the work stimulated by the great prototype. *Adult Education After the War* (1945) is a brief volume issued by the British Institute of Adult Education and developed by a group of distinguished leaders; it sets forth a basic charter for the future with recommendations for each sector of adult education and suggestions for profitable lines of future development. In an independent venture, Shearman (1944) surveyed the British adult education scene both generally and with regard to specific activities and agencies. His attitude was one of pride in the past and a strong determination to work collaboratively and democratically for a better future.

The system of adult education created in Britain during the 1920s became firmly established by legislation, custom, and precedent. When existing arrangements were threatened in the mid 1950s, the storm of protest that arose led to the creation of a commission headed by Eric Ashby. Its report, published by the U.K. Ministry of

Education in 1954, began by reviewing the situation, a valuable contribution to the understanding of the existing program. It also made recommendations for change but essentially left the system intact.

A half century after the *1919 Report*, the U.K. Department of Education and Science made still another assessment of the provision for adult education in a document published in 1973 and officially entitled *Adult Education: A Plan for Development* (usually called the Russell Report after Sir Lionel Russell, chairman of a governmental committee appointed to look into the provision of adult education in England and Wales and to recommend to the government any policies that it should follow in this field). This report provides a sober analysis of the existing situation and contains a measured list of recommendations, but it has little of the fire or eloquence of the *1919 Report*. In a follow-up survey three years later, Rogers and Groombridge (1976) concluded, "In April, 1973, the then Minister, Norman St. John Stevas, promised that the government 'would not drag its feet' over Russell. Nothing was heard subsequently but the resonant scrape of feet being dragged" (p. 23). Scotland has always held itself distinct from the other parts of the United Kingdom so far as adult education is concerned, and in 1975 a report on Scottish adult education was issued by the Scottish Education Department, recording the deliberations of a committee chaired by K.J.W. Alexander. It follows the general lead of the Russell Report and describes the need for special attention to Scottish adult education.

Britain has had a national organization for adult education since 1921, when the British Institute of Adult Education was founded. In 1946, as a result of a strongly felt desire to have a more broadly based association than the institute, a National Foundation for Adult Education was created. For three years, the two associations existed side by side, but in 1949 they merged and became the National Institute of Adult Education (England and Wales). Hutchinson (1971) commemorates the fiftieth year of the founding of the first institute. In his preface, a history of the two bodies is given; the remainder of the book is made up of a series of essays, most of which made their first appearance in the journals of the two associations.

Reorientation of the Field in Terms of Life-Span Learning

The quarter-century following World War II was essentially a time of expansion of the various sectors, themes, and institutions of adult education, whose literature will be noted in later parts of this book. From time to time, sponsors of one or another of the parts attempted to reorient the field around their own goals; in the United States, notable examples were group dynamics and liberal education. But forces were also at work to rethink the whole endeavor. Although a profound change in its conceptualization occurred that would not become fully evident until the 1970s, Hely (1962) perceived it clearly. Unesco held two world conferences on adult education in this period, one at Elsinore in 1947 and the other at Montreal in 1960. (The latter, called the *Second World Conference on Adult Education*, was reported in 1962. The primary accomplishment of the meeting was the drafting and adoption of the so-called Montreal Declaration, given in full in the report.) Hely develops the case that the chief change in the thirteen years between the conferences was that "adult education was no longer seen as a 'continuation' after formal school but as part of a 'continuous' educational process" (p. v). He comments that this altered conception had not yet influenced very much practice in either adult or preadult years and also makes shrewd suggestions as to how that situation might be changed.

The idea of life-span learning had been suggested often in the past. Seay (1938) titled his book on the Tennessee Valley Authority program *Adult Education: A Part of a Total Educational Program*, and even Yeaxlee (1929) had expressed something of the same idea. Jacks (1946) sought to visualize the education of the total person throughout a total life. His primary emphasis lay, however, on reaching all aspects of the person, particularly the child, not on the longitudinal dimension of lifelong education. Green, in his *Adult Education: Why This Apathy?* (1953), attributed a decline in registrations in WEA classes to the poor education given to children. "Adult education," he declared with great emphasis, "must start in the school" (p. 120). The term *continuing education*, which came into widespread use in the 1950s and 1960s, was sometimes used to identify learning activities directly related to earlier schooling in the professions or elsewhere, though it was most commonly used as a synonym for adult education.

Extending the focus of attention to life-span education became pronounced in the 1960s. It was emphasized by Kidd (1966), among other authors, in a book full of insights and expressed by a man deeply interested in the field. Kidd was attempting to see beyond current practices in an effort to achieve a broader conception of education than could be encompassed by current thought and procedure.

In the early 1970s, different formulations of life-span learning appeared in three international organizations based in France. *Permanent education* was espoused by the Council of Europe, *recurrent education* was sponsored by the Organisation for Economic Co-operation and Development (OECD), and *lifelong education* was advanced by Unesco. These three were oriented somewhat differently, and each had its vigorous advocates, especially in Europe. An effort to define and differentiate among the three terms is presented by Dennis Kallen in Schuller and Megarry (1979). As time went on and discussions proliferated, they seemed to overlap one another more and more. Finally, the first two merged into the third—at least in American practice.

Permanent Education (1970) is a compendium of studies written by distinguished European scholars who celebrated the idea that educational systems should be established to offer programs for people at all ages of life. Probably the ultimate development of permanent education is to be found in the book by Schwartz (1974), which presents a masterful and comprehensive plan for reshaping all European education for the whole life span, aiming toward the twenty-first century. Schwartz and the study group that worked with him were concerned not only with institutional provisions for instruction but also with increasing the opportunities for self-education for all who desire it, including entitlement for study leaves.

Permanent education has always been less well accepted than *recurrent* or *lifelong education*, perhaps because the original French term, *éducation permanente,* has connotations in that language that do not carry over into its literal English translation. (The founders of the movement would accept no other term.) Yet it is hard for

English-speaking people to discern how the sense of *éducation permanente* differs from lifelong education unless it implies a comprehensiveness and perhaps a uniformity of planning and curriculum that is hard for most people in non-French educational traditions to accept.

The work of Simpson (1972) illustrates this difficulty. Though using the term itself, he does not pause to defend it but presents an overall analysis of the major currents of growth and development of adult education throughout Europe. Displaying an impressive command of various national shifts and identifying trends and patterns of alteration, Simpson goes from the root conceptions of the field to the specifics of the programming required if adult education is to achieve both its present and its emergent purposes.

A report of the Council of Europe (1975) presents a conception of permanent education some years after it had first been advanced. This book did little, however, to clarify the difficulties in making distinctions between the two terms. More than one person has therefore concluded that *éducation permanente* can best be translated into English as *lifelong education,* though it is clear that the terms originated within two different traditions.

Recurrent Education (1973), published by OECD, is based on the key idea that learning periods should be scheduled throughout the life span, alternating with times devoted principally to work, recreation, or other pursuits. Prototypes in the adult years are the sabbatical-year study arrangements in academic life and alternating duty and study times in the military services. Tied to this general framework is the practice of providing paid educational leave, either by employers or as a right conferred by government or some other funding source. In the late 1960s and early 1970s, a good deal of thought was given to recurrent education in western Europe, particularly by international cultural organizations. The International Labour Conference (1974) reports on the responses from sixty-seven countries to an inquiry made by the International Labour Office of the United Nations on the subject of paid educational leave. It also includes a statement spelling out in elaborate detail the principles that should be followed in evolving a national policy on such leave. The Centre for Educational Research and Innovation of the OECD issued a document in 1976 that details the provisions for leave followed in nine European countries. This book stresses strongly its importance to recurrent education. Von Moltke and Schneevoigt (1977) make a somewhat comparable analysis of European programs, paying special attention to legislative enactments.

In the mid 1970s, the National Institute of Education (NIE) became interested in importing the idea of recurrent education into the United States. Mushkin (1973) provides the report of a conference held on the subject by the NIE at the behest of the OECD. The papers, by both Americans and Europeans, are varied in their approach, but all present the topic in a hardheaded fashion, not as a panacea. Levine (1977) offers a summary prepared for American distribution of arrangements for paid educational leave in ten European countries. Kurland (1977) makes available a collection of papers written by American social scientists (mainly academic economists) on the general theme of paid educational leave, most of them assessing its nature and prospects in the United States. Wirtz (1975) reviews an attempt by a panel of distinguished Americans to develop a national policy for work-related education. It may well be the high point of American discussion of recurrent education.

The idea of recurrent education has apparently been somewhat better established in Great Britain than in the United States. Houghton and Richardson (1974) deal with the introduction of the idea to England and offer a new paradigm for considering the whole educational scene, using John Dewey's ideas as paramount. Charnley (1975) analyzes the subject from an English point of view, though drawing on the experience of several continental European countries. Flude and Parrott (1979) furnish a sober and thoughtfully reasoned statement of the meaning of recurrent education, both generally and as it might be translated into national programming for the United Kingdom. The authors' main point is that recurrent education should not be regarded as simply an addition to present provisions but requires the rethinking and reconstruction of all provisions for learning. Killeen and Bird (1981) report on a study of paid educational leave in England and Wales in 1976–1977. The authors are concerned not only with the number of people involved in various systems, but also with their characteristics, their purposes, and the ways that they reacted to their study programs. Molyneux, Low, and Fowler (1988) show that recurrent education remains a viable idea in British life.

From its beginning, recurrent education has drawn heavily on economic theory. Stoikov (1975) projects the possible economic consequences of an as yet unrealized system of recurrent education. Following a conventional economic analysis of education as a process of capital formation and examining the logical consequences of various forms of policy and strategy, he comes ultimately to the same conclusion as Flude and Parrott (1979): recurrent education cannot simply be added to current practices. Stoikov argues that if such education is "not introduced with considerable preparation and care, it may only make the whole educational system an even more unmanageable colossus than it already is" (p. 115). Levin and Schütze (1983) edited a collection of essays, written by both American and European authorities, concentrating on various plans for financing recurrent education: for example, the legal entitlement of everyone to a certain amount of funds to be spent over a lifetime; single employer financing; and government financing of all education in a plan similar to that now used only for the education of children. The authors believe that an evolutionary plan is best, with opportunities for life-span study growing along with the economic resources made available as a result of such learning.

Recurrent education has merged gradually into lifelong education. Schuller and Megarry (1979), in an excellent collection of essays chiefly by European authors, sum up the attainments and problems of recurrent education at the end of its first decade. Because of the continuing (though perhaps lessened) interest of OECD in that field, it has fostered a line of research and analysis. Jourdan (1981) refers to his book as a "reader" on the subject of recurrent education. The main body of the work is made up of a relatively large number of essays on lifelong learning, most of them relating to some aspect of that subject in a specific nation in western Europe. Of special interest also is the detailed analysis of what each of the key terms had come to mean by the time Jourdan's book was published. Schütze and Istance (1987) provide a substantial report of fifteen years of work. Though the authors acknowledge that recurrent education is now considered synonymous with lifelong education, they believe that its unique thrust has given rise to an extensive world literature, which they here summarize. Of particular importance is the economic focus of recurrent education as manifested in the assessment of material values attained, the cost of various systems, and the methods of financing.

The Unesco concept of lifelong education was powerfully introduced by Lengrand (1975) in a book first published in 1970, but later reprinted in an enhanced version. Written in the tradition of lucid French rationalism, it aims to do no more than sketch the dimensions of a full conception of lifelong education as it might emerge from further experience—which, in turn, rests upon what we already know and can do. Lengrand states, "If, for example, we did not have the benefits of the appreciable contributions made by adult education, and more generally by out-of-school methods of training, if countries had not built up extensive networks of communication through radio and television, and if the means of universal instruction were not at hand, then our thoughts concerning lifelong learning would be without meaning and would doubtless not even have begun to take shape" (pp. 88–89). The revised edition of this work has new material on the history of the central concept and provides illustrations and demonstrations of it. Lengrand gives particular attention to self-education and observes that adult education is the "locomotive" that leads and energizes the whole system of lifetime learning.

Faure (1972) is believed by many people to have provided the full-scale treatment of lifelong education that Lengrand anticipated. Entitled *Learning to Be,* the book is a charter for education at all ages of life throughout the world. It was sponsored by Unesco and carried forth under the guidance of a committee of seven eminent educational scholars from around the world. Faure, the chairman, had been prime minister and minister of education of France. The book signifies the emergence of a new era in which adult education is seen in the perspective of life-span learning. Although its scope parallels or even transcends that of the *1919 Report,* its impact in the United States has been less than that of the earlier work, for reasons that are far from clear. Elsewhere in the world, *Learning to Be* has been received with great acclaim.

During the years immediately before and after the publication of the works by Lengrand and Faure, several other authors have explored the general theories and practice of lifelong education. In an English symposium by several authors, Jessup (1969) concludes that the ultimate conception of such education is "a temper, a quality of society, that evinces itself in attitudes, in relationships, and in social organization" (p. 31). Simpson (1972), writing just as the new concept was emerging, reflects a shifting orientation; the author moves away from a fundamental concern with the education of adults to that of the learning patterns of people of all ages. Parkyn's analysis (1973) appeared shortly after the publication of Faure's work. A widely experienced educator, Parkyn presents a scholarly outline of the many factors that must play a part in designing a national program of lifelong education. Because of their worldwide scope, Parkyn's proposals are not anchored to any one political system. Hummel (1977), a Swiss educator, gives a history of lifelong education and describes its major applications. He asserts that "the development of the concept of lifelong education, which can be compared with the Copernican revolution, is one of the most striking events in the history of education" (p. 32). Peterson (1979) deals comprehensively with the application of this concept, beginning with the description of how the phrase came into the American vocabulary. Chickering and Associates (1981) suggest what individuals should learn throughout their whole lives. His book includes analyses by experts in many fields of study. Himmelstrup, Robinson, and Fielden (1981) present a symposium written by both European and American authors, which starts with the ideas put forward by Faure and develops them in either general or specific terms. The book relies on clear definitions and declarative statements to help build a collective approach and a community of understanding. In 1989, the General Conference of Unesco voted to issue a periodic *World Education Report,* the first volume of which was published in 1991. This document is perhaps the fullest expression of lifelong education yet to have appeared; in it, the adult years are given full attention throughout, in both statistical tables and textual presentations and analyses.

The full development of lifelong education requires not only the growth of provisions for adult education, but also the rethinking of schooling for children. *The School and Continuing Education* (1972) pursues that latter theme by speculating on the changes that will be required in schools if they are to play appropriate roles in the new era; greatest attention is paid to France and the United States. Menson (1982) and her associates develop their ideas around three central purposes: to indicate how the development of adults influences their learning as distinguished from that of the younger people traditionally served by colleges and universities; to suggest ways by which institutions of higher learning may best plan for the education of mature learners; and to describe some programs and services that reflect an adult development perspective. Squires (1987) uses patterns of thought commonly found in curriculum research to examine four phases of the life span and the education appropriate to each. The author is most deeply oriented to the thought and practice of the United Kingdom but is in firm command of the relevant literature of other countries.

A series of somewhat overlapping monographs, treating all aspects of continuing education but especially its implications for the years of schooling, was published by the Unesco Institute of Education in Hamburg. Each volume is independent, but the series should also be considered collectively. Dave (1973) explores the "concept characteristics" of continuing education and outlines further research in the field. He is thoroughly familiar with both American and European sources. Dave and Stiemerling (1973) present English and French abstracts of a number of papers dealing with lifelong education throughout the world. Dave (1975) offers another collection of papers on the topic, with an excellent statement by the editor expressing his own views. Hawes (1975) reports the general deliberations of a seminar of representatives from seventeen countries in Africa and Asia; he suggests that an idea often thought to be restricted to advanced nations can have significant meaning, when carefully interpreted, to nations still in the early stages of economic development. Dave (1976) has also edited a deeply theoretical work by a cluster of non-American scholars, analyzing the concept of lifelong education in light of its philosophical, historical, sociological, psychological, anthropological, ecological, and economic foundations. He also provides a summarizing synthesis of these various approaches as regards the field of practice. Skager and Dave (1977) detail the efforts of teams of educators from Japan, Romania, and Sweden to study the impact of lifelong education on the curriculum of schools for the young. Cropley (1977), while providing a discursive book on the psychological foundations of the field, also gives special attention to the school curriculum and teacher education. Cropley and Dave (1978) describe a study of how teachers were trained in the concepts of lifelong education in six institutions in five Asian and European countries. The study concludes with the rueful observation that "the prospects for lifelong education may be favorable, but it will probably be necessary for its proponents to be patient" (p. 208). Ingram (1979) analyzes theoretically how this approach to learning can be incorporated into the thoughts of children. Presenting a symposium of authors drawn from around the world, Cropley (1980) deals particularly with the adult educational aspects of the field. Hameyer (1979) gives an overview of the literature of the school curriculum to assess how it can be interpreted in the light of the concept of lifelong learning. Knapper and Cropley (1985) examine how the university as a social institution should engage in a comprehensive program of continuing education.

Other concepts and terms parallel to the three major ones just described have also been advanced. One of them is the *learning society,* variously defined but generally signifying the enrichment of all social life so that everyone can be helped to develop her or his potential. Husén (1974 and 1986) presents the collected papers of a distinguished Swedish educator on this broad theme. Perhaps the most thorough statement of the idea, though concentrating on the university, is a report by the Carnegie Commission on Higher Education (1973); this document reflects the considered judgment of a group of prominent American educators about the learning society.

Another term that has some currency is *open learning.* MacKenzie, Postgate, and Scupham (1975) conclude their lengthy book on this subject with the observation that "open learning is an imprecise phrase to which a range of meanings can be, and is attached. It eludes definition. But as an inscription to be carried in processions as a banner, gathering adherents and enthusiasm, it has great potential" (p. 498).

Biographies

Most of those whose contributions to adult education have seemed great enough to warrant the writing of their biographies have excelled in specific programs, institutions, or fields of work; books about them will be considered later in connection with other works dealing with such topics. But the field itself has had its eminent scholars and accomplished practitioners, and books about them will be noted here. Moreland and Goldenstein (1985) selected outstanding individuals in American history who have had significant viewpoints on adult education or who have created outstanding programs and institutions. The work of some of these, such as Sequoyah and Margaret Fuller Ossoli, occurred during the precursor years; others, such as Alvin Johnson and Robert M. Hutchins, were pioneers of adult education itself. Each brief essay in this book sets the person concerned in a historical perspective and attempts to assess his or her contributions. Long (1991) gives cameo biographies of some of the American men and women whom he regards as innovators in the period before adult education became recognized as a field. He identifies the formative era (1607–1789), the establishment era (1790–1859), and the national era (1860–1920) and names a number of pioneering adult educators in addition to the individuals he memorializes.

Other collections of brief biographies are also available. Mansbridge ([1948] 1970) presents a gallery of portraits of the people influential in developing the adult educational movement in Great Britain. Individually, these portraits are of varying interest, but collectively they show how strongly the idea of working-class adult education penetrated throughout all of English society in the first third of the twentieth century. Ulich (1965) offers brief histories of adult education in Denmark, England, Germany, and the United States that highlight a number of the individuals who served as leaders. Thomas and Elsey (1985) furnish about three hundred short biographical and analytical statements concerning adult educators throughout the world. The results not only provide useful information about the individuals concerned, but also help define the field and indicate its scope. The entries are markedly uneven (as might be expected in a first effort of this sort). Jarvis (1987b) presents intellectual biographies of thirteen men whom the author believes to have been influential thinkers in the field. The careers of most of the subjects were concerned centrally with adult education; six are American, three are English, two are Canadian, and one each came from Italy and Brazil.

Full-scale accounts of the lives of single individuals have also been written. Corbett (1957), the founder of the adult educational movement in Canada, wrote his autobiography covering the period beginning shortly after the end of World War II and ending in 1951. The book is an anecdote-filled description of what it was like to encounter the primitive conditions of rural Canada as an extension lecturer and subsequently to create many institutions and programs. The volume gives a vivid sense of the vitality often involved in the intensely human processes of adult education. Cochrane (1986) edited an account of the life of J. R. Kidd, who succeeded Corbett as the central figure of adult education in Canada and later became perhaps the field's most internationally known leader. This book, a collaboration of a number of authors, is a very full account of the progression of his life and thought, from his earliest days until his death (1915–1982).

Stewart (1987) provides an account of the life of Eduard Lindeman, whose writings and thought have been deeply inspirational for many leaders of the adult education movement. The book is based largely on primary sources and recounts the tale of Lindeman's rise from humble rural conditions to a position of national influence. The author has retained careful objectivity about his subject, avoiding the uncritical adulation with which some observers have regarded him. Brookfield (1987) offers an account of Lindeman's intellectual growth, including a generous sampling of his writings; the biographer selected papers "which contained writing of passion and creative fire, rather than research reports or summations of distilled wisdom on completed inquiries" (p. v). Elizabeth Lindeman Leonard (1991) presents a filial but candid portrait of her father's personality and thoughts. His interests and concerns with adult education are here seen as aspects of a life filled with many other interests that engaged his thoughts and actions. Her book brings him alive to the reader more fully than any other available resource.

Collins (1977) provides an account of the life of Paulo Freire, a Brazilian intellectual born in 1921. Freire became committed to the idea of aiding the poor to improve themselves through the power of education. His success in these endeavors in Recife and elsewhere led him to develop both his theoretical and his practical formulations. His work, first in Brazil and later in other countries, brought him followers throughout the world, particularly among people interested in rapidly developing nations.

Another leader concerned with the empowerment of the deprived was Myles Horton, whose biography is presented by Adams (1975). Horton created and maintained the Highlander Folk School in Tennessee, whose first task was to help build leadership for the union movement and whose subsequent concern was the strengthening of the leadership of the civil rights movement. For many years, Highlander remained a strong educational force, amidst strife and turmoil, and Horton was the principal guide of the institution throughout that period. Though their work is presented as an autobiography, Horton, Kohl, and Kohl (1990) are relatively little concerned with the events of Horton's life. Some of these are briefly noted, but most of the book is made up of the expression of his principles of action, presented aphoristically and anecdotally, rather than in a systematic fashion. Shortly before Horton's death, he and Freire were brought together for several days to talk about their lives and thoughts. The results of these conversations have been skillfully edited into a book (Horton and Freire, 1990), which offers personal, anecdotal, and unstructured accounts of their ideas (all of which appeared to be similar or compatible). Although not a central source on the thoughts of these men, the book is useful in rounding out their conceptions of education and certain aspects of their points of view.

Since the mid 1930s, Malcolm Knowles has been active in adult education, and he has been a national leader in the field since the late 1940s. Knowles (1989) has written a highly personal autobiography in which he covers only briefly the externals of his life and career and concentrates on the growth of his distinctive approach to his work. He has always been a deeply respected but individualistic leader, impatient with forms and routines and concerned with human relationships—an orientation obvious in this book.

Summations

One small cluster of works, sure to be augmented as the twentieth century draws to a close, is based on the effort to appraise longitudinally the overall accomplishments of the field of adult education. Most such assessments are favorable. Unesco (1982) has published, under the title *It's Never Too Late to Learn,* a "coffee table" book made up of pictures and captions conveying the idea that life-span learning is present in all countries. The book especially celebrates the humanistic quest of individuals for personal fulfillment at all stages of life. Fragnière (1976) reports on a massive study conducted from 1968 to 1975 under the auspices of the European Cultural Foundation. It seeks to discern the probable nature of life in Europe in the year 2000. The people studied, drawn from many European nations, were considered in terms of four so-called cornerstones: equal educational opportunity for all; lifelong learning patterns; participative and autonomous learning; and counseling. Each theme is considered separately, and then the interacting ramifications of the four are analyzed. Avakov (1980) reviews a conference of European and Asian experts on educational planning held in Paris in 1978. This document, which expresses the ideal of lifelong learning, employs idealistic and abstract language in considering world problems of adult education. Evans (1985) provides a broad exposition of the idea that more of the attention of educators should be devoted to ongoing learning and less to various institutional arrangements. His fundamental concern is with English practice, but he uses many American sources. Coombs (1985) surveys the world educational scene from the implicit perspective that the learning of adults and that of children is a seamless whole. Thomas and Ploman (1986) present the diverse and rather idiosyncratic papers given at an international conference to discuss how a truly global approach to learning might best be conceived and carried out. Cassidy and Faris (1987) celebrate the fiftieth anniversary of the Canadian Association for Adult Education. The book is a collection of papers written by major leaders of what they clearly regard as a movement. They describe the history of adult education in their country, discuss some of its most successful programs, outline the challenges it confronts, and argue that it must recapture a sense of dedication and mission that it once had and that they collectively feel it now lacks. Long (1987) examines adult education, principally as it is reflected or analyzed in the literature, and gives his views on where the field is going and what he believes to be lines of productive thought. Quigley (1989) provides the work of several authorities in the field of adult education, who appraise how well it has achieved its purposes as a movement or as a profession; no consensus is reached. In the same book, another series of authors, while indicating their own ideas of what the field has accomplished, are more concerned with how it should grow in influence. Bhola (1989) deals systematically with the major themes and influences related to adult education worldwide in the years since Unesco was founded, with specific reference to its international conferences on the subject. The author has had much international experience himself and is familiar with the literature of many countries. He is thus able to treat the various aspects of theory and practice with unusual comprehensiveness and in a fashion unfamiliar to those who think only in national terms. Cassara (1990) offers a collection of papers by North American authors who take a fresh look at the influence of multiculturalism on adult education, particularly in the United States. Each of the papers is concerned with one or more ethnic groups and the special stance that each takes in considering adult learning for its members. Attention is also paid to the ways by which diverse populations can be integrated harmoniously into society.

A Final Word

Those who think about adult education or lifelong learning are, by nature, planners of the future, not surveyors of the past. In their view, education tends to be concerned with needs and aspirations; with imperfections or inadequacies in people, institutions, and communities; and with how life can be made better by learning. But, as my retrospective citing of the books about adult education in this century suggests, it is sometimes possible to look backward with a sense of pride at all that has been accomplished, even in adjusting to turbulent times. As Stocks noted in 1953:

> In tracing the fortunes of the W. E. A. through the succeeding half-century it will be seen that the aims of its leaders, and for that matter their methods, were largely conditioned by the social environment in

which they started their work at the turn of the century and by the changes which have since transformed the social structure of England: its appearance, its class-composition, the factors which shape and the ideas which inspire its politics, and the material require-ments which direct its economic endeavor. These changes, acting and reacting on one another, have been spectacular, potent and profound [p. 9].

It may be hoped that those who assess adult education at the end of this remarkably variable century will take equal satisfaction in its attainments.

TWO

Comprehensive Works on Adult Education

Adult education is, by definition, the education of people whose main business is not learning but living.

—Flesch, 1943, p. 1

Ever since adult education has become recognized as a field, authors have tried to discern both its essence and its limits. Chapter One cited some of the books resulting from such efforts. This chapter will enlarge on their number. The works included are grouped according to the special intent of their authors: to define and analyze the whole field; to provide a comprehensive handbook of information about it; to survey the offerings of some geographically defined area; to gather together the ideas of several authorities on the basic nature of the field or some significant part of it; or to identify the major books and other resources available. These topics will be considered more specifically in later chapters as well, but here they will be merged—perhaps submerged—into the larger framework into which they fit.

General Treatments

The books noted in this section are the results of the attempts of one writer or a team of authors to report comprehensively on adult education, almost always as it is carried out in a single nation (though this limitation may not be noted in the work itself). The authors vary greatly in the extent to which their own concerns are reflected in the selection or interpretation of their themes.

Hart (1927) wrote his book at the time that the adult educational movement was being established in the United States, but his ideas and aspirations were not deeply shaped by association with the leaders of that movement; instead, they came from the classics of pedagogy and the early beginnings of the social sciences. He interpreted adult education as a reaction to the narrow teaching of children and also as a natural evolution of human activity made necessary by the growth of modern social institutions. His book is filled with quotations, many of them unfamiliar to a modern reader.

Bryson (1936) prepared the first general textbook designed to be used by the "thousands of students of the social scene and of education in America who have been wanting a systematic account of adult education" (p. iii). In the compass of only two hundred pages, he presents many ideas, often inspirationally, but the modern reader is likely to be impressed by how little was known about the field at the time he wrote.

The Journal of Adult Education was the official publication of the American Association for Adult Education (AAAE) which (as noted in Chapter One) was founded in 1926 with support from the Carnegie Corporation. The journal contained some of the most perceptive and elegant writing ever published on the subject of adult education. Mary Ely was its editor in its early years, and in 1936 she published a generous sampling of the journal's best essays. *Adult Education in Action,* the resulting volume, provides a kaleidoscopic picture of the range of goals and programs in the first effervescent years of the movement.

Two other extensive treatments of the field also resulted from the work of the AAAE. Beals and Brody (1941) cast their work as a bibliography—and it will be so treated later in this chapter. But its themes and the overall structure of its analysis make it an excellent discussion of the field of adult education. It is one of twenty-seven studies, all cited at various places in this book, that the AAAE published between 1937 and 1944. The need was felt by the editors of this series for a synthesizing volume "which would seek to interpret the entire American experience in adult education as an important manifestation of a folk culture within the nation" (p. ix, Adams, 1944). The man selected to carry out this assignment was the distinguished American historian James Truslow Adams. The resulting book-length essay, *Frontiers of American Culture* (1944), is his intensely personal commentary. His book is easy to read, particularly for those who like a historical approach.

Debatin, in his *The Administration of Adult Education* (1938), included several chapters that deal with such matters as publicity and finance; essentially, however, his is another general overview of the field, beginning with fundamental definitions and going on to goals and broad descriptions of activities. In a brief and eloquently written book, Waller (1946) celebrated the nature of adult education and described the program in existence in England at the close of World War II. Essert (1951) systematically covered the entire field, dividing it into three areas: self-directed study, group study, and community development. Creative leadership, variously defined, seemed to Essert to be an essential goal of all adult study, and he tried to show how it can be achieved.

Sheats, Jayne, and Spence (1953) edited a beautifully designed and artfully presented book composed of a large number of quotations from the literature, woven together with bridging passages, so that the book makes a coherent presentation. Each of the major agencies and themes of the field as then perceived is dealt with in turn. This book was an early example of the modern, creatively designed university textbook. For a period of years after its publication, it was generally considered the best single treatment of adult education.

Powell (1956) offered a simply written, discursive, and idiosyncratic "general survey of the present state and future prospects of adult education in this country" (p. vii). Verner and Booth (1964) wrote one of a large series of relatively brief volumes, each of which was given over to a single topic in the field of education. All of the volumes in the series were required to follow a master format, one that did not suit the complex nature of adult education. Yet the authors transcended this limitation admirably. Rogers (1969) developed a book to accompany a television series on adult education shown in Britain in prime time in 1968 and repeated in 1969. Although the topics chosen do not purport to give full coverage of the field, they do present a broad view of the ideas and information that the producers felt to be suitable for the general public.

In 1972, Peers issued the third edition of a book that had long been accepted as a major interpretation of the field—especially in England, where the author was a distinguished educational administrator. His work focuses fairly sharply on British history and institutions but also offers a good measure of theoretical analysis and some description of the programs and practices of other countries. Peers holds fast to his conviction that adult education is and should be essentially concerned with liberal studies, an orientation that permeates his book.

Two general descriptions of British adult education, sharply critical of the prevailing system, appeared in 1976. Ellwood's (1976) major purpose was to deal with university adult education, but she broadened her theme by providing an account of the development of the field since the *1919 Report*. She believed that the immediate problems identified by the report were now solved and that it was time for a new and more cohesive adult educational service. Rogers and Groombridge (1976) moved much more sharply to the attack. The authors began by asserting, "As this country lurches unsteadily from crisis to crisis, we agree with the adage that a country which is backward in adult education will be backward absolutely" (p. 13). They demonstrated forthrightly that the caliber of adult education was far below even a minimum level of acceptability. As provision of service in Great Britain was (and is) highly nationalized, the government (under both major parties) was regarded by the authors as the chief villain. The final part of the book deals with a suggested program of reform and identifies both long-range and "instantly possible" ways of strengthening the current situation.

Hiemstra (1976) prepared his relatively slender volume as an introduction for serious readers to the field of adult education. Though he begins with simple definitions of key terms and ideas, he does not hesitate to review some of the more sophisticated aspects of the field.

Duke (1976) writes very succinctly of his major views on lifelong learning, particularly that which occurs in the adult years. He was based in Australia at the time this book was written, but his presentation is more a reflection of worldwide thought and practice than it is an expression of a nationalistic interest.

Broschart (1977) summarized a number of "study documents" commissioned by a federal bureau. The book's themes are broad and are handled in general terms. Its notable aspects are its introduction of the concept of lifelong education as an importation from Europe and its references to the stages of life through which people pass. Axford (1980) issued a second version of a book originally published in 1969 under the same title but by a different publisher. These comprehensive works on adult education include both descriptive and prescriptive passages, containing many quotations and illustrations. The total effect conveys the spirit and practice of adult education with a distinctly evangelical emphasis on its importance and values. Barton (1982) made a broad analysis of what is going on in adult education, particularly as it is related to the work careers of people in managerial positions in business. Jarvis (1983a) based his work on the literature of the field, but his clear, critical intelligence is constantly brought to bear upon the basic sources. Though one of his chapters describes the provision of adult education in the United Kingdom, his source orientations are heavily American.

Townsend Coles (1977) focused his work on the nature of adult education in the less developed countries of the world: what it really means, how it is administered, how it is provided, and what the discernible results may be. But his analyses run far deeper than his immediate place of application, for he develops a clear sense of what adult education can be and might become. The scope of the book covers the entire world and is written by a man who brings both intellect and conviction to the expression of his ideas.

Lowe (1982) prepared this second edition of a major conceptualization of the entire field of continuing education. He notes that at Unesco's Third International Conference on Adult Education, held in Tokyo in 1972, that international body "decided that a book should be published for a wide non-professional audience of people who, in national and local decision-making bodies can do much to promote the education of adults" (pp. 5-6). Lowe's book is the result of that decision, and in its broad sweep and all-embracing presentation of a worldview in relatively brief compass, it is unparalleled. The author takes up, one by one, the major concerns of adult educators everywhere and considers them in magisterial fashion. He draws on a vast array of data but brings to its presentation the unifying perceptions gained from his own experience in many countries. The result is a sophisticated and clear summary, realistic in appraisal but optimistic in tone.

Merriam and Caffarella (1991) concentrate on the act of learning in adulthood and its examination by scholars in the field and in a few allied disciplines. These authors cover the context and environment of adult learning, the adult learner, the learning process, the theoretical base for adult learning, and the issues faced by those who wish to foster adult learning. The authors base their work upon the literature in the field and summarize both its conclusions and their own ideas. This is a mature and scholarly book, one that is likely to be helpful to everyone interested in the subject.

Handbooks

Like the works just noted, handbooks seek to cover all of adult education. Authors expert in specific sectors are asked to describe their essence in relatively brief fashion. The resulting statements are then assembled to make up a compendious collection of treatments of particular areas. Such unifying syntheses as exist do not lie in the minds of individual authors or closely associated coauthors, but in the patterns designed by editors and in the sequencing or clustering of chapters. The resulting book is usually a work designed to be kept at hand to be consulted as needed.

The first such effort was the *International Handbook of Adult Education* (1929), published in England by the World Association for Adult Education (which proved to be short lived, chiefly because of the Depression). This work, written by many authors, describes the programs of sixteen nations, most of them European.

In the United States, a sequence of handbooks has appeared steadily since the 1930s and provides the best available continuing record of how the field was observed by its leaders as it grew in size. The later versions have paid careful attention to the earlier ones, thus establishing an intellectual continuity despite varying editors, authors, and institutional sponsors. The *Handbook of Adult Education* (1934), issued under the auspices of the AAAE, presented a comprehensive national picture of what was occurring in the United States eight years after the organization's founding. Edited by

Dorothy Rowden (though her name does not appear on the title page), this work brings together a number of short sections, each of which deals with some program, goal, activity, or aspect of adult education. Heavy emphasis is given to the institutional providers of educational opportunities, and lists of key programs are furnished, as are bibliographies. The 1934 edition proved to be more popular than expected, and the AAAE therefore commissioned a completely new analysis of the field; this version was issued in 1936, this time listing Rowden as editor. It dealt with much the same topics as before but with a more spacious perspective. For example, the 1934 edition had an entry for agricultural extension, whereas the 1936 version contained one on rural adult education. In neither volume was there any attempt to group topics to help build up a concept of the field as a whole.

The two original handbooks were so well received that plans were made to issue them every five years, but 1941 proved not to be a good year for such a publication. Not only was there World War II to contend with, but also the operation of the AAAE became a function of Columbia University during that year as a result of a changed granting policy by the Carnegie Corporation. In the transition, some activities had to be dropped, and the issuance of a handbook was one of them.

It was not until 1948 that the next handbook in the series appeared. Its editor, Mary Ely, had long been associated with the AAAE, and the new volume had a maturity that transcended that of its two predecessors. It remains a handbook to be consulted for quick reviews and for names and addresses, but it is also a rounded work, organized into categories and subcategories and edited with clarity and style. It brings to a brilliant close the era when the AAAE was a dominant force in the field.

The 1960 handbook, edited by Malcolm Knowles, demonstrates the growth and change that occurred in the years immediately after World War II. Then the executive head of the Adult Education Association (AEA), the dominant association in the field, Knowles rethought the whole nature of a handbook. Much of the informational emphasis (such as directories of institutions, places, and people) was dropped. An almost completely new roster of authors was chosen to write the chapters, with little overlap with those of previous editions. More important, the themes chosen for analysis tended to be more general, penetrating the field's essence and showing less concern for types of institutions and specific program emphases.

The next edition, edited by Smith, Aker, and Kidd in 1970, moved even farther away than its predecessors from factual information and toward general interpretive essays. Many of the writers had contributed to the 1960 version. Yet whereas earlier handbooks had been prepared almost entirely by eminent practitioners, more of the 1970 version was written by those engaged in the academic study of adult education. The collective professoriate had clearly emerged as a major force in the analysis and description of the field.

A radical change occurred in the publication of the 1980 edition. The AEA, the official sponsor, decided to issue a group of volumes that together would describe the whole field with a scope and amplitude not possible in a single work. The general editors of this large enterprise, which eventually produced eight books, were William S. Griffith and Howard Y. McClusky. They did not issue any synthesizing volume; the closest approximation to a general statement is to be found in the forewords to the specialist works. Each of these had its own editor who drew upon a group of associates deeply versed in the topic assigned. By this time the academic students of adult education had come to dominate the roster of contributors. Each of the eight specialized volumes will be cited in this book where it seems most relevant, but the authors and titles are given here to provide a sense of the coverage of the collective 1980 yearbook:

> Peters and others, *Building an Effective Adult Education Enterprise* (1980)
>
> Long, Hiemstra, and Associates, *Changing Approaches to Studying Adult Education* (1980)
>
> Knox and Associates, *Developing, Administering, and Evaluating Adult Education* (1980)
>
> Boyd, Apps, and others, *Redefining the Discipline of Adult Education* (1980)
>
> Boone, Shearon, White, and Associates, *Serving Personal and Community Needs Through Adult Education* (1980)

Charters and others, *Comparing Adult Education World-wide* (1981)

Kreitlow and Associates, *Examining Controversies in Adult Education* (1981)

Grabowski and others, *Preparing Educators of Adults* (1981)

The 1989 *Handbook of Adult and Continuing Education,* edited by Merriam and Cunningham, returns to the earlier one-volume format but does so with a fullness and mastery not found earlier. Some of the authors in the volumes of the 1980 handbook were again asked to contribute, but many new names are present as well. The dominance of academic authors was now virtually complete. Most of the people most frequently cited in the index are also known chiefly by their association with the professoriate. Either because of that fact or despite it, this handbook transcends all previous efforts to describe and interpret the American field of adult education as a whole and in the clarification of its parts.

The *International Yearbook of Adult Education,* more commonly known internationally under its German title, *Internationales Jahrbuch der Erwachsenenbildung,* has been published annually since 1969 under the editorship of Joachim H. Knoll and the guidance of an international committee. Each volume has a central theme dealing with national systems, programs, or themes of adult education. Some of the papers are in English. Annually from 1975–1976 through 1980–1981, a *Yearbook of Adult and Continuing Education* was published. Each of the six volumes was an all-embracing collection of material about the field, including papers already published elsewhere and various tabulations of useful information. Apparently, this publishing program did not secure adequate funding to become firmly established and to grow into the enormously useful series of books that it had seemed destined to become.

Surveys

Surveys of adult education within defined geographic units had a substantial vogue in the 1920s, though few were published as books. The *1919 Report* itself was a searching inquiry, seeking out all organized manifestations of the idea of adult education in Britain, and it set a model for similar studies of other communities of various sizes. Usually such studies were undertaken because of a desire to improve circumstances: to fill in gaps of service, to reward excellence, or to suggest methods of fruitful collaboration. Excluded from this section are unintentional surveys; though their authors intended to write general treatises, they actually described only the country that they knew.

An analysis of the early survey movement was published in 1934 by Ozanne, who used the term broadly. Among the twenty-seven surveys he studied were those that examined specific institutions and clusters of students. Three additional works reporting early municipal surveys are among the most interesting reports on the provision of adult education ever made. Marsh (1926) analyzed the offering of adult education in Buffalo, New York, his study being undertaken by the local adult education council with help from the University of Buffalo. This early survey went far beyond a simple canvass of opportunities and enrollments to a consideration of a number of profound questions not ordinarily considered. The study of adult students, for example, opened up two lines of inquiry that would later arouse research interest: the sequence of events that caused students to leave school in youth and later find their way back to learning; and the relatively negligible relationship between specific motivations for learning and the content of the courses for which students were enrolled. The author found to his manifest surprise that "though the adult education movement is one of the youngest of our social enterprises, it is, nevertheless, big; big in numbers concerned, big in extent of program, big in achievement, and big in promise" (p. 1). Lorimer (1931) presented a broadly conceived account of adult education in Brooklyn. Its title, *The Making of Adult Minds in a Metropolitan Area,* suggests its scope. The book is, in essence, a series of approaches to the massive question of how adults absorb ideas from the urban culture. It uses many techniques: an inventory of institutions, accounts in depth of the learning habits of individuals, an effort to estimate the number of adults in formal courses, a survey of the instruments of mass culture, an inquiry into clubs and voluntary associations, and other less clear-cut bodies of data. Another early survey of New York City was published by the New York Adult Education Council in 1934. Entitled *A Picture of Adult Education,* it suggests in broad and panoramic fashion how numerous and varied were the offerings of adult education in the great city.

Almost thirty years later, Kidd (1961) demonstrated how the municipal survey had grown in the maturity of its approach. He provided a systematic and massive study of adult educational activities in a complex, highly developed city: metropolitan Toronto. He analyzed the basic demographics of the city; the early history of its adult educational institutions (including some that had disappeared); the scope of service of about a thousand institutions; the nature of the students, teachers, and administrators who took part in the total offering; and such special problems of the field as promotion, counseling, research, and finance. Some basic conclusions and recommendations are provided. This volume sets a very high standard for municipal surveys.

Many statewide surveys of adult education have been made, but only two book-length published reports have been located. The first, by Reeves, Fansler, and Houle, was issued in 1938 as one volume of a massive study of education throughout New York State. This monograph is a struggle to cast a net around the whole field of adult education as it was developing throughout an extraordinarily complicated and diversified state. The authors' definition and description of adult education were thought at the time to be innovative, as were their statement of the central aims of the field and their prescription for a broad program for action. Levin and Slavet (1970) later surveyed adult education in Massachusetts and proposed a program for further development.

The status of adult education in the United States has often been surveyed in one fashion or another, and (as noted earlier) it is sometimes difficult to determine whether the basic purpose was to make a survey or to outline generally the nature of adult education. Three book-length reports, however, appear to have had the primary objective of making a survey. In 1968, Liveright undertook such a study at the behest of the federal government. It presents a broad and somewhat general account of the prevailing principles and major trends at that time. In 1972, a document entitled *Perspectives of Adult Education* was issued by the U.S. Office of Education to be used at the Third International Conference on Adult Education, sponsored in that year by Unesco in Tokyo. It has four parts: the adult participant, adult education and the economy, the organization and administration of adult education, and innovations and future directions. Peterson and Associates (1979) sought to describe the educational institutions, the learners, and the public policies of the preceding decade. He provides a compendium of useful information, and the major value of this work is probably its use as a resource for facts, rather than as an integrated work.

Five volumes with the same purpose as the foregoing works, but with more analysis and interpretation, were issued in Britain in the 1970s and 1980s. In 1970, the National Institute of Adult Education published a report entitled *Adult Education—Adequacy of Provision.* A distinguished steering committee made studies in seven geographic areas of the country. The results are rich in statistical reports and personal analyses, as well as in comments by various categories of respondents, but the question of "adequacy" proved to be ultimately unanswerable. Lowe (1970b) built an analysis of the contemporary state of the field in Great Britain around a pervasively British issue. Because of actions following the *1919 Report,* the term *adult education* had acquired the strong connotation of being concerned only with liberal studies or, at any rate, with those that were not clearly vocational. This restrictive point of view had gradually atrophied, and by 1970 leaders in the field were insisting that a broader frame of reference had to be adopted. In this book, Lowe makes the case, first theoretically and then descriptively, that adult education must be organized and developed to achieve many personal and social purposes. As his title suggests, Legge (1982) discusses *The Education of Adults in Britain.* No single principle of organization is used. Some chapters deal with themes, such as work-related instruction, leisure-related study, or education with a social dimension. Some consider formats of learning, such as self-education and residential education. Still others offer comprehensive analyses: definition of terms, objectives and needs, and cooperation and coordination. The Advisory Council for Adult and Continuing Education was established by the secretary of state for education and science in 1977; its membership was drawn from many sectors of the field. Published in 1982, the coun-

cil's report was a broad summary of the nature of continuing education in Great Britain, to which are added the council's major
conclusions and recommendations. This document reflects the
highly organized and centralized provision of adult education that
has become traditional in the country, but it deals succinctly and
well with the total conception of the field, its strengths, and the
areas where growth is required. Jarvis (1988) aims "to present a
picture of continuing education as it is in 1988 in the United Kingdom" (p. 1). He provides opening and summarizing chapters, treatments of various specific providers and themes, and an assessment
of the implications of British practice for that of the United States.

Surveys of adult education in other countries abound, and
only a few varied examples can be listed here. Kidd depicted Canadian adult education in three survey-anthologies, two by himself in
1950 and 1963 and one with Selman in 1978. Each is a collection
of brief papers, the sum of which is designed to provide a picture
of the national offering. Although all three books contain both
factual statements and analytical points of view, the particular at-
tractiveness of each collection comes from the papers that deal with
the immediate and vital aspects of adult education, particularly as
they have been encountered on Canada's great frontier. Selman and
Dampier (1991), in a creative work by these two "self-confessed Ca-
nadians," bring the story up to date. They portray in an interesting
and personal fashion what they believe to be the essence of their
country's provision of adult education, most of it indigenous but
some of it assimilated from thought and practice elsewhere. A full
description is given, both historically and analytically, of the forces,
forms, and leaders of programs, as well as of the international viewpoint that has always been such a pronounced part of the adult
educational enterprises of the country.

In a fashion similar to that employed by Kidd in his three
Canadian surveys, Bordia, Kidd, and Draper (1973) present a collection of fifty-nine relatively short papers about adult education in
India. Growing out of Kidd's stay at the University of Rajasthan,
the papers are kaleidoscopic in theme so that the total picture appears through the reader's own synthesis; however, almost all of the
papers are well written, and the editors have done a skillful job of
putting them together.

Hall (1970) undertook a more idiosyncratic survey than most. His first chapter is an original and sparkling account of what he believes the people of New Zealand hold as their major credos, a description that he uses as a background for his subsequent report on their adult educational practices. He does not hesitate to express his disagreement with certain current ways of doing things and his frustration that his imminent retirement will prevent him from challenging them. In 1970, Whitelock issued a description of Australian adult education; in 1974, he offered a lively historical narrative of adult education in Australia from the days of the convicts onward. The influence of English thought and practice on the Australian programs was pronounced, and the author begins his book with an excellent brief treatment of developments in the mother country. His study is not intended to be a comprehensive statistical report, but an evocative statement enlivened by quotations from many authors. Tennant (1991) edited a collection of essays about various aspects of adult education in Australia, each focusing on an institution, a target audience, or a programmatic thrust. The collection gains a sense of unity from the feeling, asserted by the authors or implicit in their work, that the contemporary adult educational scene is, in the words of the editor, "a ferment of activity" (p. xi). The authors are all active in the field, and their writing has a resulting freshness of expression.

Bown and Tomori (1979) define the meaning of adult education in West African terms and suggest the structures and policies of greatest value there. The writing is vigorous and forthright, and the description of the advances already made may come as a surprise to those unfamiliar with the programs of that economically underdeveloped part of the world. Townsend Coles (1982) includes two long essays written by the author, an Englishman, who was then head of nonformal education in Botswana. His first essay, which presents a worldwide survey of this form of education, uses the international literature on the subject but expresses the view implied by the title of his work, *Maverick of the Education Family*. His second essay describes in lucid detail how the program in Botswana was structured and operated.

Boucouvalas (1988) provides a solid and substantial account of the changing meaning of adult education throughout the long recorded history of Greece and of the nature of the program there at the present time. The author is an American of Greek descent. She is careful to provide a historical setting in both ancient and modern times and has developed impressive governmental and political sources to support and inform her research. Among many other themes, she gives an excellent account of *paideia,* a term related to but even broader than the educative society.

In the early 1980s, the International Council for Adult Education sent two study teams to China to survey practices in that country. Hunter and Keehn (1985) analyze the results of this investigation. They provide a probing and clearly written overview of Chinese history in this century and its influence on the patterns and offerings of adult education. Maorong and other Chinese adult educators (1988) describe the practices of their country so far as the major audiences, the range of opportunities, and the academic field are concerned. Thomas (1985) centers his study on Japan, starting with the way that certain social values emerged in a markedly homogeneous society. He shows how this ancient tradition was reshaped and radically changed by World War II and by the military conquerors in the postwar years; the theme of the book is expressed by its title, *Learning Democracy in Japan.* He then moves to a description of the major forces and institutions of adult education in modern times. His analysis differs from that of many interpreters of national systems in that it flows directly from indigenous sources and does not merely look for parallels to what is found in Western Europe or the United States.

Groups of Essays

Many of the books already identified have been collections of essays; other general speculative treatments with the same format but not classifiable in other categories will be mentioned in this section. They appear in *symposia,* in which several authors are asked to deal with a common theme; in *collections,* in which separate articles by a single author are presented; and in *anthologies,* in which a number of short works by different writers are gathered together from other sources.

Symposia have been numerous in the literature of adult education; some of the most notable ones published in book form will be included here. Parry (1920), already mentioned in Chapter One, is a collection of powerful statements about the humanistic aspirations of the field written in a tone of sustained intellectual idealism. Seyfert (1937) edited a collection of lectures given at Harvard by major innovators of adult education. The hopes of the authors seemed visionary at the time, but a modern reader is likely to be impressed that the actual growth of the field has been greater and more far-reaching than that prophesied. A somewhat similar work, with much the same implications for modern readers, was assembled by Wilson (1937), though its authors were drawn more from academic than from administrative circles. Jessup (1969) reported the results of a week-long conference at Oxford, in which a group of leaders of continuing education, most of them British, considered current developments and future trends in various institutions and programs. Gilder (1979) compiled the papers delivered at a conference of community college administrators by outstanding political and academic leaders of the time. They present an optimistic view of the future of adult education.

The foregoing symposia deal with the field as an essential element of an established society. More recent volumes have tended to argue that present patterns of work should be subject to vital changes. In essays collected by Thompson (1980), the authors insist that British systems cannot cope with changes already wrought in society, especially with the increasing needs of working-class people for more education. Some of the essays are historical, some theoretical, some interpretive, and some descriptive. They are alike only in their questing for new approaches. Costello and Richardson (1982) adopt the conception that society has now entered the postindustrial age and argue for the imperative need for greater attention to adult education. Some of the major issues are how to make better use of the leisure time that increased productivity makes possible, how to retain the central place of the individual in a society increasingly dominated by automation and new technologies, and how to use information technologies for instruction, particularly in distance learning. *Power and Conflict in Continuing Education* (1980) reports on a conference held by a number of American adult educators; it includes both the papers presented and an interestingly abridged version of the discussion. As the title implies, the theme of as yet unresolved challenges was present throughout the meetings. In Brockett (1987), the authors try to discern some major trends in the field and predict where they will have led by the year 2000.

Collections of essays by single authors have enriched the field chiefly by preserving the contributions of busy and active leaders who had not previously had time to organize their thoughts into coherent book-length form. When Alvin S. Johnson was head of the New School for Social Research, a major institution in New York City, he wrote a number of brief notes for its bulletin, and in 1934 a collection of some of the more pungent and interesting of his observations was published. Robert Redfield, the anthropologist, published in 1955 an elegantly written and provocative group of essays on learning in adulthood. Through anecdotes, quotations, and—most of all—his own power of phrasing, he evokes profound insights about the inherent nature of education in the adult years.

John Schwertman was a brilliant, emerging leader of adult education who died early in his career. In 1958, a group of his former associates published a number of the addresses that he had given to various audiences. His ideas are fresh and vivid and are expressed in a clear and striking style. They deal directly and personally with the broad problems with which the field of adult education is perennially confronted. John Gardner, in a book aptly called *Self-Renewal* (1981), suggests how both the individual and society can be continuously refreshed by many means, most of which involve some form of learning. Gardner's aphoristic style stimulates thought, as do his vivid and apt quotations. Robert Blakely, a long-time powerful presence in the field, has collected some of his addresses (1958) dealing broadly with the themes of the intellectual, moral, spiritual, and social goals of adult education; these essays are idealistic in their general framework and approach. Sharer (1969) presents a group of brief and poetic essays concerning the nature and importance of adult education as seen by one whose career was based in that field. J. R. Kidd, the Canadian who spent much of his life building international bridges among adult educational institutions and movements, published a collection of his addresses in 1969. They "were heard by audiences in various countries, in four continents, over two decades" (p. ix) and are, as a result, impossible to describe in narrow terms. The author is always idealistic and often eloquent. He has the unusual facility of being able to provide the right quotations from world literature to illustrate the points that he is making. Rogers (1976) provides a selection of papers by Harold Wiltshire, an outstanding English leader of adult education who was at the forefront of much of the innovation in the United Kingdom during a particularly significant time of change. In addition to Wiltshire's own writings, the book contains other essays discussing his contributions and the ideas and institutions that he believed to be of importance. The social psychologist Nevitt Sanford offered in 1980 a collection of essays written over a period of years. Concerned with both graduate and adult students, his primary interest is in the personality characteristics and, especially, the moral development present when adults are students in higher education. *Learning at the Back Door,* a book published by Wedemeyer in 1981, takes its title from a comment made by Jonathan Swift in 1704: "For to enter the palace of Learning at the Great Gate, requires an expense of time and forms; therefore men of much haste and little ceremony are content to get in by the back door" (p. 18). The author of this book, a world-traveled leader in the field, draws together his thoughts on the forms and processes of learning of those who have entered through the back door. On such matters as the nature of life-span learning and of nontraditional study, he develops systematic formulations, but his book is essentially an exploration of learning by those with nonconventional ways of entering the "palace."

The most deeply respected and enduring anthology of previously published essays is that by Ely (1936), to which reference was made earlier. *Adult Education: Current Trends and Practices* (1949) includes essays drawn from addresses and reports made by distinguished Europeans and Americans. They range from lofty and eloquent topics ("Adult Education and the Crisis of Civilization") to reports on the work of innovative institutions. Taken collectively, the papers fulfill the hope of the unnamed editor that "the book gives less a cross-section than a sample—a typical and vigorous one—of the most characteristic achievements of adult education in our time" (p. 4).

Hutchinson (1971) chose most of his papers from the pages

of the journals of several national adult education organizations in Britain. The authors are persons of eminence and achievement, and the papers selected from the riches available are of a very high order. Gross (1982b) collected an unusually wide-ranging selection of passages from ancient to modern times, some of them from familiar authors, some from less well-established ones. Other anthologies, noted at other places in this book, do not have the generality of reference required for inclusion here.

Bibliographies

General bibliographies of adult education have been especially important in the growth of the field because they have helped to show its scope to those concerned with only one institution or theme. Such a work is that prepared by Kelly (1974), incomparably the best bibliography available, which shows how rich and deep the organized provision of learning opportunities for adults has been, especially in Great Britain. He includes not only those works that intentionally refer to the field, but also citations to precursor institutions and to background materials that underlie practice. Though the focus is upon Great Britain, important works from other countries are also included. The third edition by the same author, this volume has profited greatly from its cumulative development, which reflects the growing and changing nature of the field and reappraises older sources, even as it adds new ones. Davies and Thomas (1988) extend Kelly's (1974) work with the same high level of competence. The authors note, "The extent and quality of published work on adult education in recent years indicates a significant move towards maturity in the discipline of the subject itself" (p. v).

A reader ordinarily expects that a bibliography will be useful, not interesting, but Beals and Brody (1941) managed to achieve both purposes. Their aim was to concentrate on the American literature of adult education during the 1930s and to present citations that would interest a "serious student," not an "average reader." To achieve this end, they were highly selective, choosing about one out of every four items available, thus eliminating the "printed flotsam" of the field. In analyzing and presenting the selected references, the authors say that their book "is not at all like a pie neatly sliced into seven pieces; rather it is like a mass of tangled string or yarn shaped roughly into a heptahedron. On each of the seven faces there have been detached a number of clues which the reader may unravel by means of the appended references. . . . The relation of these references to the text is opposite the conventional: the references have not been added to support or document the text; the text has been written to introduce the references" (p. xvii). In fact, the text encompasses far more than neat lists of references, as the authors provide a commentary upon the contemporary adult educational scene; they inform it with humanistic insights that give extraordinary depth to their quick surveys of limited subjects.

Many comprehensive bibliographies of adult education have existed in nonprinted form, and some have been maintained in such a way as to allow for frequent revision. The best-known of these, the only one that a reader of this book might hope to find without great effort, was that provided by Knowles (1980a). For some years, in compiling an annual bibliography for his students in adult and higher education, he searched for all aspects of knowledge that might be relevant. A somewhat similar effort has been commonly made in other graduate programs of adult education. Two of the early examples of such ventures are the works compiled at Stanford, published by Proctor (1934), and at Michigan State University, published by Congdon and Henry (1934). At the time of publication of this present book, the most extensive listings of the literature (principally that of the United States) are probably to be found in the citations given by the chapter authors in Merriam and Cunningham (1989) and in Peters, Jarvis, and Associates (1991).

Cotton (1968) wrote an essay based on the literature of the field. The first part is organized in chronological form, using these periods: 1919-1929; 1930-1946; and 1947-1964. The rest of the book dwells on major themes in the literature, with heavy reliance on early authors whom Cotton believes to be more eloquent than those who followed them. The literature, he argues, has had five central themes: the problem of living in a new world; the challenge confronting democracy; the failure of traditional education; the nature of adult needs and responsibilities; and the control of man's destiny.

Other bibliographies will be more briefly noted. Boshier

(1979) covers the literature on adult education in New Zealand comprehensively; his presentation not only is alphabetical but also contains an intricate subject-matter categorization. Mezirow and Berry (1960) offer a selective annotated list of references published in North America and Great Britain between 1945 and 1957. Although the emphasis is on *liberal education,* this use of the term is broadly conceived. Aker (1965) identifies the works on the methodology of adult education that appeared from 1953 to 1963. *Fostering the Growing Need to Learn* (1974) is focused directly on the continuing education of health professionals but broadens that theme to include an excellent general bibliography, carefully organized and with unusually well-written citations. Concentrating on leadership development, Knox (1979b) also includes "a basic reading list of professional literature on the continuing education of adults" (p. vii). This list ranges widely through many fields. Kulich has performed a valuable service by reporting in a series of monographs, published in 1971, 1975, and 1982, on the literature of adult education in continental Europe.

To round out this bibliographic account, it should be noted that a number of institutions, particularly in Europe, publish periodicals or occasional papers listing the literature of adult education. For some years, the *Review of Educational Research* in the United States made surveys of the literature in all fields of education. Three issues were devoted to adult education: June 1950, June 1953, and June 1959. The *Directory of Adult Education Periodicals,* 1985, is the seventh revised edition of this work. It gives full information about 209 periodicals in the field—international, regional, and national—that are printed in English, French, and Spanish.

A Final Word

One volume transcends the others mentioned earlier in this chapter in its breadth, penetration, and modernity of viewpoint. Titmus (1989) draws together the whole field of adult education from a lifelong-learning perspective and does so in a comprehensive and mature fashion. The book was originally planned by J. R. Kidd, who did not live to complete it. Contributions from many authors have been assembled in such a way as to stress balance and integration. The major strength of the book lies in the introductory, interstitial, and summarizing sections written by the editor. It is also truly international, not merely a compilation of accounts of national programs, and is written in language that rises above special and cultural usages. If one had to choose the most outstanding book in the field today, Titmus (1989) would be my choice.

THREE

The Underlying
Concerns of
Educators of Adults

There is, perhaps, no branch of our vast educational system which should more attract within its particular sphere the aid and encouragement of the State than adult education. How many must there be in Britain, after the disturbance of two destructive wars, who thirst in later life to learn about the humanities, the history of their country, the philosophies of the human race, and the arts and letters which sustain and are borne forward by the ever-conquering English language? . . . The mental and moral outlook of free men studying the past with free minds in order to discern the future demands the highest measures which our hard pressed finances can sustain. I have no doubt myself that a man or woman earnestly asking in grown-up life to be guided to wide and suggestive knowledge in its largest and most uplifted sphere will make the best of all pupils in this age of clatter and buzz, of gape and gloat. The appetite of adults to be shown the foundations and processes of thought will never be denied by a British Administration cherishing the continuity of our Island life.

—Winston Churchill, as quoted in U.K. Ministry of Education, *1954, pp. 66–67*

Most people who work in the field of adult education do not look beyond the immediacies of their own programs. They devote their attention to patterns of service with fairly well established goals and ways of achieving them—in libraries, in museums, in industry, in university-extension divisions, in labor unions, in military service, or in a myriad other settings. But many such people find within themselves a desire to look beyond their specific endeavors to understand the larger scope of the field. Sheer intellectual curiosity is the spur for some of these people; others seek new ways to improve their present performance; still others glimpse larger horizons or opportunities. As a result of this broader perspective, some practitioners redefine themselves as teachers, planners, administrators, providers, counselors, or mentors of services for adult learners. For want of a better term, they usually call themselves adult educators, or (when considered in contrast to learners) leaders. Though their numbers are still comparatively small, they are the chief figures in defining, establishing, and maintaining the field.

This chapter deals with books about some of the central concerns of those who look above daily practice to discern the essential nature of adult education. What are its basic philosophical conceptions? How can it best be defined as a body of knowledge and practice? How can adult educators be prepared to fulfill their responsibilities? How do they attract and retain learners? How are their accomplishments appraised? What are the national and international patterns of their work? As the literature reviewed in this chapter indicates, such topics as these have been considered by many writers.

The Philosophy of Adult Education

The term *philosophy* is as variously applied in adult education as it is in other fields of knowledge. Some writers merely voice a purpose and leave all other aspects of theory and practice to be inferred; an excellent collection of such statements was made by Ely (1936). Other people view the field from a special vantage point—community needs, the development of individual potentiality, liberal education, social and economic reform, or some other—and build a general construct that fits that orientation. Still others adopt a rigorous analytical approach, almost geometrical in its nature. Examples of these and other approaches are considered here. The literature also abounds in what has been called "good old-fashioned homely philosophy," but this book mentions few such unrooted advocacies and speculations.

In the mid-twentieth century, two writers—Eduard Lindeman and Paulo Freire—gained numerous followers as philosophers of adult education. Both believed adult education to be an instrument of social reform, though their approaches differed greatly. Lindeman, whose biographies were mentioned in Chapter One, came from a humble, rural background and entered adult education, as many others did, through employment in the Cooperative Extension Service. Ultimately, he became a member of the New York liberal establishment. He argued that complex, urban societies needed to develop and purify themselves, a task that he believed could best be accomplished by adult education. His book *The Meaning of Adult Education* (1990), first published in 1926 by New Republic, expresses the values of the field in a sweeping and exuberant fashion. His approach is within the tradition of John Dewey and also, and more profoundly, of Walt Whitman. This book greatly reinforced the acceptance of the fundamental ideas of adult education and has been read and valued ever since its publication. Brookfield (1987) presents a selection of Lindeman's other writings on adult education, as well as a comprehensive expression of his philosophic position.

As also noted in Chapter One, Freire developed an adult literacy program based on the need to encourage political self-awareness in adults belonging to almost destitute segments of society. His highly structured methodology has been most fully explained in English by Brown (1975); his theories on adult learning, which are linked to but rise far above his methodological practice, have attracted worldwide attention, particularly after he changed his base of operations to the international world centered in Geneva. Books by and about him are numerous and have been published in many languages. His best-known work, vividly called *The Pedagogy of the Oppressed* ([1970] 1984) has gone through many editions (the one cited here is the twenty-first). In it, he focuses on people at or near the bottom of the economic scale, who he feels are oppressed by dominating elites. The task of education, according to Freire, is to give the oppressed an awareness of what they have lost and are losing, to teach them the skills of literacy, and to show how it can be used to improve their health, their way of life, their occupational competence, and, especially, their participation in social affairs. In this process, they become conscious of themselves as individuals and as a class of people.

Freire's language is so difficult and complex that it is often hard to puzzle out its meaning. He has himself given many further interpretations and elaborations of his thought. For example, Freire (1978) makes clear his belief that adult education should be placed within the context of revolutionary thought and the overthrow of authoritarian regimes. Freire (1985) provides additional information about his ideas and his reflections on his own reputation.

Freire has had many interpreters. Mackie (1981) presents a collection of supportive essays on Freire's life and work that help to explain his ideas about the purposes and pedagogy of his approach to the teaching of adults. Elias (1976) explores the ideas of both Freire and Ivan Illich, another radical theorist. Elias believes that their work has not been sufficiently interpreted in light of the Roman Catholic traditions from which they spring, and he proposes in his book to fill that void in the literature. Kirkwood and Kirkwood (1989) provide a detailed account of how they carried out the ideas and principles of Freire in a densely populated part of the city of Edinburgh. Of particular value is the description and interpretation of Freire's ideas as they might apply to an urban European situation. A useful glossary of Freire's terms is also provided.

At least nine additional authors have put forward more or less systematic philosophical approaches to the whole field of adult education. They will be presented here in the order of their books' appearance.

Kallen (1962) offers four essays written in the 1950s that express the Dewey-derived, pragmatic philosophical views of a longtime supporter of adult education. He examines the central ideas of the people in that field; and though his references are to the issues of the period in which he wrote, his general approach is timeless.

Barton (1964) puts adult education, particularly that which is self-directed, at the apex of organized learning efforts. Barton's writing is so compressed, aphoristic, and cryptic that his argument is hard to follow, but the persistent reader gains insights and finds categories useful for dealing with some of the more difficult aspects of knowledge.

Bergevin (1967) asserts his belief that "one purpose of a philosophy is to establish a common point of reference, an integrated viewpoint, toward certain beliefs, ideas, attitudes, and practices" (p. 3). He seeks in this book to explicate such a philosophy based on twenty-two propositions, but his work is not so much a closely reasoned demonstration as it is an assertion of beliefs, some of them evangelically stated.

More (1974) has written a highly personal volume, growing out of his experiences and feelings and with almost no citations of other sources or appeals to authority. He argues strongly that emotions are dominant in learning and teaching and shows how their primacy influences all aspects of practical education and the theories on which it is based—from the simplest skills to the most profound truths.

Drawing from deep wellsprings in both ancient and modern writings, McKenzie (1978) bases his analysis on the field of philosophy itself. For those who have not accompanied him in his quest for knowledge, he reviews sources and fundamentals before coming to his own complex position. Though rooted in existentialism, his ideas are distinctively expressed in seven propositions that are stated in clear and precise terms. In the manner of the Scholastics, he then states the key arguments against his own position and gives his responses to them. He presents his work, not as an accomplished position, but as an exercise in inquiry.

Paterson (1979) desires to establish a rigorously defined, theoretical way of thinking about adult education. He reasons carefully, starting with definitions and building basic principles of action and interpretation upon them. R. S. Peters, the editor of the series in which this book appears, points out that its author's ultimate conclusions are "controversial and unlikely to be popular both with many of his colleagues in adult education and with many philosophers of education. He is, for instance, uncompromising in his refusal to harness education to practical or social purposes. Education, he claims, is concerned with the development of 'the person in his person-hood.' He vigorously defends the importance of subject-matters and their intrinsic criteria of worth" (p. viii).

Gelpi (1979), an Italian, offers a two-volume work translated by English proponents of the author's philosophy (particularly Ralph Ruddock); they view him as an emerging world theoretician of adult education who seeks the reform of social injustice without recourse to revolutionary concepts. Gelpi, who speaks several languages, was chief of the lifelong education unit at Unesco at the time of the publication of this book. As he seeks to address the whole world, his writing is highly theoretical and abstract, without direct guides to action. A collection of essays rather than a single unified work, the book sometimes seems to be a series of pronouncements. Yet the reader has the sense that, given more space, the various points in his philosophic statements could be translated into practice.

Lawson (1979) attempts to provide a truly philosophical analysis rigorously applied to the leading terms and concepts of adult education. He believes that the field has not been adequately concerned with modern conceptions of linguistic analysis and also that the philosophers of education have not taken adequate account of the distinctions between the teaching and learning of children and that of adults. He argues that adult education can appropriately be defined as "something specifically and uniquely related to adulthood in terms of what is taught, how it is taught, and how it is organized" (p. 114). The effort to demonstrate that proposition is perhaps the major purpose of this book. In another work, Lawson (1982) presents a collection of papers concerned with the philosophical underpinnings of adult education and particularly with the relationship between theoretical constructs in the field and active practice in it. These papers are subtle and closely reasoned. The background of the book is English, though some reference is made both to other European authors and to such world figures as Freire and Illich.

Wain's work (1987) is a serious philosophic treatment. He identifies lifelong education as being a Unesco invention, flowing from Faure, Lengrand, Gelpi, Dave, and other sources. The author's thought, however, springs from the deep tradition of the philosophy of education that includes Dewey and emphasizes the ideas of humanism.

The intention of the foregoing books has been to analyze all of adult education. Others seek to build a philosophy in which some learning goal or body of content is paramount. The first such major effort was that of Yeaxlee (1925), in a massive two-volume work entitled *Spriritual Values in Adult Education.* Yeaxlee was a distinguished leader of the Church of England and a member of the committee that produced the *1919 Report.* His book is deeply scholarly and written with broad humanity, clarity of expression, and an unusual command of resources. His references rest on classical and British traditions. The author's intent is nothing less than to explore all the religious, spiritual, and nonmaterialistic dimensions of adult education as they may be observed both historically and analytically. His central ideas are summarized in a chapter entitled "Ad Unum Omnes," which is found about halfway through the second volume (pp. 201–216). Here Yeaxlee argues eloquently that the true end of adult education is the "harmonized personality" of the individual, a harmony that must be based essentially on the spiritual values required for personal growth, as well as for productive interaction and institutionalization.

Another broad approach to adult learning is treated philosophically in a small cluster of works that seems likely to grow in size and significance. Brookfield (1988a) identifies and describes what he calls critical thinking, the habit of examining experiences reflectively to assess their truth or value so as to transform ideas and beliefs. His emphasis is on adulthood, as it is during the mature years that the most varied and responsible of such experiences occur. The book is celebratory and definitional rather than prescriptive. Brookfield (1990) carries these ideas further by discussing how a teacher may best bring about such changes within many instructional settings. The author pays a great deal of attention to lessons learned from his own experience. Mezirow and Associates (1990) treat this same broad theme, in a series of essays by scholars, chiefly American. Some are concerned with how critical thinking and transformative learning happen naturally. Others examine its application in psychiatry, social movements, women's consciousness raising, the workplace, and elsewhere, but always within the context of achieving profound educative changes in the individual. Mezirow (1991) presents the fullest expression of the nature of transformative learning yet developed. This book is intended as a companion piece to his 1990 work but goes much beyond it in its theoretical depth and its incorporation of the work of Habermas, other social theorists, and various analysts of aspects of general perceptual and interactive processes. Direct reference is made throughout to the theory and practice of adult education. Collins (1991) suggests the distinctiveness of this general approach by observing, "From the viewpoint of a transformative pedagogy, the growing irrelevance of contemporary mainstream adult education as a distinctive field of practice stems initially from its unquestioning compliance with the imperatives of an ideology of technique" (p. 118).

A recurrent theme in the literature of adult education has been the fostering of creativeness. Davis and Scott (1971) assess the general philosophical basis of this goal. The twenty-three annotated papers included in the book also describe various theories and techniques, such as synectics, bionics, and brainstorming.

Brockett (1988) edited a group of papers written by academic adult educators that consider questions of ethics in the field as a whole or some part of it, such as planning, administration, evaluation, counseling, or research. Each author deals with the major moral questions, dilemmas, or issues to be found in the topic under discussion, in some cases making the reader aware that behavior and practice have ethical dimensions not previously perceived.

Livingstone (1944) centers his book on the importance of the classical conception of liberal education, especially in adulthood, in creating the well-rounded person. This work, written in England in 1941 during the darkest days of World War II, identifies liberal study as the keystone of education in the postwar era and suggests the Danish folk school as a model for British adult education. Livingstone was a distinguished classicist, and his book gives perhaps the clearest brief explanation of the traditional aims of liberal education to be found anywhere in the literature.

Powell (1949) develops the point of view that maturity is the time when inquiry can best be fostered, especially by book-based discussion. He gives lengthy illustrations from several institutions, particularly the School of Social Studies founded by Alexander Meiklejohn in San Francisco.

For many adult educators, the *community* has been the concept around which thought and activity have been focused. Though this term has many definitions, it ordinarily connotes some definable unit separated from the rest of the world by geography, political system, or a complex interaction between people and groups. Some authors argue that in the analysis of the nature, needs, concerns, and desires of this unit are to be found the goals of education and that in the separate and collective activities of its institutions are to be found the means of accomplishing them. Seay (1974) presented a comprehensive treatment of the ideas and practices that he developed during his years, stretching from the 1930s to the 1980s, as a leader of community education. Galbraith (1990b) uses a different approach, extolling the idea of the community as a reinforcement of learning, particularly in settings in which education is allied with other functions. In addition to a general discussion of the idea of community, attention is given to the specifics of social and fraternal organizations, libraries, religious institutions, museums, and human services organizations. Many other community-oriented works will be mentioned throughout the later pages of this book.

A number of authors (for example, Freire and Illich) have been ardent advocates of change in the social order. Boyd (1969) reports on a conference held to explore the philosophical position that the aim of adult education is to change society and that the adult educator is best viewed as a change agent. In recent years, some interest has been expressed in examining forms of radicalism as philosophical systems. Youngman (1986) offers a sustained and rigorous analysis of Marxism as it applies to adult education—to which (the author contends) the basic theories of Marx, Lenin, and Mao have a natural and desirable application. The author himself favors the Marxist approach, but he does not proselytize or denigrate the ideas of dissenters. Though the book was published in England, the author draws on the worldwide literature in the field. Evans (1987) writes more generally about radical adult education. He makes it clear that he is for basic change in society; yet because his immediate frame of reference is practice in the United Kingdom, his study focuses on the shaping and execution of national governmental policy, not structural change in the government itself.

Collins (1991) urges that the adult educator should have a vocation, a sense of mission. He examines the ways by which it may be achieved by providing a wide-ranging survey of the North American and European literature on social and political theory, as well as on adult education. As yet the only rigorously comparative study of philosophies of adult education is that provided by Elias and Merriam (1980). They identify six conceptions of adult education and show how they apply, both analytically and practically. The six are liberal adult education, progressive adult education, behaviorist adult education, humanist adult education, radical adult education, and analytical adult education. These are sketched rapidly. The book approaches its topic from the field itself, thus moving inductively, rather than starting with basic philosophic propositions and working toward their application. In 1984, Merriam published a collection of substantial segments of a number of authorities' writings on education, so chosen as to present a picture of the breadth of philosophic viewpoint characteristic of the field. Lowy and O'Connor (1986) establish themselves as humanistic in orientation (in terms of the Elias and Merriam definition) and then, in an elaborate literature-based analysis, make the case for the importance of lifelong learning.

In recent years, the attention of some scholars in the field has turned to basic philosophical ideas and movements. Bright (1989) includes papers by several American and English authors who explore adult education, employing epistemology as a form of analysis. The editor summarizes these contributions by saying, "The major conclusion . . . is that the study of adult education does represent serious epistemological issues and problems and that these are all concerned with its postulated lack of rigor in relation to the conventional disciplines" (p. 174). Stanage (1987) applies the *phenomenological* approach to adult education, using Spiegelberg's definition of the key term as being "the name for a philosophical movement whose primary objective is the direct investigation and description of phenomena as consciously experienced, without theories about their causal explanation and as free as possible from unexamined preconceptions and presuppositions" (p. 43). Stanage explores the movement in its various manifestations, especially as it may be used as a way of viewing adult learning. The reader has a sense that this is a work in progress, not a final summation of its author's beliefs. It is not easy reading for those unfamiliar with technical philosophical approaches.

The effort to develop a personal philosophy has been attempted by many educators of adults. Apps (1973) reflects on the ways by which he went about working out a basis for thought and action in the field. He examines many principles and systems and takes from them the ideas that he finds creative and useful. He does not espouse any fundamental system, while always working, he says, for consistency in his beliefs. Long, Apps, and Hiemstra (1985) write three substantial essays on the same theme: what are the essential meaning and the ultimate dimensions of the term *lifelong learning?* The authors' analyses differ, but all three focus on adult education, giving little attention to learning in infancy, childhood, and youth. Jarvis (1987b) draws together thirteen essays by various authors, each devoted to the ideas of a leading twentieth-century author, ranging in time from Albert Mansbridge to Ettore Gelpi.

The effort to build a complete and coherent framework for education at all ages has probably been realized most fully by Dave (1973). In presenting and defending twenty propositions about lifelong learning, he has established a sound basis for emerging conceptions. Knowles (1980b) expresses the distinction between the study of the education of children (pedagogy) and the study of the education of adults (which he calls andragogy). This differentiation is also made in other books by Knowles and is extensively discussed in the periodical literature.

The relationship between the theory and the practice of adult education has long been of interest and is now coming to the forefront. As already noted, Lawson (1979 and 1982) deals with this topic. Squires (1975) offers an interesting case study of how a philosophy of adult education can be worked out in an innovative program; the Learning Exchange embodies the basic idea of Ivan Illich and Everett Reimer that society should be "deschooled," so that learning becomes spontaneously sought and provided. Kreitlow and Associates (1981) show how different viewpoints are brought to bear on some of the major controversies now present in the field. Should the adult educator be involved in social intervention? Should the continuing education of the members of professions be made mandatory? Should adult education require support from learner fees? Each of these questions, as well as others, is examined by two authorities; these do not give positive or negative answers but express complex viewpoints, with qualifications and distinctions arising from deeper philosophic positions.

Merriam (1982) has edited a group of papers about the relationship between general conceptions of the way life is or ought to be (philosophy) and the actual ways that lives are planned or occur (practice). This symposium delves deeply into the relationship between thought and action, but the central concern of the authors is with adult educational activities. The heart of the work consists of seven case examples; in each, practice is analyzed according to a fundamental idea of what it should be in broad theoretical terms. Among these examples are the outreach of a women's liberal arts college, the training division of a large insurance company, a program for improving life in primitive villages, and the continuing educational activities of an urban community college.

Usher and Bryant (1989) enlarge the discourse about theory and practice by introducing research as a third consideration. The authors believe that these three elements are not linear in nature but exist as an interrelated triangle; if there is one that dominates, the authors argue that it lies within practice and particularly in the mind of the adult educator. Though caught up in the specifics of a situation, this educator tries reflectively both to advance theories about work practice and to discover or undertake the research that will test theory and illuminate the processes being undertaken. This book is highly theoretical and requires study, rather than simple perusal, to be fully comprehended.

Adult Education as a Body of Knowledge and Practice

The works cited earlier in this chapter provide ways of thinking about the total nature and scope of adult education. The works to be noted here report inquiries into key elements of the field in order to define it, to indicate its research boundaries, and to show its linkage with other (usually better-established) bodies of knowledge.

Many founders of the field were administrators or faculty members of universities. It seemed natural to them that the creation of sound theory and practice required the establishment of graduate departments that could conduct research in adult education and prepare the men and women who could carry forward the responsibilities of guiding future activities. Beginning in the early 1930s, therefore, a few institutions of higher learning initiated the study of adult education as a graduate academic field. After World War II, the number of such programs began to increase; more than a hundred of them now exist in North America, and others are to be found throughout the world. For the graduate professors involved, the establishment of some central sense of their field was essential, however much the concerns of active practitioners might require specialized operational approaches.

The major collective effort to define academic adult education was presented by Jensen, Liveright, and Hallenbeck (1964), describing a collaborative inquiry by the professors of adult education in the United States. Because of the color of its cover, this volume has come to be known colloquially as "the black book." As the product of many minds, it is not completely consistent in its presentation but serves a useful purpose in demonstrating the range of topics included in graduate curricula and graduate research programs. A follow-up volume, edited by Peters, Jarvis, and Associates (1991), is naturally more sophisticated than the earlier book. Although the chapter authors have been left free to handle their topics in ways that seemed best to them, the editors help their readers to examine the whole field and to identify the strengths, weaknesses, and directions in which the content is moving. In 1980, Boyd and Apps presented a conceptual model of the whole field based on three dimensions: transactional modes, client focus, and social or cultural systems. The rest of their book is composed of clusters of brief chapters by various authors, essentially organized by individual, group, and transactional modes. The book ends with a critique of the system by another author and a rejoinder by Boyd and Apps. Campbell (1977) based his work on Canadian thought and practice. From that vantage point, he first gives an overview of adult education in Canada and then narrows his perspective to look closely at graduate study in that field, even as he includes thought and practice in Britain and the United States. He then reports the findings of a survey of practicing adult educators about training; his respondents were engaged in many different types of work in Alberta. He concludes by making the case for a more effective program of graduate study in that province.

A number of other efforts have been made to discover the essential nature of adult education, most of them by academic adult educators. Verner (1962) brought rigor to the task of denoting the key terms of the field and classifying its central ideas. Apps (1979) deals with what he calls the recurring problems of adult education—the perennial issues that often lie beneath immediate differences of opinion. His approach is broadly based, a fact that is apparent in the range of his concerns, the aptness of his illustrations, and his well-grounded points of view. Peters (1980) offers a work in which a number of authors, most of them seasoned veterans, describe how they envision the structure of the field. These analyses flow from several origins and research methodologies, but all seek to place boundaries around adult education or understand its internal structure. In fairly brief compass, Darkenwald and Merriam (1982) provide a broad overview of the conceptual basis of the field; they consider its definition, its philosophy, the nature of adults as learners, the extent of their participation, the agencies and programs of the field, its international dimensions, and its most common problems and issues. Long (1983a) argues that "adult and continuing education in the United States can be characterized by a combination of five descriptors: it is creative, pragmatic, voluntary, pluralistic and dynamic. . . . These five characteristics help to explain the constantly changing programmatic thrusts of a variety of institutions identified as sources of educational assistance and learning for adults" (p. 4). Fraser (1980) tries "to put together a mosaic of the present education and training structure, indicating the wide range of available estimates as to how many adults, particularly workers and would-be workers, are taking advantage of this opportunity structure" (p. 3). Thomas (1991) offers a full and recent exposition of the distinction between planned education and the learning that results from experience. In analyzing the latter, he helps to define the larger field of adult education by identifying a number of insightful distinctions and categories.

Understanding of the nature and practice of adult education may be drawn from other bodies of knowledge and university disciplines. Knox (1977) presents the fullest treatment yet published of this interdependence, with varied illustrations drawn from investigators in many fields. Bown and Okedara (1981) deal comprehensively with the connection of various academic disciplines to adult education. Blackburn (1989) explores the ways by which various theoretical and practical fields are related to university outreach, particularly agricultural extension. Included are sociology and anthropology, psychology, economics, political studies, community development, organizational development, and social work. Lengrand (1986) introduces an interesting and nonacademic way of approaching the interrelationship of various fields. This collaborative effort of authors from Europe, French Canada, and Japan is not concerned with formal disciplines, but with seven basic themes: the workings of the body; the meaning of time; the role of art; the nature of citizenship; ethics and morality; science and technology; and communication. Lengrand brings these broad ideas together in introductory and concluding chapters.

Most academic adult educators orient themselves toward the social sciences. As noted in Chapter One, recurrent education has been studied chiefly using the techniques of economic analysis, and various aspects of the social milieu have figured prominently in the works cited in many other places. Sociology has been a prime area of interest. Jarvis (1985) treats the grand theory level of sociological thought as it applies to the education of adults. He is not concerned especially (as other writers have been) with the application of such approaches as group dynamics, community development, or the study of social needs, but with central sociological distinctions. In a collection of essays, Jones (1984) deals eclectically with the general concepts and specific techniques of sociology as they apply to the practice of adult education throughout the world. The book presents a panoramic view of the topic; its ideas are varied, interesting, and well expressed. Pöggeler (1990) offers perhaps the fullest and clearest exposition now available of how adult education can be considered by political scientists, especially those interested in the theory of government. His is a very substantial work, incorporating the papers from two world conferences on the subject. These papers were written by scholars from many countries and cover both basic theory and its expression in specific countries. Mezirow (1991) furnishes an excellent example of how the adult educator can use many insights from the broad field of social theory, including some by European authors not previously familiar to American readers.

Most books within the social science tradition focus on a single theme or social construct. Hallenbeck and others (1962) present the views of five distinguished authors concerning the importance of the community for adult education; they consider the nature of the community itself, the social structures that compose it, and the institutions that carry out its goals. Bennis, Benne, and Chin (1969) make a substantial contribution to what they call applied social science. The book deals with the processes of changing people in group, dyadic, and organizational settings. Rogers and Shoemaker (1971) update an earlier work by the first-named author called *Diffusion of Innovations*. Both works deal with the way by which new ideas and practices are diffused throughout society—in some cases by structured systems of learning, but more frequently by informal association. The earlier book was widely read by workers in the Cooperative Extension Service and had influence on thought and practice in that field. In a controlled study, Verner and Millard (1966) demonstrate the link between the extent to which innovations are adopted and the rate at which subjects (in this case, a number of Canadian orchardists) participate in adult educational activities. Using sociological theories and formulations to examine the work of adult education in the Los Angeles public schools, Clark (1968) has developed the concept of marginality, which has had widespread resonance throughout the whole field. Mee (1980) uses management theory to assess the structuring and processes of adult education. Among the topics considered are role conceptions, the handling of institutional change, and the nature of professionalization. Elsey (1986) looks at the social determinants of adult education and sets up useful categories for thinking about that field. The four basic models, the author argues, are the recreation-leisure model, the work-training model, the liberal-progressive model, and the radical model. Each is described and analyzed. The author then presents (in closely reasoned arguments) other sets of categories that apply generally to the field, to the nature of the adult learner, and to such problems as nonparticipation. McGivney and Sims (1986) show in substantial detail how adult education may be related to a specific social problem. They are concerned with the reduction of unemployment, a serious problem in the United Kingdom. The authors give a clear and remarkably convincing account of what might be done, both to remedy matters in general and to meet the special needs of older people, women, ethnic minorities, professionals and executives, ex-offenders, and the disabled.

The amount and kind of adult education provided in a society are influenced by social forces, sometimes acting directly and sometimes shaped by legislative bodies. Rivera (1987) presents a collection of papers dealing with policies created by government, by forces in the social system, and by leadership. Particular attention is paid to the agricultural research and extension services in the United States, to the federal basic education program, and to the operation of specialized bodies of the United Nations system. Griffin (1987) reflects on how social policies are influenced by such theoretical approaches as Marxism, conservatism, and liberalism; he also shows how policy is shaped by the reports of deliberative bodies, especially in Great Britain. He is specifically interested in the shift from considering adult education as an instrument of social policy to treating it as an independently professionalized field of service.

The field of psychology has produced many works that discuss the changes of cognitive processes throughout the span of life; most such works have profound implications for learning, including that which occurs in the adult years. Howe (1977) includes papers written by a number of British academic psychologists, each of whom delineates a concept drawn from psychological theory or research and then finds implications for the practice of adult education. Personality theory, programmed learning, and other topics are considered. The book aims to show how psychology can help adult education but does not go beyond that purpose to indicate how psychology might be advanced by the study of such applications. Tennant (1988) has a somewhat similar goal. Among the subjects that concern him are humanistic psychology, psychoanalysis, adult development, learning styles, behaviorism, and group dynamics. His intent, he says, is "to provide a critical account of those psychological theories which have informed contemporary adult education theory and practice" (p. 22).

Verner and Davison (1971) made an early and pioneering exploration of how physiological factors influence the ability to learn. They pay attention to such topics as visual and auditory acuity, psychomotor skills, perception, and memory.

A substantial body of research has been required to build up the body of knowledge that underlies the field. When Brunner (1959) presented his work on this subject, it was regarded as a landmark event: it was the first intensive effort to summarize the research findings that could be said to be distinctively related to adult education, including such topics as the extent of adult participation in learning, the motivation to learn, and the development of leaders and leadership. Long (1983b) was inspired by Brunner, though the growth of the field in the intervening years required new patterns of presentation. Long's work is organized into broad problem areas: the nature of research in informing practice, adult learning ability, participation of adults in educational activities, program development, the teaching-learning transaction, and the nature of the field of adult education. Charnley (1974) summarizes and to some extent evaluates a large number of theses and independent investigations produced in Britain. Arranging his summaries in a sequential form according to subject, he is not content with presenting abstracts but also furnishes some interpretations. Charters and Rivera (1972) present a collection of papers by a number of analysts of adult education, each of whom deals with some aspect of the question of how the professional literature is being and should be provided.

An interesting and ingenious effort to identify major needs for further research distinguishes *Lifelong Learning During Adulthood* (1978). A number of different approaches are used, including a review of the literature, interaction among groups of leaders in the field, and the development of an analytic framework chiefly devised by Alan Knox. The various themes are drawn together into a single matrix, which is of value to anyone seeking a general idea of the range of knowledge needed for the further development of adult education. Long, Hiemstra, and Associates (1980) assemble a collection of essays dealing with various themes of research. Parallel chapters are devoted to historical, survey, field inquiry and grounded theory, and experimentation as methods of conducting research. Some overall synthesis is provided in opening and closing chapters by the two editors. Merriam and Simpson (1989) offer a comprehensive overview of how various forms of research should be conducted. They deal both with the fundamentals of detailed, hypothesis-driven investigation and with broader kinds of inquiries, such as the case study and grounded theory. They also examine some essential components of research, including literature search, data collection, and reporting and disseminating procedures.

Leaders and Leadership

As noted at the start of this chapter, no convenient term has yet been devised that encompasses all those who serve in organized learning situations as mentors, teachers, guides, instructors, or occupants of other roles in helping adults to learn. Nor is there a single term for all those who initiate, plan, direct, and manage adult educational enterprises, despite the fact that this latter group has been of crucial importance in the massive and complex task of creating the field in all its ramifications. (The French call such people *animateurs,* but the English cognate of that term has overpoweringly Disneyesque connotations.) It is conventional in the literature to use the tired but concise term *leaders* to include all people in both overlapping groups—and that usage will be followed here.

No single pathway has been devised for the initial preparation or further development of leaders. At other levels of education, matters are simpler. The role of school teacher and the path to the occupation of that position are fairly well defined, as are the nature of and preparation for a career as college or university faculty member. Such is not the case in adult education; and it seems likely that, so long as it retains its vital diversity, patterns will always be complex. Substantial work has been done in preparing leaders for each of the various segments and program emphases of adult education, and reports of such ventures are included in the more specialized sections of this book.

A few works dealing broadly with leadership roles will be mentioned here. *The Training of Functional Literacy Personnel* (1973) is a basic manual on its subject. Though international in scope, it accepts the need to set every program in its specific milieu, provides for integration with other substantive efforts, and requires feedback on outcomes. Hely (1966) makes the general case for the use of school teachers in adult education but focuses specifically on their importance in underdeveloped countries as leaders of literacy and fundamental education programs. The book analyzes "the varying practices and experiences of a number of countries which have experimented fairly widely in recent years with the training and employment of school-teachers" (p. 49) for programs of this sort. Luke (1971) describes the basic process by which school teachers may be helped to broaden their ability to guide the education of adults, chiefly by participation in workshops that aid them to develop their understanding of the distinctive nature of the learning process. At the higher level of the academic ladder, Diekhoff (1956), a humanistic scholar, probes deeply into the nature of the teaching-learning style as it is practiced with both on-campus young students and adults. The book is descriptive, not prescriptive. In a more intensive fashion, Daloz (1986) reports on his experiences as mentor-teacher of adults in an external degree program, giving lengthy case studies but moving beyond them to theoretical formulations. Stenzel and Feeney (1968) are concerned with the training of volunteers in social programs, including those that offer adult educational opportunities. Their work is grounded in the research then available, and they provide many suggestions and sample forms.

An early effort to analyze the overall nature of leadership in adult education is provided by Overstreet and Overstreet (1941). *Leadership* is defined broadly to include adult educators who work in every kind of institution and undertake every kind of work. The approach of the authors is consistently humanistic, filled with examples of both excellent and inferior practice and treating personal traits and interactions as essential components of educational leadership. A more analytical approach has been made by Liveright (1959), who observed leadership patterns closely in fourteen diversified programs in order to develop typologies of leaders and of the processes that they use in various situations. He distinguishes, for example, between group- and content-oriented leadership styles and differentiates among attitudinal programs, understanding programs, and skill programs.

Several broad analyses have been made of European leaders. *Workers in Adult Education* (1966) presents the most salient facts concerning such people in six European countries. The study was commissioned by the Council of Europe and carried out by the

European Bureau of Adult Education; the final report of the results of various conferences and documents was drafted by Frank Jessup of Oxford University. The situation in each of the six countries— Belgium, Federal Republic of Germany, France, the Netherlands, Norway, and the United Kingdom—is described, and generalizations are made about the larger European situation. Scheffknecht (1975) uses the term *tutor* to designate anyone concerned with the education of adults. His book has two parts. The first deals with how tutors are trained in European countries and suggests sixteen "training units," each of which covers a topic that tutors might find it profitable to learn. The second part provides a typology of adult educators and makes useful distinctions concerning both the kinds of existing jobs and the ways by which various functions essential to adult education are carried out. Kulich (1977) presents an anthology of papers about the training of adult educators in Eastern Europe. Most of the articles included were written by the editor, but work by other authors is also included. Of particular note is a comprehensive essay on the whole theme of the book prepared by Dusan Savicevic of Yugoslavia. Elsdon (1975) examines the total pattern of recognized and structured adult education in Britain in an attempt to define the needs for leadership at instructional and administrative levels and to suggest both the theory and practice required. He has cast his net very broadly, and the results show an impressive erudition, covering both British and American sources. Hutchinson and Hutchinson (1978) describe English programs in which general liberal studies courses are provided within a framework of close counseling and helpful assistance. Jarvis and Chadwick (1991) bring together papers prepared by specialists on adult education in fifteen western European nations who discuss the provisions made for the education or (as some prefer to say) the training of adult educators in their countries. Some description is provided, but most of the authors are concerned with the meaning of key terms used in the various national settings as they have emerged from cultural and historical backgrounds. This interest is also expressed by the editors in their introductory and final summarizing chapters. As a result, this book is valuable not only for its specific content but also as a general inquiry into the nature of adult education.

Other books describe how teaching abilities may be fostered.

Brown and Copeland (1979) edited a brief but comprehensive collection of essays dealing with all aspects of the staffing of adult education programs: recruitment, selection, development, supervision, provision of support systems, and reward patterns. Also included are three essays generally concerned with teaching. Miller and Verduin (1979) analyze the theory and practice of staff development within an adult educational program. They successfully avoid linkage with any single kind of service or institution and are varied and pragmatic in their suggestion of activities. Ilsley and Niemi (1981) give a comprehensive account of the total pattern of finding and using volunteers, particularly in institutions of adult education. Knox (1979b) provides a broad overview of leadership training, which outlines the "major areas of proficiency which contribute to the effectiveness of continuing education practitioners" (p. v) and demonstrates how they apply generally to three categories of leaders: administrators, teachers and counselors, and policy makers. The book is based on an intensive survey of the literature and is intended as a broad conceptual analysis, not as a practical workbook. In another work, Knox (1982) assumes that administrators of adult educational programs must solve many problems and handle many situations, especially when they enter new positions or move into unexpected aspects of their work. He provides suggestions and illustrations showing the strategies that leaders may use in such aspects of decision making as the setting of priorities, the use of resources, marketing, coordination, staffing, and external relationships.

In the previous section of this chapter, the graduate departments of adult education in universities were treated as providers of investigation and research. In the eyes of most people, including many of their own staff members, these departments are known chiefly as advanced centers for the preparation or upgrading of those who occupy major positions in the field. Grabowski and others (1981) deal with both the advanced instruction offered by graduate departments and with (as the editors of the volume note) "the full range of training programs conducted by adult educators, from the continuing professional education of those holding professional degrees, licenses, or other certificates to the most elementary of educational programs for laborers with little formal previous education" (pp. x–xi). Brookfield (1988b) aims "to provide readers with an understanding of the history, organization, and underlying intellectual orientations of graduate adult education in the United States" (p. 1), so far as preparation for diplomas, master's degrees, and doctoral degrees are concerned. The main body of the text is made up of passages from other books, but they are woven together and introduced skillfully by the editor in this comprehensive and voluminous work. Waldron and Moore (1991) present a text for a basic course in adult education developed as a result of experience with several hundred students who have used earlier versions.

Adult educators, like those engaged in any other profession, must be concerned with their own in-service learning. Brockett (1991) offers a collection of papers focusing on ways that those who work in the field can strengthen their own competence by reading, introspection, voluntary association, writing, the preparation of presentations, and graduate study. The emphasis of all these authors is on how each person can refine and shape individual abilities, not be forced to fit into a mold. McKenzie (1991) is concerned with how the adult educator can constantly reshape his or her *worldview*, a term that means both a place in time and geography (which determines an individual's perspective) and that person's interpretation of life. This work is philosophical in character; the central authority cited is Heidegger. It is fundamentally concerned with the ways by which the individual can build a worldview by using the processes of adult learning.

Counseling, Referral, and Promotion

The task of linking a would-be learner to the forms of education best suited to his or her needs is often a challenging task, even in assessing the offerings of a single institution; it can become a mammoth undertaking, viewed in the light of the opportunities available in a total community. Men and women seek to clarify their purposes and then search for the educational programs that will help them. Alternatively, organizations and associations provide instruction but sometimes cannot find an interested clientele. In the 1920s and 1930s, these problems seemed so staggering as to be insoluble, particularly because so many adults were not aware of learning opportunities or were opposed to the idea of participating in them. The volume of service is now so great, however, that aware-ness of the field has increased and opposition to it has diminished. Also, enough sustained effort has been undertaken in counseling, referral, and promotion to furnish a helpful body of theory and practice.

An early work on counseling techniques was provided by Klein and Moffit (1946). Their central attention was directed toward orienting adults to the offerings of an instructional center, such as an evening school or a university center. The book is practical and spells out procedures in a systematic fashion. Farmer (1967) also deals with intrainstitutional personnel services; she shows how reg-istrants in an evening college can be helped to identify and adjust to the courses offered. Topics like admissions, placement, personal counseling, student activities, and financial aid are considered. In a full-scale, highly developed work, Schlossberg, Lynch, and Chick-ering (1989) review the problems encountered by adult students as they seek to fit in as "regular" students in campus programs de-signed for young full-time students. The authors not only develop useful categories of adult students in such settings, but also give case studies showing how present arrangements affect such people, often negatively. The book is organized in terms of the progression of students through the program ("moving in," "moving through," and "moving out)."

Works about counseling have been extended to include multi-institutional situations and to be increasingly concerned with the personal interaction between the counselor and the person counseled. Van Hoose and Worth (1982) describe counseling as it can be used for adults who do not have serious problems but need to talk with a trained, helpful person. The authors treat such inter-action as a process of self-discovery and, in the broadest sense, of personal learning. Thoroman (1968) is an advocate of vocational counseling, especially as it applies to such categories of people as women, veterans, the seriously disabled, and the elderly. Schloss-berg (1984) is concerned with the ways in which adults can best learn, with the help of professional counselors, to make adjustments in the wake of personal crises, whether these are caused by external events or by personal feelings of need or inadequacy. Such counsel-ing could be considered a form of dyadic education, and it is also often a precursor to programs of organized learning. Riverin-Simard (1988) used the vantage point of an adult educational counselor to frame a theory of the phases of work life; in the process, she discovered a general approach to guide her future counseling. Farmer (1971) gathers together essays by a number of authors who describe various aspects of counseling services for adults in higher educational settings. *Counseling* here is given a broad definition, both as to kinds of problems (such as vocational, financial, and legal) and as to specialized audiences (such as minority groups, inner-city adults, and white students in black colleges). Of particular value is the essay by Farmer entitled "Counseling Adults is Different," which identifies the distinctiveness of approach needed for mature people as contrasted to children. Ironside (1976) gives a brief introduction to the systems of counseling assistance provided to would-be learners and to the methods of information seeking undertaken by such people. Her main interest, however, is in the provision of a fully annotated bibliography of books and papers covering both kinds of service. Ironside and Jacobs (1977) intended initially to compile an annotated bibliography of the literature on the general subject of counseling and informational services for adults engaged in learning. Fortunately, the editors went beyond annotations to offer seven chapters integrating the literature, thus providing a useful summary of the theory and practice of adult educational counseling as it existed at the time of publication. Schlossberg, Troll, and Leibowitz (1978) have created what is probably the most carefully worked out guide available to the practice of counseling adults. The authors begin with five chapters on basic approaches and follow these with another five chapters on improvement in practice. The book is written simply and directly so that it can readily be understood by nonspecialist readers, but its insights and practical suggestions are sufficiently sophisticated to contribute to the knowledge and ability of advanced practitioners in the art of counseling.

From the beginning of the adult educational movement in the United States, the communitywide coordination of adult education has been considered important, not only to aid in counseling, but also to discover gaps and duplications of service, to gain the other advantages of collaboration, and to advance the ideas and

programs of adult education. Initially, it was thought that the best
way to achieve such ends would be the creation of local councils;
these would involve both providing agencies and interested citizens,
perhaps following the early models of welfare councils and community chest campaigns. Kotinsky (1940) takes a broad view of the
nature and operation of these adult education councils and goes
exhaustively into such topics as their social relevance, their potentialities, and the difficulties that they encounter. The adult education council has almost disappeared in the United States; as it has
turned out, this book analyzed it at its peak.

Other forms of coordination have been tried, some of them
successfully. Thomson edited the *New York Times Guide,* published in 1972. This is a vast, fact-filled document intended to provide initial guidance to potential adult students concerning the
institutions they might consult to gain further counseling and instruction. A prefatory essay notes, "This book is an attempt to provide help to adult students at a time when their world of educational
opportunity is expanding so rapidly that it is not possible to define
its limits precisely" (p. 15). The hope that this book might be periodically revised and kept in print did not materialize. Many large
city newspapers, including the *New York Times,* now issue one or
more supplements each year filled with advertising from institutions and with feature articles describing segments of the entire
educational scene with special attention to universities, perhaps
because they are the heaviest advertisers. Another attempt at coordination occurs when single institutions, most frequently public
libraries, reach out to other providers of learning opportunities to
help reinforce their services. Coplan and Castagna (1965) describe
many efforts to broaden the usefulness of the public library. Beder
(1984) and his collaborators take a fresh and sophisticated approach
to the whole question of cooperation among providers. The authors
included in this work believe that programs and institutions will
collaborate only if their managers consider it to be to their clear
advantage to do so. The kinds of cooperation discussed are cospon-
sorship, referral, donor-receiver, and continuing coordination. Examples are given of many forms of successful and unsuccessful
collaboration.

At the end of the 1970s, opinion seemed to crystallize that the existing ways of relating potential learners to resources were inadequate. DiSilvestro (1981) gives a panoramic view, created by a number of authors, of the provision of counseling and advisory services to adult learners and potential learners. The wide range of help available is emphasized, but there is an awareness throughout the book that many forms of comprehensive assistance are still lacking. An English work by the Advisory Council for Adult and Continuing Learning (1979b) furnishes a brief but comprehensive account of the ways by which linkage can be achieved between the institutions that provide adult education and their targeted audiences. Even as these arrangements are enumerated, however, it becomes apparent how much more remains undone. The strongest statement on the point was made by Cross (1978). In her book entitled *The Missing Link,* she states her belief that the greatest requirement of organized adult education is for more effective ways of relating learning needs (both felt and potential) to the best ways of meeting them.

The concept of *educational brokering* (a term originated by Stephen A. Bailey) gathered force in the 1970s and came to its fullest development at the start of the next decade. It called for the creation of a special counseling service that would help adults use education to its maximum benefit. Heffernan, Macy, and Vickers (1976) reported on the agencies that then carried out brokering services. Such agencies, it was noted, "aim to present adults with the complete range of educational and career alternatives and help them to choose those most appropriate to their needs. Brokering agencies are neutral toward the choices made" (p. 2). The authors describe the early years of the brokering movement, list the leading agencies in 1976, and indicate the general method of work used in effective brokering as it had developed to that time. Heffernan (1981) brought the story of educational brokering up to date, analyzing its central ideas, tracing its history, describing its activities, evaluating its accomplishments, and forecasting its future. A distinction is made in the book between independent brokering agencies, which exist primarily for that purpose, and brokering programs operated by more comprehensive institutions. The book concludes that the common features among educational brokers are the emphases that they place on the functions of information giving, counseling, assessment, and advocacy and their nonemphasis on instruction. What further distinguishes them is their concern with both the educational and the occupational concerns of adults. Kordalewski (1982) discusses the history and practice of the Regional Learning Service (RLS) of Syracuse, New York, an innovative brokering program established as a model for such work. The author assesses clearly, optimistically, and candidly the results of that experience and provides an evaluation of what has happened to the RLS's former clients. Miller and Musgrove (1986) examine closely the process of providing career counseling to adults. Paying special attention to the conceptual framework of such assistance, the book notes that "the effective counselor rides the waves of new theories and perspectives, always modifying new ideas in light of actual counseling practice" (p. 3).

The managers of many adult educational programs feel a sense of social responsibility that leads them to want to seek out and serve especially needy clienteles, most significantly the economically disadvantaged. Lovett (1975) describes a three-year experiment in which he tried to find ways by which such people could be served despite their deprived and even squalid living conditions. Ward and Taylor (1986) report on a project devoted to what they called pioneer work, carried out by the University of Leeds; efforts were made to find new patterns of educational service for underprivileged adults, particularly women, the unemployed, the aged, and Asian immigrants. The book describes these efforts, both generally and in case studies. It also goes far beyond local concerns to depict historically and analytically the special problems of those in British society who have less than their share of society's goods. The ideas are deeply felt, though presented in a scholarly fashion. The theme of learning is broadened by Darkenwald and Larson (1980), who include essays covering categories of individuals particularly resistant to adult education, including the little-educated, the old, and laggards in the professions. The authors do not underestimate the seriousness of the problems with which they deal and make a number of theoretical and practical suggestions. Cookson (1989) deals generally with recruiting and retaining students but also offers a number of specific and sensible proposals for interesting students in various kinds of programs, including continuing professional education, literacy and adult basic education classes, distance education, and human resource programs.

Many institutions require straightforward marketing programs to reach all who might profit from their offerings. Beder (1986) explains the marketing concept as a basic part of the normal program planning process; he considers it both theoretically and practically and provides a number of convincing illustrations of the general principles that he advances. Farlow (1979) offers a pragmatic and interestingly written book, full of suggestions and illustrations. The book can well serve as a guide for anyone who needs a basic introduction to the topic. Baden (1987) adopts a sophisticated point of view and assumes that every continuing education provider "must choose a strategy or pattern of policies and decisions that will create and sustain a competitive advantage—a strategy that will allow the provider to thrive in a crowded marketplace" (p. 1). All of the authors included in this book agree that this end will best be achieved if a provider is "able to meet more learners' needs more effectively than other providers" (p. 2). Simerly and Associates (1989) have created the most comprehensive treatment of the whole topic of marketing for continuing education. This work is directed principally toward college and university administrators but is general enough to be of interest to everyone responsible for a program of continuing education. *Marketing* is given a broad definition as "the overall concept of studying, analyzing, and making decisions about how best to serve consumers through continuing education programs and services" (p. xix); this spirit suffuses the book. Primary attention is paid, however, to the processes of making people aware of the opportunities available to them through advertising, mass media promotion, and other means, and the book is rich with examples at many levels of complexity.

Evaluation

The progress of adult learners is measured in all the same ways as it is for children and youth: course grades, performance tests, comprehensive examinations, written exercises, self-reports by students, and sometimes sheer endurance. But, in addition—as the books in this section suggest—men and women weave education into the processes of their lives; as a result, the measurement of learning accomplishment can be both diverse and immediate. The early works on this subject had a refreshing directness, perhaps best illustrated by a work by Waples, Berelson, and Bradshaw, published in 1940 and entitled *What Reading Does to People*. They deal with evaluation in its largest sense, having to do with the ultimate impact of a total pattern of reading, not just that related to a single goal or publication.

As accomplishment in childhood and youth education is heavily related to the achievement of credits, credentials, degrees, diplomas, certificates, and other validating awards, much attention has been given to the use of the same kinds of incentive in adult education. Duke and Marriott (1973) examine carefully the motives that lead adults in Britain to seek "paper awards" and the accomplishment that is demonstrated by their acquisition. A number of American university leaders have sought to establish a standardized new form of credential called the Continuing Education Unit (CEU), which would be granted for ten hours of attendance at a defined educational activity. These units, which can be given for any kind of content or skill, can be added up, like course credits, to achieve larger awards. Ordinarily, however, no measurement is made of the amount of achievement of the student. In Long and Lord (1978), the CEU concept and its practice are explored in eight papers written by leaders of university extension.

Soon after the end of World War II, modern theoretical bases for educational evaluation began to be established by Ralph W. Tyler, Benjamin Bloom, Michael Scriven, and other academic educators. Virtually all later analyses of the evaluation of adult education have been influenced by their work, sometimes very directly. For example, Frutchey and others (1959) demonstrated how Tyler's general principles could be adapted to the programs of the Cooperative Extension Service. Miller and McGuire (1961), following in the tradition of Tyler and Bloom, worked out instruments of evaluation in the political and social area, community participation, the moral and ethical area, and the arts. Groteluschen, Gooler, and Knox (1976) showed how to assess the accomplishment of adult basic education but went much beyond this immediate goal to provide a useful and workable way of describing basic techniques that might be employed in many different settings.

With the passage of time, general theories of educational evaluation have expanded, and practice in adult education has come to be seen in new aspects and dimensions. Skager (1978) has prepared a sophisticated monograph, using advanced European theories of lifelong education and evaluation to establish propositions on the meaning of various measurements of learning accomplishment. Deshler (1984) has edited a collection of papers based on the distinction between formative and summative evaluation, and indicates how they can be developed in several kinds of programs. The general principles presented are supplemented by examples and case studies so that the concepts advanced are brought home in practical terms; evaluation is seen not necessarily as a separate and formal external activity, but as a way of discerning and monitoring progress.

Michael Patton is an evaluation specialist working with many kinds of human welfare programs, including adult education. He is deeply concerned with theory but approaches it by way of specific situational analysis and utilization. His writing is quirky and aphoristic and draws quotations from many authorities. He has written extensively; three of his books will be mentioned here. In his 1981 work, he describes his experiences in Trinidad, where he was applying principles of evaluation to the West Indian experience. He proceeds (1986) to deal with agricultural extension services, both in the United States and abroad. In yet another book, Patton (1990) focuses his attention on qualitative evaluation, providing a rich account of how general conclusions about the worth of programs can be derived from such techniques as interviews, observation, and the study of documents. In these books, as in his other writing, Patton's chief aim is to help develop the readers' insight, not to give them a practical, step-by-step account of how to proceed.

Works that illustrate the application of evaluation to different kinds of programs will be included in the parts of this book where they are discussed, but three are sufficiently general to warrant mention here. Bates and Robinson (1977) describe very broadly how educational radio and television can be evaluated. Mee and

Wiltshire (1978) have studied the people associated with a group of adult educational centers in England to discover how their evaluations of success and failure could help develop typologies of institutions, curricula, and other matters. Brinkerhoff (1987), working within the setting of on-the-job training, shows how a longitudinal pattern for the progress of participants can be estimated. The author uses six definable stages, moving from determination of need to complete readjustment in the work setting.

The most compelling idea in the evaluation of adult education is that its success can be measured by direct and immediate changes in society. With children, success at any level of schooling is usually assessed by how well students do at the next level; however, as Knox (1979a) reveals, immediate social consequences can result from learning in the later years. His work aims to go "beyond measures of satisfaction and learning gain, to assessment of practical application in terms of changed performance and societal benefits" (p. vii). The strong emphasis on *impact* (the key word in the volume) on learners' lives or on society is regarded as the ultimate test of adult education. This belief is explored in a number of ways, most of them by the provision of examples in specific kinds of education, but also by a general and exceptionally well stated introduction and set of conclusions.

Some studies measure the general impact of all adult education on the life of its society. As noted in Chapter Two, Levin and Slavet (1970) provide a cost-benefit analysis of the rewards that might be gained by the state of Massachusetts if its policy makers and public administrators fully developed the state's provision of adult education. Specific recommendations and their possible financial outcomes give concrete reality to the authors' proposals. Striner (1971) expands this kind of economic analysis to the international scene by studying the Danish, French, and German efforts to use continuing education as a way of increasing national capital formation. The author, who examines these programs in their relatively early days, is optimistic about them and their implications for American policies. Applying this general theme to Sweden, Höghielm and Rubenson (1980) deal specifically with the reshaping of public policy to encourage reallocation of resources (both public and private) to strengthen adult education, even if that makes necessary some diminution of resources for other purposes. This idea is not new, but it is here worked out in serious studies that command attention. Couvert (1979) analyzes the outcomes of Unesco's attempt to find the best means of creating universal literacy in underdeveloped nations. The author is rigorous in thinking through these efforts' implications and practice of measurement.

Comparative Education

As has been made amply evident in previous pages, adult education has always had strong international orientations. The ideas and form of the Danish folk high school have spread worldwide, and Adams demonstrated as early as 1899 how the Chautauqua example of summer sessions had been adopted in other countries. Although the idea of comparative adult education is manifest throughout the literature, some scholars have focused their primary attention upon it.

Bold attempts have been made in three works to encompass the whole field of comparative adult education. Bennett, Kidd, and Kulich (1975) present an anthology of essays with five major parts: an overview of the nature of comparative education and its value to the student of adult education; a consideration of the general methodology of comparative education as seen by some of the world authorities in that field; an analysis of some of the methods specific to adult education; examples of studies in comparative education; and a bibliography of English, French, and German sources. Harris (1980) has made an extended study of the nature of comparative adult education that indicates its essential characteristics and some of its methods and approaches. He has studied deeply both the literature of comparative education (a far more complex subject than is ordinarily realized) and the distinctive aspects of adult education; because of its diverse and often unstructured character, this enterprise does not lend itself as readily to the comparative approach as does the formal schooling of young people. This book is an excellent starting point for anyone interested in the comparative approach, particularly because of the richness of its case examples. Charters and Associates (1981) furnish both national descriptions and analyses of various themes, such as adult literacy training and the use of educational technology. The book is written by American and foreign authors, and a general overview of the field is provided by Charters, who argues, "The real value of comparative study emerges only from . . . the attempt to understand why the differences and similarities occur and what their significance is for adult education in the countries under examination and in other countries where the findings of the study may have relevance" (p. 3).

When case studies of a country or region are made by a scholar based elsewhere, the result often demonstrates a comparison of value systems. Titmus (1967), an English adult educator, sketches the historical traditions and the current status of the field in France in contrast to that of his own country. He traces a number of French movements and notes their simplicity of approach. At the time of the book's writing, Titmus concludes that the awareness of adult education as a distinctive and broad movement is not as pronounced in France as elsewhere in Europe. Adult education, he says, possesses "diversity without depth and one that leaves strange bare patches. French adult education is a one-layer case; the upper layers provided in English-speaking countries by local authority and university extra-mural classes are missing" (p. 183). But Titmus also believes that the ease of transition from youth to adult education has been more skillfully developed in France than elsewhere, a fact that may help account for the development of the concept of lifelong learning there. Read's (1955) work is the product of visits to sub-Saharan Africa by its author, an English anthropologist. Her assignment was to explore how the British government could improve conditions of life. In the process, she discovered adult education. She offers several essays that incorporate the reflections that resulted from this experience.

In 1986, the International Council for Adult Education held a twelve-day symposium on adult education in Shanghai. It included substantial representation from China, as well as formal delegates from other countries. The conference sponsored visitation of activities in and around the city and a symposium on broad themes of adult education. Duke (1987) has compiled the major general addresses and accounts of the panel discussions. The book opens up a vista hitherto not available outside China and illustrates the major difficulties (only partly surmounted here) of undertaking a venture as broadly defined as the Shanghai conference.

A number of books consist essentially of parallel descriptions of adult education in several countries, though each goes beyond simple description to provide underlying or crosscutting analyses. Ulich (1965) describes the historical growth of adult education in Denmark, England, Germany, and the United States. Liveright and Haygood (1968) present the papers given at an international conference, including descriptions of the programs of nine countries. Lowe (1970a) includes eleven serious and scholarly essays, each one based on the adult educational activities of an underdeveloped country or area, such as Zambia, English-speaking West Africa, India, and the South Pacific territories. Of particular interest in this work is the broader analysis by Alan Thomas of how adult education is related to developing nationhood. Hawes (1975) reports on a seminar comparing theories and practices concerning lifelong education in a number of relatively undeveloped nations. Titmus (1979) greatly facilitates comparative analysis by providing a carefully reasoned sorting and definition of the basic terms of adult education in English, Spanish, and French. Jarvis (1990) extends this semantic analysis by a thoughtfully conceived and developed definition of about five thousand terms used in the field, not only in the United Kingdom, where the book originated, but in other countries as well. In many cases, Jarvis has added a sentence or two, putting the term defined in a useful context or illuminating its connotations in practice.

Many comparative analyses are related to only one or a few aspects of the field. Williams (1968) presents a side-by-side report on agricultural extension in the United Kingdom, the United States, and Australia. Its emphasis is on the program itself, not upon the social or economic conditions that influence national differences. Skager and Dave (1977) discuss a study in which teams of educators from Japan, Romania, and Sweden used a common set of concepts concerning lifelong education to examine changes that might be brought about in the "national curriculum" provided to young people. The differences in adult education are thus reflected, as it were, in the proposed provisions for the earlier years. *Lifelong Education and University Resources* (1978) is a group of papers describing practice in eight countries. The separate accounts all employ the same analytical framework. Peterson and others (1982) offer a compilation of separate reports describing how nine industrialized nations provide adult education for five groups: workers, older persons, women entering the labor force, parents, and undereducated adults.

Recent comparative studies have tended to be built around a central theme and to provide less description and more analysis than earlier ones. Titmus (1981) examines the provisions for adult education in eight Western European countries in an effort to determine the unique and distinctive characteristics of each national pattern. Roberts (1982) compares the programs in two deeply diverse provinces of Canada, Alberta and Quebec. In this case, a single overall political entity embraces two remarkably divergent populations, and Roberts goes deeply into both similarities and differences. Styler (1984) seeks to capture and record the political and governmental nature of adult education for all countries for which he can collect data. His information is not statistical but consists of notes, summations by others, and personal assessments. Its value lies in the fact that the descriptions are shaped by the mind of a single individual. He concludes with general observations, including his belief that "the Communist states devote much greater effort to their type of political education than the democracies do to theirs" (p. 192). Compton (1989) presents the work of fourteen authors (writing singly or in collaboration) who describe how agricultural research and extension systems can be successfully transferred to other countries, usually after adaptations. The book aims to provide "a partial assessment of the impact of U.S. experiences and traditions on agriculture in Third World countries" (p. 2). Charters and Hilton (1989) collect a series of papers, each of which examines an outstanding program: Swedish study circles, Danish folk high schools, Yugoslav people's universities, Britain's Workers' Education Association, Canada's Frontier College, the Cooperative Extension Service in the United States, France's *Peuple et Culture,* and Germany's *Volkhochschule.*

Several full-scale studies have been made about the ways such programs as these have been transferred or adapted to other countries. Edström, Erdos, and Prosser (1970) describe the adaptation of the Swedish experience in distance education, chiefly correspondence study, to the needs of the people in the black African nations. The authors present many insights into the comparative nature of adult education, particularly as less advanced nations seek to adopt the techniques of those that have progressed to a more complex state. Houle (1971) shows how the transfer of an adult educational pattern (the residential center) from one country to another can change its essential purpose and character. Raybould (1957) compares British and African university extension. The work in Africa had been modeled on that in England, and Raybould was its director in both places. These unusual circumstances create a situation that demonstrates how original patterns must be changed when initiated in a new setting. Corner (1990) edited a collection of essays presented at a conference held in Glasgow by a group of scholars interested in comparative education. Most of the papers have some reference to the provision of opportunities for adult learning in Scotland, but some describe such services in other countries as well.

As the earlier pages of this book attest, the field of adult education has long been cast in worldwide terms. The 1929 World Conference on Adult Education, held in Cambridge, England, was reported in a compendious volume published in 1930. The gathering was attended by three hundred representatives of thirty-three countries, many of whom were prestigious national or international figures or were destined to become such. Although it expresses many interesting and still applicable points of view, the chief benefit of reading this document today is to experience the general sense of wonder and surprise of those who felt they were sharing in a genuinely revolutionary movement with great future implications. After World War II, many international and regional organizations were created, and adult education became an important function for many of them. The *International Directory of Adult Education*, published in 1952, established a world basis for the comparative study of adult education. Stephens (1988) has made an effort to identify and describe the total pattern of international and regional concerns in adult education.

Major worldwide conferences have been held by Unesco: in Elsinore (1949), in Montreal (1960), in Tokyo (1972), and in Paris (1985). Similar meetings have been held by the International Council for Adult Education, most notably the one in Tanzania in 1977, reported by Hall and Kidd (1978). It was the most broadly representative gathering in the field up until then, and its dominant focus was on the role of adult education in social, economic, and political planning, especially in less advanced societies. The Unesco conferences were reported only in pamphlet form, but they have given rise to at least three substantial books. Hely (1962), an Australian, summarizes the broad themes of the conferences at Elsinore and Montreal, quoting liberally from the major speakers. His chief task was to discern the fundamental changes that had occurred in the conceptualization and practice of the field during the eleven years between the two conferences. The result is a clear statement of the main themes and emphases as they existed at that time. Kidd, in *A Tale of Three Cities* (1974), describes in panoramic fashion the nature of the first three Unesco world conferences on adult education and traces the major patterns of thought that occurred during and between them. Lowe (1982) follows up on the Tokyo conference by offering a deeply informed account of adult education on an international basis.

At least two authors have developed comprehensive world views of lifelong education. Gelpi (1985) considers how it should be conceptualized in a spectrum of nations that includes the most primitive to the most advanced. His writing is dense and aphoristic and is therefore difficult to penetrate, and he works from references not familiar to most American authorities. Coombs (1985) gives an overall view of education throughout the world, incorporating schooling, nonformal learning, and adult education. No special attention is paid to lifelong education, and none is needed; its significance is taken for granted.

A Final Word

This chapter has dealt with the underlying concerns of adult educators trying to understand the deeper meaning of the field in which they are engaged and to perfect their performance in it. They feel a need for secure grounding in essences if they are to succeed in particulars. The philosophy of the field, its definition as a body of knowledge and practice, the requirements for its leaders, its capacity to help potential learners choose from among various alternatives, the ability to evaluate results, and the ways in which patterns of national offerings vary—such matters help establish for leaders the broad base of knowledge and ability that nourishes their accomplishments. But the most significant influence on adult educators is the nature of the learners they serve. We now turn to a consideration of who those learners are and what they need or want to learn.

FOUR

Adult Learners:
Their Nature
and Needs

I know the difficulties and soul-destroying conditions that
surround the lives of very many of the workers; I know the
oppression and languor of unvarying toil at uninteresting
and unpleasant tasks, the jading weariness of repeating the
same mechanical movements every minute for fourteen
hours a day, month after month, year after year. I know what
it is to see my boyhood and youth pass away without any
oportunity for education. . . . I know what it is *not to know*,
and to be conscious of not knowing, what it is to feel a real
mind-hunger. I have many times stood wistfully, cravingly
looking into a book-shop window much as a penniless ur-
chin looks into that of a confectioner. I have known these
things and I sometimes ponder them regretfully. There is
this consolation, however. The opportunity came to me
when I understood the need for it, and I sometimes even feel
thankful that I was not born in better circumstances.
—Alfred Cobham in Parry, 1920, p. 206

A sense of justice denied and a desire to achieve personal and social
potentialities have been two main generative forces for the creation
of adult educational opportunities. As noted in Chapter One, the
first was exemplified when Birkbeck created the mechanics' institute to teach able young workmen prevented from shaping their
talents and when—a century later—the dons of Cambridge and Oxford forced open the doors of the universities to admit Cobham and
his contemporaries. The need to help the members of an underclass
systematically denied the benefits of learning has been urgently felt

by the leaders of many programs in many countries. This feeling of injustice is deepened when whole societies in Africa, Asia, South America, and elsewhere lack ways by which most of their people can become responsible citizens in a mature economic order. The enhancement of present capacities is a second major energizing force: the desire of individuals to perfect their talents and develop their latent abilities or the wish of reformers to improve the quality of society. These two powerful drives, separately or combined, serve initially to define the types of participants and their motives for learning.

As time passes, both the number and the kinds of people served begins to broaden. Successful programs expand their services and become models for other ventures created to achieve new purposes. Men and women feel rewarded by their first experiences of learning and seek additional ones. New ways are found to satisfy continuing interests, and these, in turn, serve as patterns for parallel programs. Pioneer undertakings become established institutions and acquire broader bases of operations. As the number of opportunities grows (as it has so markedly since the end of World War I in all highly developed societies), the total student body becomes large and diversified. The creation of new activities motivated by a sense of justice denied or of unreached potential still continues, but these two forces may now be seen as merely attempts to fill out a comprehensive pattern of service based on the principle that all adults could profit by education of some sort.

In the literature of adult education, much attention has been given to the analysis of learners during various stages in the birth and maturation of a comprehensive pattern of adult education.

Extent of Participation

Perhaps because of a desire to establish the appeal of the new movement, it was important to early leaders of the field to estimate how many people were taking part in organized forms of adult education. The number of children and youth enrolled in schools and higher educational institutions provided a base against which participation in organized adult education could be measured. The first efforts to make such an estimate merely added up the numbers of people involved in all of the major forms of service, though this technique was recognized from the beginning as imperfect. Should a person signed up for a single university extension lecture be counted in the same way as one registered for a complete degree program? In churches, would one count the people attending services, the registered members of the congregation, or those participating in specially designated educational programs? Similar problems of definition existed for libraries, museums, associations, and other institutions. By this system, moreover, no account could be taken of the duplicate registrations of an individual in several kinds of activities. Lacking any other method of counting and making judgments in the most reasonable fashion possible, however, the early enumerators added up their figures and, as the years went on, achieved gratifyingly increasing totals. The most carefully derived such estimates were those of Cartwright (1935) and Knowles (1960).

Techniques for interviewing representative or random samples of the population, perfected after World War II, were first applied on a major scale to the counting of adult education participants by Johnstone and Rivera in 1965. This massive volume, entitled *Volunteers for Learning*, was commissioned by the Carnegie Corporation and compiled by the National Opinion Research Center. It went far beyond the estimation of total participation to study the nature and motivation of learners and the expected outcomes of their studies. This work is, in fact, relevant to all sections of this chapter. The study used the most advanced techniques then available for sampling, interviewing, and analyzing the data collected. When first issued, it made a great impact because it provided for the first time a comprehensive view of adult learners as seen objectively by social scientists.

A second major study was that issued by the Organisation for Economic Co-operation and Development (1977c). Volume Four of an interconnected series of studies (to be described later), it is the best available quantified comparison of participation in several countries. In this case, the nations studied were Austria, Canada, Denmark, Germany, Italy, the Netherlands, Sweden, the United Kingdom, and the United States. Although the information presented in this book is valuable, even more helpful are the insights into the difficult task of collecting the necessary national data and into the way that task is undertaken by experts in each country.

An exhaustive study of adult students in the United Kingdom was reported by Woodley and others in 1987. Their investigations, lasting for almost a decade, were supported by the national government to serve as a basis for policy decisions. The studies were broad in scope, covering most major providers of courses and examining not only demographic data but also the ideas of students about their learning processes. In a relatively brief but comprehensive review, O'Keefe (1977) provides a statistical analysis of the growth of adult education, its probable size in the future, the major program and policy proposals at the time of writing, and the author's general conclusions and recommendations for overall strategy. The study was conducted at a broad level and intended to be a document for national policy planners and makers.

The U.S. Department of Education and its predecessor organizations have sponsored many studies of the extent of participation, beginning in the early days of the field. The most recent and comprehensive is that of Hill (1987), who incorporates the results of earlier investigations, particularly the triennial reports of surveys on a sampling basis conducted by the U.S. Bureau of the Census. The definition of participation used encompasses "all courses and organized activities taken part-time and identified as adult education by respondents 17 years old or older" (p. 1). In another federal study, Kay (1974) reported on a mail survey of community organizations that might be overlooked in tallies of institutional sponsorship: churches and other religious organizations, YMCAs, civic groups, social service agencies, the Red Cross, and other institutions. A sample of 4,650 organizations was studied, and the results were projected for the total national population.

Demographic Characteristics

In the 1920s and 1930s, it was widely assumed that adult education was primarily intended to help men and women make up for lost opportunities in youth; the need for adult education would largely disappear when society finally perfected its school systems. It followed, therefore, that programs should be centered on segments of the population that had had little schooling. Yet these ideas did not seem to accord with observable facts. In 1943, Kaplan conducted a major study of the characteristics of adult learners; among many other findings, it demonstrated that the level of formal schooling was correlated positively with extent of engagement in adult studies. Kaplan's ground-breaking investigation examined a sample of five thousand of the approximately one hundred thousand residents of Springfield, Massachusetts, who were over eighteen years of age. The author sought to determine how participation was related to various factors: gender, age, marital status, level of education, economic status, occupation, nationality, and accessibility of resources. Participation included use of the library; attendance at evening schools, public forums, museums, clubs, lecture and concert series, and independent institutions; and radio listening. This systematic piece of research reported many patterns of association between the factors studied and the kind of participation undertaken. Despite much subsequent analysis, Kaplan's work remains outstanding. Another thorough study is that of London, Wenkert, and Hagstrom, reported in 1963, which analyzed adult education and social class in Oakland, California. The authors were concerned with both attitudes toward learning and extent of engagement, with special attention to blue-collar workers.

The nature of participation is often based on the needs and characteristics of a defined audience. In an early work, Evans (1926) showed how young workers took part in educational opportunities. Verner and White (1965) drew together five articles earlier published elsewhere; one deals with the general nature of participation, but others treat special audiences, such as out-of-school youth and older adults. Hopper and Osborn (1975) studied full-time adult students at several British universities. Ilsley (1990) analyzed how the experience of volunteering in social agencies proves to be both unintentionally and deliberately educative.

As the idea spread that, to some extent, all men and women are actual or potential learners, the focus of participation studies shifted to the determination of the characteristics of those taking part in specific programs and institutions. Berelson (1949) gave a striking illustration of this kind of study. At the time that he wrote, the public library was often viewed as a way of reaching people deprived of other opportunities—hence, as an instrument by which learning was democratized. However, Berelson examined the current users of the library and came to the conclusion that they made up what he called a communications elite. He then argued that the institution should turn its primary attention toward serving its "natural" clientele and not waste time and money trying to extend the range of its patrons. The reverberations of this controversial study are felt even today.

With the increase in the number of adults (especially women) returning to college campuses to secure degrees, a small stream of studies has examined their characteristics. Tittle and Denker (1980) deal thoroughly and comprehensively with the nature and problems of mature women within this category. The book is enlivened by the provision of ten in-depth case studies. Weil's *Continuing Education*, published in 1979, is a light and funny novel about a wife and mother who returns to a university to complete her degree. Her problems of adjustment are touched on, sometimes uproariously, but the book accepts that seeking a degree on a university campus is a completely natural way of life. Solmon and Gordon (1981) have based their study on data (collected by Alexander Astin from 1966 through 1978) on all entering freshmen in American colleges and universities. The authors of this book made special analyses of the reports from students (both men and women) over twenty-one years of age. Data are presented comparing traditional and adult students over the entire thirteen-year period of the study; studies are made of two particular years: 1974 and 1978. Comparisons between part-time and full-time students are also made.

Lillard and Tan (1986) have compiled a technical report on who undertakes in-service job training and what effect it has on them. The authors combine five data sources, and the findings, as might be expected, are complex. Conclusions include the following: the likelihood of being offered training rises with the level of formal educational attainment, except for people at the graduate level; among the various sources of training, that provided by the company itself has the greatest effect on increasing earnings; and extent of vocational training is positively associated with a decline in the likelihood of unemployment.

Motivation for Learning

Much effort has been spent in trying to identify which of the countless and complex aspirations, drives, and incentives of mankind are
most significantly related to participation in adult education. On
the surface, the problem does not seem difficult. Those who conduct
programs often believe that they have identified important personal
or social needs that require only clear and urgent expression to
become incentives for action. This belief underlies ongoing efforts
and reappears whenever new treatments for diseases are identified,
different parts of the world attract attention, bodies of content are
clarified, inventions are perfected, or other changes create possibilities for learning.

The belief that the clarification of goals gives rise to action
runs deep in adult education. In 1839, the New England divine
William Ellery Channing first published his work *Self-Culture,*
which was to go through many editions. This essay centers on the
need for everyone to develop his or her full potential and identifies
the array of goals that should be considered in planning a program
for personal self-culture. His views were unknowingly echoed a
century and a half later by Botkin, Elmandjra, and Malitza (1979),
in a book significantly called *No Limits to Learning.* The Club of
Rome (an informally organized group of intellectuals from all over
the world, but chiefly Europe) had earlier issued a gloomy report
on the consequences of expanding population, limitation of resources, and the rise of world-threatening dangers. This later publication of the club concludes that the solution to these great
problems may be found by creating new forms of learning for people of all ages. The president of the Club of Rome suggests in the
foreword that mankind has *"inner margins* which . . . exist within
ourselves and are pregnant with the potency of unparalleled developments" (p. xv). In one of the first doctoral dissertations in the
academic field of adult education, Stacy (1935) builds the case that
adult education should be centered around what he calls "the seven
great arts": perfecting philosophies, advancing cooperation, using
science, increasing incomes, improving uses of income, improving
uses of time, and advancing beauty. Pear's book, *The Maturing
Mind* (1938), identifies maturity, not as the precondition of adult

education, but as the source of its aims. Though he never fully defines maturity of mind, some of its components are breadth of concerns, a focus on social interests, detachment of point of view, a philosophy of life, and an ability to plan realistically for the future. Gray and Rogers (1956) take the same perspective, though orienting it toward the process of reading. They define the nature of true maturity in the use of this skill and develop a typology of purposes (pp. 92-93) by which full accomplishment may be achieved.

As the first flush of interest in adult education was translated into viable programs, it became increasingly clear that the nature of the learners could not be understood simply by an awareness of formal program goals. A midcentury cliché was "we must start with the people where they *are*"; the effort to find that precise location began to influence both program building and research. An early attempt to do so was described in Gray and Munroe (1929), who inquired directly about the reading interests of adults, but whose work has strong implications for other forms of learning as well. In 1935, Thorndike and others published *Adult Interests,* an effort to examine analytically some aspects of motivation for learning. The major early work in this line of investigation was conducted by Williams and Heath (1936); making a massive effort, these authors reported on the educational life histories of more than five hundred persons taking adult classes and examined closely these learners' ideas on all aspects of their studies. Many of the students' comments are interesting and expressed in striking, fresh, and forthright fashion. The whole work is written with clarity and a mastery of perspective that illuminates the quotations. Forty years later, Charnley (1974) observed that the book by Williams and Heath "is a paradigm of research in adult education, because the human qualities revealed by the authors are timeless and, by no means least, because the faith expressed and exposed has inspired many of the men and women who have been concerned with adult education" (pp. 143-44). In a later book on the same theme, Newman (1979) provided a vivid and impressionistic account of the attitudes of both participants and nonparticipants in organized adult education in the cosmopolitan inner city of London. Meanwhile, Johnstone and

Rivera (1965) demonstrated conclusively that the self-described motives of learners were only loosely related to the content they studied.

Since midcentury, many investigations into the motivations of adult learners have been conducted. In Peterson (1979), Cross synthesized the results of more than thirty large-scale studies of the topic. Two years later, in Cross (1981), she reported her survey and analysis of research and theoretical publications that focus on four broad questions: "*Who* participates in adult learning? *Why* do they participate or, alternatively, why not? And *what* and *how* do they learn or want to learn?" (p. xii). Attention is given to all four, but the primary focus is upon the second. Cross found that no satisfactory theories had been advanced to explain why adults were motivated to learn or how participation could be made more effective. She then advanced two basic models of her own. A somewhat comparable book was written by Flinck (1977), who provided a broadly based summary of English studies on the subject.

Much attention has been devoted to speculation about whether there is more than one dominant orientation to learning. Taking a negative view of these investigations, Adam (1940b) asserted that there is "scant evidence for the belief that mature people long for specific opportunities to discipline their minds in new sciences. The process of continued learning is generally based on enticement; on some seductive promise of material advantage or of social gain, or of increased personal power. Pure learning is a Holy Grail, quested for by few, either in childhood or manhood" (p. 30). Houle ([1961] 1988), by contrast, concluded that underlying the myriad motives that led to participation by adults deeply engaged in learning were certain basic viewpoints toward education that he identified as learning orientation, activity orientation, and goal orientation. Those who held one point of view were likely to reject the other two. He based these and other hypotheses on twenty-two closely studied cases of adults who took part extensively in adult education. A number of subsequent studies have grown out of Houle's work, most of them based on a wider range of participants; a report of three such investigations was made by Solomon (1964); Boshier (1976), who issued a critical review of fourteen studies, paid particular attention to the statistical bases of their findings. Boud and Griffin (1987) present papers by various authors that probe various psychological and social psychological underpinnings of personality as they influence personal growth.

Many other approaches to motivation have been made; here are a few. Duke and Marriott (1973) ask why so many learners seek "paper awards"—diplomas, certificates, degrees, and other credentials. Why should not learning be its own reward or be assessed as it leads to a higher quality of life? The book is an extended answer to such questions; it combines data from many sources but draws particularly on a study of certificate students at Leeds University. Houle (1984) enlarges the idea of participation to include the total pattern of learning undertaken by an individual at any one time and the ways that pattern changes as life proceeds. His book is a series of loosely related essays giving case studies of outstanding men for whom learning was a paramount interest; it also includes analyses of eminent educators and educative settings. Wlodkowski (1985) is concerned with how existing motivation may be systematically enhanced (especially by the leaders in a teaching-learning situation) at the start of an episode, during its course, and as a precursor to later episodes. The heart of the book consists of sixty-eight strategies, each of which is stated concisely and then explored by use of the relevant literature. The book is practical and eclectic, not drawn from any theoretical or doctrinaire position.

Courtney (1992) deals comprehensively with the reasons adults take part in learning activities. He bases his work on the research in the field and has done a careful job of searching out sources, both published and unpublished. He presents his material clearly, in an elegant, personal style. Of particular value is Courtney's linkage of studies into lines of research and his clarification of various clusters of viewpoints.

Educationally Disadvantaged Adults

Reports already noted in this chapter indicate that nonparticipants in adult education can be distinguished from those taking part as having less schooling, lower income, poorer locations, linguistic disadvantages, foreignness of birth, and lower social class; race, age, and gender sometimes provide bases for differentiation. These factors can be combined in such a way as to create an underclass or,

in some places, a dominant culture. The need of such people for
education has been a major theme in the literature of the field.
Perhaps as many as half of the references cited in this book deal
directly or inferentially with the extraordinarily difficult problems
encountered by efforts to provide severely restricted men and women
with the benefits of learning. A few of the books that deal directly
with this theme are mentioned at this point.

Anderson and Niemi's book (1970) has the following purpose:

> To examine the role of education in altering the per-
> sonal and social characteristics of disadvantaged
> adults. Data were collected through a review of the
> literature and have been limited mainly to research
> reports on remedial adult educational programs.
> Findings show that the disadvantaged, who are ham-
> pered by psychological disabilities, have the lowest
> income, the largest families, the poorest education, the
> highest incidence of ill-health, the least chance of em-
> ployment, and little promise of a better future. Large-
> ly because of discrimination, the poverty subculture is
> compelled to evolve its own way of life and programs
> of change seem doomed if they adhere to established
> patterns of contact used by the middle and upper
> classes. These programs should cope with the funda-
> mental problem of overcoming the resistance of the
> disadvantaged to education. Specific details of edu-
> cational planning to solve the problems inherent in
> programs designed for the disadvantaged adult are un-
> available because of the scarcity of research [p. iii].

An extensive bibliography is included.

Clyne (1972) enlarges his frame of reference from the underclass to deal also with other kinds of educationally disadvantaged
adults, including the backward, the mentally disabled, the physi-
cally handicapped, the blind and partially sighted, the deaf and
hard of hearing, immigrants, and people who live in culturally and
socially poor communities. The author shows by many vivid examples what can be done to aid such people educationally, and he

ardently advocates a more extensive and imaginative provision of opportunities than now exists. His immediate frame of reference is the United Kingdom, but much of what he says has broader relevance. Burrichter and Ulmer (1972) give illustrations of the ways by which educators can reach adults who have been culturally deprived. Although the book shows the influence of Ivan Illich, it grows mainly out of the authors' own experience.

Childers (1975) has provocatively entitled his work *The Information-Poor in America*. Through a bibliographical search, he has tried to learn about people who have difficulty in taking advantage of readily available help. The author deals fully with the concept of *need*, which he calls the "recalcitrant" word. Ross-Gordon, Martin, and Briscoe (1990) make the case very powerfully that opportunities for adult learning are not shared equally by the culturally diverse populations of the United States. In considering the African American, Hispanic, and Asian populations (and such specific subsections of them as the Hmong from Laos), the authors examine important issues, such as whether it is best to encourage each cultural group to care for its own or to try to serve all groups multiculturally. Various approaches and strategies are assessed, such as the accommodation of programs to preferred settings, the utilization of existing social networks, the effort to empower learners, and the creation of intercultural staffs to carry out the program.

Efforts to reach the disadvantaged are international. An excellent account of how the problem is being addressed in many different environments is provided by the Organisation for Economic Co-operation and Development (1981) in the fifth volume of its series of studies concerning learning opportunities for adults. The book includes case studies from all over the world, but the authors go deeper than the summary of national efforts to a consideration of what it means to be disadvantaged and some of the consequences of focusing a program upon the attempt to reach such people.

Lovett (1975) reports on a three-year effort to introduce adult education into the life of working-class adults in a depressed section of Liverpool. The author was engaged in a special project that permitted him to use open and fluid methods to attract and hold

men and women in various educational ventures. Influenced by
Freire, Illich, and other social theorists, he discusses his experience
not only in terms of their ideas and principles, but also with reference to the important traditions of working-class education developed in three-quarters of a century of British practice. Lovett,
Clarke, and Kilmurray (1983), all of them based in Northern Ireland, describe how adult education is being used to help cope with
the desperate situation there. This part of the book is rich in illustrative quotations. Surrounding and permeating this account is a
more general history and interpretation of the ways that adult education has been and is being used to work in social movements and
with action elements in community life.

Bergsten (1977), in a large Swedish investigation, reports on
in-depth interviews with 945 persons who had little formal schooling. Both men and women were studied, and the sample included
people from three age groups. This work is interesting in that it
places education within the life patterns of adults at various ages.
Kasworm (1983) presents a collection of papers from the United
States analyzing how difficult-to-reach target populations can be
served by adult educational agencies. The methods range from simple marketing tactics for existing activities to broad theories of future program design. One chapter each is given to rural and isolated
learners, women, older adults, ethnic minorities, undereducated
adults, members of the armed services, and employees in high-
technology industry. Introductory and concluding chapters provide
syntheses of the general points covered in the book as a whole.

Determination of Needs and Interests

It has long been assumed that adult learners will initiate or take part
in education either because they feel some gap or deficiency in
themselves or because they wish to pursue an existing interest. The
provider of a program must therefore appeal to learners in one of
three ways: respond to a perceived sense of need; create such a sense
if it does not exist; or build upon a present interest. This task may
be difficult when undertaken on an individualized basis but can be
much harder when the sponsor is trying to reach large numbers of
people or even an entire population. Around the topics of need and

interest, so simply stated here, there has grown up an enormous literature, based on the meaning of key terms as well as their theory and practice.

Pennington (1980) deals in a sophisticated but direct fashion with the complex subject of how the educational requirements of adults should be determined in various settings and programs. Some of the essays that he includes are concerned with specific situations or audiences: for example, the educationally underprivileged, the chronically ill, and the members of a profession. Other essays address more general themes, such as the progression of a program from the assessment of needs to attempts made to meet them, and the use of a systems approach for assessment. In beginning and concluding chapters, efforts are made to come to grips with the whole concept of needs assessment and to suggest useful models of how to carry it out. Witkin (1984) expands the discussion of needs assessment to give a full account of its use in many kinds of institutions, including its scope and purpose; the methods of securing relevant data; the conversion of data into decisions; and the ways by which needs assessment actually works out in programming. The author's approach is complex; it is not intended to be immediately useful to practitioners.

Some students of needs and interests have asked why men and women do not participate in readily available learning activities. In a book titled *Adult Education: Why This Apathy?*, Green (1953) reports on a survey of 1,885 people in Britain who were asked why they thought there was so little participation. Much data is presented, but the author answers his main question by blaming the inadequacy of earlier schooling. He notes, "The great majority of the present adult generation had an elementary education. They gained neither stimulation nor interest to continue, and only where there had been conscious effort to plan the last four years at school on broadly liberal lines, as in the secondary grammar school, was there clear evidence that seed had been sown, the harvest of which would be reaped by progressive intellectual development to the age of maturity" (p. 119).

In the late 1970s, the Organisation for Economic Co-operation and Development, a major federation of highly developed nations, conducted a massive worldwide study of learning opportunities for adults; two of the volumes have already been cited in this chapter. The *General Report* (1977a) draws together a number of conclusions about access to education and participation in it. The range of discussion is very broad and includes consideration of some ideas not always taken into account in the analysis of problems of access and participation. Another volume in this report is entitled *The Non-Participation Issue* (1977b). After an introduction summarizing four American studies, papers are presented dealing with the situation in Denmark, France, Italy, the Netherlands, Spain, the United Kingdom, and the United States. The volume concludes with papers assessing efforts to stimulate participation in Germany and England.

The major American study on this general topic was written by Aslanian and Brickell (1980). The authors are interested in the question of why some adults participate in learning activities and others do not. A thorough review of the literature serves as a basis for a national representative sample of almost two thousand Americans, twenty-five years of age and older, who were questioned in face-to-face or telephone interviews. With a wealth of quantitative data, the authors describe the characteristics of participants and nonparticipants and advance at some length the thesis that the former are stimulated to take part because changes in some aspect of their lives trigger them to take action. These transitions occur in one or more of the following "life areas": career, family, health, religion, citizenship, art, and leisure. In another investigation, Aslanian and Brickell (1988) have used telephone interviews to locate a thousand adults who had taken credit courses in the previous two years. Questions were asked to identify the kinds of persons involved in the sample, the nature of the courses that they undertook, their reasons for doing so, and other salient factors. The book furnishes the data resulting from the study and makes observations on how the data can be interpreted by program planners.

A somewhat similar study was that of Chen and Hernon (1982), who reported on telephone interviews with almost three thousand people in the New England states. The respondents were asked to identify situations where they had recognized a need for information. Demographic information on those (one-sixth) unable to do so was compared with that of the other respondents. Those who could name an occasion when they needed information were guided through an interview; they were asked how they proceeded to discover a source of information, what or whom they consulted, and how they felt about the result. An overall interpretation of the results was then provided and the implications for the public library were explored.

The starkness of division between participants and nonparticipants has been modified by other approaches to the assessment of needs and interests. Houle and Nelson (1956) argue that program planners interested in specific content areas (in the case here examined, world affairs) should identify significant categories of learners and potential learners in order to know how to reach each one. The authors suggest that the categories of potential audiences for any content field are the specialists in that subject, the persons actively concerned with it, those who pay attention to it, and those who do not. Vermilye (1974) explored how universities could assess the best ways of building programs for the new clienteles that they were then beginning to serve in large numbers, rather than merely assuming that mature people would fit into the familiar molds of late adolescence and early adulthood traditionally guiding higher education. Fordham, Poulton, and Randle (1979) report on an interesting piece of "action research," detailing the efforts of the authors and their colleagues to stimulate participation in an English "housing estate"—a residential area with much public housing but with no separate community identity or political structure. The book is a thoughtful essay describing approaches tried by the authors. Their broadest policy conclusion is that informal contact and public relations work are often necessary to bring nonparticipants to the stage of action. Those who attended classes, in contrast to those who did not, "generally had a more enhanced self-concept and probably felt that they had more control over their own lives" (p. 235). This self-concept was further developed by participation. "Once the educational train has been boarded, it can contribute to the individual status of the passengers and possibly increase their degree of power in making life choices. The problem for potential passengers lies in gaining sufficient confidence to board the train" (p. 235).

Influence of Age on Learning Abilities

All efforts to involve adults in learning experiences were handicapped in the early days by the widespread belief that only children
could learn. Folk wisdom asserts that old dogs cannot learn new
tricks; this presumed basic truth was brought forward on many
occasions as an irrefutable denial of the whole field or of any new
venture in it. The massive efforts during the nineteenth and early
twentieth centuries to create and establish schools, colleges, and
universities had caused education to be thought of solely as an
activity of children and youth, despite the fact that many adults had
been engaged in systematic learning programs throughout recorded
history. When Edward L. Thorndike, then the nation's leading educational psychologist, issued his book *Adult Learning* in 1928, it
caused an immediate stir in academic circles and was widely reported in magazines and the press. The book describes studies conducted by Thorndike and his colleagues in their Columbia University laboratories; the general conclusion was that age does not
have a profound influence on the ability to learn. The authors did
not hesitate to generalize on their findings or to suggest the social
policies that should follow from them.

One important consequence of Thorndike's work was that
other investigators were led to study the influence of increasing age
on various capacities associated with learning, such as intelligence,
memory, and physical ability. Almost all of these studies were conducted within the scientific traditions of developmental psychology;
only a few were designed to suit the practical purposes of adult
education. Sorenson (1938) summarizes a number of studies of
university-extension students, identifying their characteristics, measuring their mental abilities, examining their classroom achievement,
analyzing the methods used to teach them, and studying the relationship between age and mental ability. Of special interest is the finding
that students in extension classes generally outperformed "campus"
students taking the same courses under the same instructors. Welford
(1958) reviews investigations at Cambridge University by the Nuffield
Unit for Research into the Problems of Ageing. The book itself is a
report on the nature of physical skills and the ways they change with
increasing age. One aspect of this work had to do with the influence

of age on systematic training programs intended to create new skills or refine old ones. Welford's data led him to conclude that increasing age is much less of a factor in skill training than is commonly thought and that people vary greatly in the extent of that influence. Long (1972) considers the physiological changes that occur with increasing age and estimates their influence on the ability to learn. Some (such as the decline of hearing or vision) need only to be identified to be accepted as important. Others are more complex, such as the notion that older adults grow accustomed to functioning despite pain and are therefore less hindered by it in their learning than younger adults.

The simple question "Can adults learn?" to which Thorndike and other early investigators addressed themselves has been expanded into inquiry about how increasing years influence various kinds of learning, causing some to decline and others to increase. Summaries of such findings lie at the borderline between the fields of developmental psychology and adult education. Several such references will be noted here. Botwinick (1967) offers a relatively brief but comprehensive view of the changing nature of cognitive processes during maturity and old age. More than half of the book is given over to the nature of learning, the problems of measuring it, and the allied topics of memory, forgetting, and intelligence. An excellent final chapter sums up the content of the book. Long (1971) asks whether adults are ever too old to learn. Although his answers must be complex and qualified, they are, on the whole, positive. The fear of old age as a universally constricting force is much diminished by a consideration of the distinctions that he considers. Lumsden and Sherron (1975) present a collection of essays that reviews the experimental studies dealing with the influence of age on critical thinking ability, learning, memory loss and retention, and other, similar psychological abilities. The editors place their stress on old age, but most of the other authors do not; they deal with the successive stages of life or treat it as a continuum. Birren and Schaie (1990), in a work covering all aspects of the psychology of aging, provide a realistic but essentially optimistic attitude toward the various factors related to the ability to learn, even in the latest years of life. The emphasis of the authors is upon the variables that improve or impair learning ability or performance during the course of adulthood.

Most studies of learning ability are based on people within the range of "normality," but Johnson and Blalock (1987) provide a useful corrective to this tendency. They describe the kinds of problems dealt with by the Program in Learning Disabilities at Northwestern University. General chapters examine the nature of such disabilities, their assessment and diagnosis, the intellectual levels and patterns of the clients, and other similar topics. Another series of chapters has to do with 'such specialized problems as auditory disorders, reading disabilities, and the incapacity to deal with written language or with mathematics. Relatively little attention is given to descriptions of training or therapy. The reader of this book is likely to wonder how many people in the population have, to a greater or lesser degree, the kinds of disabilities described here.

Two works celebrating the ability of adults to learn are based on humanistic rather than technical psychological backgrounds. McLeish published his book *The Ulyssean Adult* in 1976. The author, a Canadian scholar deeply involved in the adult education movement (the book is dedicated to J. R. Kidd), considers the venturesome quality of adults, particularly during their later years. His reference is to Tennyson's poem *Ulysses*, which praises this aspect of life. In warmly affirmative and richly textured prose, McLeish seeks to refute the belief that middle and old age are necessarily times of decline, decay, or passivity. He applauds the spirit of creativeness and fresh enterprise, especially when it becomes a consuming passion. Knowles (1980b) presents a learning theory based on what the author believes to be the essential attributes of maturity. As noted in Chapter Three, he calls his theory andragogy. Knowles makes a number of interesting distinctions and gives a review of the work of many students of learning theory for both adults and children. His book also traces andragogy back to its early German antecedents and down to its modern European and American usages.

Knox (1977) moves beyond the two-stages-of-life thinking implicit in discussions of andragogy to assess how education varies through the whole span of life. The author's intention is to provide "a selective but comprehensive overview of tested knowledge about adult development and learning, in a form useful to people who help adults adapt, learn, and grow" (p. ix). He achieves this purpose in a monumental volume that synthesizes research from many fields. The result is by far the most comprehensive and useful summary available on how the learning of adults is influenced by the internal and external events of their lives. A somewhat similar though more narrowly focused book was written by Riverin-Simard (1988). Her basic orientation is toward the counseling of adults in an educational setting. From this vantage point, she examines the stages of the work life. Her analysis is based on the life-span literature, and her set of sequential phases is firmly anchored to other formulations. Merriam (1983) describes how certain basic concerns of adults change throughout the life span. She deals, for example, with the need for intimacy in young adulthood, in midlife, and in old age. Other aspects include the family life cycle, the need for identity, the world of work, and the awareness of physical change. Adult learning is another subject considered, though it is not central to the whole work. The method of presentation throughout is the use of fiction to emphasize concerns and convey a sense of reality. Rossman and Rossman (1990) present various theoretical formulations that have been made about the developmental stages, chronological or otherwise, through which adults progress during their lives. The authors of the papers in this book show how such theories can be applied in practice. Included are such instruments as the Rossman Adult Learning Inventory, psychodrama, the learning autobiography, and the proseminar, which introduces adults to periods of sustained study.

Each of three major stages of adulthood—youth, middle age, and old age—has been the subject of analysis with respect to learning emphases. Darkenwald and Knox (1984) assert that "adults under age thirty-five comprise the majority of participants in organized continuing education" (p. 1) but note that this age group has been very little studied. In addition to some general consideration of this part of the life span, the authors of the various chapters probe into certain settings that distinctively serve the needs of young adults, such as education designed to meet the needs of those not going to college, high school equivalency preparation, the upgrading of young workers in hospital settings, and the development of young managers. The authors suggest that the early years of adulthood need to be treated in a markedly different fashion than the later years and conclude that in describing youth they are dealing with two stages of life, not one. Havighurst and Orr (1956) report on an interesting study of how well the middle-aged urban adults included in the sample were meeting certain needs defined by the authors. The results of the interviews conducted are examined closely to assess their relevance for adult education. Knox (1979c) calls his work *Programming for Adults Facing Mid-Life Change,* a title that exactly describes the book's contents. In a series of brief chapters, a number of authors describe programs for "middlescence." These give a sense of reality to this theme, which is then placed in a broader context. Chapters discuss the important concepts, the literature, and the key issues involved in the effort to develop adequate educational programs for this age group in view of its distinctive religious, psychological, and social needs.

The education of older people has been a major or peripheral topic of several books already cited in this chapter or earlier, but the work most immediately relevant here is Agruso's 1978 book entitled *Learning in the Later Years.* He provides a systematic treatment of what he calls educational gerontology: learning, memory, intelligence, and organized education. Agruso is primarily concerned with summarizing the literature on these topics and assembling the research into a systematic whole. Physiological findings are included, thus correcting the frequent reliance solely on psychological and sociological data. The author brings to his discussion a refreshingly different orientation from that customarily found. He defines *continuing education,* for example, as "a viable intervention strategy structured, in formal and informal ways, for both the prevention of imminent obsolescence and the enhancement of a storehouse of knowledge" (p. 120). The author's intent throughout is to supply theoretical knowledge that can serve as the foundation for practical endeavors.

A Final Word

Early psychological treatments of adult education were heavily based on studies made of people in the early years of life. For a long time, investigators had found children and college students ready at hand to serve as their subjects; they took it for granted that they could draw conclusions or construct theories of learning for all ages of life on the basis of the study of youth. Later research has suggested that this assumption is unwarranted. When a youth-based study is replicated with adults, their ability tends to be understated, in part because they refuse to learn such things as mazes or lists of nonsense syllables. If the investigation calls for the drawing of inferences or the use of existing knowledge, adults often outperform children. It was therefore a sign of profound change when, sixty years after Thorndike's early work, Jarvis (1987a) could note that "the research upon which the model of the learning processes [here presented] was constructed came from work with adult learners and it was tested with adults, rather than with children. Hence the only claims that can be made for this model are with adults, although it is suspected that it is as valid for children as it is with adults" (p. 35).

PART TWO

The Providers
and Goals
of Adult Education

The vastness of the modern field of adult education has resulted from the creation and expansion of many institutions and the pursuit of many strongly desired goals. Part Two identifies the books that deal with institutions (here called *providers*) and the major groupings of goals (here called *themes*). It contains five chapters, three of which have to do with providers, and two with themes.

Chapter Five begins with a brief section on the overall provision of adult education. The main body of the chapter, however, identifies the literature about institutions that were initially intended to school young people but that subsequently chose to serve adults as well: public schools, colleges and universities, and community colleges. Chapter Six discusses museums, libraries, the Cooperative Extension Service, and other agencies designed from the outset to provide lifelong learning. Chapter Seven covers programs originally established (some as independent institutions but most as specialized units within industry, government, labor unions, and other social entities) to educate adults.

Although Chapter Seven is third in the sequence dealing with providers, it also bears a close connection to Chapters Eight and Nine, which describe the major goals of organized adult learning. The nature of the linkage can most quickly be shown through a few examples. Hospitals are important centers for the education of both patients and staff members, but most of the literature on hospitals treats them as but one service point in a far broader movement promoting the goals of health education. Correctional education, by contrast, is based on a clearly definable set of goals, but most of those who write on the subject in the context of adult education focus on the special circumstances of penal institutions.

Other overlaps occur with the industrial company and human resource development, the labor union and workers' education, the
church and religious education, and the armed services and national
defense education. To avoid divided or repetitive presentations, I
have made the decision in each such case to follow what appears to
be the major thrust of the existing literature.

The themes that have given rise to adult education programs
may be broadly divided into two groups. Chapter Eight deals with
goals related in some fashion to formal systems of education. Some
are compensatory, providing opportunities for adults to gain
knowledge and skills usually acquired during childhood and youth;
others take up strands of learning begun in early years. Chapter
Nine deals with the goals that are not—and sometimes cannot be—
sought until the years of womanhood or manhood.

FIVE

Providers Created
to Educate
Children and Youth

Tradition itself cannot constitute a creative force. It always
has a decadent tendency to promote formalization and repe-
tition. What is needed to direct it into creative channels is
a fresh energy which repudiates dead forms and prevents
living ones from being static. In one sense, for a tradition
to live it must constantly be destroyed. At the same time, de-
struction by itself clearly cannot create new cultural forms.
There must be some other force which restrains destructive
energy and prevents it from reducing all about it to havoc.
The dialectical synthesis of tradition and antitradition is the
structure of true creativeness.

—*Kenzo Tange, as quoted in* Commission on
Non-Traditional Study, *1963, p. xxx*

Until the 1960s, most of the American literature on adult education
was devoted to its sponsorship by specific kinds of providers. This
organizational focus also pervaded the field itself. A university survey course on adult education usually took up, one by one, the
library, the public school, the church, the labor union, the professional society, and other types of institutions and reported on the
kinds of service each one offered. Meetings in the field tended to be
summit gatherings of representatives of such sponsors. The officer-
ships of general associations were as carefully balanced as the can-
didates on any political slate. This concern with providers has
diminished in the literature but remains strong in the field; in fact,
most workers in it still give principal intellectual allegiance to their
employers, not to a pervading discipline.

123

The Structure of Institutions

The institutional structure of adult education was outlined by Fisher (1927), an early popular interpreter of the field. She saw it as a group of providers and described each one in turn; among others, she included correspondence schools, university extension divisions, women's clubs, public libraries, and museums. In the years since then, the listing of relevant agencies has grown ever larger. Peterson (1979) gave a comprehensive typology of sources of lifelong learning, centering on institutions but expanding to include self-directed and experiential learning. Niemi and Jessen (1976) provided a directory of sponsors and resources that supplied names and addresses of programs relevant to adult education.

For the most part, the writers of general works on adult education (including those mentioned in Chapter Two) have been content to list institutions serially, with little attention to their larger structure; at most, they were grouped under a few generalized rubrics. However, Blakely and Lappin (1969) raise many issues about the institutional provisions and administrative patterns of continuing education. Kowalski (1988) gives a broad overview of the nature of the organizations that sponsor adult education. He is concerned with the theory of institutional analysis and refers to both its literature and that of adult education; he provides no case studies or illustrations. Barton (1982) examines the need for a richer and better-structured provision of adult educational opportunities in the United States and takes into account social requirements (particularly, the work life) and personal values. The author is unusually adept at weaving together the literature of the field.

Two of the five volumes of the massive general report on adult education of the Organisation for Economic Co-operation and Development focus fairly directly on the analysis of providers, chiefly those in highly developed nations. The second volume, entitled *New Structures, Programmes, and Methods* (1979), deals with innovation in programming, particularly in Germany, Britain, Denmark, and Eastern Europe. The final *General Report* (1977a) concludes that "the education of adults is moving from a marginal position in relation to formal education systems to take a more central place in society's overall provision for education" (p. 5).

After a long and closely reasoned treatment of the topic, four alternative futures are suggested so far as the OECD countries are concerned:

> a) to let adult education evolve, as in the past, in a spontaneous and sporadic fashion without reference to any explicit public intervention; b) to strengthen and co-ordinate the existing range of activities but not to perceive it as an active instrument of public policy in the social and economic arena; c) to strengthen and co-ordinate the existing range of activities while simultaneously pursuing a positive policy of support for specific activities judged to be national priorities, for example, secondary education equivalency programmes designed to promote equality; d) to create a comprehensive service of adult education as an integral element of broadly conceived educational systems and to relate its functions to the social, economic and cultural objectives of the state [p. 80].

The authors of the report argue that the majority of advanced nations fall into the third category but that some are moving toward the fourth.

A sharply alternative view to all of the foregoing works is presented by Illich (1970) in a book provocatively titled *Deschooling Society.* The author, an Austrian priest with much experience in both South and North America, is deeply concerned with the way that the structure of both health care and education serves to defeat the purposes of those who need or provide them. He advocates the abolition of schools (and, by extension, of all other forms of structured education) and their replacement with fluid and fluctuating patterns and systems of learning that use people's own motivations and impulses to help them learn.

Public Schools

The term *public school* is here used in the American sense to include comprehensive local educational institutions operated by the government and usually controlled by state-established but community-oriented boards. The primary function of the public school has always been the instruction of children. Elsewhere around the world, other terms are used for essentially the same entities, such as *government schools, state schools,* and *local schools.* The English public schools were originally differentiated from parallel institutions on the basis of admissions policy, not control. They are not included here, nor are other privately controlled schools.

To achieve a school system that aims at nothing less than the appropriate education of all children—whatever their abilities and wherever they live in a continental nation—was so challenging an undertaking that it has commanded the attention and strained the resources of the American people for a century and a half. The idea that local schools should also meet the learning needs of adults within their service areas was never wholly ignored; however, it was seldom carried out in practice by anything more than adjunct programs of some sort or by the opening up of buildings at night for sketchy remedial offerings.

In 1927, Glueck published a well-researched history of the idea of schools as community centers and also suggested many programs that would not emerge until later years. Her language expresses an idealistic view of the importance of the school as a center and stimulus of neighborhood activity. Alderman (1927), in a relatively brief monograph, presents basic information about public school offerings in the mid 1920s, when the adult education movement was flowering. Just under a million adults were then in part-time attendance at such institutions, in addition to their full-time programs for three and a third million children. Alderman includes case studies of the programs for adults in cities of various sizes. Friese (1929) portrays the nature of cosmopolitan evening schools, which were usually heavily vocational in character. This emphasis is stressed even further by Prosser and Bass (1930). These four books set a base line against which to examine subsequent accomplishment.

In the 1930s, broadly based programs of adult education began to flourish in smaller cities and suburbs. Torbert (1936) discusses the program at Maplewood, New Jersey—in its day celebrated as a pioneering center. He deals practically with all aspects of the operation of an adult educational center, with abundant illustrations from the Maplewood program. Dickerman (1938) provides an exuberant account of the broadly ranging school-based programs then coming into existence in the suburbs or relatively prosperous parts of cities. It was believed at the time that they would permit public schools to become true centers of community life. One such program is described by Studebaker (1935), in his account of how a local public school system (in this case, Des Moines, Iowa) can transcend usual instructional boundaries. This program was credited with helping to elevate Studebaker, then superintendent of schools in Des Moines, to national leadership as U.S. Commissioner of Education.

In the late 1960s, two volumes were issued that assessed the nature of public school adult education at that time. Thatcher (1963) drew together brief chapters by major leading practitioners. The book represents what might be called the established point of view of the national association of people engaged in administering evening schools. Shaw (1969) had a somewhat larger scope of reference. The practical essays in his book are concerned with the ways of designing and conducting any institutional program of adult education in a community, though primary attention is paid to those in public schools.

Throughout the early years of its development, public school adult education was treated as a worthy but second-class activity, its resources often begrudged by those who would have liked to use them for the schooling of children. The belief that adult education reinforces the education of children was often expressed; however, though it might be granted in the abstract, it usually did not have immediate and compelling power. As noted in Chapter Three, Clark (1968) introduced the concept of marginality. Describing public school adult education in California (particularly Los Angeles), he begins with the history of its evolution as an institution and continues with an objective description of its operation and functioning. His main purpose is to demonstrate how the entire offering has been dominated by a sense of institutional insecurity, so that the program became only a peripheral part of a decentralized system. Clark's stature as a scholar elevates his discussion far above the peevish air of complaint sometimes surrounding others expressing the same ideas. He believes the situation in the schools to be so bad that it would be impossible to maintain strong and socially significant programs of adult education; the creation of separate institutions would be necessary to carry out distinctive social missions with vigor and determination.

Yet Clark's analysis could also lead to the opposite conclusion: those who sit in the seats of power should design and conduct a total school system that includes the education of adults as a function parallel in importance to the schooling of children. As it happened, such a transformation was already well under way, arising from deep wellsprings based on the idea of the community school.

The idea that the school should serve its community as a learning and recreational center, as well as a focus of needs analysis and decision making, was far from new in either practice or theory. As already noted, Glueck (1927) was an early proponent of this concept. Clapp (1940) describes in great detail the operation of a rural community school in West Virginia and, to a lesser extent, another such school in Kentucky. She believes that a community school "meets as best it can, and with everyone's help, the urgent needs of the people, for it holds that everything that affects the welfare of children and their families is its concern. Where does school end and life outside begin? There is no distinction between them. A community school is a used place, a place used freely and informally for all the needs of living and learning. It is, in effect, that place where learning and living converge" (p. 89). This book makes concrete an idea often expressed only as a broad concept. John Dewey, in a strongly worded foreword, calls attention to "the extraordinary significance for education of the work reported in this book" (p. vii).

Engelhardt and Engelhardt (1940) give another form of concrete expression to community education by dealing comprehensively with the design of school buildings so that they can be optimally used by the members of the whole community, not merely by children. The authors are concerned with both the construction of new buildings and the rehabilitation of old ones. The rooms required for various kinds of learning functions are described and sometimes portrayed. This book was not intended as a set of plans for architects; it was intended to assist educational and lay groups to gain a sense of the dimensions of the buildings required to house a comprehensive public school, serving all ages of the population.

By far the largest and most sustained effort to develop and support community education began in Flint, Michigan, in 1935. Storey and Rohrer (1979) give a much too brief account of the history of the movement. Particular attention is devoted to the support provided to community education by the industrialist Charles Stewart Mott, who initiated the program and whose foundation supported it for many years, not only in Flint but in many other communities as well. By 1978, the movement had become influential in 1,388 public school districts.

The Mott program has inspired a number of books, a few of which will be mentioned briefly here. Minzey and LeTarte (1972) state the nature and basic principles of community education, especially when it is based on the public schools. The work is theoretical and analytical, with relatively little attention given to description or illustration. Berridge (1973) explores the meaning of community education and explains how programs can be initiated and continued. Olsen and Clark (1977) offer a visionary approach to the planning of all education, with specific reference to community education. The authors quote many early and contemporary writers and furnish analytical charts that explain various elements of education or indicate patterns of behavior that should be followed in educational programming. Burden and Whitt (1973) provide a guide detailing how the community school principal can best carry out a complex and challenging job. Berridge, Stark, and West (1977) present twenty-four case studies dealing with major aspects of initiating and operating community schools. Seay (1974) builds on his experience of about fifty years' work with community schools, beginning in the American South and including the Mott program. Although his book refers to the whole community and its institutions, Seay pays primary attention to the use of the school as both a community educator and a center of community life. Of all the works on the subject, it is perhaps the most soundly based on an understanding of how the various problems encountered in school-community relationships can be considered.

In the British tradition, the Local Educational Authorities (LEAs) are part of the general system of government, rather than

being separately structured like American school boards. There are
other profound differences between the two systems, chief among
them that the LEAs not only operate the local schools for children,
but also subsidize a number of other educational institutions that
they do not manage. As pointed out in Chapter One, further education, a broadly based range of learning opportunities, is operated
or supported by the LEAs. It was mandated by Parliament in 1944,
and Peters (1967) summarized its first two decades of accomplishments. Another account was given by Bratchell (1968), and a still
later appraisal was made by Cantor and Roberts (1983), who noted
that further education has come to mean "all forms of post-school
education, except that provided by the universities" (p. 1).

Two other works focus on how LEA programs appear to
those who use their services. Mee and Wiltshire (1978) collected their
data through interviews with the students, faculty members, and
administrators of a large number of instructional centers. The authors' results are explained using certain themes and are finally
summed up in propositions that assess the situation as they believe
they found it. Newman (1979) entitled his book *The Poor Cousin*;
this is an impressionistic and zestfully youthful account of what
adult education is really like as it exists in the inner-city areas of
London. Even the footnotes are lively. Newman concludes his book
with the following passage: "Imagine what an exciting, challenging, truly extraordinary *educational* service we could provide for the
unemployed, the employed, the young, the old, the handicapped,
the disadvantaged, the thoroughly privileged, this socio-economic
class and that, if we had a fair share of the educational budget. Sit
back for a moment, and imagine . . . " (p. 240).

A distinctively English strain of community schools was
developed through the work of Henry Morris, who, as the chief
education officer of Cambridgeshire, conceived and fostered a system of "village colleges" in the early part of this century. Ree (1973)
provides a candid biography of Morris and describes the institutions
created through his leadership. Essentially, they were centers providing general and humanistic studies for the people of a village
and its surrounding area. An appendix summarizes in Morris's own
words the ideas that he had in mind. In a collection of essays,
Fletcher and Thompson (1980) show how those ideas have been

carried out, mostly in Britain, but (in one case) in California as well. The authors concentrate on what it means to operate an educational enterprise that is truly community-based, particularly in lower-income settings. Much of the book is theoretical, and it may be hard for readers unfamiliar with the subject matter to get a sense of the reality that lies behind the generalizations. Reporting on their study of community schools, Wallis and Mee (1983) identify the "persistent ideas" expressed by them as being the following: the school as a center for social, cultural, recreational, and educational provision; the school as a base for community development and social action; and the school as a means of "needs meeting" and outreach. The authors conclude that present schools are not implementing these ideas very well and argue that greatest attention be given to the improvement of these institutions, not their replication.

In programs of educational aid to developing nations, attention is often given to local school systems and their teachers as potentially important instruments of adult education. It could hardly be otherwise. In a tribal village, the only secular gathering place may be a school; inadequate though it almost always is, it offers the only hope for providing basic knowledge to the men and women who live there. In *The School and Continuing Education*, published in 1972, Unesco presented four studies that in some fashion assess schools as instruments of adult education, particularly as part of a total pattern of lifelong education. This latter theme has been at the heart of many of the publications of the Unesco Institute of Education in Hamburg, including those cited in Chapter One. The chief such work was offered by Dave in 1973. Another especially interesting approach was made by Skager and Dave (1977), who speculated on how the curriculum of young people in schools must be changed if lifelong education ever becomes a fully realized concept.

Universities and Colleges

The sense of marginality deeply felt by many of those who introduced adult education into schools has also been present in efforts to do the same thing in colleges and universities. Certainly in the early days, the creation of such opportunities was hampered by incomprehension or active resistance from those who believed that individual and social needs could be met only by access to the knowledge traditionally available in institutions of higher education. This negative feeling is much less acute now than it used to be, and at least a few programs for adults have achieved a status higher than that of similar activities for young people.

Books on adult education in colleges and universities are abundant, more than for any other providers considered in this sequence of three chapters. In this literature, universities and degree-granting colleges are usually treated together, sometimes being linked as university-level institutions. Community colleges and other postsecondary-school organizations have such complex purposes that they are usually treated separately. This distinction will be followed here. *Higher adult education* is a variable term, sometimes including the activities of community colleges but more often referring only to those of degree-granting institutions. At this point, mention will be made only of general works, leaving to other sections (such as those on the Cooperative Extension Service, distance education, and continuing professional education) the books on specialized university programs.

The Purposes of Higher Adult Education

The ways by which the college or university should educate external publics are expressed or implied by virtually all of the authors who write on higher adult education. The strongest single purpose, dominant in the beginning and still vital today, has been to create an opportunity for adults to master the basic knowledge not acquired in youth and to earn the credentials that signify such mastery. This aim has now been supplemented by many others.

Burns and Houle (1948) present a collection of addresses on this general theme. They were given by authorities from many fields, including industry and labor, as well as such segments of higher education as land-grant universities, liberal arts colleges, community colleges, teacher-training institutions, and urban universities. Brownell (1952) expresses in a series of short essays the powerful need for the community and the university to be brought into closer collaboration so that the humanistic values of each may be reinforced thereby. Schoenfeld (1954) focuses on how a university is related to its publics. The formal teaching of adults by various extension efforts is advanced as a major way of influencing the public's perception of the university. Many of the points that the author makes forcefully to counteract opposition or apathy are now accepted without question.

In the 1970s, a number of major university leaders spoke out strongly on the importance of full participation by universities in a society that was then accepting adult education in a wholly unprecedented fashion. The Carnegie Commission on Higher Education published in 1973 the report of its lengthy discussion on the nature of a learning society and the challenges and opportunities that it offered to higher education. Hesburgh, Miller, and Wharton (1973) supplied the results of three investigations concerning the functions of a university as a lifelong learning center. The contribution by Miller is an individual essay, that of Hesburgh is the highly compressed distillation of a study carried out by a number of task forces made up of national leaders, and that of Wharton is the report (also highly condensed) of a faculty group at Michigan State University. These reports are woven together into a synthesis that captures the essential ideas expressed in all three. Harrington (1977) writes on the basis of a vast perspective on adult education, starting with extension teaching and administration and extending to the presidency of the University of Wisconsin and of the National Association of State Universities and Land-Grant Colleges. He also took the trouble to become thoroughly informed on modern movements and literature in the field. The resulting book is a relatively brief, interestingly written statement in which Harrington weighs the evidence on both sides of many issues; however, he never leaves the reader in doubt about his own strong commitment to lifelong learning and the importance of higher education in it.

The History of University Extension

Modern accounts usually trace the history of university extension to two beginning points. The first was 1862, when Congress created the land-grant college system, intended from the beginning to transmit knowledge of engineering and scientific agriculture. Direct service to adults was slow in developing but came into full flower with the creation of the Cooperative Extension Service by Congress in 1914. Eddy (1957) provides an interesting and readable account of the unfolding of the concerns of the land-grant colleges from their origins to the time of the book's publication. The other beginning point has been accepted as 1873, when Cambridge University first offered instruction to adults. The movement initiated at that time spread fairly rapidly, soon crossing the Atlantic and extending to include the work of all kinds of higher educational institutions (including, in time, the land-grant colleges). Their distinctive efforts will be included in a later section of this book on the Cooperative Extension Service.

The early days of university adult education in England were described by Jepson in 1973. He regarded extension as an aspect of the movements to reform the ancient universities and provides much factual detail about the specifics of extension and the way that it served its clientele. In 1923, the fiftieth anniversary of the Cambridge beginning of the movement, Draper issued a history of its growth, not only there, but also elsewhere in England. The book contains a valuable chronology of the events taking place during that fifty-year history.

In two works, Herbert Baxter Adams describes the history and nature of university extension. In 1900, he published his culminating report on the British developments, incorporating and enlarging upon a number of earlier papers. Adams, one of the first major academic historians in the United States, brought to this work his rare and fully matured powers of analysis. He sketches the forms and forces that led to the development of extension and presents its picture in its fullest British development—just before it became influenced by the workers' educational movement and eventually took on the form that has dominated it ever since. Adams (1899) offers an account of the summer school idea as it was put into practice at various European universities. One interesting aspect of this book is its firsthand account of some of the leaders of English adult education at the end of the nineteenth century.

Three modern works bring the story of British university extension up to date. Welch (1973) traces the history of the Cambridge class-extension program throughout its first century. A narrative account and statistical analysis are given of the number of centers offering instruction; also supplied is the number of students attending for each of the hundred years, thus providing perhaps the longest serial record of any single program in all of adult education. The author also considers other forms of instruction at Cambridge, such as that of residential centers. Welch writes with refreshing candor and makes no effort to gloss over occasional errors and dark places. Marriott (1984) offers a revisionist interpretation of the growth of extension in the British universities. He treats it as a way of building and defending institutional empires, both so far as general public opinion is concerned and as a way of securing national grants. The work is not so much a history as an interpretation of events presumably familiar to the reader. Blyth (1983) offers a straightforward account of that history, concentrating on the fifty years from 1908 to 1958 but providing a quick summary of what went on before and a postlude prediction of probable subsequent developments. It is a clear and candid analysis of personalities and policies as they operated during an eventful national period.

The history of higher adult education in the United States has not been as fully developed as that of Great Britain, but several works can be mentioned. Using primary sources dealing with the early years of extension in the United States, Woytanowitz (1974) provides a serious and well-researched monograph. Precursor movements in both England and America are described as a preface to a detailed study of how extension emerged in the United States, had a sudden growth, seemed to die out, but subsequently began to develop as a national movement. A particularly good account is given of the contribution of various leaders, including Herbert Baxter Adams. Creese (1941) offers a well-written though discursive account of the history of university extension. Portman (1978) gives an account of some aspects of that history but makes no attempt to provide a narrative flow or a sense of historic development. Rohfeld (1990) celebrates the first seventy-five years of the National University Continuing Education Association. She includes a selection of papers and quotations from the publications of the association and other sources, illustrations from early days to late, and various other materials that show the growth of university-based adult education in all its scope and variety. This material is knit together and highlighted by a historical and analytical essay by Rohfeld.

Status Reports on University Adult Education

Some of the foregoing histories end their narration with brief accounts of the status of higher adult education at the time of publication; conversely, a number of accounts of present status begin by sketching in its background. The works in this section emphasize discussion of existing circumstances.

In an early exploratory study, Hall-Quest (1926) identified and assessed the adult educational programs then being carried out by universities. His was, he said, "a reconnoitering expedition through the territory of university extension" (p. 265). Upon looking at a field of work then little understood in its totality, he discovered that many efforts were under way. Almost twenty years later, Thompson (1943) published a factual account of what was being done in university extension around the country. Ten years after that, Morton (1953) offered another statistical survey. Shannon and Schoenfeld (1965), in one of a standardized series of books covering various aspects of higher education, composed what is essentially an extended encyclopedia entry on university extension.

Three books present somewhat more interpretive surveys of this aspect of adult education. Petersen and Petersen (1960) review the whole field, the place of universities in it, and (as an in-depth treatment of one topic) the way adult education in world affairs is handled. Much of what they see they do not like, and sometimes they spell out precisely why. But the book is not a mindless attack; it is a sober, reasoned, and urbane report based on the literature and on experience and strongly tinged with a desire to purify, if necessary by cauterizing. Knowles (1969) describes the current picture, trends, and issues of higher adult education during the mid 1960s and includes a bibliography of the significant literature available at that time. Knowles's work grew out of the deliberations of the Committee on Higher Adult Education of the American Council on Education. Gessner (1987) provides a compendium of chapters dealing with topics of interest to administrators of university programs of adult education, including structural models, financing, program planning, delivery system alternatives, and marketing. Other chapters treat such topics as the history of university continuing education, the forces influencing the field, and patterns of research and evaluation.

The idea that colleges and universities should furnish continuing learning opportunities for their alumni has been discovered afresh at many times and places. For example, Ernest M. Hopkins, in his inaugural address at Dartmouth, developed the rationale for a continuing community of scholars, of which alumni would be a vital part. This 1916 message and others are cited by Shaw (1929) in his work entitled *Alumni and Adult Education*. He reports on a sketchy survey of how alumni officers of American institutions in 1928–1929 approached this idea. Though interesting examples were found and the potentialities of alumni education were explored, the author concluded, "The continued education of the alumni, their acceptance as an integral part of the college or university as an institution of higher education, and the setting up of a program to make a contact with the graduate body on this basis are still, for the most part, matters for the future" (p. 106).

Two other works on this theme appeared soon afterward. Stone and Charters (1932) describe an inquiry made among Ohio State University alumni resident in Toledo about the kinds of educational services they desired from their alma mater. The answers were varied, interesting, and thought-provoking. Beals (1935) intended his book "to follow and supplement" Shaw (1929). Although it deals directly with alumni education, its central theme is related to the education undertaken, often in a self-directed fashion, by highly educated Americans. Beals expresses his ideas about the continuum of learning from the college years throughout life.

Alumni education has continued to exist and, on some campuses, to flourish in the years since these early works brought it into focus. Such programs are usually operated as part of general alumni and fund-raising operations rather than by extension divisions. Calvert caused alumni education to surface once again in the literature by his 1987 survey of current activities. He also provides a thorough theoretical and historical base for alumni education and gives practical advice on how to establish and maintain programs.

Another focus for adult education within the university has been the summer session. At most institutions, summer terms have been intended to offer selected academic opportunities for the ad-

vancement or remediation of students also registered for the rest of
the year—or it has sometimes been said for "the bright and the
stupid." Partly, perhaps, because physical facilities may be under-
utilized in the summer, some colleges and universities have
mounted many other summer programs for adults, often compressed into abbreviated sessions. In some cases, separate administrative units are established within the university to guide these
sessions. Schoenfeld and Zillman (1967) put the whole topic of the
summer school into a historical perspective and analyze both the
program offerings and the way they are conducted. Both comprehensive in scope and gracefully written, the book outlines the prospects and problems of the summer session vis-à-vis its special
missions, rather than merely as a block of time.

Probably the strongest status report on the British program
of university provision was written by Raybould (1951). British governmental and educational authorities came out of World War II
determined that the whole national educational system must be
changed, root and branch, to bring about a more equitable sharing
of the benefits of learning. It was strongly argued that the universities should revise and expand their programs of what that country
calls extramural education. Raybould, a national leader in the field,
reviews the accomplishment of the first five years after the war. The
book is scholarly throughout; moreover, as the author of the foreword, Charles R. Morris, notes, "Mr. Raybould makes a strong case
that the time has come to think about principles. He writes in the
manner of the traditional pamphleteers, arguing with spirit that
review and reform are long overdue. He thinks that without the
universities a sound system of adult education would not be possible. There are some studies that they alone can provide. But more
important than this they are called to be the safeguards of standards;
they must on no account do anything which could damage their
integrity or their high standing in this regard" (pp xi–xii). The
book was the subject of much discussion in Britain during the next
ten years and has become accepted as the substantive statement of
traditional values in higher adult education. Meanwhile, Raybould
continued to develop his theme. In 1959 and again in 1972 (in the
latter case, with Parker as senior author), he edited collections of

essays concerned with the overall patterns of extramural work; in 1964, he issued a thematic historical account of how British university extension developed in the period just after World War II. This latter work is technical and draws heavily on official reports but leavens them with a deep understanding of the various processes and activities being undertaken.

In 1970, the Universities Council for Adult Education, the British association of university extension and continuing education departments, issued a report with the evocative title *University Adult Education in the Later Twentieth Century*. This document was not Utopian in its projections but supplied a sober and practical diagram for action for the years ahead. Ellwood (1976) also sought to identify the emerging goals of university adult education in Britain. The author has had extensive experience in England, the United States, and Germany and demonstrates a command of the relevant literature. She develops her commentary with clarity and expresses it with wit.

Soon after Unesco came into being, it turned its attention to higher adult education and issued a report entitled *Universities in Adult Education* in 1952. The book consists of three chapters on university extension in Great Britain, Canada, and the United States and one chapter integrating the others but going beyond them to identify pervasive themes. Kulich and Kruger (1980) offer a brief and literate description, country by country, of university provision of adult education in each of eleven nations, primarily in western Europe. The general conclusion is that if higher adult education exists in the continental countries, it is not being provided by universities.

Case Examples

Studies of how colleges and universities have carried out programs of adult education abound, but most of them describe efforts to achieve specific goals or to use thematic approaches. These will be included later in the sections dealing with such approaches. Included here are those works that provide all-institutional descriptions.

One of the best-known such programs is that of St. Francis

Xavier University in Antigonish, Nova Scotia, Canada. Coady (1939) offers a firsthand account of the movement. He was its creator, chief architect, and operator. The heart of the program was its development of cooperatives to provide both economic reinforcement and education to the impoverished people of the Maritime Provinces in eastern Canada. This endeavor was sufficiently successful to inspire attention throughout the world. Laidlaw (1961) carries the story further and also draws from it a philosophy of university extension based on community development.

At the opposite end of the spectrum of cosmopolitanism, Burrell (1954) gives a historical account of extension at Columbia University in New York City. This volume, part of the bicentennial history of that institution, traces its adult educational offerings back to plans made in 1830. This early venture and other proposals made in the nineteenth century did not take root, however. It was not until what might justly be called the reign of Nicholas Murray Butler in the early twentieth century that Columbia assumed the position of leadership that it maintained for some years. Burrell indicates that many major content fields now present in the university, including the study of business administration, entered the curriculum after having first proved themselves in the extension department.

Rosentreter (1957) furnishes an account of the history of extension at the University of Wisconsin, one of the fountainheads of the movement. He covers the period from 1895 to 1945 and provides a particularly good record of the activities of the early formative years.

Rockhill (1983) gives a history of university extension at the University of California, as it grew from one campus to nine. She concentrates almost entirely on organizational and administrative arrangements. Throughout this period of growth, two sets of struggles having to do with structure and content were constantly being fought: between the organized faculty (as represented in departments and senate committees) and the extension units, and between the centralized, statewide extension division and the service units based on the campuses.

Crimi (1957) reports on the kinds of adult education sponsored by various liberal arts colleges. English (1959) describes how

West Georgia College in Carrollton provided an off-campus program that brought learning to the surrounding communities. This program, starting from a slow beginning, had attracted national attention by the late 1950s.

Kelly (1950) presents a scholarly monograph on the history of extramural work at Manchester University from 1886 to 1946. His account describes how that institution came into being as the result of a merger of several programs, each with its own tradition of service. Kelly traces the influences, both local and national, brought to bear on the development of extramural services, and his book reveals a number of factors often overlooked in the sweeping history of university extension since 1873.

Raybould (1957) describes the difference between university extension in a British university and that at an African university, even though the latter was designed after British models. For many years the chief administrator of the program at Leeds University, Raybould wrote this volume after spending two terms at the University of Ibadan in Nigeria in 1954–1955.

In 1876, the University of London began its formal offering of extension courses. Burrows (1976) gives a history of the work accomplished in the hundred years since its beginning. As its author says, it is "more in the nature of a sketch rather than a definitive work" (p. x), but it suggests something of the range and variety of offerings by a highly complex university in the city that was the world's largest for most of the century concerned.

Thornton and Stephens (1977) report with amplitude on each of the various units of service and fields of study of the Extra-Mural Department at the University of Nottingham. Their work is more thoughtful and contemplative than purely descriptive, and there is a harmony among the accounts that reflects a common purpose and philosophy. The book concludes with a chapter dealing with national trends and setting the work of the university within this context.

Arrangements for Securing Degrees and Credits

As university extension was first considered and established in the United States, it consisted mainly of efforts to make organized knowledge, usually defined in terms of academic courses and sequences, available to adults at times and places convenient to them. In his 1915 annual report, Nicholas Murray Butler of Columbia University proudly wrote, "Buildings that a generation ago were closed at one o'clock in the afternoon, that ten years ago were closed at five o'clock at night are now open and fully occupied until ten o'clock at night" (Burrell, 1954, p. 80). At a growing number of institutions, instruction was also offered on the campus during weekend hours, at sites other than the campus, or by such methods as correspondence study that could be fitted into part-time learning patterns.

The long struggle to create a higher educational system for young people was based strongly on the belief that degrees and other credentials are of great value. The general public learned this lesson well. One of the most potent appeals of university extension was its ability to provide adults an opportunity to secure these highly prized awards. Houle (1973) looked closely at the external degree—that is to say, one awarded to adults who had completed a special sequence of study designed especially for them. He explored the ancient traditions of such a degree, described the various forms that it has taken in a century and a half, and appraised the claims made for and against it. He also noted that special arrangements for these degrees were proliferating so rapidly that his book would be out of date by the time of its publication (a prediction that came true). Some adult educators have always felt ashamed of "pandering" to the desire of adults for credentials, rather than for education that directly enlightens, informs, or empowers the learners. As noted previously, Duke and Marriott (1973) present a close analysis of paper awards, focusing particularly on the kinds of students who want these awards and why they want them.

The major early instrument for providing adult degrees was the evening college, about which Dyer (1956) wrote: "Behind the ivory curtain of traditional college and university education there is developing a new phase of higher education, vast in its implications and important in the services it renders. It is the university evening college, a hustling, vigorous institution, not yet mature, but conscious of its potentialities and characterized by an almost religious sense of its destiny" (p. 7). Out of a deep knowledge of such institutions, especially as they served the war-delayed or -denied needs for education in the late 1940s and 1950s, Dyer deals both descriptively and analytically with the college itself, its students, its community, and its parent institution.

The organization of the evening college as part of the university has been the subject of much scrutiny. At one extreme, it can be merely a physical site at which such departments of the university as wish can locate their offerings for adults. At the other extreme, it can be a separately structured college with its own administrators and faculty, parallel in every respect to the other major units of the university. McMahon, himself the dean of an institution of the latter sort, presented in 1960 the results of his study of ten evening colleges in the northeastern region of the country. The pattern of growth in structure and operation that he perceived is set forth in detail. Carey (1961) espouses the idea of a growth cycle; he believes that this occurs during four stages, as the provision of adult education by a university moves from departmental domination to centralization of responsibility.

In addition to the task of providing degrees, the evening colleges often offered other adult educational services. Jacobson (1970) makes a detailed case study of how this process of growth of activities takes place. In a work underlaid with sociological principles and administrative theory, she describes how the School of General Studies of Brooklyn College evolved in its interaction with its parent institution. Jacobson concludes with a broadly stated, theoretical view of how she thinks the relationship should be further developed. Hoppe (1972) reports in great detail on the method of operation of 146 evening colleges and extension divisions. The author draws few general principles of operation but reviews the arrangements at each of the institutions that he studied. Farmer (1967) focuses on student personnel services in such institutions.

In the late 1960s and early 1970s, it became apparent that a number of trends were operating in such a way as to bring about profound changes in the traditional patterns of service of college and university education. An important shift was the restructuring of how degrees, especially the baccalaureate, were offered for young people on campus. Throughout the earlier part of the twentieth century, the single coherent educative experience of the past had been replaced by an enormous system of presumably standardized courses that a student had to accumulate in fixed amounts and distribute in a prescribed fashion. This approach, designed originally for compliant young people two or three years on either side of the age of twenty, imposed on students a rigidity that did not accord with the changing life-styles of young people of that age or with a growing awareness of how much they differed from one another. A number of new devices and doctrines appeared: the early admission of young people prepared for college life; the advanced standing of those who could demonstrate special competence; the awarding of credit on the basis of examinations rather than course attendance; and the recognition of learning gained by experience rather than by formal study. These changes made it much easier for conventional students to secure credit and degrees and also opened up new avenues for adults seeking formal study.

The innovations resulted in part from the efforts of two institutions centrally concerned with degrees. The College Entrance Examination Board (as it was then known) was the most powerful arbiter concerned with national patterns of university admission. The Educational Testing Service was the creator of monitoring instruments and examinations whose revision could make change possible. These two bodies, aided by the Carnegie Corporation, created a Commission on Non-Traditional Study, made up of people drawn from various segments of higher education and headed by Samuel Gould, formerly chancellor of the State University of New York. This commission examined the implications of a new spirit pervading its discussion. As Gould said:

> Despite our lack of a completely suitable definition, we always seemed to sense the areas of education around which our interests centered. This community of concern was a mysterious light in the darkness, yet not at all mysterious in retrospect. Most of us agreed that non-traditional study is more an attitude than a system and thus can never be defined except tangentially. This attitude puts the student first and the institution second, concentrates more on the former's

need than the latter's convenience, encourages diversity of individual opportunity rather than uniform prescription, and deemphasizes time, space, and even course requirements in favor of competence, and, where applicable, performance. It has concern for the learner of any age and circumstance, for the degree aspirant as well as for the person who finds sufficient reward in enriching life through constant, periodic, or occasional study. This attitude is not new; it is simply more prevalent than it used to be. It can stimulate exciting and high-quality educational progress; it can also, unless great care is taken to protect the freedom it offers, be the unwitting means to a lessening of academic rigor and even to charlatanism [Commission on Non-Traditional Study, 1973, p. xv].

The Commission on Non-Traditional Study did its work at a time when other studies were also being made of the system of higher education. Although they sometimes included adult education at various points in their reports, the commission accepted the need for special arrangements for adult degree programs as a central element in its work. In addition to its own report, the commission sponsored three other studies, including the already mentioned one by Houle (1973). Gould and Cross (1972) compiled essays by several authors dealing with issues related to the provision of degree-level instruction to audiences not usually served by colleges and universities. Adults are not singled out for separate attention, but an underlying assumption of the authors is that mature students will be the chief beneficiaries of the nontraditional programs concerned. Cross and Valley (1974) focus more directly on adult education. They analyze two major studies on adult learning, explore a number of possible new ways of providing instruction, and discuss the problems of maintenance of quality. An excellent annotated bibliography is also provided.

The most important single event in the modern movement to create degree programs for adults occurred in Britain. The Open University in the United Kingdom first came forcefully to the attention of people throughout the world in 1963; the proposal for its establishment offered an opportunity of a wholly new sort for people to secure a degree in a program that had many aspects but was centered on the use of the electronic media for instruction. A major institution was created in a period of only three years, from 1968 to 1971. Perry (1977) provides an inside account of the development of that institution. He was its first chief administrative officer and was awarded a knighthood for his efforts; shortly afterward, he was elevated to the peerage by a grateful monarch. When Perry's book was written, the major problem was the establishment of a mature organization that would remain innovative in its programming. The Open University provides, Perry maintains, "the most difficult way of getting a degree yet invented by the wit of man" (p. ix); yet its methods have been so innovative in their adaptation to the requirements of complex adult life-styles that it has been successful beyond most early hopes. The book's chief purpose is to be informative, but it is written with a candor and verve that make it highly interesting.

A cluster of other books dealing with the Open University also appeared in the mid 1970s. Tunstall (1974) gives a general and diversified account of the institution dealing with all aspects of its structure and operation, including a good deal of anecdotal material and case studies. Ferguson (1976) offers a highly personal account (the first chapter is an autobiography) of the beginnings of the Open University, written by one of its key administrators. His main purpose being historical and descriptive, he makes no attempt to develop generalizations, and his pride in what has been accomplished is constantly evident. In 1976, the Open University itself issued a report by its Committee on Continuing Education. Although the original mission of the institution was to award the baccalaureate on the basis of unconventional study, its leaders soon realized that they could use their machinery of operation and their theories of education to develop an all-encompassing program of continuing education that would parallel and go beyond the degree work. The committee whose deliberations are reported here identified the central goals and plans that should be used to create a comprehensive program. McIntosh, Calder, and Swift (1977) provide an elaborate and heavily statistical longitudinal report on the first group of students of the Open University, describing its composition and how it progressed during its first five years. Some data are also provided concerning subsequent "intakes" of students.

In the decade of its conception and development, the Open University evoked an astonishingly strong international interest and reaction. The nontraditional movement in the United States was strongly influenced by the appearance of this new form of bac-calaureate education. In the United Kingdom and elsewhere, it was widely believed that the institution could serve as a model for sim-ilar ventures. An appraisal of how far this hope has been realized was presented in 1982 by Rumble and Harry, who focus sharply on "those few universities mainly founded in the 1970s to teach only at a distance" (p. 7). They describe not only the Open University, but also universities or university-oriented programs in eight other countries: Canada, China, Costa Rica, the Federal Republic of Ger-many, Israel, Pakistan, Spain, and Venezuela. The authors do not hesitate to report on the problems encountered by the institutions they mention, but the general tone of the book is positive and op-timistic. It suggests that though the Open University's design, methods, and materials can be widely used elsewhere, they must always be adapted to suit the social setting in which they are tried.

In addition to the major efforts of the Commission on Non-Traditional Study and the Open University, a number of other ap-proaches have been made to the provision of credits and degrees for adults. The idea that even advanced and theoretical knowledge could be achieved by the normal processes of life, as well as by formal study, has been advanced and systematized in various ways. Stern and Missall (1960) supply an early report on the work done at Brooklyn College to test this idea in its experimental degree pro-gram for adults. Much that was highly unconventional then has become accepted now, and it is interesting to see the first cautious attempts at the quantification of experiential learning results in terms of the awarding of academic credits. Meyer (1975) deals with how undergraduate credit can be given for prior learning experi-ences. Nyquist, Arbolino, and Hawes (1977) provide a straightfor-ward, simply and directly written guide for potential adult degree seekers; they furnish practical information on how to use experien-tial learning, credit by examination, and other ways of receiving instruction. A number of profiles are given of students who have succeeded. Moon and Hawes (1980) describe how part of the credit required for a degree may be achieved by an adult by means of the assessment of life experience through portfolio completion, the passing of examinations, and the use of established assessments of military instruction programs that parallel those in civilian life.

Experiential learning has been subjected to much critical analysis and will be considered more fully in Chapter Ten. Two works seem relevant here. Chickering (1971) discusses how such learning can be provided for both conventional and adult students in colleges and universities. He covers thoroughly the major elements, practices, and problems of such learning and gives many illuminating examples of his general principles. In a deeply theoretical and abstract fashion, Kolb (1984) considers the question of how experience itself educates, drawing particularly upon the writings of Dewey, Lewin, and Piaget. His own conclusions are drawn from a blend of the fundamental ideas of all three, as well as from the thoughts of many other authors who have considered the same topic. Kolb implies that an understanding of how experience naturally influences education can help an individual or group improve the impact of planned activities.

Part of the stimulus for creating new kinds of credit and degree programs has grown out of a desire to reach new students to compensate for an expected decline in enrollment of traditional college-age students when the postwar "baby boom" came to an end. Vermilye (1974) reports on a national conference concerned with whether adults might become a major clientele group ·for American higher education. The approach of the author-experts is varied in point of view, depth of insight, generality of concern, and profundity of knowledge concerning adult education. Many of the papers are excellent; the most comprehensive is that of Ernest L. Boyer, entitled "Breaking Up the Youth Ghetto," in which he describes the changes that occur on a campus as it broadens its concerns to include adult students. MacKenzie, Postgate, and Scupham (1975) use the term *open learning* to cover all the new teaching processes and systems designed to bring postsecondary education to new categories of students. This well-financed study has a worldwide scope and represents both idealistic aims and practical accomplishments. Baskin (1974) assesses many arrangements that were being made to adjust the standard curriculum patterns of American colleges and universities in order to make their programs more accessible to mature students. The authors contributing to this volume were in the thick of these new arrangements; they express the hopes and challenges with which they were concerned. Teather (1982) reports on innovative practices in the British Commonwealth countries and one American institution. The reports are grouped in four categories: adapting to new clienteles on campus; meeting course needs off campus through appropriate technology; using research and consultancy; and providing for the performing arts. The introductory paper by Teather is an insightful summary of the nature of university-based community service in the 1980s.

Some works deal with this theme by providing collections of case studies. Hall (1974) reviews a number of ventures by colleges and universities to reach new students of conventional age as well as adults. Medsker and others (1975) make a cross-cutting analysis of sixteen innovative college degree programs established for adults in the United States. The authors undertake an in-depth investigation of what was occurring and estimate the probable success of the various ventures. Greenberg, O'Donnell, and Bergquist (1980) analyze programs founded in the 1960s and 1970s (chiefly by small liberal arts colleges) to provide formal education for adults.

The optimism underlying these new ventures was not universally shared. Writing after the establishment of the Open University and other degree-granting programs, Marriott (1981) recounts the history of a British movement in the last quarter of the nineteenth century whose aim was to offer degrees to adults. This effort, a part of the more general university extension movement, was never able to establish itself. Marriott concludes that its history was "an unhappy chronicle of how a movement of great vigour and enormous optimism was forced into that marginal status that we all know to be the miserable lot of organised adult education" (p. 97).

Lifelong Education

The university was a central instrument for learning in the thoughts of those who developed the new concepts of recurrent, permanent, and lifelong education in the 1970s. To cite but one example, the continuing education of professionals seemed to be a natural form of recurrent education for the institutions that had provided basic programs of preparation. The discussion of the new vistas that seemed to open up largely occurred outside the United States but had some relevance to higher education in that country.

Most such volumes are comparative studies of programs in several nations. Harman (1976) presents a collection of essays exploring the ways by which universities in both developed and developing countries can contribute to their societies by fostering lifelong study. Williams (1977) extends the scope of investigation even farther. Brief accounts are given of practice in twenty-three countries, and other chapters are concerned with cross-cutting analysis.

Lifelong Education and University Resources, issued by Unesco and the International Association of Universities in 1978, reports on programs in eight countries: Sweden, Canada (Quebec only), Switzerland (Geneva only), Zambia, Venezuela, Poland, Ghana, and France. The unnamed editor of this volume wrote an unusually trenchant introduction dealing broadly with the nature of lifelong education and the place of universities in it.

Knapper and Cropley (1985) examine the university, not as workers in its program or apologists for it but as social analysts trying to determine how the university as an institution can best serve to advance the ideas of lifelong learning. Rather than emphasize structure or administrative concerns, they focus on the nature of the university instructional process and the evaluation of its outcomes. A valuable chapter is included indicating how change can occur within the institution to achieve the pattern of services required to carry out new missions.

Critiques of University Extension

Four books give sustained interpretations of university adult education, all of them made by people intimately familiar with it. Wedemeyer (1981), widely read and deeply experienced in the field, offers his reflections on the nature of higher education and the implication of its service for lifelong education. He also analyzes the influence of the electronic technologies for the learning process.

This is a deeply subjective statement of the author's beliefs. Taylor, Rockhill, and Fieldhouse (1985) contribute a closely reasoned theoretical work dealing with the liberal tradition exemplified in much of both British and American practice in university adult education. They argue for the further development of the ideal, even if the forms must be new, and (to use one of the authors' key words) *radicalised*. Freedman (1987) is concerned only with the assessment of quality in the adult educational service provided by colleges and universities. He believes that two different sources of standards exist: those derived from the faculty's conception of quality and those growing out of student needs, however perceived. In striking a necessary balance between these two sources, he puts forward a series of "requirements," propositional statements of policy or practice. Apps (1988) treats very broadly the opportunities and challenges to higher education presented by various aspects of the learning society. What is the proper role of the college and university in the larger structure of providers? What are the special groups that demand services of various sorts? How can an institution set priorities between traditional and emergent services? How does higher education need to change its basic methodologies of teaching? These and other central questions are answered with a comprehensive view of the institutions themselves.

Community Colleges

The junior college came into existence in two major ways: as an upward thrust of the high school and as an outward thrust of the university. In its beginnings, its principal purpose was to provide an education for young people who could not enter traditional patterns of instruction; however, from its first efforts to expand in the 1920s and afterward, it included educational services for adults, in part reflecting the ideas of the adult educational movement that was flourishing by that time. As such services grew and as the curriculum broadened to include many vocational, technical, and other courses of study relevant to segments of the adult population, the junior college was transformed into the community college, still part of higher education but a distinctive new sector of it.

Twice earlier in this volume, reference has been made to

Clark (1968) and his concept of the marginality of public school adult education. In an earlier work published in 1960, he surveys the community college, particularly as it had developed in California. In what he called the "open door college," adult education is seen as being so central to the mission of the institution that it cannot be separated for special attention. Most of the literature of community college education adopts this point of view. Only works concerned with adult education as a special theme will be mentioned here.

Harlacher (1969) reports the results of extensive field studies, visitations, and discussions with leaders. He identifies how the institution that began as a junior college has transcended its earlier role to achieve full stature as a service institution for its whole community. Adult education, conceived as both instruction and enrichment, is an important element in all such endeavors, and the author, with unusual skill and very little jargon, provides both theory and concrete illustration to develop his points. His book was so influential that much of what he advocated as innovation has since been accepted in practice.

Gollattscheck (1976) advances the case for the community college as an instrument for social change. He believes that the leaders of the institution should analyze the needs of their entire community or of significant sectors of it and develop programs that will bring about desired changes by any means available, but essentially through the processes of education. He makes the case very strongly that the community college should no longer be considered as just another form of higher education; instead, it should become a complex operational and coordinating mechanism. The book gains strength from the fact that illustrations of all the theories and principles suggested are given from contemporary practice.

The idea of community change was further stressed by Harlacher and Gollattscheck (1978). Their collection of essays was written chiefly by community college administrators concerned with how their institutions may best be brought into a closer and more productive relationship with their communities. The main theme is perhaps best expressed by Alan Pifer, then president of the Carnegie Corporation, in his comment: "I'm going to make an outrageous suggestion that community colleges should start thinking about themselves from now on only secondarily as a sector of higher education and regard their primary role as community leadership" (p. viii).

Fuller (1979) examines continuing education in the light of his basic principle: it "is always on the fringe of a new educational frontier—if, in fact, it is not the new educational frontier itself" (p. 85). He deals with his broad theme in a highly individualistic way, mixing objective evidence with anecdote and illustration.

Gilder (1979) reports on a conference dealing with the broad spectrum of lifelong learning, but with particular attention to the community college. As a result of discussions carried on at the conference, policies were developed and recommendations made to the colleges themselves, their national association, federal and state governments, the business and industrial world, and to all persons interested in lifelong education.

In exploring the mission of the community college in the United States, Gleazer (1980) uses the following statement as his keystone idea for such service: "To encourage and facilitate lifelong learning, with community as process and product" (p. 16). In developing this theme, he relies on Dave (1973) and Faure (1972). The book is essentially a collection of brief essays, many of them presenting and interpreting examples drawn from community college experience. Of particular interest is his detailed analysis of developmental tasks at various stages of life and their implications for community college programming.

A Final Word

All institutions created to educate children and youth have made decisions, deliberately or not, about how or whether they wished to modify their purposes to become providers of lifelong learning. Many have held to their original course; others have made resolute changes; most, perhaps, have made adaptations to serve a broader clientele than before. No statistics appear to be available concerning the resulting changes in the public schools, but *Lifelong Learning Trends* (1990) highlights the past and present student enrollments in university extension and suggests the factors having to do with its probable future. Some data exist for higher education as a whole, including community colleges. Between the early 1970s and the late 1980s, the percentage of part-time students increased from 32 percent to 42 percent, and the percentage of students over the age of 25 increased from 28 percent to 42 percent. The available data do not permit conclusions about whether this trend will continue or, if it does, about how far it will eventually go; however, unscientific observation suggests that many institutions are planning futures for themselves that will open up their service to new adult populations.

The books identified in this chapter, taken as a whole, appear to bear out the observations of Kenzo Tange in its epigraph. The formalizations of the past have been reshaped in part by energy arising from new conceptions of the educative community, of the range of possibilities for the individual, and of the need to enrich every stage of the life span. But the addition of services for adults has not only enhanced and expanded the need for high-quality education for young people, it has also revealed some of the ways by which it may be fostered. Tradition and antitradition have been synthesized in a new creativeness—and there is no indication that this process has come to an end.

SIX

Providers Created to Educate People of All Ages

The prospects of instituting lifelong education, and the need for it, are to be judged not in relation to other people or to a given body of knowledge external to the pupil, but in relation to the personal development of a particular individual.

—Lengrand, 1975 p. 51

Although lifelong learning has only recently emerged as a full-scale theoretical construct, its operational form is familiar. It has been practiced for many years by three American institutions: the Cooperative Extension Service, the public library, and the museum. In their early years, all three placed primary emphasis on service to adults, but for most of the twentieth century they have reached out to people of all ages, structuring or accommodating their programs with that clear intent.

The Cooperative Extension Service

The Cooperative Extension Service (CES) is the largest adult educational program in the United States and probably the least well understood at home and abroad. Its central thrust has been the improvement of agriculture and agribusiness, of the farm home, and of rural life; yet its services, particularly for youth, have broadened to serve other purposes. It operates as a cooperative effort—hence its name—of the U.S. Department of Agriculture, the land-grant colleges, county government, and private enterprise. It has counterparts in many countries, but most of them concentrate on agriculture and are operated by national ministries in programs that sometimes offer education accompanied by various forms of legal compulsion and financial rewards. The CES takes pride in its localism, its reliance upon adapting a scientific data base to meet the needs of people, its practicality, its diversity of methods, and its creative employment of volunteers. Its leaders have always been determined that education shall be its sole function, as was shown most vividly when controls over agriculture were placed in the hands of its agents during Roosevelt's New Deal; they repudiated the unwanted power as soon as they could. "Its purpose," says Liberty Hyde Bailey, referring to the CES, "is to improve the farmer, not the farm" (Rivera and Schram, 1987, p. 58).

The CES has deep roots in American history. According to folklore, Indians taught early pioneers how to increase agricultural productivity, and the founding fathers of the republic sometimes returned from Europe with seeds to be planted in the new world. The United States was a rural country until 1920. For most of the time until then, its largest economic enterprise was farming; its level of productivity was crucial to the wealth of the nation. True (1928) chronicled the development of the idea of agricultural improvement in its various manifestations, from the founding of the new nation to the consolidation of extension work at the end of World War I. For forty years, True had been employed by the U.S. Department of Agriculture and had therefore been a direct witness to many of the events about which he wrote. In a centennial account of the land-grant colleges, Eddy (1957) included descriptions of the rise of extension.

The great success of the CES has made it seem in retrospect like an inevitable accommodation to the wishes of a dominant interest group. Such was not the case. A long political battle was required to get Congress to pass the land-grant college act. When it did, President Buchanan vetoed it. The bill had to be reenacted after Lincoln assumed office; he was willing to approve it. Even after the colleges began to receive federal aid, a half-century of political struggles were required before extension could be established by Congress.

A key problem was that the interest group that stood to gain the most from extension was determined to oppose it. Scott (1970), in his book entitled *The Reluctant Farmer,* documents the strong resistance of American farmers to scientific agricultural knowledge and provides a detailed history of the efforts to overcome that opposition. Scott begins with an account of efforts at agrarian reform in colonial days and carries the story forward with a portrayal of various group and institutional endeavors in the nineteenth century. The culminating section of the book has to do with the shaping of the eventual model for influencing rural people, which would become the central methodology incorporated in the Smith-Lever Act in 1914.

Both in his own lifetime and subsequently, Seaman A. Knapp has been regarded as the master builder of the Cooperative Extension Service. Bailey (1945) presents an engrossing biography of his life and thought. After a classical education, Knapp devoted most of his life to the improvement of agriculture. His career had many twists and turns, as he devoted a restless and inquiring mind to the solution of problems in a number of fields of work and in many stations of life. He had a constant conviction that the increase of agricultural production must begin with the education of the practicing farmer. The most active phase of his career did not begin until he was seventy years old; in combating the cotton boll weevil in Texas, he devised techniques that would lead to the agrarian revolution for which he had long hoped. His most famous aphorism was "What a man hears he may doubt, what he sees he may possibly doubt, but what he does himself, he cannot possibly doubt" (p. 155). In the last eight years of his life, he worked with great energy to establish a national system of extension that would help farmers know how to practice scientific agriculture. He did not live to see the passage of the Smith-Lever Act by Congress in 1914, but it has been an enduring memorial to his leadership.

In a monograph first issued in 1933, Blauch (1969) deals with the legislative history of the CES as it became a federal concern and traces its administrative history through the 1920s. The CES is seen in broad perspective as part of the total federal interest in higher education.

Very soon after federal financing of the CES began, club programs for young people and "home demonstration" work for women were included as integral forms of service and have continued in that capacity ever since. Smith and Wilson (1930) describe the nature of the CES as it neared the end of its first era of development (signaled by the passage of the Capper-Ketcham Act of 1928, which greatly enlarged the funds available). At the time that Smith and Wilson wrote, the World War I years and the "normalcy" of the 1920s had been safely negotiated, and the Great Depression had only recently begun. Complete and scholarly, the work expresses the authority that the authors brought to the subject as senior administrators of the CES. The picture of the service here presented would long endure in the lore of workers in the field even as they faced the great changes of subsequent decades.

Baker (1939), a political scientist, focuses on the county agent—the CES's local representative—as an official combining federal, state, and local responsibilities with strong obligations to private associations. The author's observations (chiefly of agents in Iowa) show an analytical grasp of the policy and performance requirements of the position. Baker was particularly concerned with programmatic changes required if the county agent was to help impoverished farmers, an often-expressed theme in writings about the CES.

Lord (1939) provides a vivid account of the CES, one especially useful to those who have not had firsthand experience with it. His book rises above statistics to show the human roots of this most successful of all major American programs of adult education.

Brunner and Yang (1949) give a straightforward account of the development of the CES up to the end of World War II. They show how it gradually expanded its concern with the rural community, as well as with the farm home, and how other new areas of service were opened up. The authors also explain what might be called the classic model of CES, the one that long remained fixed in the minds of people not closely concerned with it. Bliss and others (1952) celebrate the history and nature of cooperative extension by reprinting a number of short presentations, extracts from addresses and documents, and other statements on extension as a whole or some facet of it. Most of those who have fostered extension are represented or noted in the papers.

The detailed operation of the CES has been the concern of

the authors of four books. Wilson and Gallup (1955) describe the way that the CES actually relates to its clients in an educative fashion and the general theoretical approach that guides its methodological procedures. Kelsey and Hearne (1955) furnish a description of both administrative and procedural matters in a work that they intended to be a textbook for courses covering the CES. Sanders (1966) has assembled an encyclopedic work on the CES as it was in the mid 1960s; this work considers every aspect of its program. Each of the thirty-eight chapters in Sanders's book was written by one or more of the leaders of the system. Prawl, Medlin, and Gross (1984) provide a comprehensive treatment of the Cooperative Extension Service and its programming activities in the United States, heavily illustrated with photographs, charts, and figures. The book also deals with the extension idea in other countries, specifically as it has been adapted from the American model.

The social orientation of the CES at all levels of government has been the subject of much interest. Beal and others (1966) have written a large-scale, complex work detailing the program-planning processes used by the CES and the results of such planning on the opinions and actions of both the staff and the persons served. The description of this entire venture is placed within the sociological field of organizational theory and research. House (1981) presents a highly personalized account of recent efforts to use the CES as a setting for the discussion of local, state, and national policy issues.

Three additional works are related to the CES but do not focus directly upon it. Allen (1963) wrote a cross-cutting analysis of papers presented at the centennial observation of the land-grant college by eminent observers, largely from outside the system. Surprisingly, general university extension and community affairs are considered at some length (and rather critically), whereas the CES is only briefly mentioned. Hightower (1972) makes a slashing attack on the land-grant college system; his argument is that "the tax paid, land grant complex has come to serve elite and private corporate interests in rural America, while ignoring those who have the most urgent needs and the most legitimate claims for assistance" (p. i). The book is filled with carefully documented examples of how (in the author's opinion) private greed had been advanced at the expense of public interest. The author contends, for example, that most tomatoes now found on the market are of lower quality than they used to be because plant breeders have produced fruit hard enough to be processed by machines, thereby producing an inferior product and driving people out of work. Although the CES is part of Hightower's target, he does not single it out for special mention. Most commentators on the CES view it with esteem, a fact leading to the frequent suggestion that it become a model for programs for city dwellers. In a report entitled *Urban Extension* (1966), the Ford Foundation discusses nine projects that it had supported with the general aim of using university resources to improve urban life. The CES was not the sole inspiration for these efforts, but it provided encouragement for them and models that they could follow.

As the economics of most nations are based on agriculture, rural extension has been an important theme for both national and international efforts to create lifelong learning opportunities. A number of books address this theme. Brunner, Sanders, and Ensminger (1945) have edited a collection of scholarly papers about the operation of agricultural extension in many parts of the world. This book establishes a context in which the massive growth of this endeavor can be understood, particularly because of the influence of the book and its authors in shaping such progress. Savile (1965) treats the improvement of agricultural and homemaking education in many countries, particularly those least well developed economically. He aimed to produce a simple, easily read manual directly focused on the relationship between extension workers and the learners that they seek to reach. Though references are made to the countries where Savile had worked, his intent is to discover the universals of rural extension. Williams (1968) supplies a detailed study of agricultural extension in the United Kingdom, the United States, and Australia, with emphasis on the latter. The author is concerned with the structure of this kind of service (principally as it relates to governmental controls), and with the programmatic emphasis of the work. Leagans and Loomis (1971) take as their theme the need for change in the practice of agriculture in both advanced and developing nations. As suggested by their title, *Behavioral Change in Agriculture*, they are interested in how science—in particular, social science—can contribute most effectively to changes in agricultural practice. Extension education is singled out as an important means of achieving that purpose, though the book is not oriented distinctively to it. Axinn and Thorat (1972) bring formidable theoretical knowledge, as well as extensive practical experience, to bear on their analysis of agricultural extension worldwide. After identifying its chief function and activities, they describe the basic elements of programs in India, the United Kingdom, Japan, Israel, Denmark, Taiwan, the United States, Brazil, the United Arab Republic, Australia, Pakistan, and Nigeria. They conclude with a general comparison of the characteristics of the programs in the twelve countries and draw conclusions and guiding principles from what they have learned in their enormous survey. Crouch and Chamala (1981) present a major two-volume "reader" on extension education, bringing together papers by fifty-one authors from twenty-three countries into a well-edited and comprehensive whole. The first volume reports experiences in the communication and adoption of innovative practices, and the second volume is concerned with strategies for planned change. The editors are Australian, and the perceived importance of this book is suggested by the fact that its foreword was written by the governor general of that country; however, the scope of the work covered is international. Jones (1986) offers a worldview of rural extension as the way by which economic and other forms of development may be achieved. The book gives an account of a conference of leaders in this field held at Reading University in England in 1985 and includes the basic papers and summaries of the ensuing discussions. Groups of chapters are organized around four themes: overall description of extension systems; definition and establishment of agricultural and extension policies; strategies followed; and methods used. Rivera and Schram (1987) have edited the papers given at a symposium on agricultural extension at the University of Maryland in 1985–1986. Those who delivered the papers were concerned with rural extension throughout the world, especially in less highly developed areas. Readers unfamiliar with the topic will probably be struck by the deep theoretical approaches and distinctions evolved since the end of World War II.

Around the world, the best-known book on agricultural extension is the volume by Ban and Hawkins (1988). It is based on a work, first published in Dutch by Ban in 1974, that has gone through seven editions. A modified version in German is also available. This English version, which builds on both Dutch and German editions, has been adapted by Hawkins, who has had widespread experience in Australia, Asia, and the United States. The authors estimate that 400,000 trained workers are now engaged in agricultural extension throughout the world, most of them in the less industrialized nations. The book is both theoretical and pragmatic and tries to perceive the universal aspects of extension, even as it takes account of the distinctiveness of national programs.

Blackburn has edited two works on rural extension from a Canadian point of view. One book, issued in 1984, is focused directly on Canadian programs: their history, their present practices, and findings about the changes that they have wrought. Basic research, such as that on learning theories, is cited, and some of the summaries of that research may well be the best to be found anywhere in the literature. In a book that appeared in 1989, Blackburn also emphasizes Canadian practice; this time, however, his scope of concern has broadened to become international. The authors of the chapters seek to deal with agricultural extension in all its intellectual dimensions. The book begins by presenting the central ideas of extension; goes on to examine how it is influenced by concepts from sociology, psychology, economics, and other fields; and concludes with a cluster of chapters on important elements in program planning and operational process.

As the discussion of worldwide rural extension has waxed, the number of book-length treatments of the CES itself seems to have waned. It is clear to everyone that an increase in farm productivity and the improvement of rural life are desperately needed in much of the world. In many places and for many people, survival itself is at stake. But the need for the CES in a changing America is not so clear. The topic has been much discussed in meetings, and some state programs have made assessments for the future, most of them optimistic. Warner and Christenson (1984) report the results of telephone interviews with a national sample of adults to determine the extent of use of the CES, the pattern of services provided, and the reaction of the users to the help that they received. The survey results provide a basis for a thoroughgoing analysis of the program and of the issues that it confronts. A recent interpretation of how leaders of extension feel about this subject was presented by

LaVerne B. Forest in Merriam and Cunningham (1989). The factual record has also been brought up to date by Rasmussen (1989) in his volume commemorating the seventy-fifth anniversary of the signing of the Smith-Lever Act. This book was developed with the help of a broadly based national committee and therefore represents a consensus viewpoint. It is currently the best single chronology on the nature and history of cooperative extension, useful for the orientation of a newcomer to the program and helpful in achieving a broader perspective for those with experience in it. Its illustrations give a vivid picture of extension at work. It does not attempt to assess the tensions and controversies that have always been characteristic of the program and continue to plague it today.

Public Libraries

Libraries are collections of instruments for enlightenment; therefore, everything that has to do with a library is, in the broadest sense, educational. However, the essential theme animating adult and lifelong learning in libraries in this century has been the desire to provide an increased and more discriminating use of those collections to achieve personal and social goals. This active thrust can be found in school, college, and university libraries; in research and special collections; and in all other places where books and other communications resources have been meaningfully assembled. Yet it is most fully expressed in the literature dealing with public libraries.

To serve their constituencies well, such libraries must carry out several functions simultaneously. Collectively with other libraries, they must preserve culture; individually, they must safeguard the records of their own communities. They must provide recreation and aesthetic enjoyment. And they must serve as sources of information for the general public, as well as for the special-interest groups that they define as significant. The kinds of service required to attempt such objectives are easily understood, though they may be hard to achieve. When the public library seeks to carry out educational missions, however, its pathway is less simple, as its board and staff must assess myriad possible activities vis-à-vis the requirements of the immediate situation. Books can be arranged and presented more skillfully than before; special collections for defined constituencies can be enriched; books can be made available at additional service points; the requirements for books at other institutions can be met; readers' advisory services can be added; groups can be sponsored and lectures held. These are but a few of the ways by which public libraries help to fulfill the lifelong learning needs of the people they seek to serve. The most comprehensive list of such activities is included in a national inventory made by Smith in 1954.

Two substantial works focus on the history of adult education in the public library. Providing an interpretive chronicle of the institution itself, Lee (1966) shows how adult education was one of its functions from its earliest New England beginnings. He divides this history into four periods. First (1854–1875), the library began as a single-purpose institution in which education was the central aim. Next (1875–1920), it became a multipurpose institution where education, recreation, and reference were the primary objectives, with recreation and reference eventually taking precedence over education. Third (1920–1955), it entered a period of appraisal, when attempts were made to revitalize its educational objective. Fourth (1955–1964), it placed major emphasis on its informational and educational aims and less on its recreational ones Monroe (1963) centers her history on what Lee would call the third period of the public library's development. She maintains her emphasis on the institution as an instrument of learning but sets it within the framework of the broader adult educational movement. In addition to a national survey, Monroe presents case studies of the programs in Kern County (California), Baltimore, and New York. Her work portrays fully both the evangelism of some proponents of library adult education and the antagonism of its opponents; yet she herself manages to maintain a tolerant, middle view.

The period of appraisal to which Lee (1966) referred was initiated when, in the early 1920s, the Carnegie Corporation made a study of the best ways that it could bestow its funds. As part of this endeavor, the foundation's trustees asked the distinguished educator William S. Learned to assess the current needs of the American public library (with whose establishment Mr. Carnegie and the corporation had been deeply involved). His report issued in 1924 defined the essential role of the library as the provision of adult learning opportunities. Learned ended with a four-point program that was influential in the future philanthropy of the corporation, and the report itself became an important document for many public librarians and library trustees.

With Carnegie support, the American Library Association carried out a major study of adult education issued in 1926. This report concluded that the development of activities in the field could best be undertaken using three guidelines: the development of consulting and advisory services to those who wished to conduct their education by themselves; the provision of informational services concerning all the adult education available in the community; and the furnishing of books and other reading materials required by the community's providers of adult education.

The impact of the well-crafted documents by Learned and the American Library Association was enhanced when Alvin S. Johnson, the distinguished leader of the New School for Social Research, published his 1938 celebration of the public library as the paramount institution of adult education in the United States. He provided a thorough treatment of various methods used by libraries for heightening their educative impact and furnished a penetrating account of the problems that remained to be solved. He concluded with the following thundering manifesto:

> It would be foolish and unjust to fail to acknowledge the fact that the American public library, as it stands today, is a remarkable achievement, indeed one of the outstanding American contributions to civilization. I know of no department in our national life that exhibits a greater proportion of able and devoted leaders, men and women of outstanding personality whose work will live on beyond them, beneficently. They have laid a broad base for an institution that will have an even greater future when it shall boldly take to itself the leadership in adult education which it alone is capable of developing, and shall make itself over into a people's university, sound bulwark of a democratic state [p. 79].

To meet this challenge fully, a library would require an elaborate structure of operations; its scope was suggested in 1939 by Chancellor in *Helping Adults to Learn,* probably the most influential work on its subject ever written. Chancellor compiled and, in some cases, abridged articles drawn from many sources that presented innovative ideas about how public libraries could undertake adult education. As he noted, "libraries are ready for fresh points of view in this adult education work" (p. v), and "they are casting ahead for some effective and far-reaching schemes of service" (p. v). Of special value is the author's synthesis of ideas in a section (pp. 227–270) entitled "A Sketch of a Library Organized for Informal Education." The author noted, "We are far from having drained dry Dr. Learned's far-visioned suggestions" (p. viii). A modern librarian would probably feel it equally true that the institution has not yet drained dry the proposals assembled by Chancellor.

Perhaps the idea of the librarian as an individualized readers' adviser is the basis for the most widely practiced form of direct educational service to adult learners. Ways of providing such help have been created afresh in many times and places. To cite only one example, the emerging indigenous leaders of countries in the British empire in the nineteenth and early twentieth centuries were often strongly motivated to win degrees on the basis of examinations set by the University of London and other credentialing bodies. All over the world, libraries provided resources for those who wanted to take such examinations, along with counsel about how the necessary books could best be used. In the late twentieth century, this idea of assisted learning is being discovered all over again. Reilly (1981) has a particular concern for people working to secure degrees by means of distance learning. She also indicates some of the ways by which advisory service can be given to other self-directed learners.

Readers' advisory services, as developed in the United States in the 1920s, were concerned with all kinds of personal and social learning as well as with that related to formal credentialing. In 1929, the New York Public Library established such a service, where persons desiring to read seriously on some topic could gain help doing so, especially in the provision of a tailored-to-measure reading list. Flexner and Edge (1934) reported the experiences of the first three years of this program, including such facts as the number of responses, the kinds of people who sought help, the subjects in which they were interested, and (insofar as data could be assembled) the extent to which the readers carried out their plans. In 1941, Flexner and Hopkins continued the description of the program, showing how it broadened the scope and depth of its operations. By that time, advisers had been stationed in some of the branch libraries of the system; referral services had begun to help people find other organized learning experiences in many kinds of institutions; and special attention had been devoted to the needs of refugees from Hitler's Europe. The authors not only described the services offered, but reported in some detail on a sample of 1,250 of the persons served. A larger picture of the influence of readers' advisory services throughout the country was offered by Chancellor, Tompkins, and Medway (1938), who begin with the assertion, "Self-education through guided reading is the public library's primary opportunity in adult education" (p. xi). They go on to explore the nature of this education as it can most desirably be carried out in a library setting. The chapters are written by library leaders who have had experience with this kind of service and who can analyze the major research on this and such allied topics as what makes a book readable.

One persistent theme in the literature on library adult education is suggested by the title of Coplan and Castagna's *The Library Reaches Out*, issued in 1965. The public library has a mandate to serve all its community; some leaders in the field believe that this mandate is fulfilled by simply keeping the doors open to everyone. Others have argued that services should be extended to reach larger or different clienteles. Haygood (1938) established a basis for discussion by asking *Who Uses the Public Library?* Surveying the patrons of the circulation and reference departments of the New York Public Library, he went well beyond the mere description of these people to include studies of how people behave in libraries, what patrons read, where they get their materials, and what they think of the public library. The book not only presents data on such topics, but extends the discussion to encompass a wealth of anecdotal and illustrative material.

Berelson (1949), in a study reported on in Chapter Four, examined the question of who uses the public library and why, when, and to what extent. He summarized all research then available and added original data collected for his book. He showed conclusively that the institution was far from serving everyone, despite its avowed intent to do so. Its patrons had more than average schooling, were skilled workers with above-average incomes, and lived in the library's vicinity. The library's users also had a wide interest in all media of communication and tended to be opinion leaders in the community. "It is not used much by the rich" says Berelson, "who tend to buy their books, or by the poor, who often find it difficult to read books" (p. 126). Most of the service therefore went to a small number of intensive users. As noted previously, he suggested that, given the need for an optimum allocation of resources, it would be best for the library to continue its service to its traditional clientele, improve the quality of what it does to help them, and thereby take its distinctive place in the total communications pattern.

Most books on library extension both before and since Berelson's study have taken a contrary view. They suggest that, through analysis of the community's needs, the library should find many new avenues for service and develop new clienteles. Carnovsky and Martin (1944) have edited a collection of essays on this theme, many of them by nonlibrarians. Joeckel (1946) has drawn together a collection of papers dealing generally with how the public library might improve and enlarge its service, including the provision of direct instruction. Coplan and Castagna (1965) have compiled a work in which seventeen of the most distinguished librarians in the United States consider many aspects of library service to the modern community: for example, revitalizing the moribund library, furnishing suburban services, moving out into city neighborhoods, providing specialized services to adults, reaching economically and culturally deprived people, and building regional and state library services. Although the authors are concerned with people of all ages, they concentrate on efforts to reach adults. Jolliffe (1968) defines his interest as "seeking by any means to increase the usefulness and the use made of public libraries" (p. 22). This breadth of scope leads him to examine many subjects, some of which come within the scope of adult education. He cites and describes countless examples and supplies many illustrations and displays. An international approach to the extension of library services, with special reference to literacy and other fundamental forms of learning, was presented by Houle in 1951. He reported on a worldwide conference held in Malmö, Sweden, at which people from many countries described how they educated adults in public libraries.

To many people, the library has seemed a natural place to help adults become literate, both by providing materials for such instruction and by offering various forms of teaching and tutoring. Lyman (1976) treats the whole topic of literacy education for adults in the library. In Lyman (1977), she follows up her earlier work by presenting a collection of comments and references on the same theme. Weingand (1986) has edited a collection of papers viewing literacy education in libraries in broad perspective; he is interested in the library's entire educative role and its concern with independent study. The authors are, for the most part, faculty members of library schools and directors of projects in public libraries.

Throughout the history of library adult education, efforts have been made to grasp the essence of its actual practice or to create a theoretical formulation for its work. Wilson (1937) reports on a conference at which national authorities in librarianship and education assessed the development of the adult educational movement up to that time, some fifteen years after its appearance. By then, the idea was no longer as uncritically accepted as it had been earlier, and a substantial body of opinion had accumulated against it. The authors of this book make evident their recognition of the existence of this negative feeling, though most of them are positive in their own attitudes. A similar point of view is expressed in the papers published by Stone in 1959. The authors of these articles show sophistication in approaching their topic; they indicate what has been accomplished but also suggest that earlier hopes have not been realized and remain as challenges in various library settings. Although Schuster (1977) centers her presentation around the idea that reading is the core of learning, she deals specifically with how the library may become the key element, the heart of learning, throughout life. Her discussion gives primary emphasis to service for children and young people. Penland and Mathai (1978) treat the library as one site for what they call a "professional helping service," in which personalized mentoring or tutoring is carried out. The work is highly technical and theoretical. *Adult Education and Public*

Libraries in the 1980s (1980) presents a collection of thoughtful papers by British authorities. Broad in scope and Olympian in their survey of the scene, these essays still make clear that some, at least, of the leaders of librarianship in the United Kingdom are thoroughly committed to the idea of adult educational service to individuals and groups and to the active participation of libraries in collaborative efforts. In a book called *The Information Professional,* Debons and others (1981) report a large investigation into the number and specific nature of those who engage full-time in the creation, processing, and diffusion of information in all parts of the American economy. There is a total number of 1,640,000 such positions, the largest subgroup being librarians. Durrance and Vainstein (1981) seek to interpret adult service in the modern public library and assume that education is only one of a collection of purposes that may be accepted, responded to, or assertively sought. Burge (1983) collects essays on the general theme of library adult education, some of them practical and some theoretical.

Another focus in the literature has been on specific communities and settings for library service for adults. Humble (1938) describes programs developed to help rural people gain access to books during the years of the Great Depression. She believes that there is "one salient characteristic of all the libraries that seem to me to be giving distinctly educational service. The emphasis of these libraries is not on mere circulation of books; their main effort is consciously directed towards stimulating interests of individuals in ways that will contribute to their mental growth. Librarians who are educators are concerned not so much with reading per se—either with or without a purpose!—as they are with creating a desire for knowledge and understanding and with helping people to see that books are a means of satisfying this desire" (p. vii). Brooks and Reich (1974) demonstrate how the facilitation of independent study can be stimulated in a large urban library. Durrance (1984) gives her attention to citizens' protest or public action groups of various sorts. She is interested to learn where they find the information that they need to work intelligently and effectively and pays particular attention to the services provided in this respect by public libraries.

Four works spread over a forty-year span give a general but balanced view of what adult education has come to mean in the public library as a goal to be sought along with others. Thomsen, Sydney, and Tompkins (1950) furnish descriptive accounts in a roughly comparable form of adult education in the public libraries of Denmark, the United Kingdom, and the United States. The papers were prepared by outstanding library leaders in the three countries concerned. The general theme of the work is well stated in its foreword by Jaime Torres-Bodet, then the director-general of Unesco: "Certain principles of library service undoubtedly appear which may be universally acceptable, but, as several of the authors have pointed out, a living library service will be so closely keyed to the social, cultural, and economic conditions of its region that there must be widely differing interpretations in practice" (p. vi).

Phinney (1956) continues this theme of diversity in unity. The major part of her book is given over to accounts of what was occurring under the name of adult education in five very different library systems in the United States. But Phinney does not stop with establishing a base in reality, though that is her most important task. She involves the reader in her analysis of the five programs: for example, the ways that libraries were influenced by their communities, the outside assistance employed, the means used to start programs, the role of the library board, and, perhaps most important, the characteristics possessed by the librarians.

Rayward (1978) presents a symposium of articles on the current state of the public library in the United States, with one chapter devoted to the United Kingdom. The book's authors deal with services for adults, young adults, and children and also consider such topics as the place of the library as a means of communication, its financial situation, its technological growth, its collaboration with other institutions, and its provision of reference and information services. The summary chapter by Robert Wedgeworth, then executive director of the American Library Association, gives an overview of the library's prospects and challenges. He also stresses the need for the continuing education of librarians so that they can keep up with new demands and requirements made necessary by the communications revolution. (Librarians will be included with other professionals in a consideration later in this book of continuing professional education.) Rayward's conception of his book is a mature one, and the specialist adult educator gains a sense that this field has now merged into the patterns of total public library service.

Heim and Wallace (1990) supply the results of a broadly based survey of the practice and literature on library adult services in the United States in this century. The book is the result of a decade-long inquiry, mounted by the American Library Association involving many authorities in the field. It examines education within an overall framework that includes information, recreation, and research. Responses to a survey of adult services were received from 4,215 individual libraries representing 1,114 systems; the sample is broadly representative of all public libraries in the United States. In addition to this massive data base, the book contains essays on various aspects of adult service, including lifelong learning theory, literacy education, and parent education. The goals of education also figure prominently in other chapters on service to various community sectors (such as the handicapped, the elderly, labor groups, and business and industry).

Museums

Museums vary from dusty collections of curios intended to titillate a passing public to majestic assemblages of unique treasures arranged to demonstrate categories of knowledge or to serve significant social purposes. The subject matter of museums covers the full range of human thought, though each institution has its own specialties. The ones sufficiently well established to be considered in the literature of adult education usually fulfill multiple purposes, each institution allocating resources among its aims in a fashion determined by the aspirations and necessities of its local situation. Among the major goals are the acquisition of unique objects, their preservation, their display, their use as a basis for research, and their employment as a resource for education. Some museums or displays within them are not object-centered but demonstrate principles or themes; museums of science are often based on this idea.

Like public libraries, museums are inherently educative, and the concern of those who would like to advance this purpose has been centered chiefly around making this latent possibility dynamic and effective. Almost all such efforts are aimed at learners of all ages of life; even children's museums have activities for parents and teachers. Educational programs often imitate the courses, lectures, and other methods used by schools and colleges and may even collaborate with them; however, many activities are based on the distinctive nature of the institution and go to the foundations of its operation, including the selection, arrangement, and annotation of its displays.

Two books provide introductions to the theory and practice of museums and would be useful to anyone seeking to become familiar with that subject. Wittlin (1949) offers a relatively brief though sweeping history of the museum in Western culture. The author's experiences have all been in European institutions. She is mainly interested in the art museum and other comparable collections of unique or historic objects, with little attention being given to scientific museums or other instructional institutions. She believes that the fundamental purpose of the museum is education. Though she allots one short passage to children, she is primarily concerned with adults. Schwartz (1967) presents a richly illustrated beginning point for those who would like to know more about museums. One section is concerned with formal instructional programs undertaken by museums, but the entire book develops the idea of such institutions as basically educative in conveying cultural richness and increasing the sensitivities that they help their visitors to acquire.

Museums for a New Century (1984) is the central modern statement about museums, a work of highly distilled wisdom on the whole subject with a wealth of specifics added to give concreteness and substance to the topic. A distinguished commission of national leaders was aided by a number of specialists in preparing the document, which does not so much describe adult education as accept it as an inherent function of the museum.

Although an enormous literature of pamphlets, brochures, and reports on special classes and other instructional offerings exists, most serious books on adult education in museums have been concerned with exploring the ways by which its inherent and distinctive services can best be developed. One such strand of investigation has been summarized under the title *The Behavior of the Museum Visitor* by Robinson (1928), a professor of psychology at

Yale. He examines closely how adult museum visitors—random visitors, those using guides, and those submitting themselves to controlled procedures—behave. His findings are not revolutionary, but they do quantify and confirm insights that people have had about visiting displays, such as the existence of "museum fatigue" and the value of various kinds of descriptive material used as adjuncts to the objects themselves. Robinson concludes with the stout assertion that "we should like to see museum directors generally become experimental psychologists" (p. 66) and identifies categories of problems to which they might turn their investigative talents. A similar approach is taken by Screven (1974), who reports and interprets several studies measuring the reaction of adults who viewed museum exhibits. These studies seem to show that serious substantive learning can occur in the museum setting, in addition to the exploratory and "discovery" elements often thought to be basic to the museum experience. Many other quantifying studies have also been made, including those using innovative methods of observation of behavior, but such reports are to be found only in the periodic literature and in investigative reports.

Ramsey (1938) provides an early work on education in museums, including that intended for both children and adults but with primary attention to the latter. Ramsey had made an exhaustive study of the literature, as well as of the practices of a large number of American museums; her account is factual, classificatory, and, for its time, complete.

In 1937 and 1939, Adam wrote two books on the adult educational nature of museums, viewing them as a self-professed outsider. His observations were made only of institutions in New York City. The first of these two works tries to discover the meaning of adult education for those establishing institutional priorities and programs. He discovers a failure to conceptualize education in any thoughtful way as integral to a museum's work, though that function is verbally accepted as one of the essential tasks of an institution. The second book is a subjective interpretation of the museum as an aspect of popular culture, particularly as it serves as an instrument for transmitting knowledge and sensitivities to the community.

Larrabee (1968) reports on a 1966 conference held by the Smithsonian Institution, at which authorities reviewed the role of the museum and education at its various levels. Though most of the authors were probably thinking of children and of collaborative work with schools, the general insights remain refreshing and novel, and the report of the discussions is especially illuminating. Solinger (1990) brings together a number of papers on the nature of the museum as an instrument of adult education; the book is more comprehensive than its title, *Museums and Universities*. Some of the essays are theoretical, some describe institutions and programs, and some deal with special problems and issues. As a whole, the work gives a lively and vital sense of the museum as a center of learning.

The art museum has had a rich literature so far as lifelong education is concerned. The central work in the field is that of Newsom and Silver (1978), a massive volume produced by the Council on Museums and Education in the Visual Arts on the basis of grants from the federal government and from private sources. It is a vast collaborative effort that assesses a large number of case studies of programs selected because of their scope and variety, each one described in depth. In addition, relatively brief introductions and summations of groups of case studies are given. There are three clusters of chapters relating to the art museum and its general public; the art museum and the young, their teachers, and their schools; and the art museum and its college, university, and professional audiences. A largely successful effort has been made to present the facts in a candid and engaging fashion.

Collins (1981) compiles chapters by specialists in adult education, curators, and scholars in the humanities who together desire to develop a view of the museum as a resource for lifelong learning. Since many writers and viewpoints are involved, Collins does not attempt an integrated viewpoint. Some amply descriptive case studies are included.

Three works seek to provide a coherent total conception of the art museum as an instrument of education. Low (1942) makes the forceful argument that the museum should use its resources to pursue vigorously the social purposes of those who guide its destiny. The book was written just as the United States entered World War II and is therefore strongly conditioned by the need to reaffirm and disseminate democracy. In a much broader study, Low (1948) first examines statements of art museum purposes in the periods from 1870 to 1900, from 1900 to 1930, and from 1930 to 1946. He then turns to an analysis of current thought, using general responses from forty-four museums and making a detailed study of nine. Finally, he provides an overall, idealistic view of broad purposes and then a statement of "the short view"—what he believes to be necessary if those ideals are to be achieved by changing present practice. Chadwick (1980) surveys comprehensively the ways that museums serve their publics, and also gives a close look at the museums in Derby, Leicester, and Nottingham. An English author, Chadwick orients his study to lifelong learning and adopts the position that museums and galleries have a function going far beyond the study of the objects that they possess. His view, which permeates his whole analysis, is stated succinctly by his observation: "If the interpretation of a museum's educational role extends beyond the aim of merely informing its public, and, instead, enables people to think more openly about others, themselves, and their environment, then the evidence would indicate that museums are important forces in the lives of their communities. There is public agreement that museums need to change, and to develop as key centers in their localities, and that the notion of enjoyment, as well as that of education, should be given corporeal as well as spiritual expression" (p. 110).

Eisner and Dobbs (1986) offer a refreshingly trenchant report on interviews that they held with the directors and chief educational officers of twenty leading American art museums. The authors are distinguished art educators, a fact that lends weight to their views. They conclude that education in the institutions that they studied is in a state of confusion shared by all parties concerned. In particular, the position of educational specialists in such institutions is occupied by people deeply uncertain about what they should be doing and why—hence the title of the book, *The Uncertain Profession*. The final work cited in this section therefore comes to the same conclusion as the earlier ones by Robinson (1928) and Adam (1937).

A Final Word

It would be interesting to speculate on how these three kinds of institutions differ from those considered in Chapter Five; however, in the absence of substantial literature on the topic, it is beyond the scope of this book to do so. It may be appropriate, however, to emphasize a crucial point. In the CES, the public library, and the museum, service is designed in such a fashion as to appeal to successive age groups with greatest attention to the years of active maturity. All three have open access and exit arrangements for the clients they hope to serve, but the general expectation is that the child who enters the program of each will continue in it throughout adulthood. The 4-H Club member is likely to remain part of the CES clientele during all the years of productive economic life and later; the same pattern is found in the library and the museum. Such continuity is now evident in the lives of millions of people. Thus, theories of lifelong learning may be relatively new, but they can be built upon long-lasting, substantial, and far-reaching practice.

SEVEN

Providers Created to Educate Adults

In no country is the history of formal structures in adult
education a lengthy one.
>   —*Titmus, 1989, p. 381*

The institutions and programs created to educate adults are now so
numerous and varied as to defy categorization. They exist in every
aspect of communal life. Any issue of a metropolitan newspaper suggests to a discerning reader many places in our society where improvement or amelioration is being attempted by some form of instruction.
Institutional hierarchies, both public and private and with varied
purposes, reveal at many points an inward- or outward-looking desire
to teach. And there is constant creation, ebb, and flow of programs
of service. The federal government has initiated many such agencies
to help cope with the Great Depression of the 1930s, the manpower
requirements of World War II, and the deep social imbalances of the
1960s. Most of the programs then conceived (some of them developed
to great size) have now disappeared, though a few remain in altered
form. Some visionaries believe that the final years of this century and
the first years of the next will be a time when many more new programs will be begun to meet emergent challenges.

Proprietary Schools

The selling of education for profit has become so pervasive in modern culture that it is readily available to everyone able and willing

to buy it. At work, at home, or at play, adults have opportunities for learning urged upon them, and salesmen even suggest that lessons can be learned during sleep by playing recorded messages. Private tutors, reinforcement groups, classes, correspondence courses, recreational skill training, and other familiar forms of instruction have been supplemented by new forms of communication developed by modern ingenuity and made profitable in part by their uses for education. No book has been found that examines the full spread of these offerings, ranging from the home piano teacher to the massive technical school. But the role of the profit motive in instruction has been examined in a few books, each of which is usually devoted to one method or format of teaching.

Proprietary education has venerable antecedents in American culture. In colonial days, skilled workmen were not plentiful and could often advance both themselves and the general economy by offering instruction in their specialties. Seybolt based two monographs published in 1925 and 1928 upon such primary sources as the newspapers and journals of the colonial era. He concluded that private proprietary ventures grew out of, and were sometimes related to, the apprenticeship system and were chiefly intended for young men (and a few young women) who wanted to gain additional vocational knowledge and ability. In some cases, instruction was offered for a private fee by local schoolmasters. In evaluating the work of these tiny institutions, Seybolt (1928) makes an observation that would be echoed today by proprietors of all forms of education for a profit: "In the extension of educational opportunities, the private schools played a unique part in colonial America. They were free to originate, and put into practice ideas that might effect improvements in their curricula and methods. The masters sought always to keep strictly abreast of the needs of the time, for their livelihood depended on the success with which they met those needs" (p. 100).

But while the attraction and retention of students are essential to would-be profit makers, other ways of evaluating accomplishment also exist. Woodyard, a professor of psychology at Columbia University, decided to see what benefits students at private correspondence schools received for their money; in *Culture at a Price* (1940), she reported on her study. The author enrolled in thirteen institutions "under various aliases and fictitious personalities, even in a few cases by surrogate" (p. 1). In each case, she developed a distinct persona in presenting herself as a student. Part of the fun of the book is her description of the responses she got from the schools in which she enrolled. Her ultimate conclusions about the amount of learning received were negative; she believed that a reading list would in most cases be preferable to a course, at far less cost. She found that the chief weakness of the schools that she studied lay in the false expectations of the students, created or reinforced by the advertising of the schools. "People expect to pay their money," she said, "and have learning pour out upon them automatically" (p. 11).

Three reports on private vocational schools are available. Clark and Sloan (1966) discuss a detailed inquiry made of institutions that "are concerned with preparing students for a particular business position in industry, skilled trade, semiprofession, personal service, recreational activity, or some other vocation or avocation" (p. vii). The authors suggest that the chief function of such schools is to close an educational gap caused by the failure of established systems of schooling to offer needed services. Hyde (1976) has studied vocational proprietary schools in the Chicago area. His primary interest is not so much the analysis of the quality of these ventures as the assessment of their economic value—particularly as they supplement and sometimes overlap the actions and offerings of public institutions, including community colleges. Hebert and Coyne (1976) state that their book "is meant to be flipped through and thumbed" (p. 2). It is written in an impressionistic fashion and presents a great deal of information about private and technical trade schools with little or no attempt at synthesis.

Wilms (1975) reports on an elaborate study comparing proprietary and public vocational training programs. Despite the enticing claims of the private schools, Wilms concludes that their graduates were no more effective in the marketplace than those who had received their instruction in public programs. The author's recommendations call for extensive governmental regulation of vocational training.

Independent Institutions

A nation acclaimed by Tocqueville as one that created organizations to serve every social purpose has naturally founded many of them to provide education to mature members of society. Such institutions are, in fact, multitudinous; they vary greatly in purpose, scope, structure, geographic coverage, and length of life. The Chautauqua Institution, described in Chapter One, was one such agency, and others have been mentioned at other places. At this point, only the ones that have been the subject of readily accessible books will be mentioned. These organizations were designed by their sponsors to educate other people; later in this chapter, associations intended to educate their own members will be noted.

As the businessmen of the new nation began to establish fortunes, some of them set aside funds to provide places or programs for instruction. A notable example was Cooper Union, at which Lincoln spoke and which is still active today. A well-documented example of such philanthropy was Boston's Lowell Institute, also mentioned in Chapter One. Weeks (1966) provides an elegant history of the program from its founding to the year of publication of his book.

Foundations have been important in the development of adult education. In modern times, a few have operated their own programs, but most have given grants to other providers. Some large foundations have taken on the support of adult education as a major endeavor. Among them are the Carnegie Foundation and other Carnegie-originated trusts, the Fund for Adult Education of the Ford Foundation, and the W. K. Kellogg Foundation. Smaller grant makers have also been active in the field. Tjerandsen (1980) reviews the origins and programs of the Emil Schwartzhaupt Foundation, whose donor was concerned with education for responsible citizenship and which supported innovative programs during the third quarter of the twentieth century.

An institution of an entirely different character, described by Bradford (1974), was the National Training Laboratories, which employed scholars of human relations who wanted both to train people to understand and work with one another and to conduct research on the processes being used.

Most of the institutions covered by the literature are independent, instruction-providing establishments. Hewitt and Mather (1937) report on the Boston Center for Adult Education. Hewitt was its executive director, and Mather was the president of its board and a distinguished Harvard scholar. The book combines a number of statements about the ominous times in which it was written with a description of some activities that could be carried on by an independent adult educational institution not constrained by the restrictions of a multipurpose institution. Overstreet and Overstreet (1938) provide an informal history of the early years of Town Hall, an auditorium in Manhattan. Its leaders were eager to develop a center for adult education and invented many flexible ways to use a facility whose possibilities might otherwise have been limited. Most notably, they evolved and established the panel presentation process, in which several people spoke briefly on a topic and then answered questions about it—a format now so common everywhere that it hardly seems possible that it was created so recently. Hutchinson and Hutchinson (1978) discuss the City Literary Institute (now officially known as the City Lit), a specially designed center for adult education in London. They devote significant attention to a program called Fresh Horizons, which operated as a unit within the much larger center. It offered a complete instructional and counseling service for adults who required substantial assistance as they created new intellectual orientations for themselves. The authors believe that this program's intensity of service has important implications for many forms of English adult education.

Powell (1942) provides a detailed analysis of the work of the School for Social Studies, an independent institution that operated from 1933 through 1940 in San Francisco. Its founder and guiding strategist was Alexander Meiklejohn, who had headed the Experimental College at the University of Wisconsin. The school maintained discussion groups that read books having to do with the philosophical foundations of society. The small faculty, mostly drawn from university teaching staffs, gained a strong sense of community, as its members developed new approaches to the discussion of serious books. Unfortunately, the school could not maintain itself financially.

In the late 1940s and early 1950s, a number of "packaged courses" were developed and distributed nationally. The best-known was the Great Books program, designed to introduce discussion groups to outstanding works of Eurocentric culture. Many institutions sponsored this sequence of readings, but the major expansion was undertaken by the Great Books Foundation. It won substantial audiences for its work and a great deal of favorable attention. Only one book dealing with the program was produced. Fitzpatrick (1952) gives a quirky, opinionated, and (mainly) critical review. He is, however, well informed about the literature with which it deals and gives a clear description of the processes used.

Institutions built around key figures have made substantial contributions to the field, with Jane Addams at Hull-House being the best-known example. Another significant institution builder was Myles Horton of the Highlander Folk School in Tennessee. Both he and the institution that he founded have been fully described in the literature (and referred to in Chapter One). Aimée Horton (1989), his wife, offers the most comprehensive account. Her book chronicles the origins of Highlander, its successive ideas, and the programs that implemented them. In its early years, the institution made pioneering efforts in the preparation of leaders for the labor movement and for racial integration. Both programs brought it to national attention and paved the way for its reputation as an innovative trainer of leaders for social movements. Glen (1988), in a heavily documented study, carries the story of Highlander through from its early origins in 1927 to the events of 1962, with an epilogue covering the history of the institution since that time. Bledsoe (1969) wrote a history of the school as an instrument for the advancement of populist causes. The author is wholeheartedly an advocate of Highlander and makes clear his conviction that it was the target of vicious opposition and hatred—a viewpoint stressed by his title, *Or We'll All Hang Separately.*

Squires (1975) describes, clearly and compactly, the Learning Exchange, an innovative program based on the theories of Ivan Illich. Its organizing concept is that people who wish to learn anything should be put in touch with those who can teach them, usually on an individualized tutorial basis. The book reports on about five hundred such "matches" and furnishes various facts about the individuals concerned and the nature of their interaction.

A somewhat similar type of institution, the free university, is investigated by Draves (1980). In it, teachers and learners come together to carry out their mutual endeavors on a wholly independent basis, remaining outside the organized educational system unless they discover a sponsor who will provide administrative services. The infinite variety of these institutions makes it hard for them to be counted or described. According to the author's calculation, at the time he wrote, there were "approximately 200 free universities and learning networks in the country, and they enroll more than 300,000 participants a year" (p. 16). The author gives voluminous examples (some of them lengthy) in his thorough analysis of the nature and prospects of these institutions.

Voluntary Associations

The myriad voluntary associations everywhere present in complex societies usually have education—of their own memberships and of external audiences—as one of their functions. Perhaps because these associations are so numerous, few studies could be found that deal generally with the kind of learning that they provide and its overall impact, either on their memberships or on the societies in which they flourish.

The YMCA was created originally as a discussion group of young men; in all its worldwide growth, it has maintained some institutional memory of its origins. Nelson (1933) examines fifty-three adult educational programs, both individually and in comparative analyses, that were conducted in American YMCAs in the early 1930s; the author stresses their informal, voluntary, and citizen-controlled nature.

In 1938, Hill published a study called *Man-Made Culture*, an anecdotal account of those men's clubs in American society that lay some claim to providing serious educational purposes for their members. Hill casts a broad net: "The chief types explored in the following pages are men's discussion clubs; city clubs and policy associations; service clubs; advertising clubs; chambers of commerce; associations of credit men; art, music, and crafts groups; and certain clubs of an industrial character" (p. v). The author goes even beyond these various forms to consider countless autonomous groups; these, he points out, are far more prevalent among upper- and middle-class men than is commonly realized.

Ely and Chappell (1938) have produced a study similar to Hill's but scrutinizing a broader range of organizations. Their focus is upon women's groups, ranging from national associations to local clubs. The authors relate their study to the women's movement; yet they are primarily concerned not with social action but with how voluntary associations help women to understand how they may elevate their status as they inform one another, discuss intellectual topics, and work for community improvement. The authors believe that such institutions help greatly to break up old patterns of educational and work life that restrict the thoughts and actions of women.

Faris (1975), in the course of a history of the Canadian Association for Adult Education, provides both a historical and an analytical account of voluntary associations in Canada.

Social Welfare and Human Service Agencies

As with voluntary associations, the social welfare and human services agencies of our society can best be understood as adult educational providers by examining their individual purposes and approaches. Some efforts have been made, however, to look systematically at how such agencies educate adults in the private sector of our society.

Hawkins's work (1940) represents an effort, on the whole successful, to explore the complex ways by which adult education and social work overlap. She reports on a study of various agencies and programs in the late 1930s, when social work was still essentially a private, voluntary enterprise, not well defined or understood. Many of the activities of social work agencies were basically educative in character, designed to help clients learn how to gain employment or cope with other difficult problems, to train the vast number of volunteers and board members required, and to build group and community reinforcements for people in trouble. The effort of social workers to gain professional status, Hawkins believes, was sometimes inimical to a full understanding of their role as adult educators. For example, she notes, "Adult education permeates the air of the Young Women's Christian Association with the insistence of a West Texas sandstorm—and when it is identified there is a noticeable choking. Give it another name—say, group work—and it appears to be a Florida balm in which all may bask" (p. 169). The reverse situation is sometimes also true: the idea of welfare can be stultifying, that of education liberating. Hawkins goes beneath differences in terminology to discover underlying similarities and, with a lucid style and keen insights, leads the reader to substantial illumination.

Lauffer (1977) and a group of colleagues have conducted sixty in-depth interviews with administrators of continuing education programs in what they designated as human services, which include medicine, psychiatry, social work, nursing, public health, and other allied occupations. An attempt has been made to get at the fundamental concerns of such people as they operated their programs; the book is filled with quotations reflecting practices and points of view. In a companion volume, Lauffer (1978) presents an exceptionally well designed and attractive volume, a compendium of information and advice about virtually every problem that might be found in the administration of continuing education in a social work program.

Penal Institutions

The sponsors or advocates of education in penal institutions confront an unusually difficult task. They must work in a setting devoted to punishment and the protection of society from convicted evildoers; at the same time, they must try somehow to elicit a response from prisoners that will not only give them the knowledge and skill required for life outside the walls, but will also help them internalize a moral code that guides their future actions in socially positive ways. These efforts require various forms of intellectual stimulation, including classroom instruction and such learning resources as libraries. Also, as prisoners are strongly conditioned by the circumstances in which they live, efforts to reorient their values may ultimately require the reshaping of the prison's plant and its policies and practices—an undertaking often hard to reconcile with the custodial and punitive purposes of the institution. The effort simultaneously to punish, to imprison, and to correct would be staggering under the best of circumstances; and, as everyone knows, conditions in most penal institutions are sometimes deplorable.

In the early days of the adult educational movement, a considerable body of material was produced dealing with the theme of prison education, almost all of it in journal articles. However, two substantial books were published during that period. MacCormick (1931), who had extensive experience in penal institutions, surveys the educational activities for prisoners in about one hundred institutions in the United States. The volume is thorough and complete, considering many aspects of the topic and profiting from the assistance of a distinguished panel of advisers. But MacCormick's basic purpose is not to describe, but to suggest essential improvements, even though they required an outlay of human and financial resources far in excess of any previous estimate. Subsequent to the publication of this book, strong effort was put forth in the 1930s by prison officials, politicians, and lay citizens to work out what they called a new penology, based on the rehabilitation of prisoners by many means, including education. Wallack, Kendall, and Briggs (1939), in a work entitled *Education Within Prison Walls*, describe an effort to follow this approach in the prisons of New York State.

A broad reconsideration of prison education has recently brought forth a number of major works. Reagan and Stoughton (1976) provide an all-embracing account of the history of prison education, the traditional and modern theories concerning it, and the nature of what was happening in American prisons at the time of the authors' large-scale study. Clearly and in brief compass, the entire sweep of correctional education is summarized, the data being gathered from extensive visitation and analysis of the literature. This work is reinforced by another study by Bell and others (1979), which reports statistically on the programs of 163 correctional institutions. *Learning Behind Bars* (1989) provides one-page descriptions of the correctional activities in ten juvenile facilities, nine local detention programs, and eleven prisons. Morin's work *On Prison Education* (1981) is an excellent source for anyone interested in the root ideas on crime, punishment, moral behavior, and correction. This collection of papers, some published previously, flows from deep wells of European philosophy and is particularly oriented to French traditions. It also reflects modern social scientific theory and assesses creative attempts to conduct programs designed to increase understanding of ethical behavior among prisoners. Although the work is published by the Canadian government, it aims to be universal in its approach.

Probably the best single way to gain an understanding of correctional education is to consult the work by Duguid (1989). The original and reprinted papers by American, British, and Canadian scholars pay their respects to the work of MacCormick and the writings of Morin and others; however, they are essentially concerned with the description of programs and the exploration of the goals and processes of education in penal institutions.

Two generalized accounts are available about British prison education of a somewhat earlier day. Banks (1958) furnishes an overview filled with anecdotal material and cast in the framework of idealistic hopes about potential achievements. Roberts (1968) sketches a portrait of adult illiterates in British prisons and suggests the ways that they can best be taught. The author is realistic in assessing the pluses and minuses of such teaching.

Some unusual approaches to prison education have been worked out by innovative leaders. Seashore (1976) discusses eight college-level programs, with detailed descriptions of each, and reports on follow-up studies to determine their effect on their students and their cost effectiveness. Campbell (1978) analyzes his efforts to reach "difficult" students and even more difficult prison authorities in the two years he spent teaching male convicts in a maximum-security California prison. The book is written with more than usual literary skill in an effort to depict what the social settings of such situations are like; the author reveals little or no desire to be didactic or prescriptive. A strikingly unusual work is presented by Andersen and Andersen (1984), who describe a year-long course conducted for inmates of California prisons who wish to prepare for careers as deep-sea divers upon their release. A heavily illustrated account is provided of one iteration of this course and of the individuals who undertake it. Also, case studies are given of some of the men who had completed the course earlier, the reasons for their entry into crime, and the effects of their special training on their lives.

The Armed Services

The military services provide the largest and most fully worked out example of recurrent education. Preparation time and service duties are alternated throughout the career of virtually everyone, and attendance at a training program is often the reward for outstanding service, as well as the basis for subsequent field duty. Because of the high priority of national defense in the country's value system, educational programs receive a degree of support and have a creativity of approach not found elsewhere, except perhaps in some of the largest industrial enterprises.

The full significance of education in the military services did not become apparent until World War II, when millions of people in many nations had to be taken from their civil pursuits and trained to carry out full-time military responsibilities. This task was undertaken in the United States with such dispatch and thoroughness—and the results on the whole were so manifestly excellent—that it was frequently argued (beginning about 1942) that the instructional practices of the military services should be widely adopted in civilian life. Many believed, in fact, that they held the answer to problems that the world of education had been too obtuse or hidebound to solve. In 1945, the American Council on Education created a commission to examine these charges and, more important, to bring the fruits of armed-service innovation to bear on the activities of civilian life. The commission planned eleven studies dealing with various aspects of this mandate. A book by Houle and others (1947) is one of these. Its specific charge was to examine educational activities chiefly designed for the personal or social growth of military personnel through off-duty courses, libraries, special residential programs, or other forms of learning that were not directly related to military assignments and that roughly corresponded with civilian adult educational activities. Although much of the book is devoted to description, it concludes with an assessment of the conclusions that civilian educators might appropriately draw from the vast military experience.

In the same year, Hawkins and Brimble (1947) depicted how adult education was purposefully used to achieve various goals by the British army. Though limited to the army, this book thus deals more directly with military experience than did its American counterpart. It is especially helpful because it suggests the history of education in the army and also illustrates military thinking on the subject.

In their work entitled *Soldiers and Scholars*, Masland and Radway (1957) broadly survey the major methods of educating military officers, both before their periods of service and subsequently. The range of educational activities undertaken by the military is now much greater than when this book was written, but the key policies and problems still remain. Clark and Sloan (1963) provide an overview and interpretation of the total pattern of education in the nation's armed forces. The authors state that their book "presents the Armed Forces educational program as one manifestation of a universal trend—the overflow of education into non-academic channels—society's response to a technological age. It sees the program as a vast complex, integrated with the entire intellectual life of the nation, and making significant contributions of its own" (p. v). Shelburne and Groves (1965) also offer a broad overview of military adult education. Their distinctive contribution lies in the clarity of their approach to the entire military establishment and their description of how education fits within the broad purposes of the armed forces.

Governmental Agencies

Most of the providers already mentioned in this and the two previous chapters function as some aspect of government: schools, universities and colleges, community colleges, the Cooperative Extension Service, libraries, the armed services, and prisons. But adult education also appears in some fashion in many other governmental agencies, as will be illustrated in the themes discussed in the next two chapters. Meanwhile, a few books that describe varied programs will be mentioned here.

Hudson (1934) deals with the establishment of Radburn, a semigovernmental community built in New Jersey in the early 1930s. It was designed as "a demonstration in building better homes and communities, conceived by a socially-minded, limited-dividends company, led by men who felt the responsibility of making a contribution toward improved living" (p. 1). This design included full provision for social amenities, including adult education. Hudson analyzed the activities of 686 adults in 336 families who shared in the planning and early occupancy of Radburn. In modern days, when much is said about the learning society, it is interesting to see that what actually happened when people first planned and then lived in such a society is both enlightening and disturbing. Hudson has a number of instructive insights into why program planning worked and how it did not.

One of the earliest and most highly regarded innovations of the Franklin D. Roosevelt administration was the Civilian Conservation Corps (CCC) in which young unemployed men were given the opportunity to participate in a work-related collective environment in which they could be helped with their health, social, and educational needs. Receiving subsistence and modest wages, these young men worked mostly on conservation or reclamation projects under semimilitary control. In retrospect, the CCC has been highly praised and has served as a partial model for other ventures with similar purposes. Hill (1935) tells the story of the educational aspects of the camps and does so in an engaging and graphic fashion; he reinforces general points with anecdotes and illustrations. The program was far from perfect, particularly because of widespread opposition to its military orientation, and Hill does not try to make it seem better than it was.

In another memorable undertaking, Congress created in 1933 the Tennessee Valley Authority, designed to do nothing less than develop the social and material resources of the entire watershed of the river and the seven states through which it and its tributaries pass. An extraordinary group of social planners set about the task of changing the nature of a subregion of the United States. One of their principal instruments was adult education, which they considered an integral part of the total educational system as carried out in schools, libraries, and countless other community institutions.

Seay (1938), the director of education for the TVA in its early years, presents a report of the entire program written by some of the people centrally involved in its administration.

Kornbluh (1987) describes and interprets an important governmental program in adult education after the passage of time has allowed for a suitable perspective. She focuses on the workers' educational program, developed in 1933 as part of the Federal Emergency Relief Administration and later transferred to the Works Progress Administration. She sets workers' education within the larger context of New Deal agencies of which it was a part; the description of that major social thrust is presented briefly but comprehensively. This book is, in fact, an excellent introduction to the "emergency" agencies of the 1930s, which were to focus major attention on adult education. These agencies also attracted to the field many of its later leaders, as well as several other outstanding figures who occupied major positions in American life (most notably, Hubert Humphrey).

A Final Word

It was noted earlier that most descriptions of institutions created for adult education are located elsewhere in this book, but the relative scarcity of references in this chapter is caused by another factor as well. Many important educational efforts have not been reported or interpreted in the literature. For example, the valuable study by Kornbluh (1987) should be paralleled by many reports of other governmental providers. On no topic in this series of five chapters is there a surfeit of works, and some institutions and ideas have given rise to few or no serious book-length analyses. It is not hard to understand why this fact is true. Adult education is primarily a field of action, and the energies of its leaders have largely been spent in advancing its programs, not in studying them. Nor does it appear likely that this situation will soon change, as the main thrust of recent scholarly books has been to find commonalities among institutions and themes, not to advance the understanding or performance of each of them separately.

EIGHT

Goals Related to
Formal Systems
of Education

Dear Sirs: This is James Washington. I have learned to read and write. I have learned to plant corn and grass and flowers and to raise fruit and potatoes and raise cattle, and how to save my soil and how to plow, and test corn and how to plant peas and how to save my teeth from decay. I learned how to sleep well and how to save my wife from walking (too much) and how to cook corn and how to make bread. I have learned about the Lord and how to say the Lord's prayer, and this is all I have to say this time. So I will close.

—A student in a literacy group

In any design of lifelong learning, childhood and youth are times for basic instruction. For some people in some countries, this may mean only learning to read and write, but it normally goes well beyond that level to provide some of the knowledge and skills regarded in each society as necessary to a good life. Adults who have not acquired this basic education at the optimum time can be compensated by being offered it in adulthood. They may need to achieve literacy and the basic skills that it makes possible to secure academic credentials usually earned in youth and to gain initial vocational competence. Many adults also carry forward in maturity a pattern of learning initiated in the formal systems of education of their youth; thus, a nurse or an architect engages in continuing professional education. This chapter will deal with all such forms of

Note: Epigraph taken from Emily Miller Danton, "Uncle Sam, Schoolteacher." *Journal of Adult Education*, 1936, *8*, 149-152.

youth-related adult education, whether continuing or compensatory, leaving to Chapter Nine the learning motivations that ordinarily do not become significant until the years of maturity.

Literacy Plus

Reading and writing may be achieved at any level—from the simple skill of writing one's name to the mastery of the complex processes required in advanced ways of life. In earlier days, a person might be said to be literate if he or she had achieved a level of accomplishment paralleling that of children at the end of the fourth, fifth, or sixth grade. Today, most people have in mind what is sometimes called functional literacy: the ability to handle successfully the tasks required in the normal course of life. Most writers make a distinction between essential literacy (the ability to interpret or to prepare written or printed characters) and mastery of various areas of content or skill (such as economic, computer, or civic literacy). This section includes only books dealing with basic functional literacy and the ways that it is taught in adulthood.

Most adults learned to read and write so long ago that they tend to think of literacy as a trick readily mastered by anybody over the age of five. Mass campaigns have been based on this idea and may in some places have had a modest success, particularly when they were directed at people who already stood on the threshold of comprehension. Most experienced literacy instructors expect to conduct longer programs, ones that are often arduous for learners. The task is hardest perhaps when texts prepared for children are the only ones available. Many a teacher—apparently, including James Washington's—uses practical instruction to supplement the bare essentials of literacy; as we shall see, theoretical systems of "basic" or "fundamental" education have been designed around this idea. More profoundly, literacy instruction has been urgently proclaimed as the essential method for achieving three of humankind's profoundest goals: eternal salvation, political power, and economic independence.

The literature on "literacy-plus education" is enormous, and only a few of its high points can be mentioned here.

The Nature of Literacy

Two works provide a reasoned basis for all other treatments of adult literacy instruction. Carroll and Chall (1975) wrote their book as a response to a noisy controversy arising from the rivalry between two systems of teaching children to read; these are popularly known as the "look-say" and the "sound-it-out" methods, the former allegedly having driven out the latter, thereby leading to a society in which Johnny and Jane could not read. Carroll and Chall (as well as their colleagues in the National Academy of Education) sought to bring reason and light to the whole subject of literacy instruction at every age of life. Reasonably enough, greatest attention is given to the learning of children, but adult literacy is also considered throughout the book. Of particular interest are the sections that consider the essential nature of literacy, the present extent of adult illiteracy, and the major institutions at work on its eradication.

Wagner (1987) brought together a collection of essays that chiefly have to do with adult literacy education, though several are concerned with the instruction of children, and other authors imply a lifelong process. This book is at a high level of sophistication, written by people who take the acquisition of literacy so seriously that they are devoting a significant part of their lives to it. Although the authors focus on advanced nations that use European languages, some attention is also given to other languages and cultures.

Broad Approaches to Adult Illiteracy and Its Eradication

In a relatively brief book, Harman (1987) presents a lucid analysis of adult illiteracy as it has confronted the United States from its earliest history, but especially in the twentieth century; campaign after campaign has been launched, each with some success but failing collectively to have adequate impact on the massive problem. Harman is quite successful in depicting the ways by which literacy education is being undertaken.

Costa (1988) offers another introduction to literacy education with an account of how it has developed, its national leaders, and major recent research findings. Also included are extensive directories of resources. The book is intended to be a practical tool for workers in the field.

The best-known popular treatment of the problems of illiteracy was written by Kozol (1980). Working in a reportorial fashion and writing clearly and directly, he reviews the facts well known to workers in the field but not well understood by the American public. His is a search for answers to the problems of adult illiteracy, though he knows that they will not be easy to find and that the task of making the nation literate will be staggeringly expensive and enormously difficult.

Two works present scholarly approaches to the topic. Griffith and Hayes (1970), in a collection of essays by virtually all the leaders in adult basic education, furnish the most advanced practical thinking available at the time they wrote. The authors' intention is not to delve into theoretical work in linguistics and communication, but to contend with the immediate settings where instruction occurred and the aspects of society that gave rise to such instruction. Mezirow, Darkenwald, and Knox (1975) report the results of the authors' attempt "to develop and apply a methodology of scientific inquiry that would illuminate the most significant qualitative aspects of urban adult basic education (ABE) in this country. Our charge was to develop a dependable, comprehensive, and analytical description of significant patterns of program operation and classroom interaction in addition to presenting in an organized fashion the perspectives of those involved" (p. v). By the use of "grounded theory," the authors consider the nature of adult basic education, classroom dynamics, students served, teachers and counselors, the use of paraprofessionals, the directors of programs, and ways of improving programs.

Illiteracy as an international concern is the subject of an eloquent account by Jeffries (1967), who concentrates primarily on its manifestations in the underdeveloped world and the means being used to combat it there. Hunter and Harman (1979) are fundamentally interested in literacy education in the United States but bring a worldwide perspective to bear on the problem—a refreshing change from the provincialism that sometimes leads Americans to believe that they are the only creators of innovative methods.

American Literacy Campaigns

Kaestle and others (1991) supply a solid history of literacy in the United States since 1880: how it has changed and developed through the years in response to various factors; how the level of ability has been modified; how it has been studied by various types of investigators; and how it is related to the declining national test scores of the latter half of the twentieth century. The author deals with literacy as a whole at all stages of life. Cook (1977) provides a chronicle, decade by decade, of adult literacy education in the United States; the author presents much factual information and brief historical interpretation but makes little effort to evaluate various programs and movements. The book has an unusually complete bibliography. Kotinsky (1941) makes a thoughtful analysis of adult elementary education as it was carried out by established institutions at the onset of World War II.

The need for adult literacy education was first brought forcefully to the attention of the American public during the early days of World War I. Hartmann (1948) points out, "During the two-year period, 1915–1916, which preceded the entrance of America into the first World War, the nation was subjected to one of those social movements or crusades, which have periodically sprung up and colored the social history of the United States" (p. 7). This Americanization crusade, as it was called, was designed to integrate into American society the hordes of people from foreign lands who had poured into the country in the previous thirty-five years, most of them peasants from Eastern Europe. Hartmann gives a broad description of this campaign and an assessment of its accomplishments; he does not stress the literacy efforts growing out of the movement. These were relatively substantial for a number of years, however, and were still significant when Kotinsky (1941) wrote.

Carlson (1975 and 1987) adopts a larger approach to acculturation than Hartmann and one treating adult education more directly. His later volume is a substantial revision and modernization of the earlier one. In both, his central theme is the continuing effort throughout American history to integrate newcomers to this land so that they can absorb American traditions and values. Most such adjustments have occurred informally, as people found they could not make economic and social headway without conforming to established ways of life; but many purposeful efforts have been made to help the processes of acculturation. The best-known of these were programs designed to prepare for formal naturalization. A primary allied activity of such ventures was, of necessity, literacy education, because many of the people concerned could not read and write English, and a large number of them were illiterate in any language. Carlson's bibliographic work in identifying such ventures is exceptional.

Kozol (1985) assesses how much the literacy programs and campaigns of the past have accomplished. His is a comprehensive effort to indicate the scope and effects of adult illiteracy in the United States. It is thoroughly researched and presents its data in gripping anecdotes and stark statistics. Kozol believes that the eradication of illiteracy calls for drastic efforts on many fronts.

Basic Theories of Literacy Education

In his worldwide campaigns, the American missionary Dr. Frank Laubach built a conception of literacy based on Christian values, using principles that he developed and refined over the years. These were shaped by cultural diversity, but they accepted literacy instruction as a method common to all cultures. Medary (1954) provides a combined biography of Dr. Laubach and a chronicle of his work to combat adult illiteracy throughout the world. It is an uncritical record, conveying the vastness of his service but making no attempt to assess either its methods or its immediate or long-term impact.

Dr. Laubach gives a full account of his work in a series of volumes. He first became active in coping with adult illiteracy in the Philippines in 1929. In 1938, in a book called *Toward a Literate World,* he defined the international problem that he believed must be tackled by right-thinking Christians; the work gave basic data about his own activities and described enough of his methodology so that the reader can understand the processes found to be useful. After each further decade, he published a book showing cumulatively how much he had done. Of these, only his 1970 work, *Forty Years with the Silent Billion,* is cited here, as it summarizes or includes much of the earlier books in the series. It reviews, largely anecdotally, the various campaigns and many of the events and people with whom Laubach had worked for forty years. His system begins with the written language of a people or a tribe and develops charts of easily recognized symbols for each letter of the alphabet. After a specialist has laid out the pattern, instruction is given on a volunteer basis, each literate person teaching an illiterate friend or neighbor—thus giving rise to the "each one teach one" slogan that Laubach made famous. The whole approach is always underlaid with a strong religious, political, and self-help mission. The author describes in a personal—and perhaps somewhat messianic fashion—the problems that he and others encountered through the years and how they were solved.

Paulo Freire has become better known as a general adult educational theorist than as the originator of a system of literacy education, but he began his work in his native Brazil with the creation of a literacy campaign intended to help people change the prevailing social order. His early work posed such a threat to the oligarchy that ran Brazil that he was expelled for a time from his country, though he has since been allowed to return. During his years away from Brazil, he had a post with the World Council of Churches in Geneva. In that capacity and others, he traveled the world, expressing his ideas about the goals of adult education; these had evolved from his early work into a complex body of ideas. His writings and speeches have brought him attention and a host of followers in many countries.

So far as could be discovered, Freire has not himself described his essential method in English. Most people who want to know what he has accomplished find it useful to begin with Brown (1975), who entitled her work *Literacy in 30 Hours*. In the Freire methodology, according to Brown, research by a highly trained team of linguists must precede every effort at literacy education. The system of instruction itself is complex, calling for the discussion in sequence of ten drawings of scenes in local life and the close study of seventeen three-syllable words drawn from the indigenous vocabulary. The teachers who carry out this process must be trained as guides and supporters of learning. Freire's system is not a method that can give rise to a mass movement.

Freire's own works describe aspects or elements of this approach as he has reflected upon it. In a work called *Cultural Action for Freedom* (1970), he explores his basic ideas about the teaching of literacy as part of a social context based on the nature of the learners, not as an exercise in education. While based in Geneva, Freire became involved in the development of literacy education for adults in the African country of Guinea-Bisset, a former colony of Portugal. In *Pedagogy in Process,* published in 1978, he includes letters written to various leaders in that country who were attempting to carry out a program according to his principles. These letters (intentionally or not, evocative of the Epistles of Paul) put literacy in a strongly revolutionary context. In the first letter, he states, "Literacy education for adults, seen in the perspective of liberation, is a creative act" (p. 71). Again, he says, "Literacy education of adults, as we understand it, is one dimension of cultural action for liberation. . . . To discuss it means to discuss also the social, economic and cultural policies of the country" (p. 72). In 1985, Freire looked back at his original techniques and revealed his later thoughts on them. In 1987, he and Macedo recorded several dialogues on educational methodology that occurred at various times and places. The prevailing theme here is that literacy is not merely the ability to read and write but also a way to perceive reality. Other works by Freire cited earlier also contain insights related to his concern with literacy instruction. Two collections of essays about Freire's work are available. Mackie (1981) has edited a group of supportive analytical papers, some of which help to explain his methodology. Grabowski (1972) includes essays by seven leaders of adult education who were asked to appraise Freire's theory and practice. All of these papers are informed by deep knowledge of the subject, an awareness of background sources, and dedication to the aims of adult education; however, they range in opinion from wholehearted support of Freire's ideas to utter disdain for them. The book is completed by a bibliography of sources by and about Freire.

As we have seen, Americanization, the Christian ethic, and political entitlement have been three powerful forces leading to literacy education. A fourth—more diffuse but no less deeply felt—is based on the idea that literacy should be one aspect of a broader program intended both to give individuals the basic skills needed to survive in a complex world and to help their society attain the capacity to thrive economically and politically. Programs designed to achieve this end have often been called basic or fundamental education. This idea was effectively expressed at the end of World War II and was intended primarily as a means of helping nations less highly developed economically than others.

At the time that the groundwork was being laid for Unesco, a large, diverse, and distinguished committee was appointed to study the problem of providing adult basic education throughout the world; it was recognized even then that the fostering of such education should become a major part of the work of the new institution. *Fundamental Education* (1947) is the report of that committee and includes some of the data on which it based its conclusions. Lanning and Many (1966) follow through on the early efforts to carry out the report's proposals. Theirs is probably still the best introduction to the surprisingly complex problem of world literacy, even though many programs have been established since its issuance. The book is essentially descriptive, not a "how-to" manual, a sermon, or an advocacy of specific goals or methods of work. It is also firmly tied into the general field of adult education. Arndt and others (1959) have edited a study by a group of distinguished American educators who started out to examine fundamental education but found the term *community education* more suitable to describe the phenomena that they were studying. They included work being undertaken not only by Unesco and other international agencies, but also by bilateral programs and those of individual nations. This study, though relatively early, is still valuable.

Harman (1974) provides a tightly reasoned and heavily documented study of the interrelationship between the level of literacy in a country and the nature of its "development," economically and socially. The author harks back to Unesco's use of the term *fundamental education* from 1947 to 1961 and seeks to give it modern currency by developing a sophisticated analysis of how literacy efforts are related to a country's development. He concludes with a theoretical model of this relationship.

The unifying concept of fundamental education began to break apart in the mid 1970s, a change documented in two books. Paulston (1972) stresses the economic significance of literacy and uses the term *nonformal education,* which became the key expression for that approach. He presents and annotates a large number of publications dealing with all aspects of this form of education. In *The Politics of Literacy,* Hoyles (1977) collects short pieces assessing how adult illiteracy is related to the class struggle. Some of the papers are serious and analytical; others are statements, sometimes emotional, that seek to portray situations in which widespread illiteracy too often exists.

A theory of literacy education may be emerging that is based, not on some general theme or system, but on the idea that the development of goals and practices should be governed in part by the wishes of the learners. Levine (1986) begins his work by an examination of the nature of literacy itself, drawing on various bodies of literature related to that field, including advanced linguistic analysis. He then examines literacy in the European, particularly English, societies of the past. Finally, he reports on how literacy students themselves see the processes that they are using and the meaning of literacy in their lives; his sample is taken from students in such programs in Nottingham in the 1970s. Fingeret and Jurmo (1989) provide a series of explorations of the idea that literacy education should be carried out, where possible, in situations where learners have some sense of control over and some power to plan their own activities. This principle can be put into practice in many ways, from the interaction between a teacher and a learner to the development of institutions built to develop the empowerment of groups of people.

World Literacy Campaigns

Most of the works cited in the previous section could be included here as well, but there the emphasis was on theory, whereas here it is on action. Arnove and Graff (1987) present a collection of scholarly essays about campaigns to achieve literacy that have been carried out in various nations from the middle of the sixteenth century to the present time. The earlier ventures described were largely European and North American, whereas later ones have taken place in the modern underdeveloped nations. In addition to the descriptive chapters, others deal in cross-cutting fashion with key topics related to literacy and its advancement. The first world campaign was that of Laubach, and works relating to it have already been cited. After World War II, a number of campaigns emerged, sponsored originally by Unesco, by the International Council for Adult Education, and by the World Bank; eventually, they blended together. The books concerned with these efforts will be organized according to these three sponsors, and the section will be concluded by the mention of more general volumes.

Beginning in 1966, Unesco conducted its own worldwide program in literacy education. At the conclusion of this five-year experiment, a commission was appointed and a staff engaged to study the results. The resulting volume is *The Experimental World Literacy Programme* (1976). In it, country profiles are given for eleven economically underdeveloped countries, and a comparative analysis is made. The report is refreshingly candid in pointing out both successes and failures in various countries and in indicating the causes of the failures. Couvert (1979) also followed up this international effort by outlining the theoretical considerations that underlie literacy efforts on a national basis and suggesting the processes and instruments that must be used in rigorous efforts to measure results in such enterprises. Bataille (1976) reports the proceedings of an international symposium on literacy held in Persepolis, Iran, in 1975. He includes papers by authorities from around the world, a description of a symposium on the subject, and the text of the Declaration of Persepolis, a statement about the worldwide need for literacy couched in elevated language and in very broad terms. In thought and conception, the papers make up perhaps the best statement of the necessity for literacy education in the whole literature on that topic.

The International Council for Adult Education (ICAE), based in Toronto, held a 1976 conference in Dar es Salaam, Tanzania. This gathered together people from all over the world who were concerned with literacy-plus education. Hall and Kidd (1978) offer a heavily edited report of that conference, including a master plan for action that it adopted. *The World of Literacy* (1979) is a report prepared by the ICAE for the International Development Research Centre, an agency of the Canadian government. The book distills a large number of research investigations and general reports on literacy education, is well designed and illustrated, and contains an admirably comprehensive bibliography. The work is for policy makers and general administrators, not for those who teach illiterates or administer programs directly concerned with that purpose. It also provides a broad understanding of the field for the general scholar interested in the subject. Duke (1985) discusses a worldwide study undertaken in 1980 by ICAE. The book presents an introduction and concluding chapter by Duke, who also provides a framework for the chapter authors—seven leaders of adult education in as many economically underdeveloped nations who describe the literacy-plus endeavors in their own countries.

For some years, the World Bank and other organizations have been making grants to improve the quality of rural life in deeply underdeveloped countries, often by means of some form of adult educational activity. Although these have more general goals, literacy is usually a component, as it is the general skill that leads to many special ones. Coombs and Ahmed (1974) give a deeply detailed, cross-cutting account of the success of such efforts, based on analysis of twenty-five international programs and practices elsewhere. On the whole, the conclusions are positive in affirming that adult education can improve the quality of life of people in such areas, but the book goes on to identify errors and necessary changes in theory and practice. Bock and Papagiannis (1983) come to more negative conclusions. Although the transmittal of content and skills was one aspect of the programs examined by the authors, the overarching purpose was usually to create individual and collective feelings of self-worth and dignity, sometimes with overall political ramifications. The authors' study of such ventures has led them to the conclusion that none succeeded in achieving their goals; in fact, they have sometimes had a deleterious effect on their participants. In a survey of the total structure of education for people of all ages throughout the world, Coombs (1985) assesses with candor the attempt to make adults literate. He comes to the conclusion that there were more illiterate people at the end of the international effort than at the beginning. He believes that there is no quick and easy way to remedy this situation but that a great deal of practical experience now exists that should be put to use in building a more literate world. LaBelle (1986) describes and appraises national programs in nonformal education in Latin America and the Caribbean. His study is based in economics but also employs other social sciences in its analysis. The various efforts appeared to him to have three main objectives: to build up the capacity of poor people to earn a better living, to advance popular education, and to foster guerilla warfare. LaBelle examines each of these purposes—not only its outcomes but also the strategy used—particularly with regard to educational processes. The conclusions are subtly but clearly expressed, and the "rhetoric-reality gap" is fully explored. An excellent bibliography is provided. Torres (1990) furnishes a carefully reasoned theoretical work on the nature of nonformal education in Latin American countries, chiefly in the last quarter century. This volume is made up of separate papers on this theme, all written by Torres and brought together with a summarizing chapter. The author identifies four major approaches to adult education: the modernization human-capital approach, the pedagogy of the oppressed, pragmatic idealism, and social engineering. The analysis of these approaches and their interaction in practice presents a fascinating, though far from easy, exercise in understanding.

Three other works also relate to worldwide conceptions of literacy. Isenberg (1964) has compiled a collection of brief papers from many sources about different aspects of illiteracy and the efforts under way to combat it; this is a useful resource for quotations. Russ-Eft, Rubin, and Holmen (1981) devote most of their work to an extensive anecdotal bibliography on adult basic education. Bhola (1984) describes campaigns for literacy in eight countries: Russia, Vietnam, China, Cuba, Burma, Brazil, Tanzania, and Somalia. Bhola uses these national reports, as well as the general literature, to draw conclusions about practice and to suggest policy and practice recommendations.

Some sustained attention has been given to fostering opportunities for bringing the newly literate to a more advanced level of competence. The Unesco Institute of Education carried out a five-year, international program of meetings, conferences, and demonstration projects dealing with this theme, especially as it is encountered in developing countries. Many special reports and documents grew out of this project, but five central works were produced, all under the editorship of Dave, Ouane, Perera, and Ranaweera (in various combinations). A general report (1985a) of the entire effort provides a cross-national perspective; the other volumes (1984, 1985b, and 1986) focus on the work carried out in the specific nations indicated. These documents examine efforts undertaken by schools, libraries, mass media, and other general instruments for learning, as well as the specific ventures appropriate to the nations concerned.

Pati (1989) gives a very full study of neoliterates in the Indian province of Orissa. A stratified sample of two hundred such people were asked what kinds of topics they would like to read about. The author's central idea is that literacy skills are soon lost if they are not exercised. As he points out, "Literacy is an open invitation to further reading" (p. 36).

Although a sense of pride and accomplishment seemed warranted in many literacy-related programs around the world, the general mood of those who conducted them appears to be gloomy. A. Deleon, long-time head of adult education for Unesco, wrote the following statement:

> [The impact of compensatory education] on society and individuals has not been appreciable. Because, if the aim of these programmes is to provide some knowledge and technical skills, they may have had some success, but if their goal is to change psychological and sociological attitudes, the results are meager; if the goal is the acquisition of privileges hitherto denied to the majority, some progress is visible, but if the goal is liberation of individuals and the deepening of their awareness, much more has to be achieved; if adult education should enable individuals to adapt themselves to the society and to new technologies, many programmes can claim tangible achievement, but if they aim at a real change of the status of those who have been "marginalized," the outcome is poor; if the role of adult literacy programmes is to initiate millions to the 3 R's, some results have been evident; but if their purpose includes the preparation of illiter-

ates for a different working and social role and responsibility . . . the results are far from these objectives."[1]

The Processes of Literacy Teaching

Most publications dealing with literacy education are related in
some fashion to instruction itself. In early days, teachers used whatever came to hand, most frequently readers intended for children;
however, as time has gone on, materials especially for adults have
been prepared and along with them teachers' manuals and guides.
Richards and Rodgers (1986) have produced a clear and candid explanation of how people have thought about teaching languages
and the systems and methods they have devised for doing so. Each
of eight language teaching proposals is described and compared
with one another; they go back in time to the mid-nineteenth century. The authors do not differentiate the age groups of the students
concerned, except to state which method appeals to one group or
another. Only a few of the other important works on the general
processes of literacy teaching can be mentioned here.

In 1929, the U.S. Secretary of the Interior appointed a committee to stimulate the teaching of illiterate adults in an effort to
improve the nation's showing on the next year's decennial census.
Few experts on literacy shared his optimism, but they were happy
to seize the opportunity. One of them, William S. Gray, developed
a manual for teachers of adult illiterates that proved to be highly
popular, particularly as the Great Depression led to various programs designed to aid the unemployed. On the basis of this experience, the volume by Gray was revised by Whipple, Guyton, and
Morriss. Published in 1934, it became the standard guiding work for
literacy teachers. In the course of its long life, it may well have had
more widespread practical results than any other work on the
subject.

As the literacy movement grew, some of its leaders began to
write books intended to serve as guides to instructors. Cass produced
two, one of them with Crabtree in 1956, the other in 1971. The first

---

[1]"Adult Education as a Corrective to Failing Formal Education," *Literacy
Discussion*, 1975, *6*, 90–91.

of these, based on a quarter-century of experience, is intended "to identify the needs, objectives, problems, methods, practices and emerging trends in adult elementary education throughout the nation and to set down and bring together the commonalities which appear in this area of adult education" (p. 14). The 1971 work is less comprehensive but might still be useful to some practitioners in the field. Ward (1961) developed an annotated bibliography on the subject. Ulmer (1969) prepared a practical work for teachers, administrators, and curriculum planners of programs for adult basic education. Otto and Ford (1967) aimed their work primarily at teachers of illiterates. It does not propose a step-by-step method of teaching, but it does offer a number of sensible suggestions.

Beginning in the 1970s, the guides for instructors began to reflect more fully the lessons learned from experience and research. Bowren and Zintz (1977) take the task of reading very seriously and provide explanations and detailed descriptions of techniques. The bibliography is a full one. The book would be helpful to most teachers of functionally illiterate adults. Newman (1980) addresses her book to "instructors, tutors, volunteers, administrators, and leaders in business or industry who are—or would like to be—involved with teaching reading to adults" (p. ix). The author is familiar with both the theory and the practice of her subject and illuminates her general suggestions with concrete examples and case studies. Jones (1981) describes the adult illiterate in today's society and proposes a program of instruction for making adults literate. Out of the wealth of their own experience and that of others, Rossman, Fisk, and Roehl (1984) supply a practical guide for adult basic education, starting with learners and their problems and continuing with the specific ways that reading abilities can be taught and reading instruction fostered.

Many public library staffs have been concerned with literacy education. Concerned broadly with the whole topic of adult literacy, specifically as it is fostered by public libraries, Lyman (1976) lays special emphasis on the materials most helpful to new readers in terms of both format and content. In 1977, Lyman issued a supplement to her earlier work. It includes a large selection of items about literacy education in libraries. Weingand (1986) provides general coverage of literacy education in libraries. In particular, it includes a paper by Barbara Bliss on dyslexia, a topic less commonly discussed in the literature than its importance warrants.

Although mass media have been used in the United States and elsewhere to teach literacy, no books could be found on that subject. The World Bank has been deeply involved in the possibilities created by such usage, as Perraton (1982) discusses. He says, "Distance teaching attracts the economist because it uses mass-production methods, which change the structure of educational costs. . . . Indeed, if radios are widely distributed, it costs no more to broadcast to a million students within reach of a transmitter than to a hundred. In theory, then, distance teaching can bring economies of scale to education. The purpose of this book is to discover how far these theoretical advantages can be achieved in practice and how far they can be reconciled with educational effectiveness and with the maintenance of educational quality" (p. 5). Perraton reports on eight programs in six economically underdeveloped countries, each using a distinctive mixture of face-to-face and distance education. Hargreaves (1980) gives an in-depth analysis of a program carried out nationally in the United Kingdom in the late 1970s, in which about 100,000 adult nonreaders were thought to have received some remedial tuition. Many institutions were involved in this national campaign, but it was centered on the services provided by the British Broadcasting Company. Kaye and Harry (1982), in a work called *Using the Media for Adult Basic Education,* document seven case studies of western European projects. These accounts are accompanied by analytical chapters that define terms and clarify concepts.

The literature dealing with specific aspects of literacy has expanded greatly. Groteluschen, Gooler, and Knox (1976) consider how all aspects of an adult literacy program can be evaluated. Karnes, Ginn, and Maddox (1980) have assembled a book, mainly for educators, made up from papers from many sources. The topics range across the whole field of adult literacy and from theoretical analyses to highly specific treatments. Johnson (1980) brings together a number of papers on the enhancement of reading skills throughout life; examples are furnished in several settings: a nursing home, a prison, an employment environment, the provision of reading and study skills for law students, a community college, and elsewhere. Attention is also given to the improvement of reading instruction by the use of computers and other new instruments. Stevenson (1985) vividly illustrates how he handled reading and writing disabilities among British armed services personnel. Taylor and Draper (1989) have compiled a substantial collection of essays on many aspects of adult literacy education. Central attention is given to Canadian challenges and approaches, but the literature base of the authors is worldwide in scope. Chisman and Associates (1990) offer another collection of papers, chiefly by people at the forefront of adult literacy movements in the United States. Each paper is a deeply serious effort to assess some important theme; examples are the federal role, the necessity to upgrade the skills of literacy professionals, ways to strengthen the knowledge base in the field, and the need for instruction in English as a second language. Anderson (1991) discusses in considerable detail and with many vivid illustrations how new techniques of communication may be used to create education programs for adult literacy. Among the methods presented, separately or in combination, are computers, teleconferencing, narrowcast television, and interactive videodisks.

In the early days of modern literacy education, all kinds of students were brought together in the same classes. As instruction became more sophisticated, it became clear that the task of imparting basic skills of reading comprehension to the absolutely illiterate was very different from teaching a second language to those who could already read one. This latter category became the basis for a related but separate movement based on the teaching of English as a second language. Diller (1978) presents a theoretical study of the fundamentals of such teaching. One chapter explores the relative ability of children and adults to learn a foreign language, concluding that the latter are usually more efficient in doing so (except occasionally so far as pronunciation is concerned). Ilyin and Tragardh (1978) examine practice, rather than theory, in their selection of brief articles targeted at teachers of English as a second language.

Book-length descriptions of literacy programs can bring out a sense of their inherent complexities. Mention has already been made of the national campaign carried out in the United Kingdom in the 1970s. Jones and Charnley (1978) make a searching examination of the many parts of this venture and assess their cumulative effects. Quotations from many individuals are included. This relatively nontechnical study brings the subject to life in a way not possible in a more statistical analysis. Charnley and Jones add another treatment (1979) of the same subject, their purposes being: "First, to identify the aims of students and tutors involved in adult remedial literacy schemes; secondly, to discuss the achievements of both illiterate adults and their tutors in relation to their stated aims; and, thirdly, to establish a schedule of appropriate aims (the word 'appropriate' in this context meaning in terms of the philosophy of adult education)" (p. 171). This book is imaginative and would influence positively any policy maker or other analyst. The Advisory Council for Adult and Continuing Education, a U.K. cabinet-level body, produced a report (1979b) "to advise on the best way of building on the adult literacy campaign of the last three years in order to create and implement a coherent strategy for the basic education of adults, including continuing provision for adult literacy" (p. 2). A vast amount of inquiry and testimony went into the production of the strategy presented in this report, much of which would be useful in other countries.

Soon after the Sandinistas overthrew the Somoza regime in Nicaragua, they established a national literacy campaign headed by a Jesuit priest, Father Fernando Cardenal. The last half of 1979 was devoted to planning and testing, and the program was carried out with volunteer help in 1980. Miller (1985) provides a record of the campaign from its inception. The author, a highly trained social scientist familiar with the country and its language, was engaged to serve as evaluator-historian from the beginning of the program, and her report is exemplary. She fully covers the social scene and stresses its relationship to the success of the campaign.

Duke and Sommerlad (1976) offer a broadly conceived and carefully reasoned analysis and set of regulations as to how Australia should foster the life and development of its aboriginal population, particularly the forms of schooling and other education that should be made available. Although the references in the book are specific to Australian conditions, these principles can be applied to other advanced societies containing indigenous populations that have not had the opportunity to advance themselves economically and whose culture is threatened.

Hesser (1978) gives a thorough account of village literacy programming in Pakistan, discussing both its origins and its progress up to the time of writing. She also makes suggestions for its improvement and analyzes its theoretical structure using a basic program model.

Soifer and others (1990) report on a literacy program established at Eastern Michigan University in 1979. Its work has expanded from straightforward reading and writing instruction to a complex set of activities employing novel ways to aid the interaction between facilitators and learners. This book includes seven interrelated essays on aspects of this program described by its staff members.

Two books report on programs long familiar to leaders of literacy education. Stewart (1922) supplies an affecting narrative about one of America's crusades against adult illiteracy, this one mainly aimed at Appalachian mountain people. She recounts the positive results of the movement and stresses the values that it brought to an isolated people, especially to those shamed by their inability to read and write. Some of the photographs are profoundly moving. In a similar campaign in South Carolina, the State Department of Education offered "opportunity schools," at which illiterate and semiliterate adults could study together in a residential setting. These schools created sufficient national attention so that in the summer of 1931 they were studied intensively by three of the nation's leading specialists in educational research; these assessed both the instruction and also the informal learning. Gray, Gray, and Tilton (1932) furnish the results of this investigation. It is interesting not only because of its content, but because the reader observes scholars groping toward adequate measures of learning outcomes and describing what they found in lucid and measured prose. The monograph also suggests to a modern reader what might have happened if the basic education movement had continued to be a subject of careful investigation and research-based development.

In something of a tour de force, Beder (1991) draws together the contents of the major recent works on literacy education, interprets and integrates them in light of his own research programs in Iowa, and presents the results in a clear and comprehensive fashion. His concern is not so much with the processes of teaching as with the learners: who they are; what their motivation is; why so many members of the potential audience do not participate; and what the impact of study is upon those who do. Upon the basis of this research, he proposes new directions for policy and practice.

No account of literacy instruction would be complete without mention of the most famous student in such classes, H*Y-*M*A*N K*A*P*L*A*N, as he always spelled his name. He emerged as a character in a sketch written by Leo Rosten and published in *The New Yorker*. This fresh and joyous account of an adult literacy class won wide acclaim and led the author to write others, first publishing them under the pseudonym of Leonard Q. Ross (used to distinguish such lighthearted work from the scholarly research the author wrote under his own name). The first fifteen sketches appeared as a book in 1937, and another twelve were issued in 1957. In 1976, Rosten published a revision of the older essays and added some new ones in his book *O K*A*P*L*A*N, My K*A-*P*L*A*N!* The high good humor and sympathetic understanding of the author for motives of the students in the class that he describes have made these sketches into a minor classic in the general cultural literature of the middle third of twentieth-century America. Rosten portrays the tensions, frustrations, and perplexities of his adult literacy students and their teacher, the unforgettable Mr. Parkhill, so that they become hilarious accounts, without ever losing sight of how difficult it is to learn another language and how complex are the ambitions of the people who do so.

Securing Academic Credentials

Those who drop out of school in youth through choice or necessity often find in adulthood both that they lack the developed abilities needed to reach their goals and that high school diplomas, college degrees, and other formal certifications of accomplishment are prerequisites to advancement. At the secondary school level, programs for diploma completion have long been available at times and places convenient for men and women. When it became evident at the close of World War II that such programs could not meet the needs of returning service people and others who had failed to complete high school, work was initiated on a General Educational

Development (GED) test, successful completion of which would be an accepted alternative to a diploma. Programs under many auspices were established to provide GED preparation; millions of adults have now passed the examination, many of them going on to collegiate-level study. Some people have felt that because the GED is based on traditional academic content, it does not adequately reflect adult concerns. Consequently, an alternative External Degree Program (EDP) was created, based on the competence usually required in personal life, in the home, at work, and in the community. Both the GED and the EDP are now administered by the American Council on Education, thus allowing flexibility of choice.

It was a visionary task in the late 1940s to develop and refine the content and methodology of the GED test and then to win the assent of the power figures in all the states and territories to let it serve as an alternative to the diploma. After winning such assent, it did not remain static. It was revised from time to time and made available in other languages than English. The EDP has not had so long a life or so rich a development, but it too required great effort in order to become acceptable. In their impact on American lives, these two tests represent an enormous achievement. Astonishingly, despite the publication of many reports, brochures, and other documents, no book has yet been written to chronicle the history of the high school equivalence movement.

The growth of alternative means for securing degrees and other forms of higher educational certification has been almost entirely in the hands of community colleges, colleges, and universities and has therefore been covered in the description of those institutions in Chapter Five. Well beyond such credentialing lies another form of education now accepted as essential for those who are to become research scholars. *The Invisible University* (1969), its authors say, "is concerned with the appointments of a temporary nature at the postdoctoral level that are intended to offer an opportunity for continued education and experience in research, usually, though not necessarily, under the supervision of a senior mentor" (p. 42). Such appointments are not often thought to be adult education but should be considered in any comprehensive study of it.

Vocational Education

Vocational education, both preservice and in-service, has been closely interwoven with nonvocational education in the various institutions established for the education of young people. From the early part of the century, however, the federal government has demonstrated a special concern for the economic life of the country and the consequent need to provide training in the world of work. Blauch ([1933] 1969) has become the established reference on the early legislative and administrative history of federal involvement in vocational education, as well as in vocational rehabilitation and the Cooperative Extension Service. Of particular value is the social and political background that Blauch provides about the growth of federal interest in these fields of endeavor.

In the early days of the modern adult educational movement, two canvasses were made of adult vocational education. Evans (1926) analyzed the services offered to young workers by a wide range of institutions in communities of all sizes. Prosser and Bass (1930) described the evening industrial school, a type of institution that was then widespread. Both books are now of interest only for historical purposes.

A perennial question has to do with how well preservice and in-service vocational education is related to the advancement of careers. Hamer (1930) reports his analysis of about four hundred men in twenty-six states who had been chosen by farm journals or associations as master farmers, outstanding achievers in the field of agriculture. At that time, agriculture was the chief source of support of about six million families and was the most common occupation in the United States. Hamer provides an exhaustive analysis of the lives of the respondents. They did not have very much formal training; half had an eighth-grade education or less. These men did not believe that they had learned most of what they knew about farming by growing up on the farm. Nine-tenths of them thought that they had gained their significant knowledge after the age of thirty, and those old enough to make this judgment felt that their greatest number of new practices had been acquired after the age of forty-five.

Hill (1940) gives a panoramic view of vocational adult education at the time when the Great Depression of the 1930s was disappearing, mainly because of the onset of World War II. He conveys the complicated effort required to help men and women find rewarding and satisfying careers for themselves. The book is enlivened by anecdotes and illustrations describing the human drama of learning how to earn a living.

For the first half of the twentieth century, British adult education was suffused with the spirit of *liberal education,* a term that came from the traditions of the universities and meant far more than nonvocational education. After World War II, it was clear that the future of the United Kingdom required a powerful growth and rationalization of vocational and technical education, and the leaders of adult education found it essential to redefine and reinterpret their movement. *Liberal Education in a Technical Age* (1955) is the report of the deliberations of a representative and influential commission that sought to deal with this task and did, in fact, help modulate traditional positions so that they could accommodate the new urgencies required for survival of the movement. Hostler (1981) shows how the former dichotomies have gradually been eliminated in actual practice, his chief source of data being the courses actually offered by university extramural departments.

Wolfbein (1967) asserts that profound changes occurred in the American conception of work and, consequently, in the way that workers were prepared in the 1960s. He identified these changes: a determined policy of eliminating unemployment, the acceptance of a national responsibility for "a well-educated and trained supply of labor working under fair labor standards" (p. 5), and a desire for a rising level in the quality of life for all workers, including those depending on manual skills. The Manpower Development and Training Acts of 1962 and 1965 gave expression to such values and established methods for achieving them. Wolfbein records, rather impressionistically but with a valuable use of illustration, what the effects of this effort proved to be.

Showing how it is taught in various institutions, Bender (1972) narrows his focus to agriculture as a vocational training field. The approach of the book is resolutely general and applies the principles of adult education to the specialized requirements of the people engaged in the occupation of farming.

Wilms (1975) reports on his large-scale study of fifty vocational schools in four metropolitan centers. His analysis included twenty-nine proprietary schools and twenty-one publicly supported schools of various sorts. He gives a great deal of data concerning all of the schools and their graduates and also makes special analyses concerning the various types of programs undertaken. Proprietary schools often argue that they are better than public schools because economic necessity requires them to be at the forefront of performance. In this study, the labor-market experiences of 2,270 graduates of both kinds of schools did not confirm this hypothesis: "With few exceptions, graduates of public schools had about the same success in the labor market as graduates of proprietary schools" (p. 171). The author also learned that "eight out of every ten graduates of professional and technical-level, postsecondary vocational programs did not get the jobs they trained for" and that "eight out of ten graduates from lower-level vocational programs got the jobs they trained for, but with the exception of the secretaries, barely earned the federal minimum wage" (p. 186).

Garner (1978) presents the third in a series of volumes collectively entitled *The Career Educator*. This book considers the whole world of work and its relationship to adult education; the theme therefore goes beyond vocational and technical education. The papers included were written by twenty-three authors, most of them resident in Illinois. The topics discussed and their method of treatment are varied in character, with many ideas being introduced.

The final three volumes to be mentioned in this section all treat the world of work with a comprehensiveness and mastery of broad concept not previously common in the field. In a book significantly entitled *The Boundless Resource,* Wirtz (1975) distills the discussions of twenty-eight business, educational, and citizen leaders, aided by a professional staff, who sought to develop the basis for a national policy for the management of manpower work policies and strategies in the United States. This report gives full attention to adult education as it has developed both in this country and in Europe and stresses recurrent education as an element of national policy. Carton (1984) was commissioned by the International Bureau of Education (part of Unesco) to create a full-scale picture of education for the world of work as it has been since the days of the early Greeks. Although the author is familiar with the theories and processes of vocational training in youth, his central interest appears to be with systems of education in the adult years. One important asset of this book is that its author's thought derives so completely from continental European sources. Thus, Americans can see familiar problems in a fresh light and with an unfamiliar theoretical orientation. Senior and Naylor (1987) are concerned with unemployment in Britain. Using both general terms and case studies, they indicate its impact upon the individual, the family, the community, and the nation. The authors assess the ways that education can help ameliorate the difficulties and the value of distance education.

Continuing Professional Education

Every occupation that regards itself as a profession has an advanced knowledge base undergirding its thought and practice. As this base is enlarged, the resulting changes should often be reflected in practice; the practitioner's judgments about the work experience must continuously be influenced by purposeful learning of some sort. As the level of professional performance has important social consequences, the right of an individual to continue in practice is sometimes influenced by his or her willingness to take part in continuing education. As a result, several groups of adult educators have been formed to study and advance continuing education in the separate professions. Each profession now has a literature of its own on the subject, with little overlap with those of other occupations and sometimes with no recognition that people engaged in different kinds of work are dealing with like problems. But there are also studies oriented to the underlying similarities of education in several or many occupations.

Perhaps because of their close cooperation in a work setting, those in the health fields have been pioneers in considering continuing professional education as a general endeavor. The idea of collaboration was powerfully developed by a blockbuster of a book entitled *Fostering the Growing Need to Learn*, issued in 1974. This volume resulted from the initiative of a federal program called the Regional Medical Programs Service, designed to improve health care. This agency gave a grant to Syracuse University to develop a general pattern for continuing education in the health professions under the leadership of Alexander Charters and R. J. Blakely. The ten monographs and substantial bibliography of the ensuing report focus particularly on the subject at hand but have broad relevance for learning opportunities in institutions whose primary purpose is not educational. The monographs were written by people at the forefront of the field and go into great depth in describing processes that can be used in many situations and circumstances. In sum, they thus become a rich resource for those who devise or guide learning programs.

Boissoneau (1980) helped further to develop a cross-disciplinary approach to such problem areas as voluntary and mandatory continuing education, the role of professional associations, government involvement, and finance. Another substantial volume was edited by Green, Grosswald, Suter, and Walthall (1984). They presented the results of a joint venture by the Veterans Administration and the Association of American Medical Colleges "to study the theoretical and experiential foundations of continuing education and to develop a set of criteria for quality continuing education" (p. xiv). This mandate was carried out in an extensive way, and the resulting papers deal fully with the establishment of quality in providing continuing education to health professionals. Still another collection of important papers on allied themes was produced by Adelson, Watkins, and Caplan (1985).

It should not be forgotten, however, that most action in the health professions, as in others, occurs separately. For example, Popiel (1973) and Cooper and Hornback (1973) give attention to continuing education in the profession of nursing. Arndt and Coons (1987) have edited an all-encompassing series of papers on continuing education in pharmacy. Its five parts have to do with overview, fundamentals of operation, planning and development, implementation and evaluation, and trends and issues. Its authors are drawn entirely from academic pharmacy, except for one professor of adult education. Although this work centers on pharmacy, it depends throughout on the more general literature of continuing professional education (and, indeed, of adult education as a whole). Similarly, Richards (1978) takes up a number of issues concerned

with continuing medical education and treats it as one of the re-
forms then under way in both the practice of medicine and the
operation of medical schools. In assessing the forces influencing the
offering of learning opportunities for practicing doctors, use is
made of Kurt Lewin's theory of force-field analysis, in which the
state of an activity is determined by the "dynamic balance between
relatively equal driving and restraining forces" (p. 147). Fox, Mazmanian, and Putnam (1989) report on their study of the changes
made by physicians in their practice and the place of education at
all stages of such changes, from inception to full implementation.
Out of this endeavor, the authors construct a theory about the revision of medical practice, including hypotheses that can be tested.
One value of this study was the deep involvement of the national
association of training directors in medical schools.

Librarianship in all its aspects and institutional settings has
been unusually productive of works that concentrate on the specifics of the occupation while still relating them to more general considerations. Stone (1971) provides an excellent example of this
approach, the authors of the papers included having looked outside
their own profession to discover principles that they could use.
Conroy (1978) offers a thorough work on library staff development,
based on theory but fundamentally devoted to how principles can
be put into practice in complex library systems to educate further
various categories of personnel. Horne (1985) has edited a massive
volume reporting the proceedings of a worldwide conference on
continuing education for librarians sponsored by the American Library Association and the International Federation of Library Associations and Institutions. The thoughts of the conferees were
directly devoted to practices within libraries; yet their discussions
were grounded in wider treatments of adult learning, continuing
professional education, distance learning, and other subjects. Asp
(1985) has compiled a collection of four monographs by various
library authorities. Once again, the continuing education of librarians is the main focus, but its treatment is illuminated by the more
general literature in the field. The work is unusually rich in illustrative material and in the quotation of various shades of opinion.
Substantial appendixes indicate the content of important documents in the field.

The precepts and practices of continuing education are used even by occupations not ordinarily thought to be established professions. Simpson (1990) interprets the need for university and college faculty members to reshape their self-conceptions from time to time. He is especially concerned with what he calls a regenerative process of renewal for those who want to reconsider and reorient their careers. The emphasis of the book is not upon process but upon the need for it to be undertaken. The book is extremely rich in case studies. The National University Continuing Education Association (NUCEA) has published (1990) a *Handbook for Professional Development in Continuing Higher Education,* "designed as both a guide to the new professional in continuing higher education and as a resource for the seasoned professional in the field" (p. iii). It contains a number of essays by leaders in the field, extensive bibliographic references, and descriptions of activities conducted by NUCEA and other institutions. Its central theme is the importance of a continuing self-directed program of study by all workers in the field. Of special interest are the accounts of practitioners about how they entered continuing higher education and what they now think of their choices.

Some professions that maintain large continuing professional educational activities have not been drawn into the orbit of the larger movement. The in-service preparation of teachers has been a staple of schools of education throughout the twentieth century, but the people involved in such work seem to resist or remain unaware of parallel activities in other occupations. For example, Griffin (1983) offers a sober and useful book dealing with the improvement of the quality of school personnel, attention being given overwhelmingly to teachers. The authors of the papers included are all absorbed in theories, principles, and general approaches, often in institutional settings. They show no awareness of the fact that they are examining a topic of interest to other professions, and they do not cite any of the relevant general literature. What is true of teaching and educational administration is also true of other occupations. At least one reason for this separation is that each profession builds up a special vocabulary for its operations and insufficient attention has been given to the discovery of commonalities. Real—not merely semantic—differences also exist and some-times overshadow points in common.

The effort to define and develop a special field of continuing professional education is as old as Beals (1935), who treated it within the total framework of professional education. When the term *continuing education* began to be widely used in the 1940s and 1950s to indicate learning that extended instruction received pre-viously, it was recognized as having application to professional life. Nakamoto and Verner (1973) have offered a collection of biblio-graphic essays on continuing education in medicine, nursing, den-tistry, and pharmacy; they go beyond mere citations to provide insights about the services provided in each of the professions. In the mid 1970s, another important factor also emerged. The univer-sities had met the needs of the postwar baby boom by growing greatly in size. Now that the number of their customary students was diminishing, they were looking at how they might reorient their services to accommodate the new currents of social life. They felt that perhaps they had an additional field of service in the pro-vision of opportunities for continuing professional education. Ver-milye (1977) has compiled papers on this theme delivered at a national conference of leaders of higher education. The authors were concerned not only with laying the foundation for further learning in the undergraduate curriculum, but also with finding ways that needs could be met in later life.

Houle (1980) has provided a general description of the growth of continuing professional education and the reasons why it has come to prominence, basing his analysis on a study of the activities of seventeen professions. He regards much of the work and the theory that underlies it as simplistic and asserts that more com-plex foundations must be evolved if it is to have optimum effect. His emphasis is on the individual, rather than on the institution, and the purpose of the book is "to advance the process by which greater conceptual coherence may be brought to the educational endeavors of practicing professionals in the United States" (p. xi).

Stern (1983), in a book dramatically called *Power and Con-flict in Continuing Professional Education*, stresses the places where issues and difficulties are to be found in practice. His book is the result of a conference of leaders: the providers of education, the regulators of the professions, and the analysts of various aspects of the subject. As might be expected, the book that records their discussions (which is presented in an unusual and interesting fashion) is an expression of widely varying and sometimes conflicting views.

Jarvis (1983b) assesses professional education from an English point of view but with a command of American literature and thought. His book encompasses the whole process of achieving the insight and skills necessary to an accomplished professional, from before practice to its end; he does not treat continuing education as merely an addition to early instruction.

An interest in the theoretical approach to continuing professional education continued to be manifested throughout the 1980s; five substantial collections of papers on this topic may be cited. Cervero and Scanlan (1985) include chapters by individuals who are chiefly scholars, rather than practitioners; their systems of thought are substantially parallel. A summary chapter is provided by William S. Griffith. Todd (1987) offers a more heterogeneous collection of essays. Most of the authors are English and therefore provide an approach somewhat different from that found in American sources. Cervero, Azzaretto, and others (1990) supply the papers given by a state-of-the-art conference. Almost all of the authors are university-based and concerned with the analysis of general continuing education, rather than with its practical applications for works in various fields. A national conference on continuing professional education held in 1986 generated enough interest to warrant the creation of study groups among leaders in that field. Each group studied one aspect of the field and produced a report summarizing conclusions and suggesting next steps for development. These reports, skillfully woven together by Queeney (1990), represent vital viewpoints on the nature of this form of adult education. A highly theoretical view is demonstrated by the authors of papers in the work edited by Willis and Dubin (1990). The authors are senior faculty members at several American universities, primarily concerned with models and systems by which professionals can be helped to maintain or improve their practice.

Nowlen (1988), a university dean of extension, is interested in practice. He thinks of his book as a link between heavy general theorizing about continuing professional education and what he believes might be developed as the needs of the field are more fully met. He believes that three learning models are now to be found in practice—the update, the competence, and the performance. Each is described and illustrated in various settings. He himself espouses the third and shows how it may be put into practice in various ways.

Cervero (1988) offers an all-embracing work that addresses most of the general themes and topics of conceptual writers. His book is specifically helpful in examining studies that have put broad formulations to the test of research or closely observed practice.

A Final Word

It has long been customary to regard compensatory and continuing education as a result of the failure of earlier schooling—a transitory field of work that will disappear as childhood and youth instruction improves. But realists must conclude that such is not the case. Some able young people are always going to find formal learning unattractive, unchallenging, or beyond their means. Some will not identify their true vocations until maturity. Even today's best school systems, colleges, and universities have their failures, dropouts, and students with lackluster motivation; presumably, this situation will still obtain, even if today's best becomes tomorrow's average. And, short of a nuclear catastrophe, the growth of knowledge is not going to diminish enough to permit men and women to go confidently throughout their careers with the degree of mastery attained at the time of their professional certification; they will always need to continue to learn.

Perhaps the most insidious enemy of compensatory and continuing education arises from the negativism with which it is often approached. If it is regarded only as a temporary problem to be cleared up quickly, qualified adult educators will not make permanent personal commitments to it. If quick results are expected, disillusionment will follow when they do not occur; a national decennial census, for example, will never reflect the results of a literacy campaign begun in the preceding year. As this chapter has shown, compensatory and continuing education rely for their appeal on profound personal and social motives. Through literacy comes self-actualization; the achievement of a diploma, a degree, or a vocational certificate opens doors that were previously barred; and the acquisition of advanced new skills makes it possible to fulfill ever more splendidly the sense of mission at the heart of a profession. These achievements are indeed valuable and the education that provides them is worth celebrating. This is the prime lesson of the literature that deals with these themes.

NINE

Goals Related to
Aspects of
Adult Life

The purpose of education for adults is the promotion of
one's personal development and function in society through
extension of knowledge, insight, and attitude, as well as
social, cultural, and technical skills.
—Statement adopted by the Dutch legislature

Many factors that create and inspire adult education arise from the
circumstances of adult life, though some preparation may have been
made for them in childhood. A good example lies in the responsibilities that citizenship imposes on every man and woman. Courses
and intramural activities can give high school and college students
some knowledge about the public order and some experience in
limited governments. Nevertheless, not until the right to vote is
conferred on individuals do they feel the full responsibility of decision making and of participation in political affairs and the need
to learn how best to take an active part in them. The other roles that
adults play offer different challenges, some of them important for
providers of learning and for the people who respond to the opportunities made available. This chapter reviews the literature dealing
with the most widely recognized of the reasons for adult education.
First, however, it will be useful to consider the various ways by
which they are related conceptually to the field.

Note: Epigraph taken from *Adult Education in the Netherlands*,
N.C.V.O.—Department of International Relations, Box 351, 3800 A. J.
Amersfoort, 1985.

Some people, including the members of the Dutch legislature, accept the perfectibility of the person as the paramount purpose of adult education, including all the specific aims required in the achievement of personal or social potential.

Others never think about adult education except as it is related to some particular or broad goal. To them, the world of learning or teaching is centered solely on, say, religion, health, or the needs of the elderly.

Still others are aware of the multiplicity of themes but believe that one is paramount. As suggested in earlier chapters, the prevailing British view for many years (reinforced by practice and validated by legislation) was that liberal study was the central theme of adult education. Some holders of this view, such as Livingstone (1944), narrowly defined liberal studies as being the core value of the field; they accepted vocational education as being equally worthy but inherently different. For many other of its adherents, however, this tradition may have been strengthened by the breadth and flexibility of its interpretation; for them, liberal education might not be capable of exact definition, but they knew it when they saw it.

A variant view is that the single basic purpose that adult education needs to give it definition has not yet emerged. Presumably, practitioners and theorists in the field should work together to identify this purpose; until they succeed, the field will not have fully evolved. Blakely (1958) expressed this idea, along with many of its variations and applications, in a series of addresses given to many groups of adult educators.

Still another perspective (probably the prevailing one) holds that the field is inherently multithematic and that the task of the analyst or theorist is to identify the clusters of goals actually being sought or that are ideally part of the field. Most historical and general works identified in previous chapters use this approach. Two books focus directly on the analysis of program emphases. Boone, Shearon, White, and Associates (1980) have identified many that had been significantly advanced in the 1970s. These authors suggest five organizing themes: a sense of self, a sense of professional growth, a sense of opportunity, a sense of community, and a sense of experimentation. Leirman and Kulich (1987), providing a number of papers delivered at a world conference in Belgium in late 1986, assess six themes that they thought would be of major importance in the 1990s: labor and employment education, environmental and ecological education, peace making and peace education, intercultural relations and multicultural education, development in relations between the Northern and Southern hemispheres, and university and adult education. The papers are packed with interpretation and written at a high level of abstraction, sometimes focusing almost entirely on the problem area rather than on education; yet the reader still gains a sense of the potential of the field as a major means of achieving a better world.

Social Interaction and Sensitivity Training

The idea that adults learn best through imaginative interactions—as opposed to the didactic atmosphere of the classroom—has appeared in the literature since the earliest days of the field. Follett (1924) offers one of the fullest philosophic expressions of this theme. The author was an independent scholar educated at both Radcliffe and Cambridge who devoted her life to studying how interaction among people could make experience creative. Her lectures and writings had a powerful influence on both political science and business management. She devoted much of her time and resources to establishing adult educational enterprises and collaborated closely for some years with Eduard Lindeman. The work here cited expresses her mature thought on the kinds of learning that flow from human interaction, particularly in small groups.

The widely felt interest in this theme became concentrated in the late 1940s, when a group of investigators engaged in what was called *group dynamics* research, though that term was disavowed by some scholars as being too narrow. This movement was viewed by its members as a study of the processes that occur naturally in groups and that may be changed or modified if necessary to make them have greater influence. As time went on, a broader purpose appeared: the desire to work out, at every level of abstraction, the achievement of a heightened awareness of human interaction and sensitivity training.

The major line of analysis of group dynamics and the name by which it became known are usually thought to have been originated by Kurt Lewin at the State University of Iowa and Massachusetts Institute of Technology (to whom I referred in Chapter Eight). These have been carried forward by scholars at the University of Michigan, the University of Chicago, and elsewhere. For a time, roughly from 1947 to 1960, the ideas originated by these researchers dominated much of the thought in adult education, mainly because they were advanced with vigor and debated with passion. Knowles and Knowles (1972) give a compact and useful narrative of the history of the movement and the sweep of its important ideas. An earlier journalistic account is given by Chase and Chase (1951), who provide a vivid report on the leaders and submovements in what was then regarded as a new science of human relations. The book is especially useful for those who want to gain a feeling for the personalities and interactions of the people espousing these new ideas.

Much of the development of the group dynamics movement occurred under the auspices of an organization first known as the National Training Laboratory (NTL) in Group Development, though its name was later modified slightly. Bradford (1974), one of the prime advocates of this work, provides a full description of the history and works of the NTL, which was simultaneously a provider of group dynamics education and a research center for group activity.

Out of the broad and initially diffuse movement, there gradually emerged a format for training known generically as the Training-Group (or T-Group). Bradford, Gibb, and Benne (1964) examine the manifestations of this format, which is defined as "a relatively unstructured group in which individuals participate as learners. . . . The data are the transactions among members, their own behavior in the group as they struggle to create a productive and viable organization, a miniature society; and as they work to stimulate and support one another's learning within that society" (p. 1). In this book, an account is given by various authors of many aspects of T-Groups as they were conducted, chiefly for adults, in a large number of theoretical and practical settings. Benne and others (1975) discuss the changes and refinements of this form of applied group dynamics research in the ten years separating this book and the aforementioned work. Appley and Winder (1973) also delineate the history and the then-current status of the T-Group and contrast it with group therapy. The authors treat group dynamics and the T-Group as a separate adult educational movement.

The lessons learned from the theory and practice of group dynamics were soon being applied in many fields. Miles (1959), in a work that went through many editions, turned his attention to applications in the schools and in other settings where young people learn. The adult educator notes this book with some pride as it is one of the early evidences that investigations into adult learning could have broader applications than at first intended. Earlier work in social psychology had rested heavily on methods and materials first developed for children; now a reverse trend could be seen. Bradford (1976) distills from the wider movement the essential practical ideas that might be used by those who wish to achieve better interaction in meetings. His book has numerous practical illustrations, and he confronts many of the problems of meetings and suggests ways to solve them. Thelen (1954) has written a treatment of the ways in which various kinds of groups, ranging from classrooms for children to people drawn together for purposes of social action, can effectively interact and thereby gain a heightened awareness of individualities, group processes, and the dynamics of social action. One of Thelen's useful contributions, reflected in this book, was his development of action groups based on city-block organizations. Lowy (1955) tries to bridge the gap between adult education and social work; he explores the nature of group processes in both disciplines and finds little that sharply differentiates one from the other. Davis (1961) offers an intensive sociological study of the factors influencing retention in book-based discussion groups. His work is interesting and significant because of its theoretical foundations and the originality of the methods used; nevertheless, the author concludes that he is not able to derive from his work any generally useful principles, retention proving to be too complicated a matter to be simply described in other than truisms. Reviewing how group sensitivity training was used in the YMCA in the 1960s, Batchelder and Hardy (1968) give both positive and negative opinions expressed by program participants. Fry (1961) attacks with vigor the effort to foster group dynamics, which (in his judgment) overrides individuality, content, and the excitement of learning.

As the literature of group and organizational analysis expanded during the 1950s and early 1960s, efforts began to survey and systematize what had been learned. The most influential book of this sort is probably that of Cartwright and Zander (1968), which has appeared in several editions and has been widely used as a textbook and standard reference. It includes not merely accounts of classical investigations, but also other studies whose focus was on education, therapy, decision making, social welfare, or some other aspect of human interaction. Schein and Bennis (1965) supply another summary of the work undertaken in what they call the laboratory approach. They describe its nature, its uses in various settings, the research still undone, and, finally, a theory of learning based on laboratory training. The authors bring a formidable level of intellect and knowledge to bear upon the topics with which they deal; their presentation, though essentially positive, does not hesitate to point out problems with each approach that they describe and the questions that its devotees must finally answer. Bergevin and McKinley (1965) focus closely on the adult educational applications of group analysis. They present a practical and carefully worked out plan for helping groups learn how to take part fruitfully in discussion. The authors identify various training roles and establish the basic rules that guide good group process. Rice (1965) moves beyond the careful analysis of group forms and structures to consider how feelings and sensitivities can be accented in meetings set up for varied purposes. Burton (1969) seeks to establish a theory and rationale for encounter groups, which are defined to include "all sensitivity, awareness, meditative, body, consciousness-expanding, and other forms of current encounter experiences which take place in more than dyadic groups" (p. 8). Most of the authors included are psychologists and psychotherapists who do not fit their analyses within the theme of adult education. However, they accept the fact that the changes occurring as a result of encounter group experiences are forms of educational accomplishment. Luft (1970) looks at the field of group dynamics as an object of both research and practice. Egan (1970) goes deeply into the literature and practices of small-group interaction, particularly that intended for education about dynamic human processes. The literature is covered thoroughly, and the depths of interaction are probed; yet the language remains clear and accessible. Dutton, Seaman, and Ulmer (1972), in a very brief book, give the highlights of what has been proposed and learned by students of human relations and sensitivity analysis. Bradford (1978) brings to a culmination his thirty-year effort to discover the adult educational implications of group study. His book is a collection of papers on group analysis and development, with special reference to the ways that groups shape and influence their members.

Health Education

Education for health, fitness, and strength is now widely available, as is education to prevent or cope with disease and poor physical and psychological conditions. Information of both sorts is conveyed by every kind of message-bearing medium—from long and arduous instructional programs to warnings on cigarette packages. Health care workers provide many forms of education, either individually or as part of a larger health setting, such as a hospital or a clinic. To realize how far society has come in offering learning activities in this field, it is instructive to read Hill's (1939) brief and lucid account of the adult health education programs and emphases of the late 1930s. Though the reader gains a sense of countless activities vigorously undertaken by varied sponsors, the author also conveys their lack of power as they struggled with the vast health problems of the country.

In the 1970s, several surveys of health education in hospitals were produced. Schechter (1974) comments on a number of themes related to education in health care institutions and reports on programs undertaken by the author and his colleagues. Their central theme, emerging in a number of places, is the need for a hospital-based training director who can develop comprehensive educational programs for all persons associated with an institution, from its board of directors to the persons whom it serves. The Hospital Research and Educational Trust (1970) issued a comprehensive manual about the management of educational programs for personnel working in health care institutions. The emphasis is on practical applications; many examples, case studies, and illustrative forms are included. In a slender and highly compressed volume, Munk and Lovett (1977) summarize the findings of a five-year study that examined in detail sixteen individual hospitals and seventeen consortiums to discover how they conducted employee education. Of particular interest are seven case studies that give a sense of concrete reality to what might otherwise seem overgeneralized conclusions. Webster, Hoffman, and Lamson (1971) provide a report of a national conference on mental health education attended by government officials, experts on various aspects of the field, and adult educators. The book furnishes the prepared papers and the panel reactions and reports of the groups that discussed them. This work explores not only how adult education and mental health are related to each other, but also how the former can be used to improve the latter.

Believing that the many health education programs of the 1970s required systematization, Green and others at Johns Hopkins University (1980) have undertaken the development of a master plan that begins with the diagnostic analysis of some specific setting and proceeds with the planning, execution, and evaluation of an educational program appropriate to it. They also include extensive case studies of how their master programming plan has worked out in practice. They are interested in both school-based environments and other settings and seem primarily concerned with reaching adults.

The 1980s brought a strong interest in *patient education,* a term that sometimes implied more than helping the ill; in practice, it became virtually synonymous with *health education.* Green and Kansler (1980) have created a bibliography of the works on this subject that indicates how far-reaching and complex this field had become by 1980. In addition to its valuable content, the book is a model of how useful a bibliography can be in providing perspective on its field. Squyres (1980) contributes a full-scale treatment by a group of collaborating authors on the various issues and problems involved in a total patient education program in a health setting. Bille (1981) has assembled a collection of papers by various kinds of health professionals, most of them nurses, dealing with all aspects of patient education. Rankin and Duffy (1983) examine patient education from the viewpoint of the nurse. This book makes many sensible suggestions and gives attention to such general approaches as the involvement of the whole health team and the importance of preventive measures. Redman (1984) supplies a highly developed treatment of patient education, complete with charts, exercises, procedural suggestions, and other theoretical and practical aids. This is perhaps the most rounded introductory volume available. In a volume entitled *Effective Patient Education: A Guide to Increased Compliance,* Falvo (1985) carefully analyzes how the health worker (most often the nurse) can work with patients to assure that they follow the prescribed rules of good health. It should be noted that *compliance education* has sometimes been used as a synonym for *patient education.*

A fully developed recent work on health education is offered by Glanz, Lewis, and Rimer (1990). The editors and other contributors to this book are eminent specialists in health promotion; for the most part, they work in universities, foundations, and other intellectual centers. Their mutual concern in this book is how various theories of changing health behaviors in the general population or among specialized groups of people may be expressed and translated into action. They are interested in the transmittal of health information and the methods by which effective intervention can occur. Although this book deals solely with health, people involved in other social purposes might well find parallels in their own work.

Family Life Education

The early emphasis of family life education was upon helping parents learn how to handle the problems arising from their relationships with their children. Carter (1938) describes the growth of the parent education movement during the 1930s, though she was well aware of the larger dimensions of family life. Her eloquent and concise volume also considers the future of this movement.

Two related works treat in depth the problems of child rearing and the ways that parents may learn to cope with them. Brim (1959) presents a profound analysis of parent education, beginning with a history of the growing efforts in this respect since 1880 and continuing with the parent-child relationship as a basis for programs that teach parents how to discharge their roles more effectively. The author is a social scientist, and the purpose of his study, conducted under the aegis of the Russell Sage Foundation, is "to provide a useful organization of what is recognized as a field that has little or no generally accepted theoretical framework; and . . . point to ways in which social science knowledge and ideas could be efficiently applied to problems of practice in the field and to problems on which basic research was needed" (p. 5). In rigorously evaluating studies in the field, Brim comes finally to the conclusion that the value of parent education in any systematic way remains to be proved. In 1980, Harman and Brim followed up Brim's earlier analysis. They point out that the data of the intervening years does not require any change in the pattern of organization. They state, "The student of the field will recognize in the two books a survey and analysis spanning some fifty years of efforts" (p. 7). The two works together are a comprehensive assessment of the nature of parent education, the root causes of parent behavior, and the detailed aims and activities designed to improve family living.

Stern's (1960) work is both broader in scope and less rigorous in its analysis than the books by Brim and by Harman and Brim. Reporting on various international conferences held in the 1950s, Stern makes the case for parent education in all its various forms, discusses common problems and themes as they are encountered in a worldwide context, and details the practices of four countries: the Federal Republic of Germany, France, the United Kingdom, and the United States.

Some works examine specific methods or settings for parent education. Taylor (1967) celebrates the educational influence on parents of cooperative nursery schools, in whose development she exerted much influence. She describes the collective experiential learning that can occur when young parents have the opportunity to reflect collectively with other parents about what they are learning. Her work both defines the nature of that learning and demonstrates how the necessary processes can best be organized and conducted. Auerbach (1968) deals more generally with parent discussion groups, especially those occurring under the auspices of the Child Study Association of America or using principles developed under its general plan.

As the body of research on family life developed and became the basis of undergraduate and graduate study in the universities, it also had an influence on adult educational endeavors. Ruud and

Hall (1974) have surveyed all aspects of the topic as interpreted in the light of American practice. The authors give a full explication of key terms and the ways that they relate to one another. Leichter (1979) collects scholarly essays by a group of distinguished educators and social scientists dwelling on the interrelated character of formal education and the family, particularly as it is influenced by the community. These papers make reference to all the major themes now guiding work in the field but do not make recommendations for change.

Workers' and Labor Union Education

In its earliest beginnings, the term *workers' education* had a clear and exact meaning. In Britain, as in continental European countries, the working class was generally accepted as a coherent and enduring entity with its own ways of life, values, restrictions, and challenges. The systematic economic deprivation of workers and other low-income people has long caused some members of the middle and upper classes to feel a sense of shame, most often when they wondered why they themselves had been exempted from such conditions. In the last quarter of the nineteenth century, the urge to help workers improve their lot was felt by a growing number of people, especially young intellectuals in the universities. This urge was expressed to the general public in many ways; for example, Thomas Hardy's novel *Jude the Obscure* powerfully describes the life of the very poor. The protagonist is a young stone mason, with excellent innate abilities but no opportunity to develop them. In one poignant scene, he works on the campus of a university, surrounded by elegant young students to whom he is no more worthy of note than the stones with which he is working. This book (in a sense, the *Uncle Tom's Cabin* of British adult education) lent powerful support to the reformers who wanted to enable members of the working class to have the benefits of university study so that they could help their fellows. An often-repeated aphorism was that workers' education should help the student to raise, not rise out of, the working class.

This idea was most fully shaped and developed by Albert Mansbridge, founder of the Workers' Educational Association

(WEA), to which reference was made in Chapter One. His book, *Adventure in Working-Class Education* (1920), shows the pure essence of the zeal for education that animated many of the founders of adult education in that country, free from political strivings, utilitarianism, or any tinge of Marxist thought. Carrying the history of the WEA forward to mid-century, Stocks (1953) examines how the workers' education crusade was fortunate enough to enlist a number of future leaders of the country among its early founders and friends; as they rose to power, so did the fortunes of the WEA, until it eventually dominated the provision of adult education in the country—both in its independent offerings and in its collaborative ventures with universities and other sponsoring bodies.

Another well-documented strand of parallel development is the labor college movement. Near the turn of the century, three young scholars at Oxford, two of them American, founded Ruskin College, a residential center for workers in the town of Oxford. Early in its history, a schism developed among its staff and students over whether the main influence on the program should derive from university disciplines or from policies and issues of concern to the labor union movement. Craik (1969), a student in Ruskin's second class, gives an account of this split and describes how one group seceded and formed the Central Labour College, which endured for a quarter-century. It was devoted to preparing leaders for militant labor unions and was strongly influenced by Marxist thought. Craik covers its origins, history, and dissolution. Millar (1979) took over the story from there. Throughout his career, he was the director of a federation of various types of union programs called the National Council of Labour Colleges (NCLC). He recounts the entire course of this organization from its first origins to its dissolution. It is a highly personal work, of interest because it presents a point of view not often found in the literature: the firm belief that working people must rise from their own foundations chiefly by a process of education that they control and guide themselves. Simon (1990) brings scholarly discipline to the analysis of the labor colleges and other ventures conducted outside the framework of state-supported systems of education. His book is a collection of related essays by scholars long associated with working-class ideas and emphases. The papers are definitive and scholarly, striking a judicious balance in the description and interpretation of programs long suffused with passion and controversy; the essays' serious treatment dignifies the efforts of various small and struggling "colleges" and movements.

Horrabin and Horrabin (1924) compare the two models of workers' education as exemplified by the WEA and the NCLC. The first, they say, was concerned with "the *extension* of the benefits of culture . . . to the class which, by reason of its lack of means and leisure, has been debarred from a full share of those benefits hitherto" (p. 9). The other sponsored "a particular *kind* of education, aiming primarily at meeting the specific needs of the workers as a class, and undertaken by the workers themselves *independently* of, and even in opposition to, the ordinary existing educational channels" (p. 9). The authors accept the second view and assess it both historically and analytically. They end by asserting, "Working-class education must aim at the ending of Capitalism and the building of a new social order" (p. 72). Hodgen (1925) reviews how workers' education had been established in Britain and had aroused interest in the United States. He also speculates on how the movement will develop.

Corfield (1969) chronicles workers' education in Britain almost three-quarters of the way through the twentieth century. He lays primary stress on the emergence of a third model: programs designed for the improvement of trade union operation and administration, not for the extension of liberal education or the creation of a group of leaders who could change the whole social order.

Workers' educational movements occurred in many nations. Hansome (1931) gives an account of worldwide programs, sponsored by labor unions, colleges, universities, and specialized institutions, that use education as a way of helping the working class to gain strength. This class-oriented education had a powerful appeal in the 1930s particularly because the Depression around the world was strengthening its grip on the economic and social life of industrial nations; many people found inspiration (some practical, some visionary) in direct efforts to work in unaggressive ways to relieve the pressures of poverty and to honor manual labor on a cultural basis. Cook and Douty (1958) offer a compressed but lucid account of what labor education meant as it evolved within a European context (especially in Britain) and how the idea was translated to the United States. Hopkins (1985) furnishes a comprehensive analysis of workers' education on an international basis. The author is English but is fully knowledgeable about other countries as well. This work is the major present resource on this aspect of adult education.

In the United States, traditional forms of workers' education proved not to have the appeal found in Europe, perhaps because American workers were all too eager to rise out of their class. Kallen (1925) focuses on how the movement entered American life and, with a high moral tone, criticizes its lack of a solid theoretical foundation. In a beautifully written and nonmilitant monograph, Carter and Smith (1934) provide perhaps the most sympathetic account of early American workers' education; they examine efforts made by many kinds of institutions to bring education to working people who desired "ardently not only to improve their economic status but to have that broad basis of education which is necessary to the fullest enjoyment of our material resources" (p. 2). Kornbluh and Frederickson (1984), describing various ventures in workers' education for women from 1914 to 1984, also convey the strongly emotional tone of the movement that enabled working women to rise above and help conquer the deplorable conditions in which they had to work. Adam (1940b) generally surveys various forms of workers' education as conducted by unions, universities, government, and voluntary bodies. Brameld (1941) has edited a collection of papers written chiefly by European emigrés and Eastern intellectuals. They explore the nature of workers' education, its history, its programs, and its prospects. At the time the authors wrote, World War II seemed imminent, and they believed that an educated citizenry was the only hope to defeat the consequences of Hitler. The largely undeveloped force of the union movement seemed to them to be the greatest potential for mass success in building a democratic society in the United States.

The largest program of American workers' education was conducted as part of the New Deal effort to alleviate the effects of the Great Depression. Kornbluh (1987) has written a scholarly monograph on that program, preceding it with a brief but thorough introduction to the whole field of workers' education. Hubert Humphrey was director of this program in Minnesota and through it gained access to his later political constituency; he thus paralleled the career patterns of many of the young English intellectuals at the dawn of the century.

Mire (1956) has contributed perhaps the major American book on workers' education. He describes efforts put forward by a number of providers—especially unions, universities and colleges, governmental bodies, and voluntary agencies—to reach the members of labor unions with various kinds of knowledge, particularly those going beyond the specifics of labor-management interrelationships. Liveright (1951) furnishes a practical handbook of tools and techniques that can be used by union leaders.

In the United States, workers' education has taken place in many settings. Ware (1946) reports on a number of ventures in existence at the close of World War II, some of them inspired by foreign models and some evolving from the research and teaching activities of university departments of industrial relations. The tale is essentially one of discontinuous endeavors, often spurred by a single individual and sometimes with brief lives. Several years later, Kerrison (1951) supplies the results of a survey that he made of what universities were doing to foster workers' education, largely through their extension divisions. Barbash (1955) defines workers' education as "any planned educational activity which a union undertakes; or an educational activity undertaken by any other agency than a union, where a major objective is to build a more effective union citizenship" (p. 3). In describing the programs offered by universities, Barbash concentrates on the then-current structures and practices of eight institutions. He also examines the diversified programs that unions carry out on their own behalf.

Dwyer (1977) provides a bibliography on workers' and labor union education, prefaced by a useful historical introduction. He suggests that its pursuit has moved through three phases: workers' education in the traditional sense, labor education as a means of improving union operations, and education as an aspect of management-labor studies.

Women's Education

The special needs of women for education have been a topic of concern in the literature since the 1930s; however, as yet no volume seems to have linked this theme with the women's movement in any deeply analytical or sustained fashion. In one sense, that movement, particularly insofar as it is concerned with consciousness raising, may be seen as a vast adult educational enterprise—both for women themselves and for the people and institutions that they seek to influence. Yet the subject remains only an often-discussed topic that awaits substantial book-length analysis.

A first approach to the subject was made by Ely and Chappell (1938), who studied the voluntary efforts of women's associations to provide education for their members. An important element of the women's movement in the United States consisted of efforts to educate women working in industry. As Kornbluh and Frederickson (1984) show, significant efforts began as early as 1914 and were still continuing at the time their book was written, though the most significant thrusts were made in response to the Great Depression of the 1930s. They were led by eminent women of the time, including Eleanor Roosevelt. McGlynn (1977) provides a historical and theoretical study of education for women and reports on a questionnaire study of the subject carried out in the Delaware Valley region. In this highly developed part of the country, the needs of women for more education and for programs especially fashioned for their requirements are great, as the author demonstrates in her recommendations for improvement.

Special services for women enrolled in colleges and universities became a topic of substantial interest in the early 1970s. Astin (1976) reported on a study of this subject conducted by the American Council on Education. The book was written by leaders of this emerging movement and vividly describes their own accomplishments and hopes. The data summarize the practices of a sample of fifteen colleges and universities and the results of a questionnaire answered by women who were current or recent students. Analyses were also made of the attitudes of the husbands of these women. Mendelsohn, in a book entitled *Happier by Degrees* (1980), contributes a practical guidebook, full of case studies and examples, concerning college reentry for women and the ways of solving the problems that they encounter. Lewis (1988) seeks to assist continuing educators to meet the requirements of nontraditional women students. The authors of the papers included define the context of returning women's participation, their characteristics, and their concerns. Not restricted to higher education, the book includes programs of business and industry, as well as community-based organizations.

Belenky, Clinchy, Goldberger, and Tarule (1986) wrote a work that does not fit completely within the framework of adult education; as its title aptly states, it is concerned with *Women's Ways of Knowing*. Focusing on women during their college years and later, this book inquires into how they believe they acquired the values and insights that largely guide their lives. The authors identify the ways women learn through discovery, chance, reflection, or other means; they also assess how women learn in various social contexts. The data was derived over a period of years from in-depth interviews with a large and varied sample; the book is illuminated by quotations from those interviewed.

Community Development

There are many ways to try to improve communities, some of them locally initiated and others by intervention from outside. Many either begin with education of the citizenry or use some form of organized study to help in processes of political restructuring, economic reform, or physical rebuilding. The literature in the field shows some of the many ways by which this process has occurred.

Many of these works concentrate on programs in specific locations, most often demonstrating how a college or university worked with residents of a community. The Antigonish movement in Canada was mentioned earlier; it is described in books by Coady (1939) and Laidlaw (1961). In a work called *Community Organization and Adult Education,* Brunner (1942) discusses a five-year experiment called the County Council for Community Development—funded by a foundation and maintained in Greenville, South Carolina—to develop greater public awareness of how community needs might be met by adult education. A frank detailing is given of the successes and failures of this program and of the reasons the council was unable to continue after the grant funds had been spent. Brunner indicates how adult education is interwoven throughout the whole process of regeneration. Poston (1950) evaluates a statewide venture in Montana (also supported by foundation funds) in which the state system of higher education served as sponsor of study groups in small towns to provide the basis for improvement of the quality of life. Poston's account is reportorial and idealistic. In 1953, he followed up his earlier volume by issuing another description of a community development program. The University of Washington had taken up the idea in 1950, and Poston was engaged to direct it. In the course of doing so, he developed a detailed study guide that might be used by persons active in community development in small towns. Over the years, this document was heavily revised in the light of experience, and this book presents its ultimate version. Fordham, Poulton, and Randle (1979) examine an unusual effort in a lower-class English community to build a support structure for adult education, an effort that met with only modest success.

Kreitlow, Aiton, and Torrence (1965), three American leaders of adult education, present a balanced and comprehensive view of how the residents of small communities can work together to mobilize forces for social change and community development. Their book deals with structures, roles, and institutions but is also concerned with the dynamics of leadership. Many case studies and vignettes are woven into the text to illuminate general principles.

Some university-extension divisions have established departments of community development to work at places within their areas of service. The best documented of these was operated at the University of Virginia during the years of World War II. Two highly respected books resulted. Ogden and Ogden (1946), in their *Small Communities in Action*, describe in brief form "thirty-four stories telling how communities have helped themselves through the efforts of their own citizens" (p. xi). For the most part, these communities were small, and the work that they undertook can be grasped and described in brief compass. The authors write engagingly and provide the reader with a sense of involvement in the processes concerned. In a second work called *These Things We Tried*, Ogden and Ogden (1947) review the results of the whole statewide effort in a lucid and objective fashion; they analyze and evaluate many endeavors and, in the process, remove community development from the aura of vagueness sometimes surrounding it.

The book moves easily from case studies to generalizations, with many interesting anecdotes along the way. And though it is very much oriented to the place and time in which it was written, the volume conveys a spirit and belief in principles that profoundly reinforce its central theme.

Community development is far from being an American monopoly. Pearl Buck (1945), the Nobel Prize novelist, describes the activities of James Yen, a member of an ancient Chinese Mandarin family. Beginning at the time of World War I, Yen developed a program of mass education based on literacy, agriculture, economics, and government for poor people, particularly those in rural areas. The book is composed as a series of conversations over several days between Mr. Yen and the author, and her literary skills are put to good effect in bringing alive his ideas and personality.

Community development as an adult educational process has probably been most fully realized in the international sphere as a way that highly developed nations or international organizations work with people of less highly developed regions. Arndt (1959), aided by other authors, has created a report on the American experience in this respect, along with illustrations to suggest how such enterprises can best be undertaken. Points of entry into primitive cultures are suggested; and though the intent is to consider all members of the community, primary focus is upon adults, as they are the most immediate creators of change. Margaret Mead begins her essay in this book with the words "From this post–World War II work there has come . . . a new evaluation of adult learning, a recognition that adults, in any culture, have learned to be human, have learned about language, social organization, tool-using, and the family; and they have learned that learning a second language, a new form of social life, a new set of tools, is profoundly different in kind from the first learning of a child" (p. 93). Poston (1962) makes vivid proposals for ways by which community development (based at least in part on adult education) could help people in underdeveloped countries to improve the quality of their lives. He spent two years in various parts of the world working with governmental and private ventures and describes his findings both analytically and using a number of case studies. Mezirow (1963) supplies an account of a very large national program of community development conducted by the government of Pakistan from 1952 until 1961. He explores the full range of social and economic development attempted in this program but gives special attention to the elements within it that might be considered as adult education. Biddle and Biddle (1965) thoroughly treat the theory and processes of community development as a movement. Their book is direct and practical and has many case studies and a well-annotated and extensive bibliography.

Shields (1967) has analyzed "the philosophy, the functions, and the operations of United States technical assistance activities in the field of community development in order to discover the role education plays in intergovernmental programs in community development" (p. 114). The key institution described is the Agency for International Development and its predecessor organizations in the federal government. Shields traces the influence of education in this massive worldwide program and establishes its central importance in the efforts undertaken.

After World War II, Britain felt a responsibility to help less well developed nations of the Commonwealth to build economic, social, and political capacities. One such effort included many activities lumped together under the general term *community development*. Batten (1962) discusses a training course for the leaders of this work at the University of London. His book deals with the major themes and issues of this course; as a result, the book is largely descriptive of community development itself. DuSautoy (1962) provides a broad overview of community development as it might be created by the government of a developing nation. As the author's major experience was in Ghana, many of his illustrations are drawn from there. The book contains a valuable listing of definitions of the key terms in the field. Hall and Kidd (1978) include papers given at an international conference in Tanzania. They range widely over the whole field of adult education, but the main emphasis is on development. As Kidd points out in his introductory chapter, all the speakers at the conference "accepted some notion of 'balanced development'; that there is a component or aspect of adult education in every economic or social or political project, that adult education can never remain neutral about the issues of development, that the institutions of adult education should enlarge and focus their energies on development tasks which are of such importance that delay cannot be tolerated" (p. 7).

Several attempts have been made to explore the relationship of adult education to the community itself and to community development. Hiemstra (1972) offers a broadly theoretical work about how the concept of community may be understood and used to facilitate the educative process. He is concerned with the learning that occurs at all ages of life and with the use of all forms of structures and institutions. Carey (1970) presents papers by a number of experienced authors who consider community development in scholarly terms, devoid of the emotional and anecdotal approaches used by many authors. A deeply experienced practitioner of both adult education and community development, Roberts (1979) brings the two fields together and shows how they interact. The author's diagrams and models help in the understanding of his basic point of view, and his comments, observations, and summations along the way are penetrating and come from varied experiences and profound observation. Christenson and Robinson (1980) have assembled a group of essays by people active in various aspects of community development in America. Their basic theme has to do with the role of universities in helping local improvement enterprises. Stubblefield (1981) surveys the growth and range of current programs in community development as they are understood by a group of modern authors. Excellent bibliographies are also provided.

Education for the Elderly

The early development of adult education was hampered by the widespread assumption that adults cannot learn. Therefore, special courage was required to build programs for the men and women most advanced in age and, presumably, least able to acquire new knowledge or skills. In their comprehensive bibliography, Beals and Brody (1941) wrote that education for the aged "is a subject all but overlooked in the literature of adult education" (p. 232). But as the field grew and adults of all ages demonstrated their ability to respond to change and instruction, responses to the needs of older adults became more numerous. By 1955, Donahue could present a collection of papers written by leading behavioral scientists and educators who expressed their view that learning processes were important in extending and enriching the later years of life. These papers are hardheaded, unsentimental, and nonpatronizing in their approach to the topic, and the book is still a useful sourcebook of ideas and proposals.

As average longevity increased, it became apparent that many people would have life spans that extended significantly after their retirement from work. Teaching such people how to manage their lives in the years after employment became an important program area in most industrialized nations. Groombridge (1960) summarizes the findings of an English committee that inquired into the relevance of education to the enjoyment of leisure in later life. In the United States, highly formalized programs of preparation for retirement began to appear. Rosencranz (1975) has produced a practical guidebook for sponsors of such education in corporations, public schools, community colleges, universities, and other institutions. The book outlines the basic essential content, the resources for study available, useful addresses, an outline of the necessary elements in a preretirement course, a sample evaluation form, and an excellent bibliography. Hiemstra (1975) reports on his interviews with a large number of older adults to discover what they would like to learn and the major reasons that they did not do so. The Academy for Educational Development (1974) briefly explores a large national inquiry on the provision of education for old people, especially by colleges and universities. Numerous illustrations are given of then-current programs and of individuals who have profited from continuing their learning activities prior to and following their retirement from active working life. Cross and Florio (1978) have expanded the study sponsored by the Academy for Educational Development. The emphasis of the book is upon the pleasures of learning for its own sake and for the enjoyable use of leisure. De-Crow (1975) provides a general and somewhat impressionistic survey of specialized programs for senior citizens, as well as of their participation in broader study opportunities. Okun (1982) has edited a collection of papers on the application of life-span developmental psychology; the scope of offerings for older adults; the nature of institutional sponsorship by the church, the public school,

the community college, and the county commission on aging; and
major issues in the field.

The special involvement of colleges and universities in education of the aging has received some notice in the literature. Weinstock's *The Graying of the Campus* (1978) is a pictorial account of
how such institutions have changed to accommodate their growing
number of elderly students. Included is a quotation by Maggie
Kuhn, founder of the Gray Panthers: "Most organizations try to
adjust old people to the system, and we want none of that. The
system is what needs changing" (p. 87). The book treats imagina-
tively and fully the changes that must occur on a campus if it is to
meet fully the needs of older students.

In the 1970s, the literature on education for later maturity
became more deeply analytical than before, perhaps because developmental psychology was more firmly established as a body of theory and therefore offered insights and conceptions not previously
available. It is, in fact, sometimes hard to distinguish between works
in that discipline and those in adult education. Craik and Trehub,[1]
for example, examine such topics as the influence of age on memory, problem solving, intelligence, and the plasticity and enhancement of intellectual functioning. The authors provide a lucid and
sometimes vivid account of the processes that influence all forms of
adult learning, but the authors did not consider themselves to be
writing in that field.

Two works offer systematic and complete accounts of the
special needs and processes required for the education of older
learners. Peterson (1983) presents perhaps the best general treatment
of the topic, partly because of its comprehensiveness and partly
because of its excellent survey of existing literature. Lowy and
O'Connor (1986) offer a full-scale theoretical argument for the importance, both personal and social, of learning programs in later
adulthood. The authors have gone deeply into the literature of adult
education, social work, and allied fields in order to knit together
their broad humanistic argument.

Several collections of essays also treat educational gerontol-

[1]F.I.M. Craik and Sandra Trehub (eds.), *Aging and Cognitive Processes.*
New York: Plenum Press, 1982.

ogy seriously. Sherron and Lumsden (1989) include descriptions of various significant aspects of the emerging field. Grabowski and Mason (1974) also delve deeply into the subject. The papers included by Lumsden (1985) are strongly research-oriented and review the current bodies of knowledge on such subjects as the history of the field, its philosophy, the educational needs and interests of older learners, the cognitive factors affecting adult learners, and other similar themes. Peterson, Thornton, and Birren (1986) summarize in detail the literature on major topics related to learning by adults, particularly those in the later years of life. Of special interest are a concise statement on research dealing with the ability to learn in the various ages of the life span; an account of how the aging population is influencing institutions of higher education; a study of how television influences the elderly, chiefly in specialized programs called narrowcasting; and several chapters about the influence of health upon the learning ability and activities of the aged. The authors have produced a serious and thoughtfully developed work.

Human Resources Development

Most organizational leaders feel the need to improve themselves and their employees by processes of training and other forms of development. Peffer (1932), in an early exploration of programs of this sort in industry and commerce, concludes that they were the largest component of adult education. Rowden (1937) assesses the educational work of major trade associations for their own staffs and those of their member agencies. Clark and Sloan (1958) offer a personal and broad sketch of education in American industry, along with comments and dicta arising from their survey. Various other strands of activity in organizational settings have also been described; however, these efforts did not coalesce until the 1960s, when they merged into a single area called human resources development (paralleling the change in titles of personnel departments in various kinds of employment settings). Nadler and Nadler (1989), who had written other books on this area, prepared a synthesizing volume defining its subject as follows: "Human resource development (HRD) is organized learning experience provided by employers within a specified period of time to bring about the possibility of performance improvement and/or personal growth" (p. 6). The book is intended as an introductory work and gives a comprehensive summary. It is divided into four parts: the conceptual and historical base, areas of activity, roles of practitioners, and relationships and trends. Nadler and Wiggs (1989) are concerned less with human resource development itself than with its structure and operation within the framework of a given institution. Chapters are given over to such topics as budgeting, staff training, planning, and managing facilities and equipment. Nadler and Nadler (1990) have compiled a very complete sourcebook; each of its thirty-one major chapters has been developed independently by its author. Though the focus is on American practice, reports are also made on ideas and activities from many other countries. A somewhat comparable volume is that edited by Craig (1987), which has forty-nine chapters written by sixty-one authorities in the field, almost all of them employed in business or industry. They deal with every imaginable aspect of the field. Like the Nadlers', this book is designed, not to be read, but for consultation and browsing.

Several extensive surveys of HRD in the United States have been made in recent years. Carnevale and Goldstein (1983) have contributed a data-filled monograph describing the nature and scope of employee training in American business and industry, as well as in certain "outside" providers, such as schools and colleges. Eurich (1985) has made an incisive examination of the educational provisions now being furnished by major American corporations to their employees. She considers the place that such training has in the future of commerce and industry, looks at the development of degree-granting programs, and assesses the lines of future growth. She is specifically concerned with the impact of such sponsorship on traditional formal educational patterns. Eurich (1990) offers a description of learning in the workplace, stressing innovative developments and practices and focusing on a number of themes. Among the particularly valuable sections are the nature, values, and limits of the major new techniques for learning; the problem of illiteracy and what is being done to solve it in the workplace; the significance of artificial intelligence; and the relationship of training to employment. Lusterman (1985) reports on a comprehensive study of education and training in 218 companies of various sizes. The main thrust of the report concerns the substantial increase of such training during the preceding five years. Of great value is the analysis of participation in training by job category. Two books, both published in 1988, grew out of a nationwide study of HRD guided by a board of distinguished citizens drawn from corporations, unions, and the public sector. Casner-Lotto and Associates (1988) have collected twenty-eight case studies of how leading American companies have shaped and reshaped their training strategies; each study is presented on its own terms by a professional writer engaged for that purpose. Rosow, Zager, and Associates (1988) draw together the data from these examples; they are particularly interested in how workers are trained to handle major innovations in technology. Carnevale, Gainer, and Villet (1990) make a global analysis of the estimated $30 billion spent on formal training and $180 billion spent each year on informal, on-the-job training. They also cite studies showing that such efforts account for two-thirds of productivity improvement since 1929. Their purpose is to describe such training in the United States "in terms of both who gets trained and how the training itself is organized, structured, and delivered" (p. xi).

The literature on HRD contains a number of works on research and theory building. Belbin and Belbin (1972) review studies undertaken at Cambridge University on the problems encountered by industry in training and retraining workers on the job. Nadler (1982) presents what he calls a critical events model, which moves from the identification of needs through various steps to evaluation and feedback. He thus sets HRD within the pattern of general program design in adult education. Charner and Rolzinski (1987) describe an effort by the Fund for the Improvement of Postsecondary Education of the U.S. Department of Education "to examine how educational institutions can be responsive to the changing needs of industry and adult workers and to suggest how continuing education can develop and enhance programs that integrate education and work" (p. 1). The book describes six projects sponsored by the fund. Marsick (1987) collects papers by authors primarily concerned with the learning that occurs within an organizational setting. Examples from practice are included, but the concern throughout the book is to discover basic models of practice (here called paradigms) that can most accurately describe learning in the workplace. In another collection of essays, Marsick (1988) emphasizes learning strategies for the orientation of staff to an organization and their continued development within it. Some chapters describe such institutional settings as community colleges, public schools, and research hospitals. Other chapters deal with such problem areas as staff "burnout" or the conflicts between the pressures of practice and those of education. Chalofsky and Reinhart (1988), focusing on the qualitative aspects of HRD, use for that purpose a Delphi technique applied to experts in HRD. Carnevale, Gainer, and Schulz (1990) furnish a comprehensive summary of the ways that technical workers, at all levels of competence (including the professional), are prepared in the United States. The authors have achieved a very broad perspective on the whole process of preparation and improvement of skilled workers. By the use of brief examples, they have also given concrete reality to their categories and distinctions between them. This book illustrates in excellent fashion how the concept of lifelong learning can be applied. Carnevale, Gainer, and Meltzer (1990b) report the results of a substantial study on the basic skills desired by employers. Among these are facility in learning, basic competencies, communication skills, group effectiveness, and adaptability. An allied book by Carnevale, Gainer, and Meltzer (1990a) was prepared for use in training for these basic skills. It contains many checklists, sample forms, budgets, case studies, and other examples designed to be helpful in practice.

In a work called *Models for HRD Practice*, McLagan (1989) has prepared four related but free-standing volumes that collectively report the results of a large-scale analysis of the basic patterns of HRD and suggest strategies for its future development. The four volumes are *The Research Report*, which describes the historical origins of the study, the work undertaken, and the major results (291 pages); *The Models*, which presents the major theoretical constructs evolved from the study (81 pages); *The Practitioner's Guide*, which shows how people who do HRD can use the models (99 pages); and *The Manager's Guide*, which is designed to help those who control and administer large programs (80 pages). The work is so closely tied to the special situations and language of HRD that those not engaged therein may have problems comprehending this massive scholarly effort.

Most of the books about HRD are guides to practice, intended either for directors of HRD in organizational settings or for the senior officers who direct their efforts. A specialized business library might well have several shelves of works of this sort, of which only a few can be mentioned here. Lynton and Pareek (1967) have contributed one of the first comprehensive treatments of HRD. They have based their work on the relevant social science literature, particularly that on group theory and practice; their book also has deep foundations in literature and philosophy. King (1968) evaluates what organizational training may accomplish. A liberal use of case studies, chiefly from Norway, aids in this process. Davies (1971) furnishes a highly analytical study of training in industry with carefully worked-out sequences of process and action. He is centrally concerned with the actual process of instruction and the achievement of practical accomplishments. Tracey (1974) has prepared a comprehensive work on HRD, with voluminous notes and illustrations. Michalak and Yager (1979) review their experiences as training consultants for business and industry. Their book is a distillation of what they have learned, with some reference to the literature in the field. They move simply and directly through each of the steps of program planning and execution—from the emergence of a problem to the evaluation of the program devised to correct it. Watson (1979) presents an exceptionally well written book dealing with the continuing development of managers in business and industry. Gretler (1972) examines the educational needs of persons in various kinds of public and private organizations who fall somewhere between low-level or first-line operators on the one hand and senior policy makers on the other. The problems of such middle-level personnel are hard to define, but Gretler handles them by presenting typologies of workers and of educational goals and by applying them in societies at various levels of economic and social development. Laird (1985) describes the major tasks of training directors in industry and government in an idiosyncratic way designed to appeal to his practical-minded readers. Bard, Bell, Stephen, and Webster (1987) have written a handbook for training directors, composed of a collection of brief chapters giving the essence of HRD and including many resource materials. Brinkerhoff (1987) focuses on the concepts of evaluation as they apply to different forms of HRD. Quick (1991) draws upon his twenty years' experience in executive and management development, which have already produced an equal number of books. In this volume, he extracts his essential advice for workers in his field (whom he addresses directly); his comments are buttressed by the results of interviews with some of his colleagues with positions comparable to his own.

A somewhat less need-oriented approach to HRD is presented by Johnston and Associates (1986). Their common purpose is to demonstrate the value of liberal education in both the preservice and in-service preparation of managers. Although primary attention is given to the undergraduate years, the book also deals extensively with managers' further development, using programs that transmit general skills rather than those directly related to the occupations concerned. Most of the authors are educators who work in various capacities, but the chief executive officers of CBS and General Motors also contributed papers.

HRD has now become an international concept. The nature of various countries' programs may vary, but basic similarities are present. Frank (1974) surveyed the state of various programs at the time his book was published and demonstrates how the approach to HRD in Europe is determined by the culture of each country. Kerrigan and Luke (1987) establish the importance of management education in both the public and private enterprises of underdeveloped nations. They then discuss the basic form of such education and indicate how programs can be carried out in various settings. The authors cover a large topic with economy and little anecdotal material. Kairamo (1989) reports on a high-level study conducted by the European Round Table of Industrialists, an influential group. Their survey included the education and training being done in major European countries. The approach is wholly favorable to adult education, and the conclusions reached could provide significant support for HRD among industrial leaders. In addition, some of the comparative data presented is unusual and interesting.

Most discussions of HRD are based on formal instructional

programs, but some effort has been made to discover how work experience itself can be made more educative. In practice, for example, a worker is often trained for a job by a more experienced employee. "Sitting next to Nellie" is what the English call it. Systematic use of this principle is now being reported in the HRD literature. Beginning in the mid 1930s, Reginald Revans, an Englishman, developed the idea that the best kind of management education was rooted in practice, where ideas could be developed inductively, sometimes by like-minded fellow managers; it was not some theoretical system of formal training. He called this idea action learning, and his 1982 book on the subject is a collection of fifty-two theoretical papers by himself and others. Marsick and Watkins (1990) examine what they call informal and incidental learning in a number of settings, including case studies in Sweden, Nepal, the Philippines, and elsewhere. The authors are mainly concerned with the work setting but are not limited to it. They also seek by a rigorous examination of the literature to move toward a theory of this form of learning.

Religious Adult Education

Most of the literature on religious adult education consists of works that concentrate on the transmission of tenets of individual faiths and denominations or on their special frameworks of instruction and reaffirmation. Only a few such books—those likely to be found in general libraries—are mentioned here; the others are too numerous to include, and no valid method of sampling them could be found. It should be said that most of the ones identified here have a Christian orientation and do not take into account the educative practices of other world religions.

Elias, in two books published in 1982 and 1986, has provided useful introductions to religious education. His 1982 volume is a systematic work applying the general principles of adult education to the field of religion. It is his intention to give an in-depth perspective on the subject, not to contend with its immediate practicalities. His 1986 volume brings together fifteen essays written by himself, each dealing with a special theme but collectively moving through the major areas of religious education. He presents his ideas and classifications clearly and completely.

A central quest in the literature has been to define the religious elements in the lives of people that could frame both the aims and the content of education in this subfield. In a lengthy and much admired book, Yeaxlee (1925) discusses the spiritual values transmitted by adult education in many kinds of institutions. Miller (1956) provides a serious and thorough analysis of all aspects of Christian education, especially as it is carried out by the church. Little (1959 and 1962) has collected the addresses and papers delivered at two conferences of national leaders in the field of Christian education for adults. The themes expressed are broad statements of aspiration and philosophy about the field, though a few are based on experience or data. Khoobyar (1963) offers a summation of the ideas about adult religious education; it is based on the participation of more than five thousand people in activities sponsored by various denominations in several states over a six-year period. The author is concerned with the meaning of religion as an aspect of ordinary life and emphasizes goals and content, not structure or methods. Moran (1979) presents a general essay on adult education, with special emphasis on its use for religious purposes and in religious institutions. The author is less interested in methodology and structure than in the key ideas and concepts that must be involved in all thought on this subject. Hughes (1981) makes an effort to work carefully through the identification of those traits desirable in a truly religious person ("a person of faith") and in those who are teacher-facilitators, program planners, and administrators of religious adult education. The disparity between these ideal characteristics and the extent to which they are possessed by an individual indicates his or her need for religious education. Stokes (1982) describes an attempt to bring together social scientists and persons concerned with religion to discuss how morals are developed. The structure of the inquiry involved the production of a basic paper on the subject, the preparation of twelve commentaries on that paper, and discussion of the documents at a national conference. In compiling discourses on the general nature of adult religious education, McKenzie (1982) uses not only the specialized literature of writers in that field, but also more general treatments of adult education.

Foltz (1986) has edited a collection of essays on religious adult education; the author deals not so much with the church as with the more general spiritual needs of mature people. Treatments of basic principles are followed by detailed approaches to the needs of young, middle-aged, and older adults, as well as to such special problems as divorce, single parentage, and death-related situations. Vogel (1991) makes an effort to get at the core of religious experience in the life of the adult. She believes that it is the task of the teacher-mentor to help people interpret the stories and allegories of their faith to get at their deeper meaning, which can then be put into practice in their own lives and that of their communities. The book would also be helpful for those who wish assistance in guiding the evolution of their own religious feelings and actions.

As the church is the major instrument of religious adult education, many manuals and guidebooks have been devoted to how it reaches learners. Only a few general works of this sort will be mentioned here. Meland (1939) supplies a profusely anecdotal account of various educational activities for adults undertaken by a number of outstanding churches of various denominations. The book includes a useful categorization of educational activities distinctive to churches. Clemmons (1958) makes the case that education can build more effective programs by creating small groups to bring people together in dynamic interpersonal ways. This idea is attacked by Fry (1961) in a strong criticism of group dynamics, which he believes to be faddish, trivial, and doctrinaire. He goes beyond this specific attack to criticize most education in the church as useless. His distrust of such methods, he says, "does not arise out of recognizing the disparity between objectives and performance, a remarkable disparity to be sure. The disenchantment has been provoked by the objectives themselves, the way they are stated, the manner in which they have been arrived at, and the kind of wistful hoping that they are so fond of" (p. 2). After a survey of adult education in churches, Bergevin and McKinley (1961) concluded that it was being poorly handled; they viewed it as no more than an adaptation of secular children's education that ignored both the spiritual nature of the institution and the distinctive characteristics of adulthood. As a result of this conviction, they evolved what they felt was a more satisfactory method of providing education, a sustained and complex system that became known as the Indiana plan (after the state where the authors resided). Their book explains in great detail the basic theoretical foundations of this plan and many of its intricacies and fundamental processes. Havighurst (1965), a distinguished social scientist, outlines in arresting fashion how the church can serve as an educational institution during each part of the life cycle. His view is broad, but his analytical exposition is enlivened by a number of brief case studies. Apps (1972) writes simply and directly about the meaning of adult education in the Protestant church and its influence on the entire work of the institution. He uses his own experience and comments from about forty pastors whose opinions he has solicited. This is not a detailed manual; its aim is to inform readers about the church's general goals and purposes in serving adults. Peterson (1984) is concerned with the general literature of adult education as it is related to Christian churches, particularly those of Protestant denominations. The book has four parts: a largely historical orientation to the subject, a summary of the methods of teaching adults, a description of the role of adults in the church, and a definition of what is required in establishing a family ministry. Vogel (1984) broadly treats the education of older adults in churches and other religious institutions and settings. The material is drawn from the literature and from the author's extensive interviews with forty-four subjects who lived in rural and village areas in Iowa.

Religious denominations are usually interested in strengthening the understanding of their distinctive traditions and tenets of faith. Goldman (1975), in a work entitled *Lifelong Education Among Jews,* celebrates a long and deep tradition but does not dwell on programs and practices. Using many quotations, he makes the case that the tradition of education among Jews is focused more on lifelong learning than on learning in childhood. In an early work, MacLellan (1935) identifies the distinctive emphases and programs of Catholic adult education, generally in the United States. In the 1950s, Catholic scholars and educators became interested in a number of approaches to adult education in their church and its allied institutions. Miklas (1959) records the papers and proceedings of a workshop on Catholic adult education, where programs were described and analyzed by a group composed chiefly of nuns and priests.

Other Themes

Four other themes have attracted sufficient attention in the literature to warrant mention here, though they have not had as great an influence as those already discussed.

Rural Adult Education

The Cooperative Extension Service, described elsewhere, has been the dominant institution in providing education for the residents of rural areas; nevertheless, many people have been concerned that the conditions there are ameliorated far too little by adult education. In their early study, Landis and Willard (1933) set the pattern for later thought and investigation. Though they recount the accomplishments that they observed, they are far from happy about what was available in rural areas; they believe that the people who lived there were systematically deprived of educational and cultural opportunities and that a national plan of action should be followed to remedy the situation. Loomis and others (1953) report on an enormous study conducted by the Association of Land Grant Colleges and Universities. The work is approached from Loomis's discipline—rural sociology—but his collaborators included experts from many fields. The book contains chapters on libraries, churches, mass media, farmers' organizations and cooperatives, service clubs, and numerous other agencies whose work fell within the broad rubric of adult education. The book concludes with an effort to fit the diverse pieces together to create an overall picture of rural adult education. English (1959) details the efforts of West Georgia College in Carrollton to bring culture and enlightenment to its neighboring communities. This case study indicates what dedicated leaders can achieve in a college outreach program in a setting that most observers would feel to be unpromising.

Adult Education in the Arts

Eisner and Dobbs (1986), in their work on art museum education, begin by asserting, "Works of art, no matter how grand, how glorious, how great, are without consequence unless encountered by a seeing eye, a thoughtful mind, and a feeling heart. Works of art live by virtue of their capacity to shape human experience. A viewer's experience becomes artistically significant when he or she is able to treat the work in a manner relevant to its artistically important features" (p. 1). This perspective would be shared by all involved in adult education in the arts and would be especially relevant to the performing arts, which are inherently interactive between artist and audience. Mearnes (1940), whose book has been widely read, focuses on the learners rather than the producers of art by asserting his view that "adults need a special education to rescue their creative spirit from the annihilating imprisonment of conformity" (p. 38). He speculates on the nature of that special education, how it might be conducted, and what it might produce. His is an inspirational and personal narrative that relies heavily on the influence of literature and the arts to create fresh and liberating insights. He has no general program to recommend, but he does argue for collaborative groups to stimulate individual development and liberation.

Two works, both published in 1938, survey adult educational activities in two art forms. Van de Wall gives a panoramic view of activities in music education, notable to a modern reader mainly because it shows how far this country has come since the late 1930s in the breadth and depth of the acceptance of good music of all types. Carter and Ogden (1938) describe and celebrate the educational values conveyed to adults by noncommercial theater offered under many kinds of auspices. The authors are never didactic as they skillfully portray the lessons learned by those who produce and act in drama and the aesthetic and intellectual values cultivated in audiences. The authors are candid about the limitations that they encountered but discern a "development, if present trends are trustworthy indicators . . . toward a theater which is polycentered both geographically and as to auspices; toward larger and more discriminating audiences; toward increased opportunities for development and utilization of talent of actors, playwrights, and the many creative artists required by the theater; toward the continuance of experimentation with new forms, new techniques, new associations, and even new purposes" (p. 129). Many people then would not have believed the extent to which this prediction has come true.

Two English works published in the 1980s are comprehensive treatments of adult education and cultural development through the arts. Jones and Chadwick (1981) present essays by experts in various art forms and people engaged in directing British adult education. They seek "to provide practical examples of ways in which adult education and arts activities can relate" (p. 7). The resulting papers have freshness, clarity, and interest. Jones (1988) concentrates on the ways that the arts are presented to adult audiences and the kinds of learning that then ensue. Summing up, Jones states, "This book has attempted to explore the nature of culture and the nature of the arts; it has looked at the different ways in which we engage with the arts and analysed the opportunities available for such engagement. Finally, it has explored the contribution that adult education can make to the way in which we relate to the arts and to the cultural context in which we live and work" (p. 206). The author strongly urges that culture should not be understood as merely the high culture of western Europe, but that it include the products of other societies.

World Affairs Education

Many institutions today foster the study of international relations as a prominent part of their educational programs. Many specialized associations also hold this aim, in one form or another, as paramount. The literature on this area of adult education comes from an earlier time, before the revolutions in transportation and communication had progressed very far. The United States was still, to some degree, under the influence of isolationist thought, and the world's distances seemed much greater than they do today. In their 1951 work, Arndt and Everett projected a view of world affairs education that then seemed far too lofty and idealistic but now appears to have been largely realized. A short time later, Houle and Nelson (1956) speculated on the major ways that universities could educate adults to know more about and have a deeper concern for international understanding. The central feature of this book is its segmentation of potential audiences for this education and its review of how the audiences could most effectively be reached. Petersen and Petersen (1960), in their general study of university adult education, take world affairs education as a topic for special inquiry. Their view is candid and often critical and is especially useful because of that fact.

Radical Adult Education

A major concern ever since the adult education movement began has been the need to reach people who have fewer of the world's advantages than their fellow men and women. Many special themes, such as adult literacy education, have been undergirded by a wish to help the poor—though, in fact, many illiterates are persons of substantial status and income. As has been shown many times on previous pages, articulate advocates and practical activists have long been motivated by a sense that education should aim to solve the pressing personal and social problems of the disadvantaged.

A generalized theme of reform or radicalization, as it is often called, has taken form and won substantial acceptance in Europe, with some devoted followers in the United States. Brown (1975) begins her description of Freire's methods with the words, "learning to read is a political act" (p. 5). Other writers as well believe that personal accomplishments should be seen in revisionist social contexts. Volume Five of the massive report of the Organisation for Economic Co-operation and Development (1981) reviews efforts throughout the world to reach the economically deprived. A number of authors from various countries examine the theoretical and practical consequences of programs designed to achieve this purpose. In an effort to define and shape the key ideas of radical education, Thomas (1982) makes the case that all adult educational programs now and in the past can be placed on a continuum that ranges from the drastic reform of some aspect of the social order to the conservation of values and activities. He then proceeds to the analysis of the radical end of this continuum, first examining such early examples as British working-class education and the Danish folk school and then looking at present ideas and programs across the world. Lovett (1988) presents a collection of papers by people active in radical movements designed to advance peace, to protect the environment, to empower some category of people, or to change the policies of economic systems and governments.

The general idea of radicalism advanced in these books stops short of recommending changes in the basic structures of government. The English are content to work within the monarchical and parliamentary systems, and the Americans accept Congress and the presidency.

A Final Word

The seventeen themes whose literature has been noted in this and the preceding chapter are the most frequently discussed in the field's content- or audience-oriented goal areas. Many other, less fully explored aims exist, however. For example, in 1935, Gruenberg argued strongly for adult education in science (particularly that taking a liberal approach) and showed how little was being done in this respect. In 1985, McGee and Neufeldt described the nature and historical growth of education for black adults. Boggs (1991) analyzes major modern efforts to foster good citizenship by means of adult education and presents strong arguments for the improvement and expansion of efforts to achieve that goal. He draws his various themes together into twenty-eight propositions that usefully define his position. Many other examples of special advocacy or procedure could be found, some of which might well grow into major perspectives in the future.

These themes are best seen independently, though they overlap at their edges—for example, health education with family life education. But anyone who compares these separate bodies of literature will find an ebb and flow among them. Some themes (such as world affairs education and education for the arts) grow out of the relative rarity of information in their content fields; the great increase in knowledge and in ways of communicating it has meant that special advocacy is no longer as necessary as it once was. Rural adult education still has its deficiencies, but they no longer appear to warrant book-length analyses. The major drama of workers' and labor union education seems to have been played out and to have become chiefly a subject for history and retrospection. Other themes are at least as active as ever: human resources development, religious adult education, radical approaches, and women's education. New concepts are constantly appearing but have not yet achieved substantial literatures.

Reflection over this chapter and the preceding one can give rise to a sense of accomplishment. Adult literacy, health, informed parenthood, and provisions for the elderly are now the concerns of far more people than before. The lessons of group dynamics are embedded in practice, as are the root ideas of community development. If certain aspects of life are now better than they used to be, adult education can possibly be granted some credit for working out approaches that could be used in the more spacious and complex settings now available, particularly those provided by new means of communication and transportation. And perhaps this alertness to adult education as a way to deal with important issues will continue to be reflected not only in the themes already identified in these two chapters but also in goals now appearing or about to emerge.

PART THREE

The Practice of Adult Education

The field of adult education centers ultimately on the internal or external experience that influences mature learners (individually or in company with others) in mind, body, or sensitivity, bringing about a desired alteration in them or their behavior. Changes in people occur for other reasons as well: they may result from heredity, maturation, or religious transformation, or they may be by-products of habitual behavior or experiences intended to achieve other purposes. These other influences are usually subject to the disciplined attention of geneticists, psychologists, sociologists, and experts in religion and other matters. They are also, of course, the subject of speculation by everyone, including adult educators. But the field of adult education itself has ordinarily been confined to the efforts of mature people to learn and attempts by other people to help them do so. Although this is the analytical essence of practice, its applications are as varied as the people who seek to learn, the situations in which they do so, the length of their endeavors, the goals that they strive for, the methods they choose, and the helpers available. Many of the books mentioned earlier have dealt in some way with practice; the two chapters in this part focus on it directly.

TEN

Theory and
Program Design

Every teacher must know that every method invented is only
a step, on which he must stand in order to go farther; he
must know that if he himself will not do it, another will
assimilate that method and will, on its basis, go farther, and
that, as the business of teaching is an art, completeness and
perfection are not obtainable, while development and perfectibility are endless.

—Leo Tolstoy

Every field of work increases its productivity by clarifying the elements and processes of its practice. Those who have tried to improve
adult education have given much thought to probing the nature of
learning and discovering the basic patterns that would increase
quality of service. The literature dealing with such basic themes is
identified in this chapter.

Theories of Adult Learning

At the forefront of books on adult learning theory is *How Adults
Learn*, by Kidd (1973). This work is a straightforward development
of its "chief message: people of all kinds, in all places, and of all
ages have a marvelous capacity to learn and grow and enlarge"
(p. 7). With an unusual command of both theoretical and practical

Note: Epigraph taken from *Tolstoy on Education.* Chicago: University of
Chicago Press, 1967, pp. 58–59.

literature, Kidd examines the adult learner; the physical, intellectual, and affective domains of learning; and learning theory and practice, so far as adults are concerned. This book has gone through several editions, has been translated (in whole or in part) into many languages, and is probably the most widely used volume on practice throughout the world.

Many writers have drawn parallels between the education of children and that of adults. The main body of this literature has probably been produced in the middle European countries and is not available in English. *Pedagogy* (a familiar term in German) has been used to signify the study of the education of children, and (as was noted earlier) *andragogy* has been coined to describe the study of the education of adults. In defining the difference between the two stages of life, relatively little attention has been given to their fundamental scientific distinctions. Hebb,[1] for example, has shown that the physiological and psychological difference between early learning and later learning are profound; however, such bodies of evidence as his are little used in the literature of andragogy, though they might help make clear how adults learn in contrast to children. Instead, the attention of writers on this subject is devoted largely to methods of teaching. The didactic, systematized instruction said to be characteristic of children's learning is contrasted with the open, free, and diversified methods used in the education of adults. In the European literature, an often-quoted work is *Andragogik*, by Hanselmann.[2] The best-known American author to take up this theme is Knowles, who sought to establish a theoretical basis for the concepts of andragogy. It underlies his general book on programming (1980b), and another expression of his approach occurs in a work entitled *Andragogy in Action*, published in 1984. In the introductory material of the latter work, he gives his own academic and intellectual history and tells how his central ideas emerged and changed over time; this section ends with a summary of his current

[1]D. O. Hebb, *The Organization of Behavior: A Neuropsychological Theory.* New York: Wiley, 1940.

[2]Heinrich Hanselmann, *Andragogik* (Andragogy). Zurich, Switzerland: Rotapel Verlag, 1951.

beliefs. The rest of the book provides case examples of the operation of his theory in business, industry, government, higher education, the professions, religious education, and elementary, secondary, and remedial education. Still another volume by Knowles (1990) has been widely influential—as is suggested by the fact that it is now in its fourth edition. Here Knowles presents the latest and fullest available account of his theory of andragogy as it is worked out in practice, particularly in nonschool settings and most especially in the workplace. A scholar or theorist will find great value in his discussion of the development of learning theories in the literature of education and his exploration of the roots of his own thinking about theorizing. But much of the work is practical and gives concrete examples of how learning activities are planned, structured, and executed. The appendix presents case studies in some depth.

Sommer (1989) begins with an analysis of andragogy; despite his awareness of criticisms of it, he believes it to be a sound theory of adult learning and teaching. He then goes on to show how its principles can be applied in many settings as the writing skills of adults are improved.

Mouton and Blake (1984) advance the term synergogy, a concept that they feel they have firmly established after twenty-five years of worldwide development and field testing. Synergogy focuses on learning as a process in which a colleague-oriented group conducts its own education, achieving wholly by itself the knowledge, skills, and attitudes that it desires. Four synergogic models are identified and fully explained, as is the role of group facilitators of learning, known as learning administrators. The authors compare their new term with pedagogy (which they take to be the teacher-student relationship in the traditional class or training room) and with andragogy (in which the instructor serves as a facilitator rather than as an authority figure). They do not dwell on distinctions among age levels.

Freire's theories of method are expressed in all his work but are dealt with most extensively in his books published in 1973, 1985, and (in collaboration with Shor) 1987. He does not concentrate on the differences between childhood and adulthood, but it is clear in context that he believes that his teaching and learning principles are applicable distinctively to adults. In these three works, he dwells with increasing firmness and clarity on his methodological principles. The fullest exposition occurs in the 1985 volume, entitled *The Politics of Education*. In this work, he reveals more fully than before the full context of such concepts and terms as *praxis, conscientization,* the *generative word,* and other political and linguistic concerns important to his thought concerning learning patterns.

The origin of theories about adult learning does not lie entirely in the desire to distinguish the patterns appropriate at various stages of life. The effort to use research findings as a basis for theory has been demonstrated in one way or another by many authors. Brundage and Mackeracher (1980) sought to discover and catalogue basic learning principles as revealed in many kinds of investigations and to apply them to general program planning. The book ends with the presentation of thirty-six learning principles gleaned from 158 references, which are listed. Belbin and Belbin (1972) describe the discovery of such principles in studies conducted at the Industrial Training Research Unit at Cambridge University. The book reports in graphic detail and usually from the viewpoint of the learners how various kinds of learning problems were encountered and handled. Among the topics are overcoming anxiety in older learners, teaching a high-speed manual skill, breaking the literacy barrier, keeping supervisors up to date, and using self-assessment as a focal point of adult retraining. The book concludes with a summary of the strategies of training identified in such research.

The learning acquired from experiences other than those of conventional instruction has been often noted and sometimes studied. One important line of investigation in this respect occurred in the nontraditional higher educational movement beginning in the 1960s. This endeavor was focused in the work of CAEL, a federation of scholars and administrators first named the Cooperative Assessment of Experiential Learning and later called the Council for the Advancement of Experiential Learning. Keeton and Associates (1976) have produced a distillation of a set of theoretical papers intended "to illuminate, and possibly to guide, the more practical work of CAEL, which was perforce proceeding at breakneck speed" (p. xvii). These papers are collected under three rubrics: rationale, characteristics, and assessment of experiential learning. The authors were free, however, to deal with an assigned topic as they wished, an approach that led to individualized variations on a common theme. Keeton and Tate (1978) present a more systematic approach to the nature of and practical approaches to experiential learning. Cell (1984) and Kolb (1984) offer more theoretical analyses of it.

The disciplines of psychology and sociology have both been used as bases for theories of adult learning. Miller (1964) treats the general aspects of adult learning, the ways in which it differs from that of children, and the major settings in which such learning occurs: small groups of various sorts; autonomous study; and large-group learning, both face-to-face and by use of mass media. Lovell (1980) has based his work on research findings but states his conclusions simply and directly. The resulting book is a brief and clear exposition of various kinds of learning, their general application, their usefulness in many situations and for different types of personality and ability, and their adaptation at different stages of life. Jarvis (1987a) expresses his belief that adult learning theory should be much more based on sociological studies than is currently the case. He seeks to redress this imbalance by examining the social context in which learning occurs and that he feels to be important in influencing the learner.

The desire to assess the literature of childhood education for its value to adult learning is exemplified in Verduin's (1980) work on curriculum building. His advanced and theoretical study is grounded in concepts of formal curriculum analysis as it has developed in graduate departments of education. Griffin (1983) is also concerned with how the customary meanings of the term *curriculum* can be interpreted in nonschool settings, particularly insofar as the concept of lifelong learning is concerned. Special attention is given to Ettore Gelpi's conception of such learning and its relationship to the ideas of Illich and Freire.

Argyris (1976) has developed what he calls a theory of "double loop" learning, which aims "to change underlying values and assumptions" (p. ix). He believes that this learning theory encourages the growth of "a learning environment that helps people to discover their present theories of action and unfreeze them, and that helps them to learn a new theory that can help slow down and ultimately reverse" the handling of problems they are encountering

(p. x). He evaluates in great depth the learning experiences, both collectively and separately, of six presidents of sizable companies who worked with him and provided examples that helped to develop and test his theories.

Collins (1987) uses the philosophical concepts of phenomenology to analyze and criticize the idea (then prevalent) that learning should accomplish sharply defined changes in the learner. He argues that emphasis on seeking competence and measuring its exact outcomes is detrimental to the growth and development that might occur if the philosophical principles that he espouses were applied.

In contrast to the foregoing references, other theories of adult learning are more loosely textured. *Open learning,* a term and concept that had some advocates in the latter half of the 1970s, called for reducing restrictions on adult students and creating new avenues of learning. MacKenzie, Postgate, and Scupham (1975) survey the nature and extent of efforts to increase learning opportunities throughout the world, with special reference to distance education. Davies (1977) has made a thoughtful attempt to describe the theories behind open learning and to provide descriptions of how it worked out in practice in a number of British programs and institutions. Cleugh (1970) reviews the learning processes of groups in various situations and shows (in an idiosyncratic foreword) how theory is influenced by the awareness of broader practice. Grabowski (1983) has edited a series of papers dealing with the ways by which learning is translated into changed performance and what the developer of programs can do to assure that the desired changes occur. Smith and Associates (1990) present a collection of papers exploring the meaning of the learning process and means of advancing it at various stages of childhood and adulthood. Although the treatment is essentially theoretical, many taxonomies of practice and lists of relevant elements are included.

Adult learning theory has progressed far enough so that existing patterns of thought have been subjected to extensive critiques. Niebuhr (1984) feels that new paradigms of learning are required to meet the challenges to our society suggested in the writings of current best-selling analysts like Naisbitt, Reich, Toffler, and others. Brookfield (1986) subjects current learning theory to a sharply detailed examination. The methodology of adult education, Brookfield contends, is flawed by wishful thinking, unverified assumptions, and dogmatic practice. He distinguishes between the additive, content-oriented thought of many practitioners and theorists and his own conception of learning; this he regards as facilitation in which a guide helps a learner, often in sophisticated ways, to progress in reaching the goals that both believe are the next achievements to be mastered. The author's extensive experience in three countries and his command of a wide range of literature help him make a convincing analysis.

Apps (1985) finds that the improvement of practice in continuing education comes about by the rigorous scrutiny of programs by the educator responsible for them. His book consists of the description of a number of the ways an analytical framework can be developed by a consideration of the elements in the program theory used by the leader. Apps stresses the need for individuals to select and refine their own methods of self-evaluation to the consequent enlargement of their understanding of whatever theory of practice they are following.

The Basic Design of Operation

Adult education would be greatly strengthened if those who worked in it believed that they followed a common pattern of action growing out of the essential nature of the field. At first glance, such similarity seems impossible. Settings, methods, and assignments are so diversified that they appear to have no common basis of action. Librarians, lecturers, counselors, administrators, broadcasters, and occupiers of other roles seem to work in unique ways. But some analysts have looked deeply at practice and believe that they have found that the many different approaches do, in fact, follow a common pattern. Moreover, many people active in the field—among them county extension directors, deans of evening colleges, and administrators of human resources education—simultaneously design and conduct a number of diverse programs, while other individuals move sequentially through several roles, all of which they believe to be concerned with adult education. This section will identify some of the efforts to discern and describe a basic design of operation.

The most widely accepted such book is *The Modern Practice of Adult Education* by Knowles, first published in 1970 and issued in revised form in 1980. In 1950, Knowles had published a precursor work known as *Informal Adult Education,* whose value has not been diminished by the popularity of the later similar work. In the 1950 volume, Knowles deals essentially with open patterns of instruction in contrast to formal learning systems. In 1970, he moved to a more complete analysis, building his thought on the elaboration of his doctrine of andragogy. The 1980 revision retains essentially the same focus as the first edition but has been complemented by the author's further experience and reflection. The book has three main focuses: a description of the emerging role and technology of adult education, a thorough treatment of how large-scale programs of adult education should be organized and administered, and an analysis of how adults can best be helped to learn. The book is full of illustrations and exhibits that create a vitality not often found in overviews of the subject.

Houle (1972) furnishes a basic structure for program design that is descriptive of the work of the field and that serves as the basis for further knowledge derived from experience and study. Houle identifies eleven basic situations in which programs are planned and develops each one by the use of principles and examples. He believes that the process of program operation is the same in all situations and outlines the fundamental framework of components that must be applied (though in different ways) to each such setting.

Davis and McCallon (1974) have called their book *Planning, Conducting, and Evaluating Workshops,* but this title is deceptive; the authors are concerned, not with a single method of instruction, but with providing a program-planning guide for all adult education. Although some principles are suggested, most of the book is a compilation of techniques, instruments, and other specific means of teaching adults.

McLagan (1978) has produced a series of flow charts designed to help course planners and analysts understand program-planning principles, from the definition of objectives to the measurement of results. This is a very lean and theoretical analysis of program planning.

Green and others (1980) report on an all-encompassing master design that they have developed for the planning, delivery, and evaluation of programs of health education. They call their design PRECEDE, "an acronym for predisposing, reinforcing, and enabling causes in educational diagnosis and evaluation" (p. 11). It would have broad applications for many forms of adult education.

Lenz (1980) begins with an analysis of the history and nature of continuing education and goes on to consider trends leading to a new future. She suggests programs likely to win a wide response in days to come. Her emphasis is on the building of new programs, not on the promotion of courses that have already been created.

Knox and Associates (1980a) present the work of a number of authors who aim to provide "a comprehensive overview of concepts and practices related to adult education program development and administration" (p. xiii). The topics consider both total program operation and such aspects of it as staffing and leadership.

Boyle (1981) is concerned with the dynamic aspects of program planning and administration. In his effort to develop a complete system of planning for adult educational activities, he uses the whole field as his base and discusses such key problems as the general character of programming, methods of fitting it into organized structures, ways to involve people at various stages of the process, the identification of problems and needs, the design of specific activities, and the determination and communication of program values. Boyle draws widely on his own experience and on the relevant literature and includes many useful lists of activities and alternatives.

As analyses of basic patterns of practice appeared, later authors began including reviews of earlier models in the presentation of their own systems. Boone (1985) provides a good example of this trend by beginning with a description and comparison of earlier program-planning formulations. He then synthesizes and fits them within his own conceptions. He also interweaves examples and illustrations that have grown out of his experience and that of his students (who, he says, often refer to his own model as "Booneology" because of its idiosyncratic nature). Langenbach (1988) argues clearly and forcefully that practical adult educators must have an awareness of program design because they, unlike the teachers of children and youth, must often engage in the task of constructing their own basic work formats. The author summarizes the major program-design models now available in the literature. He assesses, in addition, specialized programs of service, including literacy education, continuing professional education, and self-directed learning.

University extension includes many different educational formats; therefore, works on program planning and administration in that setting are relatively common. Two volumes cover a wide range of activities and processes. Strother and Klus (1982) focus on the knowledge that administrators should possess about how to initiate, design, conduct, and evaluate the programs they operate. The basic point of view is that of the generalist administrator, who wants to provide oversight without becoming involved in detail. Simerly and Associates (1987) present a collection of essays written by seasoned but relatively young university administrators and by professors of adult education. They are concerned with how an organization can design itself and its component parts in such a fashion as to retain freshness and vitality—putting new ideas into action and evaluating their accomplishments. General theories of strategic planning are analyzed, and attention is paid to several managerial problems—such as the relationship of the continuing educational program to its parent institution, to community and economic development, and to such specialized tasks as marketing.

Two other works should also be noted because of their implications for all program design, though each restricts itself primarily to one setting. The authors of *Fostering the Growing Need to Learn* (1974) were fundamentally concerned with the continuing education of health professionals, but that theme is itself so wide-ranging that the essays included have broad or even universal relevance. Thus, one monograph (by Alexander N. Charters and R. J. Blakely) defines how continuing education can be used as a model of problem-solving strategy within organizations. In another monograph in this volume, Alan Knox covers the whole subject of life-long, self-directed education. Caffarella (1988) wants to explain the essential ideas of program development to "persons responsible for planning and evaluating training programs in all types of organizations, from business and industry to hospitals and voluntary associations" (p. 1). Basic theories are quickly summarized, and

Caffarella identifies the sources of her own theoretical constructs. The book contains numerous brief case examples and provides worksheets and charts to be used by those who want to follow her general plan.

Aspects of Program Design

Most elements of program design have been accorded special attention in the literature. Some, such as counseling and evaluation, have seemed to fit more appropriately in earlier parts of this book; still others will be mentioned here.

How to Teach Adults

The rapid growth of adult educational activities in recent years has made it necessary to help many leaders do their work effectively. Some are teachers in schools and colleges but feel that they need to know how to meet the challenge of working with men and women. Some have never had any experience in guiding instruction. And others want to enhance their skills. Responding to the need for improved instruction, many institutions have issued books and pamphlets describing the principles of teaching in their special environments or with their distinctive methods. Other works have had a larger scope, dealing generally with the methods by which all adults can best be taught, usually in group settings. We are concerned here only with the books in this latter group.

Dees (1965) presents the views of British university faculty members, some of them tutors in extramural departments, on the best ways to teach categories of subject matter, such as economics, foreign languages, and psychology. A full bibliography of British sources is included.

Mills (1977) has published the third version of his book, one that benefits from lessons learned by the users of the previous editions. He incorporates not only the fruits of his own lifetime as an instructor, but also the products of research on the learning process. He has worked in a number of countries and believes that his principles are widely applicable. He also includes a number of adages and quotations found to be stimulating to earlier audiences.

Dickinson (1973) considers the nature of adult learning, the characteristics of the adult learner, course planning, instruction, and evaluation. On each of these topics, a brief description of content is given, along with advice on how to put the knowledge into practice. A self-instructional feature is also built into the volume by the provision of pre- and postreading tests for each chapter.

Langerman (1974) has edited a group of essays by seasoned teachers of adults who examine various topics related to a general theme. The material is presented simply and directly and is centered on the perceived needs of teachers, particularly those just beginning to serve. Sample chapter themes are facing fears about teaching adults, recognizing how the group environment affects learning, selecting appropriate instructional materials, and evaluating student progress.

Curzon (1976) focuses on teaching in *further education* programs. This British term refers "to education, full- and part-time, provided outside the school system for those above the statutory school-leaving age, excluding the work of the universities and colleges of education" (p. 181). This book, brief but full of highly condensed knowledge, serves as an introduction to learning theory and its application to the myriad forms of instruction included within further education.

Verduin, Miller, and Greer (1977) have chosen the provocative title *Adults Teaching Adults*. At the heart of their book is a treatment of the central aspects of the teaching-learning process, with attention to such matters as objectives, program plans, methods, and evaluation. Of special value are the illustrations of various principles. Preceding and following the basic analysis are assessments of adult educational topics.

Knox (1980b) is perhaps more interested in describing good teaching than in prescribing principles to be followed. Each of the chapter authors in his book deals with an aspect of the teaching of adults. Thus, one of them provides five accounts of how successful teachers do their work, another describes how instruction should occur in adult basic education, and still another discusses correspondence instruction. Knox, as volume editor, provides an overall summary on the effective teaching of adults.

Hiemstra and Sisco (1990) advocate the importance of personalizing instruction in all forms of adult learning facilitation. They describe many methods of achieving individualization in a variety of situations by the use of many processes. Brief case studies and practical guides are introduced throughout.

Eight works seek to state the essentials of adult teaching in an accessible fashion. Lenz (1982) offers a collection of notes about teaching adults that is loosely organized and intended to be immediately helpful to people who are working with groups. Moore and Poppino (1983) furnish a practical volume, complete with exercises and study plans, for everyone who guides the learning of another. Draves (1984) has produced a simply written compendium of useful advice about how to teach what might be called low-cognitive popular courses for adults. Cranton (1989) provides a methodical approach to the sequence of processes beginning with the appraisal of the audience and continuing through to the evaluation of learning and of instruction. Another work by Cranton (1992) is primarily concerned with transformative learning, self-directed learning, and other less established forms and processes of education. Crux (1989) deals with methods of teaching adults who have learning disabilities. Cantor (1992) is primarily concerned with designing instructional systems for adult audiences. Apps (1991) contributes the counsel of an experienced master teacher of adults on the processes and techniques of his craft. The book is written directly in the second person and would be instantly useful to any teacher-mentor of adults. Little attention is given to theory, but an underlying point of view is implicit.

Two authors go systematically beyond classroom teaching. Rogers (1989), in the third edition of her work, incorporates learning by discovery, by the use of mass media, by correspondence, and by other means. As a straightforward and direct guide, it grows out of the wide experience of its author and is encouraging and helpful throughout. Though generally concerned with the facilitation of learning, Daloz (1986) focuses directly on the mentoring process, particularly of a sustained sort. Daloz analyzes the many and subtle levels characterizing such a relationship and portrays this complex form of learning in several carefully analyzed case studies.

Methods of Teaching

It is sometimes assumed that adult education has only one technique or that there is a recognized hierarchy in which some methods are always better than others; in earlier days, for example, discussion was believed by some people to be the best way to provide the pooled experience that would assist the learning of mature people. The major thrust in the literature, however, has been to identify and describe all the techniques that might be used, assuming that educators could choose the ones most appropriate to the overall pattern of the instructional design. Some books concentrate on methods themselves, whereas others stress the selection and mastery process that leads ultimately to a personal style for each leader.

An early comprehensive work is supplied by Mueller (1937), who reviews the major methods of teaching and learning, such as the lecture, the discussion, and the use of learning aids. Bergevin, Morris, and Smith (1963) provide a compressed handbook, intended to give beginning leaders a broad perspective on the essentials of program planning, with specific reference to the techniques and aids used in a wide variety of settings. Verner and White (1965) have compiled an anthology of previously published papers dealing in some fashion with the instructional processes of adult education. Aker (1965) has assembled an annotated and classified bibliography of research studies, descriptions of practice, and essays on methodology during the period from 1953 through 1963. Stephens and Roderick (1971) have collected a group of essays by leading educators of adults in Britain. They treat many themes and topics concerning the learning and teaching of adults. By covering many different forms of instruction and practices used in a variety of situations, the authors attempt to knit together the whole field of adult education in a descriptive rather than a prescriptive way.

Morgan, Holmes, and Bundy (1976) have completed the third edition of a widely popular book. The democratic principles of the field are set firmly in place, and attention is given to what the authors regard as the basic principles of adult education. The authors' overriding interest, however, is in methods of face-to-face instruction—one chapter being devoted to each method or cluster of methods.

Two more recent comprehensive treatments of the formats and methods of instruction are available. Seaman and Fellenz (1989) evaluate the various ways that adults can be taught and the distinctive values of each method as a strategy for encouraging learning. Their book is clearly and fully developed and informs its ideas and suggestions with the use of both research and extended personal experience. Galbraith (1990a) draws together papers written for the most part by academic adult educators. Introductory chapters lay the groundwork for later treatments of such specific methods as lecturing, discussion, correspondence study, and computer-enriched discussion. This work is an interesting contrast to those published earlier and demonstrates the growth of maturity in the field.

Over a period of twenty years, Klevins has published four editions of a work entitled *Materials & Methods in Adult and Continuing Education;* only the 1987 edition is cited here. This book is a labor of devotion. As a young instructor in the UCLA extension program, the author sensed the widespread national need for the improvement of methods and materials in adult education, worked out an elaborate outline, and persuaded a substantial number of leaders in the field to write chapters. In subsequent editions, the pattern of topics and authors has changed somewhat, though the theme remained the same. In the 1987 edition, emphasis is placed on international topics and on the eradication of illiteracy.

Several works emphasize the analysis and description of methods less than their incorporation into the practice of the leader. In an effort to get away from the atomistic use of separate techniques and processes, Solomon, Bezdek, and Rosenberg (1963) consider the total teaching style of an instructor. The authors explore the extent and nature of previous research and present the results of a study they undertook. Rogers (1986) assumes that teachers will find themselves in a multitude of situations for which they need to be prepared. The aim of the book is to serve as a guide to leaders when they assume their first responsibility and later throughout their careers as they find new and different ways to carry out their missions. Hayes (1989) offers a symposium wherein the authors use various meanings for the key terms; however, they are all concerned with examining the distinctive approach that a leader in any teaching-learning transaction uses to achieve desired instructional purposes. Hayes argues that "the most important skill for teachers ultimately may not be expertise with particular methods as much as it is the ability to engage in a process of critical reflection on the process and outcomes of instruction in relation to the demands of a particular context and an explicit set of values" (p. 1). Galbraith (1991) is concerned with the precise point at which the adult learner interacts with a facilitator of some sort or with resource materials necessary to provide and support learning. Many theories and methods are suggested for analyzing this interaction and for applying such analysis to learning theory and planning. Hiemstra (1991) defines a learning environment as "all of the physical surroundings, psychological or emotional conditions, and social or cultural influences affecting the growth and development of an adult engaged in an educational enterprise" (p. 8). Each chapter author describes one or more elements, including the physical environment, the initial social contact, the external barriers and tensions of the learner, and the difficulties imposed by racism and sexism. The introduction and final chapter provide syntheses of these various strands of influence. Sork (1991) presents the reflections of several highly experienced educators of adults on what the educator can learn for future reference when mistakes are made in some activity or program. Among the book's specific topics, usually handled in fresh and interesting ways, are identifying the most common kinds of mistakes and ways to prevent them, deciding ultimately whether a program has been a failure, detecting and remedying crucial flaws, and profiting from mistakes. This book is an interesting and rewarding exploration of the pathology of adult education.

Two authors base their ideas upon their experience as facilitators of learning. Bateman (1990), thinking chiefly about instruction in the community college classroom, is interested in how learners can be stimulated to seek information and understanding and thereby acquire a sense of fulfilled inquiry. His book is styled and written in an unorthodox fashion. Brookfield (1990) offers a personalized account of what the author has learned about teaching in twenty years of experience with graduate-level sessions or courses where many students are experienced practitioners of adult education. The first third of this book describes how he came to have an orientation to method broader than before; the second two-thirds is made up of sharply worded dicta (such as "be ready to admit your errors" or "evolve consensual rules"); these might be useful to teachers in many kinds of instructional settings if they are stimulated to reflect on their own experiences.

Supplementing the generalized approach of the foregoing books are others that deal broadly with the methods used in a specific setting or subject area of adult education. Several will be mentioned briefly here. Wilson and Gallup (1955) give an overview of the major methods used in the Cooperative Extension Service. Particular attention is paid to informal contact methods, the use of indirect influences, and the employment of nonprofessional local leaders. These methods are here treated one by one, but they are also reinforced by statements having to do with motivation, evaluation, and other topics. A great deal of practical wisdom and procedure is packed into brief compass. Zoll (1969) provides a detailed manual describing simulation methods used in industry. Among the suggested techniques are case studies, role playing, in-basket response, and business games. Mackie (1981) offers a collection of essays by American devotees of Paulo Freire, with emphasis on his techniques of teaching (especially his use of generative words). Lippitt and Lippitt (1986) offer essays by authors with long experience as consultants in personal and social situations. They view the range of techniques used as having purposes and consequences of an educative sort.

Helping Adults Increase Their Learning Skills

We turn now to learners to ask how they may be helped to acquire the ability to make the most of their educative opportunities. This section deals first with books focused directly on actual or potential participants in instructional activities and then on works intended for leaders who want to foster good learning habits in others.

Books designed to aid learners or would-be learners tend to be written simply and directly and to offer support and encouragement. Houle (1964) uses the results of a large-scale inquiry to address the chief problems reported by adult students and to help them map out a learning program and accomplish its various processes. Hoping to encourage adults to learn, Shute (1968) uses a wide range of appeals, cites arguments from many sources, and is sometimes evangelistic in his approach. Lenz and Shaevitz (1977) are concerned chiefly with adults who wish to enter or reenter formal patterns of higher education. Their book is unusually attractive in format, provides many pictorial and verbal illustrations, and makes excellent use of the literature. It is directed more at interpretation and understanding than at how-to procedures. Moore and Bostaph (1979) also design their work specifically for adults who want to resume formal schooling in some form or at some level. Their writing is accessible, and their ideas are practical; much use is made of organizing and simplifying diagrams. This book was written after the establishment of many of the new forms of nontraditional learning, and the reader is advised about how to take advantage of the opportunities that they offer. Apps (1978) provides a sensible and useful book, combining reassurance about the feasibility of further study with helpful exercises and principles. The returning learner is helped to solve the problems likely to be found in formal systems of study, and the suggested exercises and other aids are based on sound theory and illuminated by anecdotes illustrating successful practice. Apps (1982) goes beyond his 1978 book by focusing on writing skills, suggesting exercises helpful to people having difficulty in this respect, and indicating how they can develop learning plans. Smith (1982) argues that it is important for learners to strengthen their personal learning styles. He also deals with practical matters, chiefly those related to the various ways that learning occurs: self-direction, collaborative study, educational institutions, reflection about experience, use of mentors, use of mass media, and use of computers. Smith's emphasis is on conveying insight more than on giving rules or practical hints. In a second edition of their work, Haponski and McCabe (1985) have created a useful guide to educational and career planning for adults that examines general approaches, as well as the multitude of problems that such people often encounter. The authors include many interesting profiles of men and women who have successfully participated in study programs.

A second cluster of books is intended to help teachers, administrators, mentors, and other leaders who want to aid their students to learn better in their present settings or to develop broader or longer programs of study. Brew (1948) offers an engaging essay celebrating the idea that learning can be introduced into the lives of all adults. Beneath its lively and anecdotal surface, the book makes excellent methodological points. Gibbs's work (1981) was written for beginning students in institutional settings. It provides several group exercises that can help internalize good habits of independent learning for those whose only experience has been with classroom and other didactic instruction. Boud (1981) includes essays from scholars all over the world who write about the practical ways in which the independent capacity to learn is developed, particularly among students in postsecondary institutions. The authors realize that it is not easy to become a self-directed learner, but they have realistic and insightful suggestions about how to bring about the desired change. Apps (1981) has prepared his book for teachers and administrators on college and university campuses who want to know how to handle the increasing number of adults enrolling for postsecondary study. He has supplemented his own experience and a close study of relevant literature with interviews on several campuses with faculty members who have gained reputations as outstanding teachers of adults. Smith (1983) has collected essays about how learning can be internalized as a continuing lifelong process. Among the topics are the reorientation of adults to formal instruction, means of fostering self-directed learning, the improvement of autonomous groups' collaborative learning, ways to help students extract meaning from experience, and the potential of state-of-consciousness psychology to create new patterns of awareness. Rosenblum (1985) unites the work of several contributors who believe "that the most significant learning occurs when adult students and their instructors together plan the learning process and together participate in carrying it out" (p. 1). One chapter deals with discussion as a way of drawing upon the experience of learners. Another assesses guided learning experiences in cultural institutions. The tone throughout is more theoretical than pragmatic. Knox (1986) offers guidance for any individual who serves as a teacher, mentor, counselor, or other leader of adult educational activities. He writes in the second person and aims to provide help to the nonspecialist adult educator in understanding the whole learning "transaction," as the author refers to it. The main value of this book is that it brings the entire theoretical literature on the subject to an appropriate focus in actual practice.

Learning Materials

The distinction between methods and materials has proved to be harder and harder to draw. In earlier years, the differentiation appeared to be clearer than it is today. Lyon (1937), for example, devotes her attention to the selection of books for adult study groups. She pays greatest attention to the inherent elements of the materials themselves and relatively little to the situations in which they will be used. Today, methods and materials blend together to such an extent that any of the works mentioned in the previous section might well have been included in this one. But there are still some books concentrating on materials.

Wilson (1983) brings together the work of several authors who consider how instructional materials can be chosen or shaped by planners of or participants in various adult educational activities. Although this theme resists generalization, the authors succeed in giving substance to such topics as adaptation of materials to the physical and psychological changes of older adults, selection and use of resources in adult basic education, materials available for nontraditional study and the natural learning of adults, and resources for teaching problem solving to adults.

Noble (1980), using the term *resource-based learning*, advances the idea of a system of instruction in which "students are given direct access to stored knowledge, teachers taking on a role more as consultants and tutors than as instructors" (p. 15). The author provides an illustration: "Picture the learner in a resource-based system: busy with set tasks from a course workbook; submerged in a world of sound with head-set and cassette player; trying to solve decision-making problems with other students before rejoining a patient computer terminal; tuning in to radio and television transmission; scanning a set of slides to find essential information; seeking out a teacher for help or guidance to other sources" (p. 15). In a fully developed and well-illustrated fashion, the author analyzes the learners and the institutions in which resource-based education occurs. Clarke (1982) describes the proliferation of materials of instruction produced both in customary ways and in such learning formats as distance education, the use of mass media, and computerized instruction. His fundamental concern is with the way that these resources can be used by British adult students engaged in formal processes of instruction.

Lewis (1986) moves to the borderline between methods and materials in a book entitled *Experiential and Simulation Techniques.* It includes chapters by various authors covering resource-based techniques—such as educational videos, computer simulations, trips and tours, and theater—and their use in achieving general and specific goals: removing cultural blinders, enhancing managerial functions, and learning by doing in the workplace.

Learning contracts have been an important form of experiential education for both young people and adults. Berte (1975) defines such contracts as "written agreements or commitments between a student and a faculty member or faculty committee regarding a particular amount of student work and the institutional reward or credit for this work" (p. vii). Berte shows how such agreements can ensure the individualization of education both on campus and off and outlines their use in a number of experimental programs. Knowles (1986) considers both institutional programs and separate mentor-learner relationships. His basic emphasis is upon the free, open, and self-initiated study that he believes to be characteristic of adults.

Administration

Complex adult educational programs require supervision to strengthen and coordinate specific teaching and learning situations where direct services are provided to learners.

Snow (1955) believes that "the total adult education movement in America is vast, experimental, formless and diverse" (p. vii), and contends that an important way to develop it systematically would be for administrators in local communities to work more efficiently. He examines such matters as the definition of goals, the identification and use of resources, the training and supervision of leaders, and the development of better public relations. Kempfer (1955) has written a similar work, intended "primarily as

a practical guide for directors of adult education in a broad range
of agencies and community organizations" (p. vii). Although
Kempfer is especially interested in how public school adult education operated at the time of publication, the book's reference base
is broader than that. Shaw (1969) also focuses on the local public
school, but he is generally concerned with how institutions can best
plan, develop, and channel their supporting services to make them
most effective in providing learning opportunities.

Langerman and Smith (1979) deal realistically (and using a
wealth of illustrations) with the establishment of a sound framework on which planning and innovation must ultimately be based.
Such topics as budgeting and fiscal management, program evaluation and follow-up, needs assessment, managerial role and style,
and staff leadership are discussed. The book is particularly valuable
because its general principles have been arrived at inductively, rising out of practical experience. The authors move well beyond the
"recipe" stage to relate the principles of good management to the
essential purposes of adult education.

Votruba (1981) assesses the situation in which adult education is but one of the services performed by institutions (such as
schools, community colleges, universities, libraries, industrial corporations, and professional associations). In such cases, as has been
noted in previous chapters, adult education is often perceived to be
of marginal importance. In this book, a group of authors address
the topic of how greater institutional support can be provided for
this function.

Financing and Budgeting

One aspect of administration that has been marked in the literature
for special study has to do with securing and managing funds. This
subject was first addressed by Kidd (1962) in a study that touches on
most aspects of finance but analyzes none of them deeply. Another
comprehensive work is by Shipp (1982), who explains basic financial concepts and procedures; the thrust of his book makes it more
of a procedural resource for administrators than a study in the field
of adult education itself.

Aspects of financial management have been given special

attention by several authors. Matkin (1985) provides both an understanding of budgeting procedures and advice on undertaking them by those who operate adult educational programs. He begins with making cost analyses for courses and programs and proceeds to the larger structure of institutional budgeting. His experience in university extension inclines him somewhat toward that environment, but his general intention is to examine budgeting as a basic process in all agencies. Anderson and Kasl (1982) make a comparative analysis of costs incurred in the sponsorship of various forms of adult education offered by public schools, colleges and universities, proprietary occupational schools, private tutors, community organizations, professional associations, labor unions, and profit-seeking employers. In addition to detailed analyses of finances in all these situations, the authors provide a useful summary of comparative cost-benefit financing and give an analysis of its implications. Buskey (1981) has edited a practical guide in which several expert authors identify and offer approaches to sources of outside funds for the support of adult educational programs. Particular attention is given to governmental agencies and foundations as income resources.

A Final Word

The literature reviewed in this chapter has been designed to be of practical help to many kinds of workers in the field. Among them are beginners who seek assurance in making a start, experienced practitioners who have problems to solve, people who want to prepare themselves for advancement, and others who feel they could gain competence if they fully understood what it meant to be an adult educator. The sources already reviewed are supplemented by others dealing with major formats and settings of adult education; to them we now turn.

ELEVEN

Formats and Settings for Adult Learning

Knowledge knows no boundaries except the opportunity to learn.

—World Education Report, 1991 (p. 44)

Some people think about adult education in terms of complex formats or special settings in which various elements of program design fit together in distinctive ways, as in self-directed study or distance education. Seven will be considered in this chapter, though one of them (widely found throughout the United States) has not yet produced a significant literature. The dividing line between formats and methods cannot be sharply drawn. For example, in such a format as residential adult education, many methods are used; most of them are considered separately elsewhere in this book. But substantial groups of works center on the formats themselves and it is that literature which will be considered here.

Classroom Teaching

Despite all the creative inventions and special methods developed in adult education over the last century, the classroom remains the most familiar format for instruction. Its use in meeting the special requirements of mature learners has been the concern of many authors, only a few of whom can be mentioned here. Cleugh (1970) establishes a perspective on this approach by stating that his purpose is "to consider how the educative process works when its subjects are not young persons but older ones, not willing or unwilling prisoners but voluntary contractors, not green twigs but sturdy and often unbending timber—are, in short, adults with a formed outlook on life, family responsibilities, a wealth of past experience, favourable or unfavourable, and special interests, training, or expertise" (p. 9). The book is full of sensible suggestions and is expressed in the chatty, friendly manner of an experienced person talking to a beginner; the author includes many bits of good advice on such topics as "getting things going," lecturing, supervising practical work, and assessing performance in examinations. Much emphasis is placed on personal relationships between teacher and students and among students. Ratcliff (1938) presents a somewhat similar book, simply written and with comments that would be useful for beginning instructors in almost any subject.

Staton (1960) sees his book as a general guide to modern classroom instruction, but its lessons would also be helpful for directors of training in industry and the people who work under their supervision. Davies (1981) clearly intends his work for use by industrial and commercial trainers. Its language and illustrations reflect that fact, as do the experience and literature on which it is based.

Interactive Processes

The adult educational movement has helped to dissolve the stiffness and formality of established didacticism and to foster interactive processes intended to stimulate learners and bring new content and viewpoints into the stream of their learning. In most cases, boldly proclaimed innovations were not wholly new but built upon or added to existing patterns of instruction. Neglected or rarely expressed ideas were thus brought to the forefront of attention and often became widespread practices or principles. To an extent undreamed of in the early part of the century, people now learn systematically from fellow learners.

One group of books on interactive processes evaluates how they are used to illuminate and personalize formal presentations of content. Lecture-discussions and reading circles existed in the eighteenth century, though they were far from common. But in the early 1930s, John Studebaker, then superintendent of schools in Des

Moines, Iowa, created a series of meetings that he called forums; these enabled citizens to hear outstanding lecturers on current subjects and to ask questions or express their own views. Studebaker (1935) discusses this program in detail and makes a fervent statement about the importance of participative democracy and of the forum in achieving it. The idea was taken up in other cities, and Ely (1937) describes her visits to forums offered under varied sponsorship throughout the country. Having a clear preference for interaction and continuity in education, she felt that forums were deficient as forms of learning—however valuable they might occasionally be. She concludes "first, that the chief feature of a forum program is generally a lecture, supplemented by a period of audience participation which is not group thinking but most commonly consists of disconnected questions about the lecture and a few comments upon it; second, that the recognized weaknesses of the forum as an educational medium are not offset for most members of forum audiences either by subsequent discussion or by reading" (p. 206). Another effort to illuminate formal presentations by discussion occurred in the 1950s, when there was a vogue for packaged materials (usually books or excerpts from them), read and discussed by small groups. Kaplan (1960) reports on efforts of this sort sponsored by the Fund for Adult Education in southern California in the late 1950s. The fund was interested in liberal arts and helped support the Great Books program, courses in world politics, and other similar packaged presentations. Kaplan summarizes the results of interviews in depth with participants in such courses. Oliver (1987) recounts the history of study circles, which arose from American prototypes but which have had their fullest development in Sweden (which adopted and adapted them). The author believes that the pattern should be reintroduced into American practice and reviews some modest efforts to do so.

The discussion method—or, as Ely (1937) called it, group thinking—has been much talked about in the literature and has gradually spread in practice to become the central or adjunct method in many programs. Fansler (1934) contributes an urbane analysis of the process, a valuable part of which is the inclusion of several sample discussions accompanied by the author's commentary on what presumably lay behind the comments and the nature of the discussion's flow. Using the second person, Fansler (1950) presents the essential ideas of discussion in a simple and colloquial fashion. The four sections of the book are how to be a good group member, how people behave in a group, how cooperative thinking can solve problems, and how to lead a discussion. In Zelko's *The Business Conference* (1969), a revision and elaboration of an earlier work, the author's ideas about group communication do not flow centrally from the business setting; rather, they are derived from an analysis of interpersonal relations as they are used by leaders and other participants in meetings where intellectual interaction is a part of the effort to create understanding and achieve new systems of thought.

Unlike other applications of interactive processes, the group dynamics movement did not build on past efforts. It was an original and independent line of research and action designed to help people understand the nature of groups by participating in one. This movement has been described earlier, but it seems appropriate to mention three works that make practical suggestions about how groups can set out to inquire into the ideas, feelings, and interactions of their members. Bradford, Gibb, and Benne (1964) have supplied the best-known work on the theory and practice of the T-Group, as this form of organized interaction was called. Strauss and Strauss (1951) use popular language to discuss a number of the lessons learned from the then-burgeoning study of group dynamics. Knowles and Knowles (1972) offer a brief introduction to group dynamics written in an exceptionally clear fashion. The original version of this work, published in 1959, reflected the first ten years of the organized movement; this revised edition brings the account up to date.

As the pioneering ideas of that movement were tested and accepted, they began to be incorporated into earlier ideas of group processes. Bergevin and Morris (1954) concisely describe the essential characteristics of settings that use interactive processes, including symposiums, forums, institutes, seminars, and workshops. Each of these forms has a distinctive pattern of operation, and the authors perform a useful service in differentiating among them. Beal, Bohlen, and Raudebaugh (1962) furnish an extended summary of the principles and theories of group work and social interaction as found in the literature of the social sciences, but the major part of their book is given over to the presentation of specific techniques of instruction and evaluation. Utterback (1964) presents a comprehensive work on the themes identified in his title, *Group Thinking and Conference Leadership.* It is particularly rich in illustrations and case examples. Bergevin and McKinley (1965) contribute a carefully worked-out plan for helping members of groups be better participants, thereby increasing the rewards of discussion for themselves and others.

The findings first developed with adult educational groups or by authors regarding themselves as adult educators have entered the college curriculum in several textbooks. As Bormann (1975) points out, "Group discussion owes its new prominence both to new information and to new applications. The new information has come not only from large-scale research programs being conducted at some of the leading graduate schools in speech but also from extensive research in many other disciplines" (p. ix). Other innovative college texts that use much of the research undertaken in adult education have been presented by Keltner (1957) and Gulley (1968). Such books as these may be helpful for educators of adults not familiar with group processes.

Autonomous action groups—street gangs, neighborhood improvement societies, block groups, promoters of social causes, and others—are found everywhere in democratic societies but have not been deeply studied by educators of adults. However, two works may be cited. Doddy (1952) reports on the nature of these groups in a depressed area of New York City. Using ingenious techniques, the author was able to trace the existence of a large number of groups even in this unpromising setting. Fifty such groups were studied closely and generalizations made about their nature and activities. Doddy found, for example: "Groups appear to pass through three stages of development, each being characterized by different qualities of relationships existing among members. These stages may be described as *collections of individuals, habit groups,* and *purpose groups.* Purpose groups may grow out of collections of individuals as a result of either internal or external stimulation brought about by a condition which forces an evaluation of the association in terms of purposive factors. Out of these evaluations continuous group purposes are defined" (p. 33). The author was interested in discovering how seriously these groups took their mutual education and the extent to which they could be used by more formal institutions to penetrate the community. Durrance (1984), in a work entitled *Armed for Action*, made a study of autonomous action groups to find out how they gained the knowledge that they needed to pursue their ends; special attention was paid in this study to the public library.

Crane (1972) examines interactive processes at a knowledge level that would seem stratospheric to most people. She analyzes the patterns of informal affiliation and relationship of the members of advanced scientific specialties to show how they collectively refine knowledge in their field and inform one another of its new developments. These collectives are called invisible colleges.

Ashby (1955) aroused a great deal of attention when *The Pathology of Adult Education* was first issued because of his eminence in Great Britain, his recent chairmanship of a national commission on adult education, and the strength of his attack upon the prevailing system. He traces the ultimate failure of two earlier patterns of instruction and suggests drastic and (in his view) fatal deficiencies of the provisions in existence at the time he wrote. His solution lies in the development of "thousands of small voluntary groups"; these could regenerate adult education at its source and help to create and preserve the individuality of mankind. He does not specify how this broad new movement is to be brought about.

Residential Adult Education

In this format, people are assembled to live and learn together, usually focusing their major efforts on shared educative processes. This setting has qualities that commend it in many cases: it provides for intensity of study; it brings together people who would otherwise be dispersed geographically; it can be linked effectively with other formats in a total program of education; and it can allow the efficient use of human and material resources that might not otherwise be available. These virtues have long been recognized, and an early analysis of them was provided by Adams (1899) in his description of residential summer schools at various places in Europe. His book suggests some of the most important humanistic outcomes of shared residential learning as perceived by one of the keenest intellects who ever observed adult education closely and who had the literary style to write about it with clarity and conviction. Another early study was provided by Gray, Gray, and Tilton (1932), who explore the nature and results of residential education for two groups of lower-class, illiterate and semi-illiterate adults. The authors' description—and especially their careful statistical analysis of achievements—provides a refreshing contrast to the analysis of middle-class students usually found in such formats.

Mead and Byers (1968) were interested in what they called the small substantive conference, which they regarded as a new method of communication, having deep roots in the past but emerging as a new form in modern times. "All members of such a conference," they say, "are accorded participant status; the method of communication is mutual multisensory interchange with speech as the principal medium; attitude, shifts in attention, gestures and the types of expressiveness that cannot be adequately represented in print, play an important part. Such a conference is self-contained, generating its own style and its own solutions" (p. 5). An interesting feature of the book is its use of photographs; these, often taken in close sequence, can be interpreted in a perceptive fashion to indicate what is occurring during the process of interaction. The book gains added value from the acute anthropological observations of its distinguished senior author, Mead.

Since World War II, the international conference has become an important means for the advanced learning of specialists. In 1960, Capes issued the report of an international conference on international conferences. Her book presents the working papers prepared for that session (held in Eastbourne, England) and an abstract of its proceedings. The group members were veterans of many such conferences (including Margaret Mead) and therefore brought to their task the ability to make sharp and analytical approaches to the subject. Each of the many aspects of conference design is evaluated, including preplanning, group atmosphere, agenda formation, small-group and plenary sessions, and emergent leaders. A somewhat similar book was issued by Rice in 1965; he examines the subculture that grows up in all groups but is most fully developed within residential environments. All elements of a conference—its setting, its plenary sessions, its work groups, and so forth—are assessed to determine how their underlying human structure can be used to foster learning.

The planning and operation of conferences has become a subspecialty of adult education, and a number of books deal with the theory and mechanics of such work. Burke and Beckhard (1976) provide a collection of papers on many aspects of conference design, including conventions, small local gatherings, collaborative group-planning efforts, and many other forms of activity. Loughary and Hopson (1979) were moved to prepare their book because they had observed so many disastrous examples of short-term training. In a straightforward, clear, and direct fashion, they seek to remedy that situation by taking readers through every step of planning and operation, with very helpful hints and suggestions. Seekings (1981) surveys the practical aspects of planning and conducting conferences and other meetings, going into extraordinary detail about processes and procedures. The book is written for an English audience, and an interesting feature is the inclusion of advertisements by agencies that provide services for conference operators. Sork (1984) is primarily concerned with the workshop, here defined as "a relatively short-term intensive, problem-focused learning experience that actively involves participants in the identification and analysis of problems and in the development and evaluation of solutions" (p. 5). The authors of papers in this book believe that this very commonly found type of temporary learning system has special characteristics that make it worthy of study. Ilsley (1985) presents the work of a group of authors broadly interested in the theme of conference design. This book is not only a practical guide for planners but a useful introduction to its general topic. Nadler and Nadler (1987) contribute a massive and magisterial work covering all aspects of the planning, conduct, and evaluation of conferences. The work is intended primarily for professionals but would be helpful to any conference planner, particularly as a handbook or reference tool. Of special utility are the many checklists on specific aspects of planning or operation. Simerly (1990) offers an eminently practical book that gives 172 suggestions for programming conferences and workshops, each explained in a paragraph or more; the suggestions are grouped in seven chapters. A final section provides useful addresses, a listing of key resources, and a bibliography. Among the suggestions made are diligently research the competition, negotiate a written contract for all meal functions, and calculate complimentary registrations as fixed expenses. An understanding of the principles underlying such practical advice helps the practitioner to acquire the overall conceptions of conference operation.

In the late 1940s, the W. K. Kellogg Foundation became interested in residential learning in university centers for continuing education. Alford (1968) chronicles the ensuing movement. By the time his book was written, the foundation had endowed nine American universities and Oxford with buildings that could contain and foster conferences. Although Alford describes the buildings, his primary attention is devoted to the programs they make possible.

In a pair of books, the tradition of residential education in Britain and the United States is reviewed and interpreted. Houle (1971) begins by saying, "The theme of this discursive essay is residential continuing education: its definition; its development along somewhat different lines in Europe and in America; and its practice in university centers in the United States" (p. vii). In the development of this three-part theme, the author uses history, personal observation and analysis, and the results of research to analyze the various elements that have gone into the operation of residential adult education and its development (along several different lines) as a specialized form of learning by adults. Jessup (1972) offers a graceful essay drawing upon many ancient and modern sources concerned in some way with residential learning. He gives scope and dimension to this way of learning.

As residential adult educational centers have proliferated, the people familiar with their deep traditions have worried that growth may have diminished the advantages of this form of learning. Simpson and Kasworm (1990) have edited a work designed to restate inherent values and indicate how the residential conference center can be a true learning sanctuary for adults. One chapter describes the history of such centers in Europe and explores their distinctive purposes; another provides a similar history of those that have emerged in the United States, with special reference to the ones sponsored by universities. Attention is paid by other authors to defining the essential character of residential study and suggesting how its values can be reinforced by the methodologies of learning used.

An ultimate expression of residential education is presented in *Lust for Learning* by Nielsen (1968), an account of life in a college in Denmark; this institution grafted some American symbols (such as credits and degrees) onto the pattern of a Danish folk high school, with its mixture of ancient traditions and modern freedoms. Teachers and students are differentiated for some purposes, but everyone learns and everyone teaches in a wholly self-contained living situation; all elements of life (including the housework) are shared. The expression of personal feelings is an important part of the learning experience. The book is not so much written as compiled from various kinds of documents, some of great frankness and often presented without a glint of humor.

Self-Directed Learning

Works on self-directed learning focus on the role of individuals (or, in some cases, groups) in choosing and guiding their processes of education. In the largest sense, all adult education is self-directed. The act of registration in even the most content-oriented course represents a personal decision by the student, and the amount and kind of effort subsequently expended are determined by that person. Most works on this theme, however, are concerned with more active, more determined, and longer-range forms of personal planning and control over the processes of acquiring knowledge. The range of treatment is indicated in the works here cited.

The idea of self-directed learning is far from new, and references to it may be found even in antiquity. Only two book-length examples will be provided here. In 1839, William Ellery Channing, the distinguished Boston clergyman, issued a work called *Self-Culture*, which was to go through many later editions. He first identifies the areas of knowledge that adults should have in mind as they seek to improve themselves through formal education and in other ways. The author treats successively the moral, the religious, the intellectual, the social, and the practical realms of content. He then sets forth a number of specific rules on the establishment of self-culture as a fundamental aim in life, the control of the animal appetites, intercourse with superior minds (especially through the use of books), the need to remain true to one's own highest convictions, the use of a person's condition or occupation as a source of knowledge, and the importance of social and political relationships. Eggleston's *How to Educate Yourself*, first issued in 1872, is an example of a type of self-help volume widely found in the nineteenth and twentieth centuries and often derided by sophisticates. This particular manual offers helpful advice to adults (the author's language suggests that he has young men primarily in mind) who, "with or without masters," seek to educate themselves. It is not a study guide so much as it is an effort to help potential learners understand the methods and materials of education that might be useful to them.

Some authors examine self-directed learning within the framework of the individual's total experience. Hirschberg (1966) equates learning with all aspects of existence and seeks to show the advantages to be gained by a creative reaction to physical and human surroundings. At considerable length, he details his own efforts to learn and the lessons acquired thereby. He also gives advice to readers on how they can do likewise. He is not deeply concerned with such familiar formats as disciplined instruction, collaborative study, or group discussion. Addressing directly the adult who wishes to learn, Gross (1977) provides an inspirational approach grounded in common sense and including practical suggestions about how to proceed with a personally designed program and where to go for help in pursuing it. Gross also emphasizes the experiential learning provided by the environment, citing Socrates' aphorism "Not I but the city teaches." Houle (1984) has compiled essays describing how individuals devise patterns of learning for themselves that change as they grow older. Although this general theme is considered analytically, much of the book is given over to case examples, most of them biographical. Some of the people discussed, such as Montaigne and Thoreau, were self-directed learners. Some, such as Edward Everett and William Osler, were designers of learning systems. In one case, educational travel, the example is the city of Florence. Other briefer examples are provided in a chapter on the conceptions, goals, and major methods of learning in adulthood.

The attempt to quantify the nature of self-directed learning was first undertaken in the 1960s by Tough and his associates at the Ontario Institute for Studies in Education. The basis for evaluation was the learning project as devised and carried out by an individual. In 1979, Tough published the second edition of his summary of numerous studies analyzing such projects as they were undertaken by people in various conditions of life. In 1982, he published another work reflecting a change in his focus of investigation. His new emphasis was upon the intentional changes that people make in their lives and the ways by which they accommodate to them by the use of organized and purposeful learning. The data are drawn from interviews with 330 men and women in variously sized communities in Canada, England, and the United States.

In the 1970s and 1980s, self-directed learning began to be stressed in the periodical literature, and several books have since resulted. Brookfield (1984) explores the ways that adults, acting both independently and in groups, learn in either self-designed or established ways within the opportunities provided them by their communities. He is interested in how learning operates naturally in ways not determined by formal structural procedures, but he also considers how organized cultural resources can have their fullest effect as resources for independent learners. Along with a group of collaborators, Brookfield returned to these themes in 1985. The authors wish to show how the principles of self-directed learning can be introduced into health education, hospitals, universities, libraries, museums, adult education centers, and colleges. They also assess the problems and rewards of learning in this nontraditional format. The authors take full account of the fact that self-directed learning is no panacea, especially because many adults do not want to learn on their own initiative. Long and others (1989) have produced a collection of scholarly papers on various theoretical aspects of self-directed learning.

Gross and Gross (1983) demonstrate how such learning applies to the life of the independent, nonacademically affiliated scholar. Their book reports on a two-year study of people in this category. The authors believe strongly in the value of such advanced inquiry, not only for the persons involved, but also in the results of their research for society. The book has many suggestions as to how such endeavors can be assisted.

Efforts to aid and counsel adults seeking education have been mentioned in earlier chapters, but several general guides will be noted here. Under the auspices of the *New York Times*, Thomson (1972) has issued a massive volume, most of which was given over to brief descriptions, institution by institution, of the services provided to adults by colleges, universities, and other similar agencies. Several essays also advise students on how to direct their approaches to learning in accredited educational institutions. Knowles (1975) contributes a simply written, second-person book on independent study, which addresses first the learner, then the teacher or helper, and finally both together. The learner is told how to develop and carry out a learning plan or contract, using help as needed. The teacher is informed about how to work with such learners and how to help them to set and achieve goals for themselves. Marshall and Rowland (1983) provide a full account of various forms of study in Great Britain and the ways that they may best be utilized by those who want to learn. The emphasis in this work is on how each individual can best exercise his or her own responsibility for learning programs. Rowntree (1986) offers a direct and pragmatic set of instructions on going about the task of constructing a self-instructional program of learning. This useful, specialized work offers illustrations from many content fields. Brockett and Hiemstra (1991) furnish a broad-ranging interpretation of the concept and practice of adult self-directed study. The book deals with the emergence and subsequent history of the concept, the various lines of research into aspects of the subject, institutional and other practical consequences, and the probable direction of further endeavors. Illuminating case studies reveal the nature and implications of this kind of learning. Candy (1991) reports comprehensively on the literature of self-directed learning, which began to proliferate in the 1960s and has continued to flourish ever since. The author demonstrates that this term is far more complex than is usually supposed, and he reviews the themes and topics explored in the relevant literature.

As suggested in several places above, the learner may have a closely associated mentor supporting his or her endeavors. Both fiction and biography offer many descriptions of this relationship, the best known being Eliza Doolittle of Shaw's *Pygmalion* and Lerner and Loewe's *My Fair Lady*. Eliza could scarcely be called self-directed, though she was more so than DuMaurier's Trilby. In Russell's *Educating Rita*, however, Rita was clearly the assertive figure. The details of a learner-mentor relationship are identified in *College of One* (1967), in which Sheilah Graham describes how F. Scott Fitzgerald guided her education in a three-year learning plan, centered on reading, listening to music, and looking at art. This last work differs from the other ones mentioned in that it is centrally concerned with the processes of adult education.

Several kinds of institutions specialize in helping independent learners. Draves (1980) discusses the free universities then in vogue, which are wholly voluntary institutions in which students and teachers come together outside the auspices of established schools and colleges and study together without any desire for credentials or other paper awards. Public libraries, as already noted in the section describing them, have long been concerned with readers' advisory services. Some recent works have underscored the importance of a fuller range of services. Brooks and Reich (1974) offer a detailed account, with many illustrations of forms and procedures, of the Dallas Public Library's attempt to serve creatively as a center for independent study. This well-funded venture shows what can be undertaken with ample resources. Reilly (1981) gives a thorough statement of the ways that both English and American public librarians can assist individuals to engage in systematic study, particularly when working in degree-related programs. Robinson (1928) shows how museums can understand and respond to the behavior of those who visit them. Gross (1982a) not only celebrates the value of the independent scholar, but also suggests how such a person can find needed supports and resources. Niemi and Gooler (1987) examine technologies of learning as they influence nontraditional study, especially as engaged in by the individual learner. The authors cover such familiar media as radio, television, and print and also still-emerging forms of learning like interactive video, computers, and the combinations of technology that stimulate new kinds and complexities of learning.

Distance Education

This term came into widespread use in the 1970s as a way of identifying instruction where teachers (of any sort) are not in immediate face-to-face contact with students. In times past, the major method used was correspondence instruction, but as new media (radio, television, computers, audio and video recorders, flexible uses of the telephone, and others) appeared and were used singly or in combination, the range of possibilities of distance education was greatly extended. These media are also used for diffusion of knowledge to the generalized public or to specialized segments of it, but these usages are different from those of distance education, which serves specific students.

Correspondence instruction emerged in many parts of the world in the late nineteenth and early twentieth centuries as a way of dealing with various challenges. It offered a hope for education to people isolated from other resources and to those denied opportunities to learn because of their race, their gender, their age, their poverty, or other similar circumstances. MacKenzie, Christensen, and Rigby (1968) analyze the use of the method by many suppliers in the mid 1960s. They give a clear and compressed history of correspondence study and describe the difficulties faced by both providers and users. They conclude with a chapter that offers blueprints for further development. Macken and others (1976) report the results of a literature search on correspondence instruction in the United States, including summaries of the major data contained in that literature.

In the United States, the best-known form of correspondence study has been that carried out by for-profit institutions, which advertised their offerings widely in the public press. Noffsinger (1926) provides a complete evaluation of such schools, including their methods of teaching. He strikes the theme that recurs in all later treatments of this subject: the variable quality of the institutions. "The first great need in this field," he comments, "is an almost automatic separator of the sheep from the goats" (p. 89). Woodyard (1940), a Columbia professor, took fifteen courses and recorded her experiences, good and bad. She felt that the chief fault of the institutions involved was that they played on the gullibility of their students. Pugni (1965) gives a positive view of such schools. He emphasizes the great breadth of opportunity afforded by this means of study and tells students and potential students how they may best reap its values.

The other major form of correspondence study in the United States has been that conducted by universities, often under the label *home study.* Bittner and Mallory (1933) give a comprehensive view of the traditions of such study and tell the history of how it became part of the American academic scene. The book is essentially factual, but its authors face up directly to some of the vexing problems created by correspondence teaching, particularly when it is carried out within the structure and value systems of a university. Smith (1935) gives a vivid case study of the correspondence education program at Columbia University, his investigation being set within the larger framework of adult education. It was undertaken with an optimistic viewpoint, but its findings were obviously dismaying to the author, especially in terms of the low completion rates achieved.

In other countries—England, South Africa, Sweden, and elsewhere—correspondence study seems to have been more successful, perhaps because more talent and resources were used in its provision. Erdos (1967) presents a practical description of how correspondence teaching can be carried out in many ways. The book is aimed at the educational administrators and policy makers of less highly developed parts of the world where the need for instruction is great. MacKenzie and Christensen (1971) offer a book of readings, worldwide in scope and written over a hundred-year period, which paints a broad picture of the nature of correspondence study as it has been viewed by many authors and carried out in a multitude of situations. This distinguished volume, with broad perspectives and meticulous editing, deals with both the aspirations and the mechanics of this form of learning.

The creation of the Open University (OU) in Great Britain brought international attention to distance education. Glatter and Wedell (1971) describe the opportunities available in that country at the time the OU was being considered. They supply a full report, as their title page says, on "an enquiry into correspondence study for examinations for degrees and other advanced qualifications" in the United Kingdom, with roughly parallel observations on practice in other countries. The general conclusion of the authors is that correspondence study is an admirable method for learning (at least for some students), but it is not widely known, understood, or accepted. This view suggests the atmosphere into which the OU was introduced, with its emphasis on the use of the newer media and its introduction of the concept of *distance learning,* a term that the able young intellectuals on its staff (and their colleagues elsewhere) devised as a way to describe their work. The introduction of the OU has been most memorably described by Perry (1977), who gives a vivid account of the challenges faced and the victories achieved. In an apt phrase, Perry refers to "the loneliness of the long-distance learner" (p. x); however, the author makes it clear that distance education is not merely a way of alleviating that loneliness but also of making solitary study more rewarding for those who undertake it.

Even before the OU was inaugurated, its plans were being studied throughout the world, and comparable institutions were being considered. Chang and others (1983) have produced a carefully worked-out proposal for an open university, their treatment ranging from an abstruse theoretical base to the cost analysis of various kinds of services. The OU held a tenth-anniversary conference, reported by Neil (1981) and attended by participants from nearly fifty countries, more than half of them in the Third World. Essays were presented on the theory and practice of distance education, but the major part of Neil's book summarizes the ideas discussed at the conference. Many other works have resulted from the experience of the OU. Some of these are mentioned elsewhere in this book, but an especially thoughtful one was written by Harris (1987). Called *Openness and Closure in Distance Education,* this volume is concerned primarily with the extent to which the OU has been able to open access to higher education to the poor, the working class, and other underserved people who in the founding days were intended to be its major beneficiaries. The author also evaluates the extent to which the OU may itself have become an instrument for closing doors of opportunity for some people. As the author demonstrates, the new patterns of communication used by the OU and the pressures and counterpressures exerted by its enormous growth have become highly complex; his analysis as a result is informed and intricate at every point.

Other British commonwealth countries have also developed distance education programs. Mugridge and Kaufman have composed a work entitled *Distance Education in Canada* (1986). Though it contains contributions from thirty-one authors, the editors have maintained an admirable tightness of construction and presentation and have made an obvious (and, on the whole, realized) effort to be clear, comprehensive, and candid. Garrison (1989) has also written on the basis of Canadian experience but with a worldwide scope of reference. His central thesis is that distance education will eventually be seen as part of the mainstream of educational thought; yet its principles need to be worked out somewhat differently than in other settings in view of new forms of "mediated communication," which the author sees as "the quintessential characteristic of distance education" (p. 122). India has had substantial experience with distance education, a fact made evident by Borah (1987). His book is a collection of essays by Indian educators with some experience of the programs of forty open universities. The papers are intended to be resources for the planners of a new institution, the Indira Gandhi National Open University, created by Rajiv Gandhi as a memorial to his mother on the occasion of his becoming prime minister in 1985. At its inauguration, an international seminar was organized. Reddy (1988) presents the papers delivered on that occasion with some additional essays. The book is essentially composed of case studies of thirteen open universities, most Asian and some European. Khan (1989) furnishes a symposium of papers on distance education, chiefly by Indian authors. Although some papers are general and theoretical, several have to do with aspects of Indian practice (such as rates of completion and discontinuance) and techniques of instruction (such as lesson writing).

The use of distance education in economically underdeveloped countries had already been well established when the only method used was correspondence instruction. Edström, Erdos, and Prosser (1970), in a volume entitled *Mass Education*, describe how Swedish programs in this format worked in African countries. In Sweden, one of the chief forms of study had long been correspondence instruction, and some of the most advanced and creative thought on this topic had occurred in that country. Concerted effort was therefore made to translate tested principles into African practice, this work being supported by the Dag Hammarskjold Foundation. The authors focus on distance education but also pay attention to other forms of learning. Young and others (1980) broadly study the use of the techniques of distance education in the relatively underdeveloped countries of the Third World, particularly those in Africa. A number of case illustrations are given, as are listings of distance education projects under way at the time the book was published. The authors are close to their subject and are writing for other people in a similar situation; others may have difficulty understanding the problems that they regard as significant.

Beginning in the late 1970s, the effort to describe and analyze distance education has produced a number of general works, both by individual authors and by groups of essayists. Holmberg has written four books in this vein. In *Distance Education* (1977), he defines the key term as covering "the various forms of study at all levels which are not under the continuous, immediate supervision of tutors present with their students in lecture rooms or on the same premises, but which, nevertheless, benefit from the planning, guidance, and tuition of a tutorial organization" (p. 9). He presents a comprehensive bibliography of the field and, in brief compass, summarizes the essential aspects of distance learning and his own conclusions about each aspect of this approach. In *Status and Trends of Distance Education* (1981), he states a series of sequential propositions, each explained and defended as necessary. He does not seek to describe actual activities but to penetrate to the essence of his topic. He pursues his thought further in *Growth and Structure of Distance Education* (1986), in which his presentation is both historical and analytical, and he treats this form of education as a distinctive and inherently valuable form of instruction. In *Theory and Practice of Distance Education* (1989), he furnishes a comprehensive world view of distance education as both a practical enterprise and as a field of academic research.

Keegan is deeply experienced in the establishment and operation of distance education universities. In his book *The Foundations of Distance Education* (1986), he attempts to interpret both this experience and the worldwide literature on the topic. This volume is extremely probing; it defines the needed terms, examines the usage of various authors, and builds a positive and constructive basis for the theoretical field and a platform for practice. An important part of the book is the discussion of the comparative costs of distance education institutions and those based on residential instruction.

Six collections of essays written by authors in many nations describe the facets of what has become an international movement, though it is less well represented in the United States than in some other countries. Kaye and Rumble (1981) have compiled the papers given at an international seminar held by the OU in 1979, which dealt comprehensively with many aspects of the format. Daniel, Stroud, and Thompson (1982) contribute a beautifully edited work, presenting 118 papers on various aspects of distance learning, as well as integrative material by the editors, a bibliography, a glossary, and other useful items. For anybody wishing a complete viewpoint on distance education, it is probably the best volume available; however, it is so bulky that some readers will want only to scan it, paying close attention to the sections that interest them. Sewart, Keegan, and Holmberg (1983) supply an anthology of papers (most of them previously published), mainly by European authors who consider all aspects of distance education and who have tried to give perspective to the topics that they describe. For example, the major paper on theory by Hilary Perraton begins with the comment "Distance education has managed very well without any theory" (p. 34). Smith and Kelly (1987) include writings from many different nations. The authors have varying topics and points of view but agree that distance education and the more established forms of instruction (which they call the mainstream) should converge more fully than at present, each acquiring some of the advantages of the other. Fresh and interesting insights emerge from the authors' analyses. Garrison and Shale (1990) focus their studies on North American and Australian practice. The contributing authors have sought to consider afresh the issues and problems found in study by correspondence or by the use of the mass media. Moore (1990b) provides a collection of detailed studies of the literature dealing with distance education and includes an annotated bibliography on the subject. The author concludes, "The weight of evidence that can be gathered from the literature points overwhelmingly to the conclusion that teaching and studying at a distance, especially that which uses interactive electronic communications media, is effective, when effectiveness is measured by achievement of learning, by the attitudes of students and teachers, and by cost effectiveness" (p. 34).

Faith (1988) presents studies operating at two closely interrelated levels. Most directly, the book explores the special advantages that distance education has for women in opening up to them new opportunities for study. As part of this approach, the authors are concerned with the ways that the curriculum should best be structured to meet the needs and desires of women. At another level, the authors of the essays try to create a sisterhood among those women who work in important posts in distance education throughout the world.

As noted earlier, the practice and theory of distance education have not been as great in the United States as elsewhere in the world. In an effort to help it become less of an unknown quantity, Verduin and Clark (1991) begin with its fundamentals and proceed by illustration, example, and exposition to develop a complete description, including the presentation of some of its most abstruse theories. The authors also try to ascertain the promise of distance education for American adult education. Moore (1990a) suggests that more is going on than is generally realized. In an exceptionally well edited fashion, his book brings together the papers prepared for a national symposium on distance education held at Pennsylvania State University in 1988. These essays are largely research-based and deal with many topics grouped in four categories: institutional contexts; learners and the assistance given to them; course design and instruction; and theory, policy and research. The book centers on American thought and practice, but it has a firm orientation toward the international movement.

Mass Media

As the term implies, the basic idea of such media of communication (books, television, computers, and all the others) is that they are directed toward a general audience, not toward identified learners. *Mass* never means *everyone;* even the most widely diffused television programs on commercial channels are aimed at segments of the population in the sure knowledge that selectivity will be displayed by the viewers themselves. The task of the educator working in a mass medium is to identify the kinds of people that it can reach, the message appropriate to the occasion, and the ways by which it can best be communicated.

A concern for the educational impact of mass media has been evident for a long time, and Ohliger and Gueulette (1975) have made a listing of the references about this theme. The authors have summarized, often with telling quotations from the works themselves, the substantial contributions to be found in this literature and have arranged the citations within an analytical framework.

Two collections of essays reflect varied ideas and viewpoints. Niemi (1971) has collected papers written by American, Canadian, and British authorities on numerous aspects of the topic. Chamberlain (1980) includes brief essays having to do with television, radio, computers, and newspapers. The authors deal with the general use of such media, suggest how they can aid in the offering of university courses, and describe how media can be used in business, government, and medicine.

The educative impact of print in all its various forms has been more fully subjected to study than any other mass medium. A basic work was presented by Buswell in his book *How Adults Read* (1937), a laboratory study of the silent and oral reading processes of 1,020 adults at every level of reading skill. Special machines had to be devised and coordinated to measure eye movements, lip movements, the oral enunciation of words, and the extent of vocalization in silent reading. To the author, "the most mature process of silent reading consists in the fusing of groups of words into units of meaning, which in turn flow into, and become a part of, a larger stream of thought constituting the total substance of the material being read" (p. 117). Buswell used his research findings to train fifty readers to increase their speed and comprehensiveness of reading. He thus established the basis (since supplemented by countless other investigations) of the so-called speed reading courses that are now familiar. Although Buswell's investigative techniques and educational processes were primitive—a fact he fully recognized—his concluding chapter contains reflections and warnings that seem surprisingly modern.

Most of the research in adult reading has been carried out with people who possess few or no skills in the process. Gray and Rogers (1956), in their book *Maturity in Reading,* went to the upper end of the continuum so far as such abilities are concerned. In their investigation, the authors seek to identify the characteristics of highly sophisticated readers who operate at the level of competence required to meet the demands and fulfill the rich potentials that reading makes possible. By thus identifying the truly mature reader, Gray and Rogers lay the foundation for measuring competence in reading ability.

Two significant works treat the topics that most interest adult readers. Gray and Munroe (1929) have made a thoroughgoing survey of the practice of reading with attention to both gross statistics and individual case studies. The authors considered a wide range of topics: "the status of reading in American life; the amount of adult reading; the character of the material read; the interests and motives of readers; the influences that affect the development of reading interests and habits; and the importance of establishing permanent reading habits early in the life of an individual" (p. 259). Waples and Tyler (1931), in a work concisely titled *What People Want to Read About,* consider the total pattern of voluntary reading, not merely that undertaken for self-enrichment purposes. As they point out, "More people read to forget than read to learn. Yet the two types of reading are never entirely distinct. One obtains some pleasure from anything interesting enough to get itself read, and some additional knowledge from anything read merely for fun" (p. 187). Accepting this range of motivation, the authors undertake a broad study of reading patterns among various groups of people, and this book reports their extensive findings.

Waples recounts in two striking works the results of his reflection and research on adult reading. In a book called *People and Print* (1937), he gives a brilliantly concise presentation of what was known and what could be inferred about the use of print by adults, particularly during the Depression years. Throughout the book are the evidences of a truly creative mind, willing to accept no easy answers to problems and trying hard to get at the evidence to substantiate hypotheses. In a 1940 work entitled *What Reading Does to People,* written with Berelson and Bradshaw, Waples deals precisely and elegantly with the area defined by the title. The authors review the salient literature, but, more important, they assess fully all aspects of the topic. Though all kinds of reading are within the authors' scope of concern, their focus is on the influence of total reading patterns, not merely those chosen for self-educative purposes.

Much of the research concerning the impact of print has had to do with readability, a subject that Gray and Leary (1935) opened up in an original fashion. Their book carries out three purposes: "to make an initial survey of current opinion concerning what makes a book readable for adults of limited reading ability; to study objectively a small but important area of readability commonly designated 'ease' or difficulty; and to suggest possible application of the findings to the work of librarians in selecting the right book for adult readers as well as to the task of writers and publishers in preparing readable materials for different reading groups" (p. vi). In a work that proved influential, Flesch (1943) sought to develop an objective measure of readability. He noted, "The fact was undeniable that books differed in degrees of difficulty and . . . these differences were obviously related to certain differences in the language structure of the text" (p. 3). He therefore set about the task of discovering and measuring those differences and combining them into a formula; this, when applied to samples of prose, would yield an index of difficulty. These two works helped to create a sizable literature on the subject of readability, which is summarized by Klare (1963).

A general statement of all aspects of adult reading, with specific emphasis on educative consequences, is presented in a substantial collection of papers by Clift and others (1956). The book contains chapters written by American authorities on reading, each dealing with a basic aspect of the topic: what do adults read; how well do they do so; why do they read; how are readable materials developed; and so on.

Before television became a significant force, the educative impact of radio was considered by a number of writers. In the 1920s and 1930s, the use of radio for instruction had become a familiar phenomenon. Hill (1937) provides a panoramic view of what had occurred in this respect in the previous fifteen years and made an estimate of the success achieved in the various spheres of work. Of special interest to adult educators is the idea of listening groups. Hill and Williams (1941) evaluate efforts to give radio a greater educative impact through the organized or spontaneous operation of adult listening groups. The book pulls together the records of various ventures and exploratory research efforts on this theme in both Britain and the United States. The authors are clear about their skepticism on several counts: whether listening groups will prove to be significant efforts in education; whether the impending world war will hamper existing programs; and whether television, then looming on the horizon, will overshadow the influence of radio. Ohliger (1967) reviews the further development of listening groups during the next quarter-century. He describes then-existing ventures, analyzes their strengths, and suggests why such groups have always remained a minor influence in educational circles.

From the first appearance of television, its impact as a means of influencing public awareness of various topics has been evident, and attempts to channel its power in the service of education have been numerous. Groombridge (1966) compiles accounts of the progress of educational television in Canada, Czechoslovakia, and Japan, written by experts in the three countries. In his own preface and conclusion, Groombridge looks realistically at the nature and accomplishments of television as a learning mechanism. Trenaman (1967) describes a pioneering study conducted by the British Broadcasting Company concerning the learning outcomes of several kinds of television programs by various audiences. Bates and Robinson (1977) present the papers and summaries of discussion at a conference held in England in 1976. About 230 people attended, with thirty countries being represented. The papers and discussion concerned education for young people, as well as adults, and ran the full range from televised courses to nonformal learning activities. Robinson (1982) gives a historical narrative of the educational aims and procedures of the British Broadcasting Company as viewed by one who considers himself an adult educator. In his book *Video*, Moss (1983) analyzes the use of VCRs as a supplemental way of reinforcing television as an educative instrument. He takes a broad view of the usefulness of television in direct instruction, in distance learning, and in personal programs of continuing education.

In the United States, the development of local channels for educational television has been closely linked to the field of adult education, and the channels themselves have been greatly aided by grants from the Fund for Adult Education. Powell (1962) gives a journalistic account of these stations during the first stage of their development, when they had few traditions and much hope. The account is essentially descriptive, rather than analytical. Schramm, Lyle, and Pool (1963) report on a pioneering study of the nature and outreach of nine educational television stations in the United States, with primary attention to the audiences reached. Blakely (1979) traces the development of educational broadcasting—first by radio, then by television—in the United States beginning about 1920. This work is basically a chronicle of institutions and individuals; it makes an effort to assess their contributions to a pattern of development often confusing to those trying to understand the complexities of a high-stakes field.

The role of especially developed television programs in supporting literacy instruction has been significantly developed in Europe. Hargreaves (1980) furnishes a fully documented account of such a program in Britain in the late 1970s. Kaye and Harry (1982) describe such ventures in Britain and on the European continent. The authors give clear definitions and briefly stated concepts for such work.

Adam (1940a) presents a book-length essay considering many aspects of the motion picture as an educative device, including commercial, documentary, and educational films.

The use of computers for education dates back to their progenitors, the so-called teaching machines, whose designs led to much thought about the best ways to introduce and reinforce knowledge. A computer has a built-in capacity to interact with a learner that is not shared by any other mass medium of communication. The major books on computer usage in adult education were produced in the 1980s, and all of them indicate that their authors recognize that this instrument and its possibilities are still in their preliminary phases of development. Gueulette (1982) supplies a collection of essays on personal computers as instruments of teaching and learning. The basics of computer construction and usage are considered, as are the applications of the computer in a number of situations and fields of work. Gerver (1984) is an enthusiastic English advocate of computers in adult educational programs. The author includes many illustrations that show how computers are actually being used and that suggest other possible applications. Heermann (1986) explores three major ways of using personal computers for adult learning: as teaching machines (as in computer-aided instruction programs), as learning tools (as in word processors), and as learning resources (as in computer networks). Mason and Kaye (1989) offer a cluster of papers dealing with the application of computers to various learning situations; these describe both the nature of such processes and their impact on students. The authors are basically sympathetic to this innovative method but are admirably ready to look at both its potential limitations and its drawbacks.

Fairs and Expositions

Everyone who ponders the subject would probably agree that modern fairs and expositions have significant educational purposes or outcomes, but the literature has given little or no consideration to this element of their operation. The trade fairs so prominent in medieval social history were solely for purposes of commerce, though they had the concomitant effect of helping spread ideas and understandings. By contrast, the worldwide expositions of the last century and a half have placed notable emphasis on enlarging horizons, even if their ultimate effect is suggested by the title of the major work describing them, *Ephemeral Vistas*, by Greenhalgh.[1] State and county fairs, ubiquitous in American life, have activities and displays intended to provide instruction and, perhaps more important, offer opportunities for evaluating learning. Both children and adults display the products of their instruction or their power to perform in many arts, particularly in the home or work-

[1]Paul Greenhalgh, *Ephemeral Vistas: The Expositions Universelles, Great Expositions, and World Fairs, 1851–1939*. Manchester, England: Manchester University Press, 1988.

place. The exposition or fair is a format designed, if only in part, for lifelong learning. However, if serious book-length efforts have been made to describe or analyze it, I have failed to find them.

A Final Word

The various strands of purpose and practice mentioned in this long book can ramify in so many directions as to produce a sense of suffocation or impatience. Some leaders of adult education believe that their lives would be simpler if they defined the field as having fewer aims or ways of work. But as Parts One and Two have shown, the institutions and goals sought are numerous and complex; none could be cut away without significant disfigurement of the whole. And the learning theories, designs, and formats mentioned in Part Three are multitudinous but essential, needed to cope with the endless variety of people who seek knowledge. But, as I hope I have shown, this diversity can be encompassed within the central unifying concept that all adults need to learn throughout their lives in order to develop their personal and social potentialities. This idea has never been expressed more profoundly than in the great Unesco report *Learning to Be* (Faure, 1972, pp. 181–182): "The idea of lifelong learning is the keystone of the learning society. . . . It is the master concept for educational policies in the years to come for both developed and developing countries."

Conclusion:
Achievements and
Future Prospects

Adult education can be taken seriously as a discipline because, while it may not wish to own it, it does indeed have a body of knowledge that it can respond to and wrestle with. Adult education in the United States contains an amazingly rich body of ideas, folk-knowledge, bona fide theory and impeccable philosophy. . . . The legacy which earlier adult educators have left the current generation is ill-served if we continue to trade in defensive postures and do not submit our ideas and theories to the good light of our colleagues' opinions. The benefits to be derived from a dialogue among researchers and between researchers and practitioners can do much to strengthen our beliefs and commitment to intervention . . . [to remedy] human inadequacy and injustice. Ultimately, this dialogue is necessary to insure that we survive as a recognizable entity into the twenty-first century.

—Sean Courtney, 1991, p. 159

Those who read widely and deeply in the literature of adult education are likely to agree with the belief expressed in the early pages of this book that most workers in that field are able to undergird their art with disciplined knowledge. Those who occupy specific roles (such as distance education coordinators, trainers in industry, community activists, and deans of extension) can take advantage of existing resources to help them achieve a higher level of performance and bring tangible rewards to their institutions. Those with career aspirations can be helped to prepare for future responsibilities. Those who are interested intellectually in the field or who want to contribute to its writings find that it has overall shape and well-developed emphases.

Some people have always disagreed with this conclusion. Their views resemble those expressed in an address by a distinguished leader of higher education, a man who had headed two universities and chaired major national commissions. Among other autobiographical comments, he noted that he had prevented the creation of graduate programs in adult education at two universities on the grounds that the field had no knowledge base. Perhaps this book will persuade him otherwise; perhaps not.

Two major categories of the total literature add to the influence of the books included here. One is made up of nonbook resources: journal articles, monographs, brochures, separately published chapters of symposiums, and similar serious works. As with most well-established fields of social endeavor, such publications abound in adult education, often at the frontiers of knowledge. The other category is composed of volumes that are centered in other fields but that have proved useful in the theory and practice of adult education. As noted in the Preface, both categories had to be omitted here because no manageable way of defining the scope of either could be found. Perhaps someday works dealing with them or, indeed, covering all the literature will be available. Other fields, more advanced in this respect than adult education, already have such compendiums, sometimes in volumes that undergo periodic revision.

However significant the literature, the practice of learning and instruction is so widespread in the modern world that it cannot all be depicted and analyzed. Adult educators are said to be so eager to meet the challenges of the present and the future that they pay little attention to the past. Thus, adult education as a practical endeavor is not adequately defined or described. People write about events and activities that interest them or that can be readily observed. Those who read such writing respond to it; sequences of study and communication result. The literature devoted to some themes therefore flourishes, whereas other kinds of equally worthy learning remain virtually ignored. Generally speaking, lofty aspirations and motivations are considered more frequently than immediate and pedestrian ones. Liberal and political studies are more amply described than vocational training, and the development of recreational skills gets relatively cursory treatment. Examples abound of such incongruities between practice and its written description or evaluation.

Nor does the serious study of adult education draw for its resources and analytical methods on the whole world of scholarship as seen in its four well-established categories: the humanities, the social sciences, the mathematical and physical sciences, and the biological sciences. Most scholarly writers on adult education would define themselves as social scientists and, in particular, as oriented toward psychology, sociology, economics, and (in recent years) political theory. The humanistic disciplines of philosophy and history are also represented in the writings in the field. The mathematical and physical sciences are found chiefly as they help establish an exact methodology for investigation by the use of research designs, statistics, and various forms of measurement. But one searches almost in vain for any use of the biological sciences either to explain or to enhance human learning. The body changes dramatically throughout life, the hemispheres of the brain set different styles of behavior, and biological rhythms and cycles of the passing days influence thought and action. Every person has a distinctive pattern of physiological strengths and weaknesses, heredity has its powerful influences, and chemical substances exert their effects: these and other determinants of aspiration or behavior are virtually absent from the study of adult education.

The literary arts are also not strongly represented. In the foregoing pages, it has occasionally been noted that imagination and literary skill can create works of art from the settings and practices of adult learning. Even so familiar an activity as a literacy class can be used for such a purpose, as the triumphant figure of H*Y*M*A*N K*A*P*L*A*N attests. But his equal is hard to find. Few novels, plays, poems, and short stories have been based on the complex hopes, emotions, and struggles of those who try to perfect themselves by some form of study or on the places and patterns of learning that they use, many of them colorful.

A few specific lacunae have been noted—sometimes emphasized—throughout the book. Among them are the descriptions or analyses of such major efforts as the development of the GED test;

the special services provided by the federal government, especially in the New Deal and Great Society years; and the educative purposes and impact of fairs and expositions. Readers will doubtless discover other gaps. Some of the future literature may well result from filling them or by supplementing works perceived to be inadequate.

The major future course of the literature is almost impossible to chart. Any effort made in 1978 (when this exercise began) to guess what would be the important future books or trends would probably not have predicted any of the substantial works or movements of the subsequent fifteen years. Nor does past experience lead to confidence in a master plan of needed research. Such projections, some of them large-scale, have been made in the past, but they appear to have had little effect in stimulating their proposed plans of investigation.

The future literature seems likely to be primarily influenced by the summative effect of many kinds of investigations, each undertaken by a scholar who sees an opportunity to be of service. One incentive for investigators may well be the work now available. Every one of the books cited here could serve as an inspiration for some inquirer to carry on its theme or, alternatively, to refute its approach or conclusions. Such challenges will arise not only from the interests of individuals but also from the specifics of an ever-changing culture. A literature grows through a multifaceted development of ideas, controversy, the discovery of new techniques of investigation, and the interaction of researchers and other analysts with one another and with scholars in other fields.

In the epigraph to the preface, James Truslow Adams remarked that at first sight (in the early 1940s), the literature of adult education reminded him of an impenetrable jungle, complete with venomous snakes. An initial descent into the same terrain fifty years later might create the same impression, though if any snakes remain they appear to have been defanged. Even after intensive study, nobody would argue that the body of work in the field is now neat and tidy, like a formal French garden, but in its complexity and its tangled and interactive parts, it is perhaps best regarded as an ecosystem.

References

A small girl whom I once knew had a passion which I fear
was never gratified. She wanted a baby elephant as a pet. It
is amusing to reflect upon what might have happened if
some good fairy had granted her request. For she lived in a
small house with a negligible garden. Evidently she did not
foresee "whereto this thing might grow." I was in like case
when, five years ago, I began this inquiry which has ended
in the writing of this book.

—*Yeaxlee, 1925, vol. 1, p. 5*

The list of 1,241 works cited in this book is here presented in a
single alphabetical sequence by author or, failing any named person, by title or by issuing authority. Multiple items by a single
author, combination of authors, or other source are listed by date
of issuance. When more than one item from one source appeared
in a single year, a letter is added to the date of each one; thus, three
books published by one writer in 1987 would be entered under her
name as 1987a, 1987b, and 1987c.

 Little effort has been made in the past to establish the relative
quality of items in the literature. Three ways of identifying outstanding books will be used here. (1) For some years, the American
Association for Adult and Continuing Education (AAACE) has selected (usually annually) books to receive awards named for Im-
ogene Okes and Cyril O. Houle. Ten awards have been made for the
first award and ten for the second. (The list of awards was provided
by Judith Ann Koloski, executive director, American Association

for Adult and Continuing Education.) These works will here be designated with the letters *O* or *H*. (2) In 1989, Syracuse University (with the leadership of Roger Hiemstra) asked the professors of adult education in North American universities to identify the English-language works in their field that they thought to be outstanding; it was suggested that each person limit choices to not more than forty items[1]; 135 people responded. The fifty-nine works that received the votes of one-fifth or more of these highly qualified judges are here marked with an *S* (for Syracuse). (3) When all these notable books had been identified, there remained a number of others whose eminence seemed to me to deserve recognition. Perhaps they were too old, too new, too foreign, too obscure, or too formidable to have captured the attention they should have received. About each such work, a number of questions were raised. Did it deal with a major or probably important emergent theme? Was it written with freshness and style? Did it show striking originality? Did it have unusual weight and substance? Would anyone broadly familiar with the books in the field tend to rate it highly if it were drawn to his or her attention? Many books did not survive such questioning, but the ones that did are marked with an *X*. As the two AAACE lists and the Syracuse list overlap, only 66 books total were designated by them as outstanding. To that number, I have added 64 works for a total of 130, or 10 percent of all those listed here.

Academy for Educational Development. *Never Too Old to Learn.* New York: Academy for Educational Development. 1974. 109 pages.

Adam, T. R. *The Civic Value of Museums.* Studies in the Social Significance of Adult Education in the United States, no. 4. New York: American Association for Adult Education, 1937. 114 pages.

Adam, T. R. *The Museum and Popular Culture.* Studies in the Social Significance of Adult Education in the United States,

[1]Reported in Roger Hiemstra, Albert Mgulambwa, and Brent Snow, *English Language Adult Education Books: Their Value to Adult Educators,* Technical Report no. 4, Syracuse University Kellogg Project, 1991.

no. 14. New York: American Association for Adult Education, 1939. 177 pages.

Adam, T. R. *Motion Pictures in Adult Education*. Studies in the Social Significance of Adult Education in the United States, no. 18. New York: American Association for Adult Education, 1940a. 94 pages.

Adam, T. R. *The Worker's Road to Learning*. Studies in the Social Significance of Adult Education in the United States, no. 21. New York: American Association for Adult Education, 1940b. 162 pages.

Adams, Frank. *Unearthing Seeds of Fire: The Idea of Highlander*. Winston-Salem, N.C.: Blair, 1975. 255 pages.

Adams, Herbert B. "Summer Schools in England, Scotland, France, and Switzerland." In *Report of the Commissioner of Education for the Year 1897–1898*, vol. 1. Washington, D.C.: Government Printing Office, 1899, pp. 83–131.

Adams, Herbert B. "University Extension in Great Britain." In *Report of the Commissioner of Education for the Year 1898–1899*, vol. 1. Washington, D.C.: Government Printing Office, 1900, pp. 957–1055.

Adams, Herbert B. "Educational Extension in the United States." In *Report of the Commissioner of Education for the Year 1899–1900*, vol. 1. Washington, D.C.: Government Printing Office, 1901, pp. 275–379. (*X*)

Adams, James Truslow. *Frontiers of American Culture: A Study of Adult Education in a Democracy*. New York: Charles Scribner's Sons, 1944. 364 pages.

Addams, Jane. *Twenty Years at Hull-House*. New York: Macmillan, 1910. 462 pages. (*X*)

Adelson, Richard; Watkins, Fran S.; and Caplan, Richard M. (eds.). *Continuing Education for the Health Professional: Educational and Administrative Methods*. Rockville, Md.: Aspen, 1985. 249 pages.

Adler, Mortimer J., and Mayer, Milton. *The Revolution in Education*. Chicago: University of Chicago Press, 1958. 224 pages.

Adult Education: Adequacy of Provision. London: National Institute of Adult Education, 1970. 203 pages.

Adult Education After the War. Oxford, England: Oxford University Press, 1945. 64 pages.

Adult Education and Democracy. New York: American Association for Adult Education, 1936. 85 pages.

Adult Education and Public Libraries in the 1980s: A Symposium. London: Library Association, 1980. 94 pages.

Adult Education: Current Trends and Practices. Paris: Unesco, 1949. 147 pages.

Adult Education: A Plan for Development. London: Her Majesty's Stationery Office, 1973. 211 pages.

Advisory Council for Adult and Continuing Education. *Links to Learning.* Leicester, England: Advisory Council for Adult and Continuing Education, 1979a. 71 pages.

Advisory Council for Adult and Continuing Education. *A Strategy for the Basic Education of Adults.* Leicester, England: Advisory Council for Adult and Continuing Education, 1979b. 107 pages.

Advisory Council for Adult and Continuing Education. *Continuing Education: From Policies to Practice.* Leicester, England: Advisory Council for Adult and Continuing Education, 1982. 213 pages.

Agruso, Victor M., Jr. *Learning in the Later Years: Principles of Educational Gerontology.* San Diego, Calif.: Academic Press, 1978. 149 pages.

Aker, George F. *Adult Education Procedures, Methods, and Techniques: A Classified and Annotated Bibliography, 1953–1963.* Syracuse, N.Y.: Library of Continuing Education, Syracuse University, 1965. 163 pages.

Alderman, L. R. *Public Evening Schools for Adults.* Department of the Interior, Bureau of Education Bulletin, 1927, no. 21. Washington, D.C.: U.S. Government Printing Office, 1927. 31 pages.

Alford, Harold J. *Continuing Education in Action: Residential Centers for Lifelong Learning.* New York: Wiley, 1968. 153 pages.

Allen, Herman R. *Open Door to Learning.* Urbana: University of Illinois Press, 1963. 193 pages.

American Library Association. *Libraries and Adult Education.* New York: Macmillan, 1926. 284 pages.

Andersen, Brian David, and Andersen, Kevon. *Prisoners of the Deep.* New York: HarperCollins, 1984. 150 pages.

Anderson, Darrell, and Niemi, John A. *Adult Education and the Disadvantaged Adult.* Occasional Papers, no. 22. Syracuse, N.Y.: Syracuse University Publications in Continuing Education, 1970. 96 pages.

Anderson, Jonathan. *Technology and Adult Literacy.* London: Routledge, 1991. 219 pages.

Anderson, Richard E., and Kasl, Elizabeth Swain. *The Costs and Financing of Adult Education and Training.* Lexington, Mass.: Lexington Books, 1982. 328 pages. (*O*)

Appley, Dee G., and Winder, Alvin E. *T-Groups and Therapy Groups in a Changing Society.* San Francisco: Jossey-Bass, 1973. 209 pages.

Apps, Jerold W. *How to Improve Adult Education in Your Church.* Minneapolis, Minn.: Augsberg, 1972. 110 pages.

Apps, Jerold W. *Towards a Working Philosophy of Adult Education.* Syracuse, N.Y.: Syracuse University Publications in Continuing Education, 1973. 65 pages.

Apps, Jerold W. *Study Skills for Those Adults Returning to School.* New York: McGraw-Hill, 1978. 238 pages.

Apps, Jerold W. *Problems in Continuing Education.* New York: McGraw-Hill, 1979. 204 pages. (*S*)

Apps, Jerold W. *The Adult Learner on Campus: A Guide for Instructors and Administrators.* Chicago: Follett, 1981. 264 pages. (*S*)

Apps, Jerold W. *Improving Your Writing Skills: A Learning Plan for Adults.* Chicago: Follett, 1982. 239 pages.

Apps, Jerold W. *Improving Practice in Continuing Education: Modern Approaches for Understanding the Field and Determining Priorities.* San Francisco: Jossey-Bass, 1985. 225 pages. (*S*)

Apps, Jerold W. *Higher Education in a Learning Society: Meeting New Demands for Education and Training.* San Francisco: Jossey-Bass, 1988. 241 pages.

Apps, Jerold W. *Mastering the Teaching of Adults.* Malabar, Fla.: Krieger, 1991. 150 pages.

Argyris, Chris. *Increasing Leadership Effectiveness.* New York: Wiley, 1976. 286 pages.

Arndt, Christian O., and Everett, Samuel (eds.). *Education for a*

World Society: Promising Practices Today. New York: Harper-Collins, 1951. 273 pages.

Arndt, Christian O., and others. *Community Education: Principles and Practices from World-Wide Experience.* 58th Yearbook, National Society for the Study of Education. Part 1. Chicago: University of Chicago Press, 1959. 417 pages.

Arndt, Jack R., and Coons, Stephen Joel. *Continuing Education in Pharmacy.* Alexandria, Va.: American Association of Colleges of Pharmacy, 1987. 374 pages.

Arnove, Robert F., and Graff, Harvey J. (eds.). *National Literacy Campaigns: Historical and Comparative Perspectives.* New York: Plenum, 1987. 322 pages.

Ashby, Eric. *The Pathology of Adult Education.* Belfast, Northern Ireland: Queen's University, 1955. 24 pages.

Aslanian, Carol B., and Brickell, Henry M. *Americans in Transition: Life Changes as Reasons for Adult Learning.* New York: College Entrance Examination Board, 1980. 172 pages. (O,S)

Aslanian, Carol B., and Brickell, Henry M. *How Americans in Transition Study for College Credit.* New York: College Entrance Examination Board, 1988. 123 pages.

Asp, William G., and others. *Continuing Education for the Library Information Professions.* Hamden, Conn.: Library Professional Publications, 1985. 348 pages.

Astin, Helen S. (ed.). *Some Action of Her Own: The Adult Woman and Higher Education.* Lexington, Mass.: Lexington Books, 1976. 180 pages.

Auerbach, Aline B. *Parents Learn Through Discussion.* New York: Wiley, 1968. 358 pages.

Avakov, R. M. (ed.). *The Future of Education and the Education of the Future.* Paris: International Institute for Educational Planning, 1980. 369 pages.

Axford, Roger W. *Adult Education: The Open Door.* Scranton, Pa.: International Textbook, 1969. 247 pages.

Axford, Roger. *Adult Education: The Open Door to Lifelong Learning.* Indiana, Pa.: Halldin, 1980. 492 pages.

Axinn, George H., and Thorat, Sudhakar. *Modernizing World Agriculture: A Comparative Study of Agricultural Extension Systems.* New York: Praeger, 1972. 216 pages.

Baden, Clifford (ed.). *Competitive Strategies for Continuing Education.* New Directions for Continuing Education, no. 35. San Francisco: Jossey-Bass, 1987. 107 pages.

Bailey, Joseph Cannon. *Seaman A. Knapp: Schoolmaster of American Agriculture.* New York: Columbia University Press, 1945. 307 pages. (X)

Baker, Gladys. *The County Agent.* Chicago: University of Chicago Press, 1939. 226 pages.

Ban, A. W. van den, and Hawkins, H. S. *Agricultural Extension.* New York: Wiley, 1988. 328 pages. (X)

Banks, Frances. *Teach Them to Live.* London: Parrish, 1958. 287 pages.

Barbash, Jack. *Universities and Unions in Workers' Education.* New York: HarperCollins, 1955. 206 pages.

Bard, Ray; Bell, Chip R.; Stephen, Leslie; and Webster, Linda. *The Trainer's Professional Development Handbook.* San Francisco: Jossey-Bass, 1987. 346 pages.

Barton, George E., Jr. *Ordered Pluralism: A Philosophic Plan of Action for Teaching.* Chicago: Center for the Study of Liberal Education for Adults, 1964. 27 pages.

Barton, Paul. *Worklife Transitions: The Adult Learning Connection.* New York: McGraw-Hill, 1982. 197 pages.

Baskin, Samuel. *Organizing Nontraditional Study.* New Directions for Institutional Research, no. 4. San Francisco: Jossey-Bass, 1974. 93 pages.

Bataille, Leon (ed.). *A Turning Point for Literacy.* Elmsford, N.Y.: Pergamon Press, 1976. 277 pages.

Batchelder, Richard L., and Hardy, James M. *Using Sensitivity Training and the Laboratory Method: An Organizational Case Study in the Development of Human Resources.* New York: Association Press, 1968. 128 pages.

Bateman, Walter L. *Open to Question: The Art of Teaching and Learning by Inquiry.* San Francisco: Jossey-Bass, 1990. 221 pages.

Bates, Tony, and Robinson, John (eds.). *Evaluating Educational Television and Radio.* Milton Keynes, England: Open University Press, 1977. 410 pages.

Batten, T. R. *Training for Community Development: A Critical*

Study of Method. Oxford, England: Oxford University Press, 1962. 192 pages.

Beal, George M.; Bohlen, Joe M.; and Raudebaugh, J. Neil. *Leadership and Dynamic Group Action.* Ames: Iowa State University Press, 1962. 365 pages.

Beal, George M., and others. *Social Action and Interaction in Program Planning.* Ames: Iowa State University, 1966. 510 pages.

Beals, Ralph A. *Aspects of Post-Collegiate Education.* New York: American Association for Adult Education, 1935. 137 pages.

Beals, Ralph A., and Brody, Leon. *The Literature of Adult Education.* Studies in the Social Significance of Adult Education in the United States, no. 26. New York: American Association for Adult Education, 1941. 494 pages. (*X*)

Beder, Hal (ed.). *Realizing the Potential of Interorganizational Cooperation.* New Directions for Continuing Education, no. 23. San Francisco; Jossey-Bass, 1984. 94 pages.

Beder, Hal (ed.). *Marketing Continuing Education.* New Directions for Continuing Education, no. 31. San Francisco: Jossey-Bass, 1986. 110 pages.

Beder, Hal. *Adult Literacy: Issues for Policy and Practice.* Malabar, Fla.: Krieger, 1991. 182 pages. (*O*)

Begtrup, Holder; Lund, Hans; and Manniche, Peter. *The Folk High Schools of Denmark and the Development of a Farming Community.* (3rd ed.) Oxford, England: Oxford University Press, 1936. 176 pages.

Belbin, Eunice, and Belbin, R. Meredith. *Problems in Adult Retraining.* Portsmouth, N.H.: Heinemann Educational Books, 1972. 224 pages.

Belenky, Mary Field; Clinchy, Blythe M.; Goldberger, Nancy R.; and Tarule, Jill M. *Women's Ways of Knowing: The Development of Self, Voice, and Mind.* New York: Basic Books, 1986. 256 pages.

Bell, Raymond, and others. *Correctional Education Programs for Inmates.* Washington, D.C.: National Institute for Law Enforcement and Criminal Justice, 1979. 123 pages.

Bender, Ralph E., and others. *Adult Education in Agriculture.* Columbus, Ohio: Merrill, 1972. 225 pages.

Benne, Kenneth D., and others (eds.). *The Laboratory Method of*

Changing and Learning: Theory and Application. Palo Alto, Calif.: Science and Behavior Books, 1975. 589 pages.

Bennett, Clif; Kidd, J. Roby; and Kulich, Jindra. *Comparative Studies in Adult Education: An Anthology.* Syracuse, N.Y.: Syracuse University Publications in Continuing Education, 1975. 257 pages. *(X)*

Bennis, Warren G.; Benne, Kenneth D.; and Chin, Robert (eds.). *The Planning of Change.* (2nd ed.) Troy, Mo.: Holt, Rinehart & Winston, 1969. 627 pages. *(S)*

Berelson, Bernard. *The Library's Public.* New York: Columbia University Press, 1949. 175 pages.

Bergevin, Paul. *A Philosophy for Adult Education.* New York: Seabury Press, 1967. 176 pages. *(S)*

Bergevin, Paul, and McKinley, John. *Design for Adult Education in the Church.* New York: Seabury Press, 1961. 320 pages.

Bergevin, Paul, and McKinley, John. *Participation Training in Adult Education.* St. Louis, Mo.: Bethany Press, 1965. 108 pages.

Bergevin, Paul, and Morris, Dwight. *Group Processes for Adult Education.* Bloomington: Community Services in Adult Education, University of Indiana, 1954. 86 pages.

Bergevin, Paul; Morris, Dwight; and Smith, Robert M. *Adult Education Procedures: A Handbook of Tested Patterns for Effective Participation.* New York: Seabury Press, 1963. 245 pages. *(S)*

Bergsten, Urban. *Adult Education in Relation to Work and Leisure.* Stockholm, Sweden: Almquist & Wiksell, 1977. 245 pages.

Berridge, Robert I. *The Community Education Handbook.* Midland, Mich.: Pendell, 1973. 118 pages.

Berridge, Robert I.; Stark, Stephen L.; and West, Philip T. *Training the Community Educator: A Case-Study Approach.* Midland, Mich.: Pendell, 1977. 150 pages.

Berte, Neal R. (ed.). *Individualizing Education by Learning Contracts.* New Directions for Higher Education, no. 10. San Francisco: Jossey-Bass, 1975. 103 pages.

Bhola, H. S. *Campaigning for Literacy: Eight National Experiences of the Twentieth Century with a Memorandum to Decision-Makers.* Paris: Unesco, 1984. 203 pages.

Bhola, H. S. *World Trends and Issues in Adult Education.* London: Kingsley, 1989. 177 pages.

Biddle, William W., and Biddle, Loureide J. *The Community Development Process: The Rediscovery of Local Initiative.* Troy, Mo.: Holt, Rinehart & Winston, 1965. 334 pages. (X)

Bille, Donald A. (ed.). *Practical Approaches to Patient Teaching.* Boston: Little, Brown, 1981. 363 pages.

Birren, James E., and Schaie, K. Warner. *Handbook of the Psychology of Aging.* (3rd ed.) San Diego, Calif.: Academic Press, 1990. 552 pages.

Bittner, Walton S., and Mallory, Hervey F. *University Teaching by Mail.* New York: Macmillan, 1933. 355 pages.

Blackburn, Donald J. (ed.). *Extension Handbook.* Guelph, Canada: University of Guelph, 1984. 167 pages.

Blackburn, Donald J. (ed.). *Foundations and Changing Practices in Extension.* Guelph, Canada: University of Guelph, 1989. 159 pages.

Blakely, Robert J. *Adult Education in a Free Society.* Toronto: Guardian Bird, 1958. 184 pages.

Blakely, Robert J. *To Serve the Public Interest: Educational Broadcasting in the United States.* Syracuse, N.Y.: Syracuse University Press, 1979. 274 pages.

Blakely, Robert J., and Lappin, Ivan M. *Knowledge Is Power to Control Power: New Institutional Arrangements and Organizational Patterns for Continuing Education.* Syracuse, N.Y.: Syracuse University Publications in Continuing Education, 1969. 88 pages.

Blauch, Lloyd E. *Federal Cooperation in Agricultural Extension Work, Vocational Education, and Vocational Rehabilitation.* New York: Arno Press and New York Times, 1969. (Originally published in 1933.) 297 pages.

Bledsoe, Thomas. *Or We'll All Hang Separately: The Highlander Idea.* Boston: Beacon Press, 1969. 266 pages.

Bliss, R. K., and others (eds.). *The Spirit and Philosophy of Extension as Recorded in Significant Extension Papers.* Washington, D.C.: Graduate School, United States Department of Agriculture and Epsilon Sigma Phi, 1952. 293 pages.

Blyth, John A. *English University Adult Education, 1908–1958: The Unique Tradition.* Manchester, England: Manchester University Press, 1983. 363 pages.

Bock, John C., and Papagiannis, George J. (eds.). *Non-Formal Education and National Development: A Critical Assessment of Policy, Research, and Practice.* New York: Praeger, 1983. 390 pages.

Bode, Carl. *The American Lyceum: Town Meeting of the Mind.* New York: Oxford University Press, 1956. 275 pages.

Boggs, David L. *Adult Civic Education.* Springfield, Ill.: Thomas, 1991. 140 pages.

Boissoneau, Robert. *Continuing Education in the Health Professions.* Rockville, Md.: Aspen, 1980. 322 pages.

Boone, Edgar J. *Developing Programs in Adult Education.* Englewood Cliffs, N.J.: Prentice-Hall, 1985. 244 pages.

Boone, Edgar J.; Shearon, Ronald W.; White, Estelle E.; and Associates. *Serving Personal and Community Needs Through Adult Education.* AEA Handbook Series in Adult Education. San Francisco: Jossey-Bass, 1980. 338 pages.

Borah, Swapna (ed.). *Distance Education.* Delhi, India: Amar Prakashan, A-1/139B, Lawrence Road, 110035, 1987. 306 pages.

Bordia, Anie; Kidd, J. R.; and Draper, J. A. (eds.). *Adult Education in India.* Bombay, India: Nachiketa Publications, 1973. 532 pages.

Bormann, Ernest G. *Discussion and Group Methods: Theory and Practice.* (2nd ed.) New York: HarperCollins, 1975. 395 pages.

Boshier, Roger. "Factor Analysts at Large: A Critical Review of the Motivational Orientation Literature." *Adult Education,* 1976, *27,* 24-47. (O)[1]

Boshier, Roger. *Adult and Continuing Education in New Zealand, 1958-1978: A Bibliography.* Vancouver: Adult Education Research Centre, Faculty of Education, University of British Columbia, 1979. 157 pages.

Botkin, James W.; Elmandjra, Mahdi; and Malitza, Mircea. *No Limits to Learning—Bridging the Human Gap: A Report to the Club of Rome.* Elmsford, N.Y.: Pergamon Press, 1979. 157 pages.

Botwinick, Jack. *Cognitive Processes in Maturity and Old Age.* New York: Springer, 1967. 212 pages.

Boucouvalas, Marcie. *Adult Education in Greece.* Vancouver: Cen-

[1]This is not a book but is included here because it won the Okes award.

tre for Continuing Education, University of British Columbia, 1988. 139 pages.

Boud, David (ed.). *Developing Student Autonomy in Learning.* New York: Nichols, 1981. 222 pages.

Boud, David, and Griffin, Virginia (eds.). *Appreciating Adults Learning: From the Learner's Perspective.* London: Kogan Page, 1987. 248 pages.

Bown, Lalage, and Okedara, J. T. (eds.). *An Introduction to the Study of Adult Education: A Multidisciplinary and Cross-Cultural Approach for Developing Countries.* Ibadan, Nigeria: University Press, 1981. 323 pages.

Bown, Lalage, and Tomori, S. H. Olu (eds.). *A Handbook of Adult Education for West Africa.* London: Hutchinson, 1979. 296 pages.

Bowren, Fay F., and Zintz, Miles V. *Teaching Reading in Adult Basic Education.* Dubuque, Iowa: Brown, 1977. 409 pages.

Boyd, Robert D. (ed.). *Beyond the Four Walls: Adult Educators as Urban Change Agents.* Madison: University Extension, University of Wisconsin, 1969. 98 pages.

Boyd, Robert D.; Apps, Jerold W.; and others. *Redefining the Discipline of Adult Education.* AEA Handbook Series in Adult Education. San Francisco: Jossey-Bass, 1980. 219 pages.

Boyle, Patrick G. *Planning Better Programs.* New York: McGraw-Hill, 1981. 244 pages. (S)

Bradford, Leland P. *National Training Laboratories: Its History, 1947–1970.* Bethel, Maine: Bradford, 1974. 348 pages.

Bradford, Leland P. *Making Meetings Work.* San Diego, Calif.: University Associates, 1976. 121 pages.

Bradford, Leland P. (ed.). *Group Development.* (2nd ed.) San Diego, Calif.: University Associates, 1978. 234 pages.

Bradford, Leland P.; Gibb, Jack R.; and Benne, Kenneth D. (eds.). *T-Group Theory and Laboratory Method.* New York: Wiley, 1964. 498 pages.

Brameld, Theodore (ed.). *Workers' Education in the United States.* New York: HarperCollins, 1941. 338 pages.

Bratchell, D. F. *The Aims and Organization of Further Education.* Elmsford, N.Y.: Pergamon Press, 1968. 158 pages.

Brew, J. Macalester. *Informal Education: Adventures and Reflections.* London: Faber and Faber, 1948. 383 pages.

Bright, Barry P. (ed.). *Theory and Practice in the Study of Adult Education: The Epistemological Debate.* London: Routledge, 1989. 248 pages.

Brim, Orville, Jr. *Education for Child Rearing.* New York: Russell Sage Foundation, 1959. 362 pages.

Brinkerhoff, Robert O. *Achieving Results from Training: How to Evaluate Human Resource Development to Strengthen Programs and Increase Impact.* San Francisco: Jossey-Bass, 1987. 248 pages.

British Institute of Adult Education. *Adult Education After the War.* Oxford, England: Oxford University Press, 1945. 64 pages.

Brockett, Ralph G. (ed.). *Continuing Education in the Year 2000.* New Directions for Continuing Education, no. 36. San Francisco: Jossey-Bass, 1987. 102 pages.

Brockett, Ralph G. (ed.). *Ethical Issues in Adult Education.* New York: Teachers College Press, Columbia University, 1988. 217 pages.

Brockett, Ralph G. (ed.). *Professional Development for Educators of Adults.* New Directions for Adult and Continuing Education, no. 51. San Francisco: Jossey-Bass, 1991. 107 pages.

Brockett, Ralph G., and Hiemstra, Roger. *Self-Direction in Adult Learning: Perspectives on Theory, Research, and Practice.* London: Routledge, 1991. 276 pages.

Brookfield, Stephen. *Adult Learners, Adult Education and the Community.* New York: Teachers College Press, 1984. 229 pages. (S)

Brookfield, Stephen (ed.). *Self-Directed Learning: From Theory to Practice.* New Directions for Continuing Education, no. 25. San Francisco: Jossey-Bass, 1985. 94 pages.

Brookfield, Stephen. *Understanding and Facilitating Adult Learning: Comprehensive Analysis of Principles and Effective Practices.* San Francisco: Jossey-Bass, 1986. 375 pages. (O,H,S)

Brookfield, Stephen (ed.). *Learning Democracy: Eduard Lindeman on Adult Education and Social Change.* London: Croom Helm, 1987. 238 pages.

Brookfield, Stephen. *Developing Critical Thinkers: Challenging*

Adults to Explore Alternative Ways of Thinking and Acting. San Francisco: Jossey-Bass, 1988a. 293 pages. (*H,S*)

Brookfield, Stephen (ed.). *Training Educators of Adults.* New York: Routledge, 1988b. 344 pages.

Brookfield, Stephen D. *The Skillful Teacher: On Technique, Trust, and Responsiveness in the Classroom.* San Francisco: Jossey-Bass, 1990. 233 pages.

Brooks, Jean S., and Reich, David L. *The Public Library in Non-Traditional Education.* Homewood, Ill.: ETC Publications, 1974. 244 pages.

Broschart, James R. *Lifelong Learning in the Nation's Third Century.* HEW publication no. (OE) 76-09102. Washington, D.C.: U.S. Government Printing Office, 1977. 47 pages.

Brown, Cynthia. *Literacy in 30 Hours: Paulo Freire's Process in North East Brazil.* London: Writers and Readers Publishing Cooperative, 1975. 47 pages. (*X*)

Brown, M. Alan, and Copeland, Harlan G. (eds.). *Attracting Able Instructors of Adults.* New Directions for Continuing Education, no. 4. San Francisco: Jossey-Bass, 1979. 98 pages.

Brownell, Baker. *The College and the Community.* New York: HarperCollins, 1952. 248 pages.

Brundage, Donald H., and Mackeracher, Dorothy. *Adult Learning Principles and Their Application to Program Planning.* Toronto: Ontario Ministry of Education, 1980. 126 pages.

Brunner, Edmund deS. *Community Organization and Adult Education.* Chapel Hill: University of North Carolina Press, 1942. 124 pages.

Brunner Edmund deS.; Sanders, Irwin T.; and Ensminger, Douglas (eds.). *Farmers of the World: The Development of Agricultural Extension.* New York: Columbia University Press, 1945. 208 pages. (*X*)

Brunner, Edmund deS., and Yang, E. Hsin-Pao. *Rural America and the Extension Service.* New York: Teachers College Press, 1949. 210 pages.

Brunner, Edmund deS., and others. *An Overview of Adult Education Research.* Chicago: Adult Education Association, 1959. 279 pages. (*S*)

Bryson, Lyman. *A State Plan for Adult Education.* New York: American Association for Adult Education, 1934. 69 pages.

Bryson, Lyman. *Adult Education.* New York: American Book Company, 1936. 208 pages. (S)

Buck, Pearl S. *Tell the People.* New York: Day, 1945. 84 pages.

Burden, Larry, and Whitt, Robert L. *The Community School Principal: New Horizons.* Midland, Mich.: Pendell, 1973. 250 pages.

Burge, Elizabeth J. (ed.). "Adult Learners, Learning, and Public Libraries." *Library Trends,* 1983, *31*(4), 513–686.

Burke, W. Warner, and Beckhard, Richard (eds.). *Conference Planning.* (2nd ed.) La Jolla, Calif.: University Associates, 1976. 174 pages.

Burns, Norman, and Houle, Cyril O. (eds.). *The Community Responsibilities of Institutions of Higher Education.* Chicago: University of Chicago Press, 1948. 88 pages.

Burrell, John Angus. *A History of Adult Education at Columbia University: University Extension and the School of General Studies.* New York: Columbia University Press, 1954. 112 pages.

Burrichter, Arthur W., and Ulmer, Curtis. *Special Techniques That Work in Teaching the Culturally Deprived.* Englewood Cliffs, N.J.: Prentice-Hall, 1972. 40 pages.

Burrows, John. *University Adult Education in London: A Century of Achievement.* London: University of London, 1976. 122 pages.

Burton, Arthur J. *Encounter: The Theory and Practice of Encounter Groups.* San Francisco: Jossey-Bass, 1969. 207 pages.

Buskey, John (ed.). *Attracting External Funds for Continuing Education.* New Directions for Continuing Education, no. 12. San Francisco: Jossey-Bass, 1981. 134 pages.

Buswell, Guy T. *How Adults Read.* Chicago: University of Chicago Press, 1937. 158 pages.

Caffarella, Rosemary S. *Program Development and Evaluation Resource Book for Trainers.* New York: Wiley, 1988. 266 pages. (X)

Calvert, Steven L. *Alumni Continuing Education.* New York: American Council on Education, Macmillan, 1987. 311 pages.

Campbell, Duncan D. *Adult Education as a Field of Study and Practice: Strategies for Development.* Vancouver: Centre for Continuing Education, University of British Columbia, 1977. 230 pages.

Campbell, Olive Dame. *The Danish Folk School: Its Influence in the Life of Denmark and the North.* New York: Macmillan, 1928. 359 pages.

Campbell, W. Reason. *Dead Men Walking: Teaching in a Maximum-Security Prison.* New York: Marek, 1978. 274 pages.

Candy, Philip C. *Self-Direction for Lifelong Learning: A Comprehensive Guide to Theory and Practice.* San Francisco: Jossey-Bass, 1991. 567 pages. (*H*)

Cantor, Jeffrey A. *Delivering Instruction to Adult Learners.* Toronto: Wall & Emerson, 1992. 212 pages.

Cantor, Leonard M., and Roberts, I. F. *Further Education Today: A Critical Review.* (2nd ed.) New York: Routledge & Kegan Paul, 1983. 265 pages.

Capes, Mary (ed.). *Communication or Conflict?* New York: Association Press, 1960. 228 pages.

Carey, James T. *Forms and Forces in University Adult Education.* Chicago: Center for the Study of Liberal Education for Adults, 1961. 229 pages.

Carey, Lee J. (ed.). *Community Development as a Process.* Columbia: University of Missouri Press, 1970. 213 pages.

Carlson, Robert A. *The Quest for Conformity: Americanization Through Education.* New York: Wiley, 1975. 188 pages.

Carlson, Robert A. *The Americanization Syndrome: A Quest for Conformity.* New York: St. Martin's Press, 1987. 197 pages.

Carnegie Commission on Higher Education. *Toward a Learning Society.* New York: McGraw-Hill, 1973. 112 pages.

Carnevale, Anthony P.; Gainer, Leila J.; and Meltzer, Ann S. *Workplace Basics: The Essential Skills Employers Want.* San Francisco: Jossey-Bass, 1990a. 477 pages.

Carnevale, Anthony P.; Gainer, Leila J.; and Meltzer, Ann S. *Workplace Basics Training Manual.* San Francisco: Jossey-Bass, 1990b. 304 pages.

Carnevale, Anthony P.; Gainer, Leila J.; and Schulz, Eric R. *Training the Technical Work Force.* San Francisco: Jossey-Bass, 1990. 196 pages. (*X*)

Carnevale, Anthony P.; Gainer, Leila J.; and Villet, Janice. *Training in America: The Organization and Strategic Role of Training.* San Francisco: Jossey-Bass, 1990. 261 pages.

Carnevale, Anthony P., and Goldstein, Harold. *Employee Training: Its Changing Role and an Analysis of New Data.* Washington, D.C.: ASTD Press, 1983. 84 pages.

Carnovsky, Leon, and Martin, Lowell (eds.). *The Library in the Community.* Chicago: University of Chicago Press, 1944. 238 pages.

Carroll, John B., and Chall, Jeanne S. (eds.). *Toward a Literate Society: The Report of the Committee on Reading of the National Academy of Education.* New York: McGraw-Hill, 1975. 370 pages.

Carter, Jean. *Parents in Perplexity.* Studies in the Social Significance of Adult Education in the United States, no. 11. New York: American Association for Adult Education, 1938. 143 pages.

Carter, Jean, and Ogden, Jess. *Everyman's Drama.* Studies in the Social Significance of Adult Education in the United States, no. 12. New York: American Association of Adult Education, 1938. 136 pages.

Carter, Jean, and Smith, Hilda W. *Education and the Worker-Student.* New York: Affiliated Schools for Workers, 1934. 72 pages.

Carton, Michel. *Education and the World of Work: Studies and Surveys in Comparative Education.* Paris: Unesco, 1984. 237 pages.

Cartwright, Dorwin, and Zander, Alvin. *Group Dynamics: Research and Theory.* (3rd ed.) New York: HarperCollins, 1968. 580 pages. (S)

Cartwright, Morse Adams. *Ten Years of Adult Education.* New York: Macmillan, 1935. 220 pages.

Case, Victoria, and Case, Robert Ormond. *We Called It Culture.* New York: Doubleday, 1948. 272 pages.

Casner-Lotto, Jill, and Associates. *Successful Training Strategies: Twenty-Six Innovative Corporate Models.* San Francisco: Jossey-Bass, 1988. 429 pages.

Cass, Angelica W. *Basic Education for Adults.* New York: Association Press, 1971. 160 pages.

Cass, Angelica W., and Crabtree, Arthur P. *Adult Elementary Education.* New York: Noble and Noble, 1956. 275 pages.

Cassara, Beverly Benner (ed.). *Adult Educatiion in a Multicultural Society*. New York: Routledge & Kegan Paul, 1990. 236 pages.

Cassidy, Frank, and Faris, Ron (eds.). *Choosing Our Future: Adult Education and Public Policy in Canada*. Toronto: Ontario Institute for Studies in Education, 1987. 245 pages.

Cell, Edward. *Learning to Learn from Experience*. Albany: State University of New York Press, 1984. 245 pages.

Centre for Educational Research and Innovation. *Developments in Educational Leave of Absence*. Paris: Organisation for Economic Co-operation and Development, 1976. 237 pages.

Cervero, Ronald M. *Effective Continuing Education for Professionals*. San Francisco: Jossey-Bass, 1988. 191 pages. (*H*)

Cervero, Ronald M.; Azzaretto, John F.; and others. *Visions for the Future of Continuing Professional Education*. Athens: University of Georgia, 1990. 246 pages.

Cervero, Ronald M., and Scanlan, Craig L. (eds.). *Problems and Prospects in Continuing Professional Education*. New Directions for Continuing Education, no. 27. San Francisco: Jossey-Bass, 1985. 114 pages.

Chadwick, A. F. *The Role of the Museum and Art Gallery in Community Education*. Nottingham, England: Department of Adult Education, University of Nottingham, 1980. 158 pages.

Chalofsky, Neal E., and Reinhart, Carlene. *Effective Human Resource Development; How to Build a Strong and Responsive HRD Function*. San Francisco: Jossey-Bass, 1988. 146 pages.

Chamberlain, Martin N. *Providing Continuing Education by Media and Technology*. New Directions for Continuing Education, no. 5. San Francisco: Jossey-Bass, 1980. 104 pages.

Chancellor, John (ed.). *Helping Adults to Learn: The Library in Action*. Chicago: American Library Association, 1939. 296 pages. (*X*)

Chancellor, John; Tompkins, Miriam D.; and Medway, Hazel I. *Helping the Reader Toward Self-Education*. Chicago: American Library Association, 1938. 111 pages.

Chang, T. M., and others. *Distance Learning: On the Design of an Open University*. Boston: Kluwer-Nijhof, 1983. 195 pages.

Channing, William E. *Self-Culture*. Boston: Munroe, 1839. 57 pages.

Charner, Ivan, and Rolzinski, Catherine A. (eds.). *Responding to the Educational Needs of Today's Workplace.* New Directions for Continuing Education, no. 33. San Francisco: Jossey-Bass, 1987. 102 pages.

Charnley, Alan H. *Research in Adult Education in the British Isles.* London: National Institute of Adult Education, 1974. 361 pages.

Charnley, Alan H. *Paid Educational Leave.* St. Albans, England: Hart-Davis, 1975. 148 pages.

Charnley, A. H., and Jones, H. A. *The Concept of Success in Adult Literacy.* Cambridge, England: Huntington, 1979. 200 pages.

Charters, Alexander N., and Hilton, Ronald J. (eds.). *Landmarks in International Adult Education: A Comparative Analysis.* New York: Routledge & Kegan Paul, 1989. 207 pages.

Charters, Alexander N., and Rivera, William M. (eds.). *International Seminar on Publications in Continuing Education.* Syracuse, N.Y.: Syracuse University, Publications in Continuing Education, 1972. 112 pages.

Charters, Alexander, and Associates. *Comparing Adult Education Worldwide.* AEA Handbook Series in Adult Education. San Francisco: Jossey-Bass, 1981. 272 pages.

Chase, Stuart, and Chase, Marian Tyler. *Roads to Agreement.* New York: HarperCollins, 1951. 250 pages.

Chen, Ching-chih, and Hernon, Peter. *Information Seeking: Assessing and Anticipating User Needs.* New York: Neal-Schuman, 1982. 205 pages.

Chickering, Arthur W. *Experience and Learning: An Introduction to Experiential Learning.* New Rochelle, N.Y.: Change Magazine Press, 1971. 89 pages.

Chickering, Arthur W., and Associates. *The Modern American College: Responding to the New Realities of Diverse Students and a Changing Society.* San Francisco: Jossey-Bass, 1981. 810 pages.

Childers, Thomas. *The Information-Poor in America.* Metuchen, N.J.: Scarecrow Press, 1975. 182 pages.

Chisman, Forrest P., and Associates. *Leadership for Literacy: The Agenda for the 1990s.* San Francisco: Jossey-Bass, 1990. 277 pages.

Christenson, James A., and Robinson, Jerry W., Jr. (eds.). *Com-*

munity Development in America. Ames: Iowa State University Press, 1980. 245 pages.

Clapp, Elsie R. *Community Schools in Action*. New York: Viking Penguin, 1940. 429 pages. (*X*)

Clark, Burton R. *The Open Door College: A Case Study*. New York: McGraw-Hill, 1960. 207 pages.

Clark, Burton R. *Adult Education in Transition: A Study of Institutional Insecurity*. Berkeley: University of California Press, 1968. 202 pages. (*S*)

Clark, Harold F., and Sloan, Harold S. *Classrooms in the Factories: An Account of Educational Activities Conducted by American Industry*. Rutherford, N.J.: Institute of Research, Fairleigh Dickenson University, 1958. 139 pages.

Clark, Harold F., and Sloan, Harold S. *Classrooms in the Military: An Account of Education in the Armed Forces of the United States*. New York: Teachers College Press, Columbia University, 1963. 154 pages.

Clark, Harold F., and Sloan, Harold S. *Classrooms on Main Street*. New York: Teachers College Press, Columbia University, 1966. 162 pages.

Clarke, John. *Resource-Based Learning for Higher and Continuing Education*. London: Croom Helm, 1982. 211 pages.

Clemmons, Robert S. *Dynamics of Christian Adult Education*. New York: Abingdon Press, 1958. 143 pages.

Cleugh, M. F. *Educating Older People*. (2nd ed.) London: Tavistock, 1970. 187 pages.

Clift, David H., and others. *Adult Reading*. 55th Yearbook, National Society for the Study of Education. Part 2. Chicago: University of Chicago Press, 1956. 279 pages.

Clyne, Peter. *The Disadvantaged Adult: Educational and Social Needs of Minority Groups*. White Plains, N.Y.: Longman, 1972. 147 pages.

Coady, M. M. *Masters of Their Own Destiny: The Story of the Antigonish Movement of Adult Education Through Economic Cooperation*. New York: HarperCollins, 1939. 170 pages.

Cochrane, Nancy J., and others. *J. R. Kidd: An International Legacy of Learning*. Monographs on Comparative and Area Studies in Adult Education. Vancouver: Center for Continuing Education, University of British Columbia, 1986. 320 pages.

Collins, Denis E. *Paulo Freire: His Life, Works, and Thought.* New York: Paulist Press, 1977. 94 pages.

Collins, Michael. *Competence in Adult Education.* Lanham, Md.: University Press of America, 1987. 152 pages.

Collins, Michael. *Adult Education as Vocation: A Critical Role for the Adult Educator.* New York: Routledge & Kegan Paul, 1991. 146 pages.

Collins, Zipporah (ed.). *Museums, Adults, and the Humanities.* Washington, D.C.: American Association of Museums, 1981. 399 pages.

Commission on Non-Traditional Study. *Diversity by Design.* San Francisco: Jossey-Bass, 1973. 178 pages.

Compton, J. Lin (ed.). *The Transformation of International Agricultural Research and Development.* Boulder, Colo.: Lynne Rienner, 1989. 237 pages.

Congdon, Wray H., and Henry, David D. *Adult Education: A Bibliography with Annotations and an Introduction.* Lansing: Michigan School Service, 1934. 39 pages.

Conroy, Barbara. *Library Staff Development and Continuing Education: Principles and Practices.* Littleton, Colo.: Libraries Unlimited, 1978. 296 pages.

Cook, Alice H., and Douty, Agnes M. *Labor Education Outside the Unions: A Review of Postwar Programs in Western Europe and the United States.* Ithaca: New York State School of Industrial and Labor Relations, Cornell University, 1958. 148 pages.

Cook, Wanda Dauksza. *Adult Literacy Education in the United States.* Newark, Del.: International Reading Association, 1977. 139 pages.

Cookson, Peter S. (ed.). *Recruiting and Retaining Adult Students.* New Directions for Continuing Education, no. 41. San Francisco: Jossey-Bass, 1989. 118 pages.

Coombs, Philip H. *The World Crisis in Education: The View from the Eighties.* New York: Oxford University Press, 1985. 353 pages.

Coombs, Philip H., and Ahmed, Manzoor. *Attacking Rural Pov-*

erty: How Nonformal Education Can Help. Baltimore, Md.: Johns Hopkins University Press, 1974. (X)

Cooper, Signe Scott, and Hornback, May Shiga. *Continuing Nursing Education.* New York: McGraw-Hill, 1973. 261 pages.

Coplan, Kate, and Castagna, Edwin. *The Library Reaches Out.* Dobbs Ferry, N.Y.: Oceana Publications, 1965. 416 pages.

Corbett, E. A. *We Have with Us Tonight.* Toronto: Ryerson, 1957. 222 pages.

Corfield, A. J. *Epoch in Workers' Education: A History of the Workers' Educational Trade Union Committee.* London: Workers' Educational Association, 1969. 272 pages.

Corner, Trevor (ed.). *Learning Opportunities for Adults.* New York: Routledge & Kegan Paul, 1990. 238 pages.

Costa, Marie. *Adult Literacy/Illiteracy in the United States: A Handbook for Reference and Research.* Santa Barbara, Calif.: ABC-Clio, 1988. 167 pages.

Costello, Neil, and Richardson, Michael. *Continuing Education for the Post-Industrial Society.* Milton Keynes, England: Open University Press, 1982. 146 pages.

Cotton, Webster E. *On Behalf of Adult Education: A Historical Examination of the Supporting Literature.* Boston: Center for the Study of Liberal Education for Adults, 1968. 82 pages.

Council of Europe. *Permanent Education: A Framework for Recurrent Education. Theory and Practice.* Strasbourg, France: Council of Europe, 1975. 30 pages.

Courtney, Sean. *Why Adults Learn: Towards a Theory of Participation in Adult Education.* London: Routledge, 1992. 191 pages.

Couvert, Roger. *The Evaluation of Literacy Programmes: A Practical Guide.* Paris: Unesco, 1979. 168 pages.

Craig, Robert L. (ed.). *Training and Development Handbook: A Guide to Human Resources Development.* (3rd ed.) New York: McGraw-Hill, 1987. 878 pages.

Craik, William W. *The Central Labour College, 1909-29: A Chapter in the History of Adult Working-Class Education.* London: Lawrence & Wishart, 1969. 192 pages.

Crane, Diana. *Invisible Colleges: Diffusion of Knowledge in Scientific Communities.* Chicago: University of Chicago Press, 1972. 213 pages.

Cranton, Patricia. *Planning Instruction for Adult Learners.* Toronto: Wall and Thompson, 1989. 215 pages.

Cranton, Patricia. *Working with Adult Learners.* Toronto: Wall & Emerson, 1992. 234 pages.

Creese, James. *The Extension of University Teaching.* Studies in the Social Significance of Adult Education in the United States, no. 27. New York: American Association for Adult Education, 1941. 170 pages.

Crimi, James E. *Adult Education in the Liberal Arts Colleges.* Notes and Essays on Education for Adults, no. 17. Chicago: Center for the Study of Liberal Education for Adults, 1957. 38 pages.

Cropley, A. J. *Lifelong Education: A Psychological Analysis.* Elmsford, N.Y.: Pergamon Press, 1977. 196 pages.

Cropley, A. J. (ed.). *Toward a System of Lifelong Education: Some Practical Considerations.* Elmsford, N.Y.: Pergamon Press, 1980. 219 pages.

Cropley, A. J., and Dave, R. H. *Lifelong Education and the Training of Teachers.* Elmsford, N.Y.: Pergamon Press, 1978. 245 pages.

Cross, K. Patricia. *The Missing Link: Connecting Adult Learners to Learning Resources.* New York: College Entrance Examination Board, 1978. 80 pages.

Cross, K. Patricia. *Adults as Learners: Increasing Participation and Facilitating Learning.* San Francisco: Jossey-Bass, 1981. 300 pages. (S)

Cross, K. Patricia; Valley, John R., and others. *Planning Non-Traditional Programs: An Analysis of the Issues for Postsecondary Education.* San Francisco: Jossey-Bass, 1974. 263 pages.

Cross, Wilbur, and Florio, Carol. *You Are Never Too Old to Learn.* New York: McGraw-Hill, 1978. 226 pages.

Crouch, Bruce R., and Chamala, Shankariah. *Extension Education and Rural Development.* 2 vols. New York: Wiley, 1981. Vol. 1, 361 pages; vol. 2, 313 pages. (X)

Crux, Sandra C. *Learning Strategies for Adults: Compensations for Learning Disabilities.* Toronto: Wall & Emerson, 1989. 130 pages.

Curzon, L. B. *Teaching in Further Education.* London: Cassell, 1976. 218 pages.

Daloz, Laurent A. *Effective Teaching and Mentoring: Realizing the Transformational Power of Adult Learning.* San Francisco: Jossey-Bass, 1986. 256 pages. (*H,S*)

Daniel, John S.; Stroud, Martha A.; and Thompson, John R. (eds.). *Learning at a Distance: A World Perspective.* Edmonton, Canada: Athabasca University, 1982. 338 pages.

Darkenwald, Gordon G., and Knox, Alan B. (eds.). *Meeting Educational Needs of Young Adults.* New Directions for Continuing Education, no. 21. San Francisco: Jossey-Bass, 1984. 110 pages.

Darkenwald, Gordon G., and Larson, Gordon A. *Reaching Hard-to-Reach Adults.* New Directions for Continuing Education, no. 8. San Francisco: Jossey-Bass, 1980. 96 pages.

Darkenwald, Gordon G., and Merriam, Sharan B. *Adult Education: Foundations of Practice.* New York: HarperCollins, 1982. 260 pages. (*H,S*)

Dave, R. H. (ed.). *Lifelong Education and the School Curriculum.* Unesco Institute for Education, monograph 1. Hamburg, Germany: Unesco Institute for Education, 1973. 90 pages. (*X*)

Dave, R. H. *Reflections on Lifelong Education and the School.* Unesco Institute for Education, monograph 3. Hamburg, Germany: Unesco Institute for Education, 1975. 80 pages.

Dave, R. H. (ed.). *Foundations of Lifelong Education.* Elmsford, N.Y.: Pergamon Press, 1976. 382 pages. (*X*)

Dave, R. H.; Ouane, A.; and Perera, D. A. (eds.). *Learning Strategies for Post-Literacy and Continuing Education in China, India, Indonesia, Nepal, Thailand, and Vietnam.* Hamburg, Germany: Unesco Institute for Education, 1986. 284 pages.

Dave, R. H.; Ouane, A.; and Ranaweera, A. M. (eds.). *Learning Strategies for Post-Literacy and Continuing Education in Brazil, Colombia, Jamaica, and Venezuela.* Hamburg, Germany: Unesco Institute for Education, 1986. 282 pages.

Dave, R. H.; Perera, D. A.; and Ouane, A. (eds.). *Learning Strategies for Post-Literacy and Continuing Education in Mali, Niger, Senegal, and Upper Volta.* Hamburg, Germany: Unesco Institute for Education, 1984. 206 pages.

Dave, R. H.; Perera, D. A.; and Ouane, A. (eds.). *Learning Strategies for Post-Literacy and Continuing Education: A Cross-National*

Perspective. Hamburg, Germany: Unesco Institute for Education, 1985a. 269 pages.

Dave, R. H.; Perera, D. A.; and Ouane, A. (eds.). *Learning Strategies for Post-Literacy and Continuing Education in Kenya, Nigeria, Tanzania, and United Kingdom.* Hamburg, Germany: Unesco Institute for Education, 1985b. 256 pages.

Dave, R. H., and Stiemerling, N. *Lifelong Education and the School: Abstracts and Bibliography.* Unesco Institute for Education, monograph 2. Hamburg, Germany: Unesco Institute for Education, 1973. 154 pages.

Davies, Ivor K. *The Management of Learning.* New York: McGraw-Hill, 1971. 256 pages.

Davies, Ivor K. *Instructional Technique.* New York: McGraw-Hill, 1981. 369 pages.

Davies, J. H., and Thomas, J. E. (eds.). *A Select Bibliography of Adult Continuing Education.* (5th ed.) Leicester: National Institute of Adult Continuing Education (England and Wales), 1988. 209 pages.

Davies, T. Charles. *Open Learning Systems for Mature Students.* London: Council for Educational Technology, 1977. 145 pages.

Davis, David C. L. *Model for a Humanistic Education: The Danish Folk Highschool.* Columbus, Ohio: Merrill, 1971. 132 pages.

Davis, Gary A., and Scott, Joseph A. *Training Creative Thinking.* Troy, Mo.: Holt, Rinehart & Winston, 1971. 302 pages.

Davis, James A. *Great Books and Small Groups.* New York: Free Press of Glencoe, 1961. 237 pages.

Davis, Larry Nolan, and McCallon, Earl. *Planning, Conducting, Evaluating Workshops.* Austin, Tex.: Learning Concepts, 1974. 310 pages.

Debatin, Frank M. *The Administration of Adult Education.* New York: American Book Company, 1938. 486 pages.

Debons, Anthony, and others. *The Information Professional: Survey of an Emerging Field.* New York: Dekker, 1981. 271 pages.

DeCrow, Roger. *New Learning for Older Americans: An Overview of National Effort.* Washington, D.C.: Adult Education Association, 1975. 150 pages.

Dees, Norman (ed.). *Approaches to Adult Teaching.* Elmsford, N.Y.: Pergamon Press, 1965. 198 pages.

Deshler, David (ed.). *Evaluation for Program Improvement.* New Directions for Continuing Education, no. 24. San Francisco: Jossey-Bass, 1984. 109 pages.

A Design for Democracy. New York: Association Press, 1956. 222 pages.

Dickerman, Watson. *Outposts of the Public Schools.* Studies in the Social Significance of Adult Education in the United States, no. 10. New York: American Association for Adult Education, 1938. 76 pages.

Dickinson, Gary. *Teaching Adults: A Handbook for Instructors.* Toronto: New Press, 1973. 108 pages.

Diekhoff, John S. *The Domain of the Faculty in Our Expanding Colleges.* New York: HarperCollins, 1956. 204 pages.

Diller, Karl Conrad. *The Language Teaching Controversy.* Rowley, Mass.: Newbury House, 1978. 174 pages.

Directory of Adult Education Periodicals. Paris: Unesco, 1985. 151 pages.

DiSilvestro, Frank R. *Advising and Counseling Adult Learners.* New Directions for Continuing Education; no. 10. San Francisco: Jossey-Bass, 1981. 113 pages.

Dobbs, A. E. *Education and Social Movements, 1700–1850.* White Plains, N.Y.: Longman, 1919. 257 pages.

Doddy, Hurley H. *Informal Groups and the Community.* New York: Teachers College Press, Columbia University, 1952. 34 pages.

Donahue, Wilma (ed.). *Education for Later Maturity: A Handbook.* New York: Whiteside, Morrow, 1955. 338 pages.

Draper, William H. *University Extension: A Survey of Fifty Years, 1873–1923.* Cambridge, England: Cambridge University Press, 1923. 255 pages.

Draves, Bill. *The Free University: A Model for Lifelong Learning.* Chicago: Follett, 1980. 321 pages.

Draves, William A. *How to Teach Adults.* Manhattan, Kans.: Learning Resources Network, 1984. 117 pages.

Duguid, Stephen (ed.). *Yearbook of Correctional Education, 1989.* Burnaby, Canada: Institute for the Humanities, Simon Fraser University, 1989. 310 pages.

Duke, Christopher. *Australian Perspectives on Lifelong Learning.*

Victoria: Australian Council for Educational Research, 1976. 104 pages.

Duke, Christopher (ed.). *Combatting Poverty Through Adult Education: National Development Strategies.* London: Croom Helm, 1985. 253 pages.

Duke, Christopher (ed.). *Adult Education: International Perspectives from China.* London: Croom Helm, 1987. 254 pages.

Duke, Christopher, and Marriott, Stuart. *Paper Awards in Liberal Adult Education.* London: Michael Joseph, 1973. 301 pages.

Duke, C., and Sommerlad, Elizabeth. *Design for Diversity: Further Education for Tribal Aborigines in the North.* Canberra: Australian National University, 1976. 161 pages.

Durrance, Joan C. *Armed for Action: Library Responses to Citizen Information Needs.* New York: Neal-Schuman, 1984. 190 pages.

Durrance, Joan C., and Vainstein, Rose (eds.). *Public Libraries and New Directions for Adult Services.* Ann Arbor: School of Library Science, University of Michigan, 1981. 73 pages.

DuSautoy, Peter. *The Organization of a Community Development Programme.* Oxford, England: Oxford University Press, 1962. 156 pages.

Dutton, M. Donnie; Seaman, Don F.; and Ulmer, Curtis. *Understanding Group Dynamics in Adult Education.* Englewood-Cliffs, N.J.: Prentice-Hall, 1972. 64 pages.

Dwyer, Richard E. *Labor Education in the U.S.: An Annotated Bibliography.* Metuchen, N.J.: Scarecrow Press, 1977. 274 pages.

Dyer, John. *Ivory Towers in the Marketplace: The Evening College in America.* New York: Bobbs-Merrill, 1956. 205 pages.

Eddy, Edward Danforth, Jr. *Colleges for Our Land and Time.* New York: HarperCollins, 1957. 328 pages.

Edström, Lars-Olof; Erdos, Renée; and Prosser, Roy (eds.). *Mass Education.* Stockholm, Sweden: Almqvist & Wiksell, 1970. 380 pages.

Edwards, H. J. *The Evening Institute.* London: National Institute of Adult Education, 1961. 192 pages.

Egan, Gerard. *Encounter: Group Processes for Interpersonal Growth.* Pacific Grove, Calif.: Brooks/Cole, 1970. 419 pages.

Eggleston, George Cary. *How to Educate Yourself: With or Without Masters.* New York: Putnam, 1872. 151 pages.

Eisner, Elliot W., and Dobbs, Stephen M. *The Uncertain Profession: Observations on the State of Museum Education in Twenty American Art Museums.* Los Angeles: Getty Center for Education in the Arts, 1986. 106 pages.

Elias, John L. *Conscientization and Deschooling: Freire's and Illich's Proposals for Reshaping Society.* Philadelphia: Westminster, 1976. 170 pages.

Elias, John L. *The Foundations and Practice of Adult Religious Education.* Malabar, Fla.: Krieger, 1982. 301 pages.

Elias, John L. *Studies in Theology and Education.* Malabar, Fla.: Krieger, 1986. 229 pages.

Elias, John L., and Merriam, Sharan. *Philosophical Foundations of Adult Education.* Malabar, Fla.: Krieger, 1980. 212 pages. (S)

Ellwood, Caroline. *Adult Learning Today: A New Role for the Universities?* Newbury Park, Calif.: Sage, 1976. 266 pages.

Elsdon, K. T. *Training for Adult Education.* Nottingham, England: Department of Adult Education, University of Nottingham, 1975. 202 pages.

Elsey, Barry. *Social Theory Perspectives on Adult Education.* Nottingham, England: Department of Adult Education, University of Nottingham, 1986. 171 pages.

Ely, Mary L. (ed.). *Adult Education in Action.* New York: American Association for Adult Education, 1936. 480 pages. (X)

Ely, Mary L. *Why Forums?* Studies in the Social Significance of Adult Education in the United States, no. 2. New York: American Association for Adult Education, 1937. 220 pages.

Ely, Mary L. *Handbook of Adult Education in the United States.* New York: Institute of Adult Education, Teachers College, Columbia University, 1948. 555 pages.

Ely, Mary L., and Chappell, Eve. *Women in Two Worlds.* Studies in the Social Significance of Adult Education in the United States, no. 7. New York: American Association for Adult Education, 1938. 179 pages.

Engelhardt, N. L., and Engelhardt, N. L., Jr. *Planning the Community School.* New York: American Book Company, 1940. 188 pages.

English, Mildred E. *College in the Country.* Athens: University of Georgia Press, 1959. 120 pages.

Erdos, Renée F. *Teaching by Correspondence.* White Plains, N.Y.: Longman, Unesco, 1967. 218 pages.

Essert, Paul L. *Creative Leadership of Adult Education.* Englewood Cliffs, N.J.: Prentice-Hall, 1951. 333 pages.

Eurich, Nell P. *Corporate Classrooms: The Learning Business.* Princeton, N.J.: Carnegie Foundation for the Advancement of Teaching, 1985. 163 pages.

Eurich, Nell P. *The Learning Industry: Education for Adult Workers.* Princeton, N.J.: Carnegie Foundation for the Advancement of Teaching, 1990. 298 pages.

Evans, Brendan. *Radical Adult Education: A Political Critique.* London: Croom Helm, 1987. 245 pages.

Evans, Norman. *Post-Education Society: Recognising Adults as Learners.* London: Croom Helm, 1985. 157 pages.

Evans, Owen D. *Educational Opportunities for Young Workers.* New York: Macmillan, 1926. 380 pages.

The Experimental World Literacy Programme: A Critical Assessment. Paris: Unesco, 1976. 198 pages.

Faith, Karlene (ed.). *Toward New Horizons for Women in Distance Education: International Perspectives.* New York: Routledge & Kegan Paul, 1988. 343 pages.

Falvo, Donna R. *Effective Patient Education: A Guide to Increased Compliance.* Rockville, Md.: Aspen, 1985. 244 pages.

Fansler, Thomas. *Discussion Methods for Adult Groups.* New York: American Association for Adult Education, 1934. 149 pages.

Fansler, Thomas. *Creative Power Through Discussion.* New York: HarperCollins, 1950. 211 pages.

Faris, Ron. *The Passionate Educators: Voluntary Associations and the Struggle for Control of Adult Educational Broadcasting in Canada, 1919–52.* Toronto: Peter Martin, 1975. 202 pages.

Farlow, Helen. *Publicizing and Promoting Programs.* New York: McGraw-Hill, 1979. 277 pages.

Farmer, Martha L. (ed.). *Student Personnel Services for Adults in Higher Education.* Metuchen, N.J.: Scarecrow Press, 1967. 211 pages.

Farmer, Martha L. (ed.). *Counseling Services for Adults in Higher Education.* Metuchen, N.J.: Scarecrow Press, 1971. 172 pages.

Faure, Edgar, and others. *Learning to Be: The World of Education Today and Tomorrow.* Paris: Unesco, 1972. 312 pages. (S)

Ferguson, John. *The Open University from Within.* New York: New York University Press, 1976. 165 pages.

Fingeret, Arlene, and Jurmo, Paul (eds.). *Participatory Literacy Education.* New Directions for Continuing Education, no. 42. San Francisco: Jossey-Bass, 1989. 96 pages.

Fisher, Dorothy Canfield. *Why Stop Learning?* Orlando, Fla.: Harcourt Brace Jovanovich, 1927. 301 pages.

Fisher, Dorothy Canfield. *Learn or Perish.* New York: Liveright, 1930. 43 pages.

Fitzpatrick, Edward A. *Great Books: Panacea or What?* Milwaukee, Wis.: Bruce, 1952. 116. pages.

Flesch, Rudolf. *Marks of a Readable Style: A Study in Adult Education.* New York: Teachers College Press, Columbia University, 1943. 70 pages.

Fletcher, Colin, and Thompson, Neil (eds.). *Issues in Community Education.* Lewes, England: Falmer Press, 1980. 214 pages.

Flexner, Jennie M., and Edge, Sigrid A. *A Readers' Advisory Service.* New York: American Association for Adult Education, 1934. 59 pages.

Flexner, Jennie M., and Hopkins, Byron C. *Readers' Advisers at Work: A Survey of Development in the New York Public Library.* New York: American Association for Adult Education, 1941. 77 pages.

Flinck, Rune. *Why Do Adults Participate in Education?* Lund, Sweden: Department of Education, University of Lund, 1977. 67 pages.

Flude, Ray, and Parrott, Allen. *Education and the Challenge of Change: A Recurrent Education Strategy for Britain.* Milton Keynes, England: Open University Press, 1979. 176 pages.

Follett, M. P. *Creative Experience.* White Plains, N.Y.: Longman, 1924. 303 pages.

Foltz, Nancy T. (ed.). *Handbook of Adult Religious Education.* Birmingham, Ala.: Religious Education Press, 1986. 272 pages.

Fordham, Paul; Poulton, Geoff; and Randle, Lawrence. *Learning Networks in Adult Education.* New York: Routledge & Kegan Paul, 1979. 250 pages.

Fostering the Growing Need to Learn: Monographs and Annotated Bibliography on Continuing Education and Health Manpower. DHEW Publication no. (HRA) 74-3112. Washington, D.C.: Division of Regional Medical Programs, Bureau of Health Resources Development, Department of Health, Education and Welfare, 1974. Part 1, 446 pages; part 2, 160 pages.

Fox, Robert D.; Mazmanian, Paul E.; and Putnam, R. Wayne (eds.). *Changing and Learning in the Lives of Physicians.* New York: Praeger, 1989. 104 pages.

Fragnière, Gabriel (ed.). *Education Without Frontiers.* London: Duckworth, 1976. 207 pages.

Frank, H. Eric. *Human Resource Development: The European Approach.* Houston, Tex.: Gulf, 1974. 248 pages.

Fraser, Bryna Shore. *The Structure of Adult Learning, Education, and Training Opportunity in the United States.* Washington, D.C.: National Institute for Work and Learning, 1980. 75 pages.

Freedman, Leonard. *Quality in Continuing Education: Principles, Practices, and Standards for Colleges and Universities.* San Francisco: Jossey-Bass, 1987. 195 pages.

Freire, Paulo. *Cultural Action for Freedom.* Cambridge, Mass.: Harvard Educational Review, 1970. 55 pages.

Freire, Paulo. *Education for Critical Consciousness.* New York: Seabury Press, 1973. 164 pages.

Freire, Paulo. *Pedagogy in Process: The Letters to Guinea-Bissau.* New York: Seabury Press, 1978. 178 pages.

Freire, Paulo. *Pedagogy of the Oppressed.* New York: Continuum, 1984. (Originally published 1970.) 186 pages. (S)

Freire, Paulo. *The Politics of Education: Culture, Power, and Liberation.* South Hadley, Mass.: Bergin and Garvin, 1985. 209 pages.

Freire, Paulo, and Macedo, Donaldo. *Literacy: Reading the Word and the World.* South Hadley, Mass.: Bergin and Garvey, 1987. 184 pages.

Friese, John F. *The Cosmopolitan Evening School.* New York: Century, 1929. 388 pages.

Frutchey, Fred P., and others. *Evaluation in Extension.* (4th ed.) Topeka, Kans.: Ives, 1959. 107 pages.

Fry, John R. *A Hard Look at Adult Christian Education.* Philadelphia: Westminster, 1961. 150 pages.

Fuller, Jack W. *Continuing Education and the Community College.* Chicago: Nelson-Hall, 1979. 127 pages.

Fundamental Education: Common Ground for All Peoples. New York: Macmillan, 1947. 325 pages.

Galbraith, Michael W. (ed.). *Adult Learning Methods: A Guide for Effective Instruction.* Malabar, Fla.: Krieger, 1990a. 414 pages.

Galbraith, Michael W. (ed.). *Education Through Community Organizations.* New Directions for Adult and Continuing Education, no. 47. San Francisco: Jossey-Bass, 1990b. 97 pages.

Galbraith, Michael W. (ed.). *Facilitating Adult Learning: A Transactional Process.* Malabar, Fla.: Krieger, 1991. 216 pages.

Gardner, John. *Self-Renewal: The Individual and the Innovative Society.* (2nd ed.) New York: Norton, 1981. 141 pages. (S)

Garner, Donald P. (ed.). *The Adult Learner, the World of Work, and Career Education.* Dubuque, Iowa: Kendall/Hunt, 1978. 237 pages.

Garrison, D. R. *Understanding Distance Education: A Framework for the Future.* New York: Routledge & Kegan Paul, 1989. 139 pages.

Garrison, D. Randy, and Shale, Doug (eds.). *Education at a Distance: From Issues to Practice.* Malabar, Fla.: Krieger, 1990. 144 pages.

Gelpi, Ettore. *A Future for Lifelong Education.* 2 vols. Manchester, England: Department of Adult and Higher Education, Manchester University, 1979. Vol. 1, 81 pages; vol. 2, 110 pages. (X)

Gelpi, Ettore. *Lifelong Education and International Relations.* London: Croom Helm, 1985. 206 pages. (X)

General Conference of Unesco. *World Education Report.* Paris: Unesco, 1991.

Gerver, Elisabeth. *Computers and Adult Learning.* Milton Keynes, England: Open University Press, 1984. 124 pages.

Gessner, Quentin H. (ed.). *Handbook on Continuing Higher Education.* New York: American Council on Education, Macmillan, 1987. 261 pages.

Gibbs, Graham. *Teaching Students to Learn: A Student-Centered*

Approach. Milton Keynes, England; Open University Press, 1981. 111 pages.

Giere, Ursula, and Maehira, Yasushi. *Directory of Writers on Lifelong Education*. Hamburg, Germany: Unesco Institute for Education, 1980. 62 pages.

Gilder, Jamison (ed.). *Policies for Lifelong Education: Report of the 1979 Assembly, American Association of Community and Junior Colleges*. Washington, D.C.: American Association of Community and Junior Colleges, 1979. 128 pages.

Glanz, Karen; Lewis, Frances Marcus; and Rimer, Barbara (eds.). *Health Behavior and Health Education: Theory, Research, and Practice*. San Francisco: Jossey-Bass, 1990. 460 pages. (*X*)

Glatter, Ron, and Wedell, E. G. *Study by Correspondence*. White Plains, N.Y.: Longman, 1971. 361 pages.

Gleazer, Edmund J., Jr. *The Community College: Values, Vision, and Vitality*. Washington, D.C.: American Association of Community and Junior Colleges, 1980. 190 pages.

Glen, John M. *Highlander: No Ordinary School, 1932–1962*. Lexington: University Press of Kentucky, 1988. 309 pages.

Glueck, Eleanor T. *The Community Use of Schools*. Baltimore, Md.: Williams & Wilkins, 1927. 222 pages.

Godard, John George. *George Birkbeck: The Pioneer of Popular Education: A Memoir and a Review*. London: Bemrose, 1884. 242 pages.

Goldman, Israel M. *Lifelong Learning Among Jews: Adult Education in Judaism from Biblical Times to the Twentieth Century*. New York: KTAV Publishing House, 1975. 364 pages.

Gollattscheck, James F., and others. *College Leadership for Community Renewal: Beyond Community-Based Education*. San Francisco: Jossey-Bass, 1976. 160 pages.

Gould, Joseph E. *The Chautauqua Movement: An Episode in the Continuing American Revolution*. Albany: State University of New York Press, 1972. 108 pages.

Gould, Samuel B., and Cross, K. Patricia (eds.). *Explorations in Non-Traditional Study*. San Francisco: Jossey-Bass, 1972. 137 pages.

Grabowski, Stanley M. *Paulo Freire: A Revolutionary Dilemma for the Adult Educator*. Occasional Paper no. 32. Syracuse, N.Y.:

Syracuse University Publications in Continuing Education, 1972. 136 pages.

Grabowski, Stanley M. (ed.). *Strengthening Connections Between Education and Performance*. New Directions for Continuing Education, no. 18. San Francisco: Jossey-Bass, 1983. 86 pages.

Grabowski, Stanley M., and Mason, W. Dean. *Learning for Aging*. Washington, D.C.: Adult Education Association of the USA, 1974. 358 pages.

Grabowski, Stanley M., and Associates. *Preparing Educators for Adults*. AEA Handbook Series in Adult Education. San Francisco: Jossey-Bass, 1981. 164 pages.

Graham, Sheilah. *College of One*. New York: Viking Penguin, 1967. 246 pages.

Grattan, C. Hartley. *In Quest of Knowledge: A Historical Perspective on Adult Education*. New York: Association Press, 1955. 337 pages. (S)

Grattan, C. Hartley (ed.). *American Ideas About Adult Education, 1710–1951*. New York: Teachers College Press, Columbia University, 1959. 140 pages.

Gray, William S.; Gray, Wil Lou; and Tilton, J. W. *The Opportunity Schools of South Carolina*. New York: American Association for Adult Education, 1932. 141 pages.

Gray, William S., and Leary, Bernice E. *What Makes a Book Readable?* Chicago: University of Chicago Press, 1935. 358 pages.

Gray, William S., and Munroe, Ruth. *Reading Interests and Habits of Adults*. New York: Macmillan, 1929. 305 pages.

Gray, William S., and Rogers, Bernice. *Maturity in Reading*. Chicago: University of Chicago Press, 1956. 273 pages.

Green, Ernest. *Adult Education: Why This Apathy?* London: Allen & Unwin, 1953. 145 pages.

Green, Joseph S.; Grosswald, Sarina J.; Suter, Emanuel; and Walthall, David B. III (eds.). *Continuing Education for the Health Professions: Developing, Managing, and Evaluating Programs for Maximum Impact on Patient Care*. San Francisco: Jossey-Bass, 1984. 438 pages.

Green, Lawrence W., and Kansler, Connie Cavanaugh. *The Professional and Scientific Literature on Patient Education: A Guide to Information Sources.* Detroit, Mich.: Gale Research, 1980. 330 pages.

Green, Lawrence W., and others. *Health Education Planning: A Diagnostic Approach.* Palo Alto, Calif.: Mayfield, 1980. 306 pages.

Greenberg, Elinor; O'Donnell, Kathleen M.; and Bergquist, William (eds.). *Educating Learners of All Ages.* New Directions for Higher Education, no. 29. San Francisco: Jossey-Bass, 1980. 110 pages.

Gretler, Armin. *The Training of Adult Middle-Level Personnel.* Paris: Unesco, 1972. 164 pages.

Griffin, Colin. *Curriculum Theory in Adult and Lifelong Education.* London: Croom Helm, 1983. 218 pages.

Griffin, Colin. *Adult Education As Social Policy.* London: Croom Helm, 1987. 274 pages.

Griffin, Gary A. (ed.). *Staff Development.* 82nd Yearbook, National Society for the Study of Education, Part 2. Chicago: University of Chicago, 1983. 276 pages.

Griffith, William S., and Hayes, Ann P. (eds.). *Adult Basic Education: The State of the Art.* Chicago: Department of Education, University of Chicago, 1970. 240 pages.

Groombridge, Brian. *Education and Retirement.* London: National Institute of Adult Education, 1960. 159 pages.

Groombridge, Brian (ed.). *Adult Education and Television.* London: National Institute of Adult Education, 1966. 143 pages.

Gross, Ronald. *The Lifelong Learner.* New York: Simon & Schuster, 1977. 190 pages.

Gross, Ronald. *The Independent Scholar's Handbook.* Reading, Mass.: Addison-Wesley, 1982a. 261 pages.

Gross, Ronald (ed.). *Invitation to Lifelong Learning.* Chicago: Follett, 1982b. 287 pages.

Gross, Ronald, and Gross, Beatrice. *Independent Scholarship: Promise, Problems, and Prospects.* New York: College Entrance Examination Board, 1983. 68 pages.

Groteluschen, Arden D.; Gooler, Dennis D.; and Knox, Alan B. *Evaluation in Adult Basic Education.* Danville, Ill.: Interstate, 1976. 274 pages.

Gruenberg, Benjamin C. *Science and the Public Mind.* New York: McGraw-Hill, 1935. 196 pages.

Gueulette, David G. (ed.). *Microcomputers for Adult Learning: Potentials and Perils.* Chicago: Follett, 1982. 228 pages.

Gulley, Halbert E. *Discussion, Conference, and Group Process.* (2nd ed.) Troy, Mo.: Holt, Rinehart & Winston, 1968. 374 pages.

Hall, Budd L., and Kidd, J. Roby. *Adult Learning: A Design for Action.* Elmsford, N.Y.: Pergamon Press, 1978. 337 pages.

Hall, David O. W. *New Zealand Adult Education.* London: Michael Joseph, 1970. 200 pages.

Hall, Laurence, and Associates. *New Colleges for New Students.* San Francisco: Jossey-Bass, 1974. 210 pages.

Hall, W. Arnold. *The Adult School Movement in the Twentieth Century.* Nottingham, England: Department of Adult Education, University of Nottingham, 1985. 244 pages.

Hallenbeck, Wilbur C., and others. *Community and Adult Education.* Washington, D.C.: Adult Education Association, 1962. 33 pages.

Hall-Quest, Alfred Lawrence. *The University Afield.* New York: Macmillan, 1926. 292 pages.

Hamer, Oliver Stuart. *The Master Farmers of America and Their Education.* University of Iowa Studies in Education, no. 6. Iowa City: University of Iowa Press, 1930. 151 pages.

Hameyer, Uwe. *School Curriculum in the Context of Lifelong Learning.* Hamburg, Germany: Unesco Institute for Education, 1979. 112 pages. (X)

Handbook for Professional Development in Continuing Higher Education. Washington, D.C.: National University Continuing Education Association, 1990. 146 pages.

Handbook of Adult Education in the United States, 1934. New York: American Association for Adult Education 1934. 384 pages. (S)

Hansome, Marius. *World Workers' Education Movements.* New York: Columbia University Press, 1931. 594 pages.

Haponski, William C., and McCabe, Charles E. *New Horizons: The Education and Career Planning Guide for Adults.* Princeton, N.J.: Peterson's Guides, 1985. 228 pages.

Hargreaves, David. *Adult Literacy and Broadcasting: The BBC's Experience.* New York: Nichols, 1980. 257 pages.

Harlacher, Ervin L. *The Community Dimension of the Community College.* Englewood Cliffs, N.J.: Prentice-Hall, 1969. 140 pages.

Harlacher, Ervin L., and Gollattscheck, James F. (eds.). *Implementing Community-Based Education.* New Directions for Community Colleges, no. 21. San Francisco: Jossey-Bass, 1978. 102 pages.

Harman, David. *Community Fundamental Education: A Nonformal Educational Strategy for Development.* Lexington, Mass.: Lexington Books, 1974. 174 pages.

Harman, David (ed.). *Expanding Recurrent and Nonformal Education.* New Directions for Higher Education, no. 14. San Francisco: Jossey-Bass, 1976. 112 pages.

Harman, David. *Illiteracy: A National Dilemma.* New York: Cambridge University Press, 1987. 113 pages.

Harman, David, and Brim, Orville G., Jr. *Learning to Be Parents: Principles, Programs, and Methods.* Newbury Park, Calif.: Sage, 1980. 272 pages.

Harrington, Fred Harvey. *The Future of Adult Education: New Responsibilities of Colleges and Universities.* San Francisco: Jossey-Bass, 1977. 238 pages.

Harris, David. *Openness and Closure in Distance Education.* London: Palmer, 1987. 174 pages.

Harris, W.J.A. *Comparative Adult Education: Practice, Purpose, and Theory.* White Plains, N.Y.: Longman, 1980. 198 pages. (X)

Harrison, J.F.C. *Learning and Living, 1790-1960: A Study in the History of the Adult Education Movement.* Toronto: University of Toronto Press, 1961. 404 pages. (X)

Hart, Joseph K. *Adult Education.* New York: Crowell, 1927. 341 pages.

Hartmann, Edward George. *The Movement to Americanize the Immigrant.* New York: Columbia University Press, 1948. 333 pages.

Havighurst, Robert J. *The Educational Mission of the Church.* Philadelphia: Westminster, 1965. 159 pages.

Havighurst, Robert J., and Orr, Betty. *Adult Education and Adult Needs.* Chicago: Center for the Study of Liberal Education for Adults, 1956. 66 pages.

Hawes, H.W.R. *Lifelong Education, Schools, and Curricula in Developing Countries.* Hamburg, Germany: Unesco Institute for Education, 1975. 146 pages.

Hawkins, Gaynell. *Educational Experiments in Social Settlements.* Studies in the Social Significance of Adult Education in the United States, no. 5. New York: American Association for Adult Education, 1937. 145 pages.

Hawkins, Gaynell. *Education for Social Understanding: Programs of Case Work and Group Work Agencies.* Studies in the Social Significance of Adult Education in the United States, no. 22. New York: American Association for Adult Education, 1940. 207 pages.

Hawkins, T. H., and Brimble, L.J.F. *Adult Education: The Record of the British Army.* London: Macmillan, 1947. 420 pages.

Hayes, Cecil B. *The American Lyceum: Its History and Contribution to Education.* Office of Education Bulletin no. 12. Washington, D.C.: U.S. Government Printing Office, 1932. 72 pages.

Hayes, Elisabeth (ed.). *Effective Teaching Styles.* New Directions for Continuing Education, no. 43. San Francisco: Jossey-Bass, 1989. 100 pages.

Haygood, William Converse. *Who Uses the Public Library: A Survey of the Patrons of the Circulation and Reference Departments of the New York Public Library.* Chicago: University of Chicago Press, 1938. 137 pages.

Hebert, Tom, and Coyne, John. *Getting Skilled: A Guide to Private Trade and Technical Schools.* New York: Dutton, 1976. 262 pages.

Heermann, Barry (ed.). *Personal Computers and the Adult Learner.* New Directions for Continuing Education, no. 29. San Francisco: Jossey-Bass, 1986. 109 pages.

Heffernan, James M. *Educational and Career Services for Adults.* Lexington, Mass.: Lexington Books, 1981. 272 pages. (X)

Heffernan, James M.; Macy, Francis U.; and Vickers, Donn F. *Educational Brokering: A New Service for Adult Learners.* Syracuse, N.Y.: National Center for Educational Brokering, 1976. 82 pages.

Heim, Kathleen M., and Wallace, Danny (eds.). *Adult Services: An Enduring Focus for Public Libraries.* Chicago: American Library Association, 1990. 524 pages. (X)

Hely, A.S.M. *New Trends in Adult Education: From Elsinore to Montreal.* Paris: Unesco, 1962. 136 pages.

Hely, A.S.M. *School-Teachers and the Education of Adults*. Paris: Unesco, 1966. 50 pages.

Hesburgh, Theodore M.; Miller, Paul A.; and Wharton, Clifton R., Jr. *Patterns for Lifelong Learning*. San Francisco: Jossey-Bass, 1973. 135 pages.

Hesser, Florence E. *Village Literacy Programming in Pakistan: A Comparative ABE Study with Guidelines*. Vancouver: Centre for Continuing Education, University of British Columbia, 1978. 207 pages.

Hewitt, Dorothy, and Mather, Kirtley F. *Adult Education: A Dynamic for Democracy*. East Norwalk, Conn.: Appleton & Lange, 1937. 193 pages.

Hiemstra, Roger. *The Educative Community: Linking the Community, School, and Family*. Lincoln, Nebr.: Professional Educators Publications, 1972. 116 pages.

Hiemstra, Roger. *The Older Adult and Learning*. Lincoln: Department of Adult and Continuing Education, University of Nebraska, 1975. 106 pages.

Hiemstra, Roger. *Lifelong Learning*. Lincoln, Nebr.: Professional Educators Publications, 1976. 114 pages. (*S*)

Hiemstra, Roger (ed.). *Creative Environments for Effective Adult Learning*. New Directions for Adult and Continuing Education, no. 50. San Francisco: Jossey-Bass, 1991. 103 pages.

Hiemstra, Roger, and Sisco, Burton. *Individualizing Instruction: Making Learning Personal, Empowering, and Successful*. San Francisco: Jossey-Bass, 1990. 304 pages.

Hightower, Jim. *Hard Tomatoes, Hard Times: The Failure of the Land Grant College Complex*. Washington, D.C.: Agribusiness Accountability Project, 1972. 308 pages.

Hill, Frank Ernest. *The School in the Camps*. New York: American Association for Adult Education, 1935. 84 pages.

Hill, Frank Ernest. *Listen and Learn*. Studies in the Social Significance of Adult Education in the United States, no. 1. New York: American Association for Adult Education, 1937. 248 pages.

Hill, Frank Ernest. *Man-Made Culture*. Studies in the Social Significance of Adult Education in the United States, no. 8. New York: American Association for Adult Education, 1938. 166 pages.

Hill, Frank Ernest. *Educating for Health.* Studies in the Social Significance of Adult Education in the United States, no. 15. New York: American Association for Adult Education, 1939. 224 pages.

Hill, Frank Ernest. *Training for the Job.* Studies in the Social Significance of Adult Education in the United States, no. 19. New York: American Association for Adult Education, 1940. 160 pages.

Hill, Frank Ernest, and Williams, W. E. *Radio's Listening Groups: The United States and Great Britain.* New York: Columbia University Press, 1941. 270 pages.

Hill, Susan T. *Trends in Adult Education, 1969–1984.* National Center for Educational Statistics publication no. CS87-307. Washington, D.C.: U.S. Government Printing Office, 1987. 57 pages.

Himmelstrup, Per; Robinson, John; and Fielden, Derrick (eds.). *Strategies for Lifelong Learning.* Esbjerg, Denmark: University Centre of South Jutland, Denmark, and the Association for Recurrent Education, U.K., 1981. 243 pages.

Hirschberg, Cornelius. *The Priceless Gift.* New York: Simon & Schuster, 1966. 344 pages.

Hodgen, Margaret T. *Workers' Education in England and the United States.* London: Kegan Paul, Trench, Trubner, 1925. 212 pages.

Höghielm, Robert, and Rubenson, Kjell (eds.). *Adult Education for Social Change: Research on the Swedish Allocation Policy.* Stockholm, Sweden: Department of Educational Research, Institute of Education, 1980. 169 pages.

Hole, James. *An Essay on the History and Management of Literacy, Scientific, and Mechanics Institutions.* London: Cass, 1970. (Originally published 1853.) 186 pages.

Holmberg, Börje. *Distance Education: A Survey and a Bibliography.* New York: Nichols, 1977. 167 pages.

Holmberg, Börje. *Status and Trends of Distance Education.* London: Kogan Page, 1981. 200 pages.

Holmberg, Börje. *Growth and Structure of Distance Education.* London: Croom Helm, 1986. 163 pages.

Holmberg, Börje. *Theory and Practice of Distance Education.* London: Routledge, 1989. 252 pages. (X)

Holm-Jensen, Paul Henry. *The People's College: Its Contributions and Its Application to American Education and Conditions.* Blair, Nebr.: Danish Lutheran Publishing House, 1939. 195 pages.

Hopkins, Philip G. H. *Workers' Education: An International Perspective.* Milton Keynes, England: Open University Press, 1985. 248 pages.

Hoppe, William A. (ed.) *Policies and Practices in Evening Colleges, 1971.* Metuchen, N.J.: Scarecrow Press, 1972. 587 pages.

Hopper, Earl, and Osborn, Marilyn. *Adult Students: Education, Selection, and Social Control.* London: Pinter, 1975. 187 pages.

Horne, Esther E. (ed.). *Continuing Education: Issues and Challenges.* New York: Saur, 1985. 434 pages.

Horner, Charles F. *Strike the Tents.* Philadelphia: Dorrance, 1954. 204 pages.

Horrabin, J. F., and Horrabin, Winifred. *Working-Class Education.* London: Labour Publishing, 1924. 93 pages.

Horton, Aimée Isgrig. *The Highlander Folk School: A History of Its Major Programs, 1932–1961.* Brooklyn: Carlson, 1989. 334 pages.

Horton, Myles, and Freire, Paulo. *We Make the Road by Walking: Conversations on Education and Social Change.* (Brenda Bell, John Gaventa, and John Peters, eds.) Philadelphia: Temple University Press, 1990. 256 pages.

Horton, Myles; Kohl, Judith; and Kohl, Herbert. *The Long Haul: An Autobiography.* New York: Doubleday, 1990. 231 pages.

Hospital Research and Educational Trust. *Training and Continuing Education: A Handbook for Health Care Institutions.* Chicago: Hospital Research and Educational Trust, 1970. 261 pages.

Hostler, John. *The Aims of Adult Education.* Manchester Monographs, no. 17. Manchester, England: University of Manchester Press, 1981. 77 pages.

Houghton, Vincent, and Richardson, Ken. *Recurrent Education.* London: Lock, 1974. 137 pages.

Houle, Cyril O. *Libraries in Adult and Fundamental Education.* Paris: Unesco, 1951. 179 pages.

Houle, Cyril O. *Continuing Your Education.* New York: McGraw-Hill, 1964. 183 pages.

Houle, Cyril O. *Residential Adult Education.* Syracuse, N.Y.: Syracuse University Publications in Continuing Education, 1971. 86 pages.

Houle, Cyril O. *The Design of Education.* San Francisco: Jossey-Bass, 1972. 333 pages. *(S)*

Houle, Cyril O. *The External Degree.* San Francisco: Jossey-Bass, 1973. 214 pages.

Houle, Cyril O. *Continuing Learning in the Professions.* San Francisco: Jossey-Bass, 1980. 390 pages. *(O,S)*

Houle, Cyril O. *Patterns of Learning: New Perspectives on Life-Span Education.* San Francisco: Jossey-Bass, 1984. 243 pages. *(S)*

Houle, Cyril O. *The Inquiring Mind.* Norman: Oklahoma Research Center for Continuing Professional and Higher Education, 1988. (Originally published in 1961.) 99 pages. *(S)*

Houle, Cyril O., and Nelson, Charles A. *The University, the Citizen, and World Affairs.* Washington, D.C.: American Council on Education, 1956. 179 pages.

Houle, Cyril O., and others. *The Armed Services and Adult Education.* Washington, D.C.: American Council on Education, 1947. 259 pages.

House, Verne W. *Shaping Public Policy: The Educator's Role.* Bozeman, Mont.: Westridge, 1981. 116 pages.

Howe, Michael J. A. (ed.). *Adult Learning: Psychological Research and Applications.* New York: Wiley, 1977. 291 pages.

Hoyles, Martin (ed.). *The Politics of Literacy.* London: Writers and Readers Publishing Cooperative, 1977. 211 pages.

Hudson, J. W. *The History of Adult Education.* London: Woburn, 1969. (Originally published in 1851.) 238 pages.

Hudson, Robert H. *Radburn: A Plan of Living.* New York: American Association for Adult Education, 1934. 118 pages.

Hughes, Jane Wolford (ed.). *Ministering to Adult Learners: A Skills Workbook for Christian Educational Leaders.* Washington, D.C.: United States Catholic Conference, 1981. 44 pages.

Humble, Marion. *Rural America Reads.* Studies in the Social Significance of Adult Education in the United States, no. 13. New York: American Association for Adult Education, 1938. 101 pages.

Hummel, Charles. *Education Today for the World of Tomorrow.* Paris: Unesco, 1977. 200 pages.

Hunter, Carmen St. John, and Harman, David. *Adult Illiteracy in the United States: A Report to the Ford Foundation*. New York: McGraw-Hill, 1979. 206 pages. (S)

Hunter, Carmen St. John, and Keehn, Martha McKee (eds.). *Adult Education in China*. London: Croom Helm, 1985. 147 pages.

Hurlbut, J. L. *The Story of Chautauqua*. New York: Putnam, 1921. 429 pages.

Husén, Torsten. *The Learning Society*. London: Methuen, 1974. 268 pages.

Husén, Torsten. *The Learning Society Revisited*. Elmsford, N.Y.: Pergamon Press, 1986. 262 pages.

Hutchinson, E. M. (ed.). *Aims and Action in Adult Education, 1921–1971*. London: National Institute of Adult Education, 1971. 150 pages.

Hutchinson, Enid, and Hutchinson, Edward. *Learning Later: Fresh Horizons in English Adult Education*. New York: Routledge & Kegan Paul, 1978. 200 pages.

Hyde, William D., Jr. *Metropolitan Vocational Proprietary Schools: Assessing Their Role in the U.S. Educational System*. Lexington, Mass.: Lexington Books, 1976. 149 pages.

Illich, Ivan. *Deschooling Society*. New York: HarperCollins, 1970. 186 pages. (S)

Ilsley, Paul J. (ed.). *Improving Conference Design and Outcomes*. New Directions for Continuing Education, no. 28. San Francisco: Jossey-Bass, 1985. 96 pages.

Ilsley, Paul J. *Enhancing the Volunteer Experience: New Insights on Strengthening Volunteer Participation, Learning, and Commitment*. San Francisco: Jossey-Bass, 1990. 170 pages.

Ilsley, Paul J., and Niemi, John A. *Recruiting and Training Volunteers*. New York: McGraw-Hill, 1981. 150 pages.

Ilyin, Donna, and Tragardh, Thomas (eds.). *Classroom Practices in Adult ESL*. Washington, D.C.: Teachers of English to Speakers of Other Languages, 1978. 209 pages.

Ingram, James B. *Curriculum Integration and Lifelong Education: A Contribution to the Improvement of School Curricula*. Elmsford, N.Y.: Pergamon Press, 1979. 115 pages.

Inkster, Ian (ed.). *The Steam Intellect Societies: Essays on Culture, Education, and Industry Circa 1820–1914*. Nottingham, England:

Department of Adult Education, University of Nottingham, 1985. 203 pages.

International Directory of Adult Education. Paris: Unesco, 1952. 324 pages.

International Handbook of Adult Education. London: World Association for Adult Education, 1929. 476 pages.

International Labour Conference. *Paid Educational Leave.* Geneva, Switzerland: International Labour Office, 1974. 75 pages.

International Yearbook of Adult Education (Internationales Jahrbuch der Erwachsenenbildung). Cologne: Bohlau Verlag. Issued annually since 1969.

The Invisible University: Postdoctoral Education in the United States. Washington, D.C.: National Academy of Sciences, 1969. 309 pages.

Ironside, Diana J. *Counselling and Information Services for Adult Learners in North America.* Bulletin of the International Bureau of Education, nos. 198–199. Paris: Unesco, 1976. 70 pages.

Ironside, Diana J., and Jacobs, Dorene E. *Trends in Counselling and Information Services for the Adult Learner.* Toronto: Ontario Institute for Studies in Education, 1977. 99 pages.

Isenberg, Irwin (ed.). *The Drive Against Illiteracy.* New York: Wilson, 1964. 164 pages.

Jacks, M. L. *Total Education: A Plea for Synthesis.* London: Kegan Paul, Trench, Trubner, 1946. 160 pages.

Jacobson, Myrtle S. *Night and Day: The Interaction Between an Academic Institution and Its Evening College.* Metuchen, N.J.: Scarecrow Press, 1970. 358 pages.

Jarvis, Peter. *Adult and Continuing Education: Theory and Practice.* London: Croom Helm, 1983a. 317 pages.

Jarvis, Peter. *Professional Education.* London: Croom Helm, 1983b. 150 pages.

Jarvis, Peter. *The Sociology of Adult and Continuing Education.* London: Croom Helm, 1985. 259 pages. (S)

Jarvis, Peter. *Adult Learning in the Social Context.* London: Croom Helm, 1987a. 220 pages. (H)

Jarvis, Peter (ed.). *Twentieth Century Thinkers in Adult Education.* London: Croom Helm, 1987b. 327 pages.

Jarvis, Peter (ed.). *Britain: Policy and Practice in Continuing Ed-*

ucation. New Directions for Continuing Education, no. 40. San Francisco: Jossey-Bass, 1988. 104 pages.

Jarvis, Peter. *An International Dictionary of Adult and Continuing Education.* London: Routledge, 1990. 372 pages. (X)

Jarvis, Peter, and Chadwick, Alan (eds.). *Training Adult Educators in Western Europe.* London: Routledge, 1991. 235 pages.

Jeffries, Charles. *Illiteracy: A World Problem.* New York: Praeger, 1967. 204 pages.

Jensen, Gale; Liveright, A. A.; and Hallenbeck, Wilbur (eds.). *Adult Education: Outlines of and Emerging Field of University Study.* Washington, D.C.: Adult Education Association of the USA, 1964. 334 pages. (S)

Jepson, N. A. *The Beginnings of English University Adult Education—Policy and Problems.* London: Michael Joseph, 1973. 372 pages.

Jessup, Frank W. (ed.). *Lifelong Learning: A Symposium on Continuing Education.* Elmsford, N.Y.: Pergamon Press, 1969. 170 pages.

Jessup, Frank W. *Historical and Cultural Influence upon the Development of Residential Centers for Continuing Education.* Occasional Papers no. 31. Syracuse, N.Y.: Syracuse University Publications in Continuing Education, 1972. 26 pages.

Joeckel, Carleton (ed.). *Library Extension: Problems and Solutions.* Chicago: University of Chicago, 1946. 260 pages.

Johnson, Alvin S. *Deliver Us from Dogma.* New York: American Association for Adult Education, 1934. 84 pages.

Johnson, Alvin S. *The Public Library—A People's University.* Studies in the Social Significance of Adult Education in the United States, no. 9. New York: American Association for Adult Education, 1938. 85 pages.

Johnson, Doris J., and Blalock, Jane W. (eds.). *Adults with Learning Disabilities: Clinical Studies.* Philadelphia: Grune & Stratton, 1987. 327 pages.

Johnson, Laura S. (ed.). *Reading and the Adult Learner.* Newark, Del.: International Reading Association, 1980. 76 pages.

Johnston, Joseph S., Jr., and Associates. *Educating Managers: Executive Effectiveness Through Liberal Learning.* San Francisco: Jossey-Bass, 1986. 242 pages.

Johnstone, John W. C., and Rivera, Ramon J. *Volunteers for Learning: A Study of the Educational Pursuits of American Adults.* Hawthorne, N.Y.: Aldine, 1965. 625 pages. (*S*)

Jolliffe, Harold. *Public Library Extension Activities.* (2nd ed.) London: Library Association, 1968. 343 pages.

Jones, Arthur J. *The Continuation School in the United States.* Bureau of Education, Department of the Interior, Bulletin no. 1. Washington, D.C.: U.S. Government Printing Office, 1907. 157 pages.

Jones, David J. *Adult Education and Cultural Development.* New York: Routledge, 1988. 228 pages.

Jones, David J., and Chadwick, A. F. (eds.). *Adult Education and the Arts.* Nottingham, England: Department of Adult Education, 1981. 82 pages.

Jones, Edward V. *Reading Instruction for the Adult Illiterate.* Chicago: American Library Association, 1981. 169 pages.

Jones, Gwyn E. (ed.). *Investing in Rural Extension: Strategies and Goals.* New York: Elsevier Science, 1986. 297 pages.

Jones, H. A., and Charnley, A.H. *Adult Literacy: A Study of Its Impact.* London: National Institute of Adult Education, 1978. 121 pages.

Jones, R. Kenneth. *Sociology of Adult Education.* Brookfield, Vt.: Gower, 1984. 159 pages.

Jourdan, Manfred (ed.). *Recurrent Education in Western Europe: Progress, Projects and Trends in Recurrent, Lifelong, and Continuing Education.* Windsor, England: NFER-Nelson, 1981. 386 pages.

Kaestle, Carl F., and others. *Literacy in the United States: Readers and Reading Since 1880.* New Haven, Conn.: Yale University Press, 1991. 338 pages.

Kairamo, Kari (ed.). *Education for Life: A European Strategy.* London: Butterworth, 1989. 190 pages.

Kallen, Horace M. *Education, the Machine, and the Worker: An Essay in the Psychology of Education in Industrial Society.* New York: New Republic, 1925. 204 pages.

Kallen, Horace, M. *Philosophical Issues in Adult Education.* Springfield, Ill.: Thomas, 1962. 99 pages.

Kaplan, Abbott. *Study-Discussion in the Liberal Arts.* New York: Fund for Adult Education, 1960. 138 pages.

Kaplan, Abraham Abbott. *Socio-Economic Circumstances and Adult Participation in Certain Cultural and Educational Activities.* New York: Teachers College Press, Columbia University, 1943. 152 pages. (*X*)

Karnes, Frances A.; Ginn, Clyde N.; and Maddox, Beverly Bell (eds.). *Issues and Trends in Adult Basic Education: Focus on Reading.* Jackson: University of Mississippi, 1980. 258 pages.

Kasworm, Carol E. (ed.). *Educational Outreach to Select Adult Populations.* New Directions for Continuing Education, no. 20. San Francisco: Jossey-Bass, 1983. 116 pages.

Kay, Evelyn R. *Adult Education in Community Organizations, 1972.* Washington, D.C.: U.S. Government Printing Office, 1974. 81 pages.

Kaye, Anthony, and Harry, Keith (eds.). *Using the Media for Adult Basic Education.* London: Croom Helm, 1982. 255 pages.

Kaye, Anthony, and Rumble, Greville (eds.). *Distance Teaching for Higher and Adult Education.* London: Croom Helm, 1981. 342 pages.

Keegan, Desmond. *The Foundations of Distance Education.* London: Croom Helm, 1986. 277 pages.

Keeton, Morris T., and Tate, Pamela J. (eds.). *Learning by Experience—What, Why, How.* New Directions for Experiential Learning, no. 1. San Francisco: Jossey-Bass, 1978. 109 pages.

Keeton, Morris T., and Associates. *Experiential Learning: Rationale, Characteristics, and Assessments.* San Francisco: Jossey-Bass, 1976. 266 pages.

Kelly, Thomas. *Outside the Walls: Sixty Years of University Extension at Manchester, 1886–1946.* Manchester, England: Manchester University Press, 1950. 124 pages.

Kelly, Thomas. *George Birkbeck: Pioneer of Adult Education.* Liverpool, England: University Press, 1957. 380 pages.

Kelly, Thomas. *A History of Adult Education in Great Britain.* (2nd ed.) Liverpool, England: Liverpool University Press, 1970. 420 pages. (*X*)

Kelly, Thomas (ed.). *A Select Bibliography of Adult Education in Great Britain Including Works Published to the End of the Year 1972.* London: National Institute of Adult Education, 1974. 220 pages. (*X*)

Kelsey, Lincoln David, and Hearne, Cannon Chiles. *Cooperative Extension Service.* (2nd ed.) Ithaca, N.Y.: Comstock, 1955. 424 pages.

Keltner, John W. *Group Discussion Processes.* White Plains, N.Y.: Longman, 1957. 373 pages.

Kempfer, Homer. *Adult Education.* New York: McGraw-Hill, 1955. 433 pages.

Keppel, Frederick Paul. *Education for Adults and Other Essays.* Freeport, N.Y.: Books for Libraries Press, 1968. (Originally published 1926.) 94 pages.

Kerrigan, John E., and Luke, Jeff S. *Management Training Strategies for Developing Countries: Studies in Development Management.* Boulder, Colo.: Rienner, 1987. 240 pages.

Kerrison, Irvine L. H. *Workers' Education at the University Level.* New Brunswick, N.J.: Rutgers University Press, 1951. 177 pages.

Khan, Inayat (ed.). *Teaching at a Distance: Some Papers on Distance Education.* Delhi, India: Amar Prakashan, A-1/139B, Lawrence Road, 11035, 1989. 167 pages.

Khoobyar, Helen. *Facing Adult Problems in Christian Education.* Philadelphia: Westminster, 1963. 140 pages.

Kidd, James Robbins (ed.). *Adult Education in Canada.* Toronto: Canadian Association for Adult Education, 1950. 249 pages.

Kidd, James Robbins. *18 to 80: Continuing Education in Metropolitan Toronto.* Toronto: Board of Education, 1961. 154 pages. (X)

Kidd, James Robbins. *Financing Continuing Education.* Metuchen, N.J.: Scarecrow Press, 1962. 209 pages.

Kidd, James Robbins (ed.). *Learning and Society.* Toronto: Canadian Association for Adult Education, 1963. 414 pages.

Kidd, James Robbins. *The Implications of Continuous Learning.* Toronto: Gage, 1966. 122 pages.

Kidd, James Robbins. *Education for Perspective.* New Delhi: Indian Adult Education Association, 1969. 369 pages.

Kidd, James Robbins. *How Adults Learn.* (Rev. ed.) New York: Association Press, 1973. 318 pages. (S)

Kidd, James Robbins. *A Tale of Three Cities: Elsinore, Montreal, Tokyo: The Influence of Three Unesco World Conferences upon the Development of Adult Education.* Syracuse, N.Y.: Syracuse

University Publications in Continuing Education, 1974. 36 pages.

Kidd, James Robbins, and Selman, Gordon R. (eds.). *Coming of Age: Canadian Adult Education in the 1960's*. Toronto: Canadian Association for Adult Education, 1978. 410 pages.

Killeen, John, and Bird, Margaret. *Education and Work: A Study of Paid Educational Leave in England and Wales (1976/77)*. Leicester, England: National Institute of Adult Education, 1981. 147 pages.

King, David. *Training Within the Organization*. London: Tavistock, 1968. 274 pages.

Kirkwood, Gerri, and Kirkwood, Colin. *Living Adult Education: Freire in Scotland*. Milton Keynes, England: Open University Press, 1989. 155 pages.

Klare, George R. *The Measurement of Readability*. Ames: Iowa State University Press, 1963. 328 pages.

Klein, Paul E., and Moffit, Ruth E. *Counseling Techniques in Adult Education*. New York: McGraw-Hill, 1946. 185 pages.

Klevins, Chester (ed.). *Materials & Methods in Adult and Continuing Education: International—Illiteracy*. Los Angeles: Klevens Publications, 1987. 446 pages.

Knapper, Christopher K., and Cropley, Arthur J. *Lifelong Learning and Higher Education*. London: Croom Helm, 1985. 201 pages.

Knowles, Malcolm S. *Informal Adult Education: A Guide for Administrators, Leaders, and Teachers*. New York: Association Press, 1950. 272 pages.

Knowles, Malcolm S. (ed.). *Handbook of Adult Education in the United States*. Chicago: Adult Education Association, 1960. 624 pages. (*S*)

Knowles, Malcolm S. *Higher Adult Education in the United States: The Current Picture, Trends, and Issues*. Washington, D.C.: American Council on Education, 1969. 106 pages.

Knowles, Malcolm S. *Self-Directed Learning: A Guide for Learners and Teachers*. New York: Association Press, 1975. 136 pages. (*S*)

Knowles, Malcolm S. *A History of the Adult Education Movement in the United States*. (2nd ed.) Malabar, Fla.: Krieger, 1977. 426 pages. (*S*)

Knowles, Malcolm S. *The Master Bibliography in Adult and*

Higher Education. Fort Lauderdale, Fla.: Nova University Press, 1980a. 91 pages.

Knowles, Malcolm S. *The Modern Practice of Adult Education: From Pedagogy to Andragogy.* (Rev. ed.) Chicago: Follett, 1980b. 400 pages. (*S*)

Knowles, Malcolm S. *Using Learning Contracts: Practical Approaches to Individualizing and Structuring Learning.* San Francisco: Jossey-Bass, 1986. 262 pages.

Knowles, Malcolm S. *The Making of an Adult Educator: An Autobiographical Journey.* San Francisco: Jossey-Bass, 1989. 211 pages.

Knowles, Malcolm S. *The Adult Learner: A Neglected Species.* (4th ed.) Houston, Tex.: Gulf, 1990. 296 pages. (*S*)

Knowles, Malcolm S., and Knowles, Hulda. *Introduction to Group Dynamics.* (Rev. ed.) New York: Cambridge University Press, 1972. 96 pages.

Knowles, Malcolm S., and Associates. *Andragogy in Action: Applying Modern Principles of Adult Learning.* San Francisco: Jossey-Bass, 1984. 444 pages.

Knox, Alan B. *Adult Development and Learning: A Handbook on Individual Growth and Competence in the Adult Years.* San Francisco: Jossey-Bass, 1977. 679 pages. (*O, S*)

Knox, Alan B. (ed.). *Assessing the Impact of Continuing Education.* New Directions for Continuing Education, no. 3. San Francisco: Jossey-Bass, 1979a. 124 pages.

Knox, Alan B. (ed.). *Enhancing Proficiencies of Continuing Educators.* New Directions for Continuing Education, no. 1. San Francisco: Jossey-Bass, 1979b. 98 pages.

Knox, Alan B. (ed.). *Programming for Adults Facing Mid-Life Change.* New Directions for Continuing Education, no. 2. San Francisco: Jossey-Bass, 1979c, 135 pages.

Knox, Alan B. (ed). *Teaching Adults Effectively.* New Directions for Continuing Education, no. 6. San Francisco: Jossey-Bass, 1980. 104 pages.

Knox, Alan B. (ed.). *Leadership Strategies for Meeting New Challenges.* New Directions for Continuing Education, no. 13. San Francisco: Jossey-Bass, 1982. 115 pages.

Knox, Alan B. *Helping Adults Learn: A Guide to Planning, Imple-*

menting, and Conducting Programs. San Francisco: Jossey-Bass, 1986. 262 pages. (S)

Knox, Alan B., and Associates. *Developing, Administering, and Evaluating Adult Education.* AEA Handbook Series in Adult Education. San Francisco: Jossey-Bass, 1980. 299 pages. (S)

Kolb, David A. *Experiential Learning: Experience as the Source of Learning and Development.* Englewood Cliffs, N.J.: Prentice-Hall, 1984. 256 pages.

Kordalewski, Jean B. *The Regional Learning Service: An Experiment in Freeing Up Lives.* Syracuse, N.Y.: Regional Learning Service, 1982. 127 pages.

Kornbluh, Joyce L. *A New Deal for Workers' Education: The Workers' Service Program, 1933-1942.* Urbana: University of Illinois Press, 1987. 175 pages.

Kornbluh, Joyce L., and Frederickson, Mary (eds.). *Sisterhood and Solidarity: Workers' Education for Women, 1914-1984.* Philadelphia: Temple University Press, 1984. 372 pages.

Kotinsky, Ruth. *Adult Education and the Social Scene.* East Norwalk, Conn.: Appleton & Lange, 1933. 208 pages.

Kotinsky, Ruth. *Adult Education Councils.* Studies in the Social Significance of Adult Education in the United States, no. 20. New York: American Association for Adult Education, 1940. 172 pages.

Kotinsky, Ruth. *Elementary Education of Adults—A Critical Interpretation.* Studies in the Social Significance of Adult Education in the United States, no. 26. New York: American Association for Adult Education, 1941. 205 pages.

Kowalski, Theodore J. *The Organization and Planning of Adult Education.* Albany: State University of New York Press, 1988. 218 pages.

Kozol, Jonathan. *Prisoners of Silence: Breaking the Bonds of Adult Illiteracy in the United States.* New York: Continuum, 1980. 113 pages.

Kozol, Jonathan. *Illiterate America.* New York: Doubleday, 1985. 270 pages.

Kreitlow, Burton W.; Aiton, E. W.; and Torrence, Andrew P. *Leadership for Action in Rural Communities.* (2nd ed.) Danville, Ill.: Interstate, 1965. 346 pages.

Kreitlow, Burton W., and Associates. *Examining Controversies in Adult Education.* AEA Handbook Series in Adult Education. San Francisco: Jossey-Bass, 1981. 290 pages. (S)

Kulich, Jindra. *Adult Education in Continental Europe: An Annotated Bibliography of English-Language Materials, 1945–1969.* Vancouver: Centre for Continuing Education, University of British Columbia, 1971. 227 pages.

Kulich, Jindra. *Adult Education in Continental Europe: An Annotated Bibliography of English-Language Materials, 1970–1974.* Vancouver: Centre for Continuing Education, University of British Columbia, 1975. 165 pages.

Kulich, Jindra (ed.). *Training of Adult Educators in East Europe.* Vancouver: Centre for Continuing Education, University of British Columbia, 1977. 130 pages.

Kulich, Jindra. *Adult Education in Continental Europe: An Annotated Bibliography of English-Language Materials, 1975–1979.* Vancouver: Centre for Continuing Education, University of British Columbia, 1982. 204 pages.

Kulich, Jindra, and Kruger, Wolfgang (eds.). *The Universities and Adult Education in Europe.* Vancouver: Centre for Continuing Education, University of British Columbia, 1980. 205 pages.

Kurland, Norman D. *Entitlement Papers.* Washington, D.C.: National Institute of Education, 1977. 225 pages.

LaBelle, Thomas J. *Nonformal Education in Latin America and the Caribbean: Stability, Reform, or Revolution.* New York: Praeger, 1986. 367 pages.

Laidlaw, Alexander Fraser. *The Campus and the Community: The Global Impact of the Antigonish Movement.* Montreal: Harvest House, 1961. 173 pages.

Laird, Dugan. *Approaches to Training and Development.* (2nd ed.) Reading, Mass.: Addison-Wesley, 1985. 315 pages.

Landis, Benson Y., and Willard, John D. *Rural Adult Education.* New York: Macmillan, 1933. 299 pages.

Langenbach, Michael. *Curriculum Models in Adult Education.* Malabar, Fla.: Krieger, 1988. 228 pages. (X)

Langerman, Philip D. (ed.). *You Can Be a Successful Teacher of Adults.* Washington, D.C.: National Association for Public Continuing and Adult Education, 1974. 186 pages.

Langerman, Philip D., and Smith, Douglas H. (eds.). *Managing Adult and Continuing Program and Staff.* Washington, D.C.: National Association for Public Continuing and Adult Education, 1979. 377 pages.

Lanning, Frank W., and Many, Wesley A. *Basic Education for the Disadvantaged Adult: Theory and Practice.* Boston: Houghton Mifflin, 1966. 411 pages.

Larrabee, Eric (ed.). *Museums and Education.* Washington, D.C.: Smithsonian Institution Press, 1968. 255 pages.

Laubach, Frank C. *Toward a Literate World.* New York: Columbia University Press, 1938. 178 pages.

Laubach, Frank C. *Forty Years with the Silent Billion: Adventuring in Literacy.* Old Tappan, N.J.: Revell, 1970. 501 pages.

Lauffer, Armand. *The Practice of Continuing Education in the Human Services.* New York: McGraw-Hill, 1977. 227 pages.

Lauffer, Armand. *Doing Continuing Education and Staff Development.* New York: McGraw-Hill, 1978. 356 pages.

Lawson, K. H. *Philosophical Concepts and Values in Adult Education.* (Rev. ed.) Milton Keynes, England: Open University Press, 1979. 120 pages.

Lawson, K. H. *Analysis and Ideology: Conceptual Essays on the Education of Adults.* Nottingham, England: Department of Adult Education, University of Nottingham, 1982. 100 pages.

Leagans, J. Paul, and Loomis, Charles P. (eds.). *Behavioral Change in Agriculture: Concepts and Strategies for Influencing Transition.* Ithaca, N.Y.: Cornell University Press, 1971. 506 pages.

Learned, William S. *The American Public Library and the Diffusion of Knowledge.* Orlando, Fla.: Harcourt Brace Jovanovich, 1924. 80 pages.

Learning Behind Bars: Selected Educational Programs from Juvenile, Jail and Prison Facilities. Pittsburgh, Penn.: QED Communications, 1989. 44 pages.

Lee, Robert Ellis. *Continuing Education for Adults through the American Public Library, 1833–1964.* Chicago: American Library Association, 1966. 158 pages.

Legge, Derek. *The Education of Adults in Britain.* Milton Keynes, England: Open University Press, 1982. 244 pages.

Leichter, Hope Jensen (ed.). *Families and Communities as Educators.* New York: Teachers College Press, 1979. 246 pages.

Leirman, Walter, and Kulich, Jindra (eds.). *Adult Education and the Challenges of the 1990s.* London: Croom Helm, 1987. 215 pages.

Lengrand, Paul. *An Introduction to Lifelong Education.* London: Croom Helm, 1975. 156 pages. (X)

Lengrand, Paul. *Areas of Learning Basic to Lifelong Education.* Elmsford, N.Y.: Pergamon Press, 1986. 251 pages.

Lenz, Elinor. *Creating and Marketing Programs in Continuing Education.* New York: McGraw-Hill, 1980. 240 pages.

Lenz, Elinor. *The Art of Teaching Adults.* Troy, Mo.: Holt, Rinehart & Winston, 1982. 132 pages.

Lenz, Elinor, and Shaevitz, Marjorie Hansen. *So You Want to Go Back to School: Facing the Realities of Reentry.* New York: McGraw-Hill, 1977. 252 pages.

Leonard, Elizabeth Lindeman. *Friendly Rebel: A Personal and Social History of Eduard C. Lindeman.* Adamant, Vt.: Adamant Press, 1991. 214 pages.

Levin, Henry M., and Schütze, Hans G. (eds.). *Financing Recurrent Education: Strategies for Increasing Employment, Job Opportunities, and Productivity.* Newbury Park, Calif.: Sage, 1983. 320 pages.

Levin, Melvin, and Slavet, Joseph. *Continuing Education.* Lexington, Mass.: Heath Lexington Books, 1970. 139 pages.

Levine, Herbert. *Paid Educational Leave.* Washington, D.C.: National Institute of Education, 1977. 44 pages.

Levine, Kenneth. *The Social Context of Literacy.* New York: Routledge & Kegan Paul, 1986. 253 pages.

Lewis, Linda H. (ed.). *Experiential and Simulation Techniques for Teaching Adults.* New Directions for Continuing Education, no. 30. San Francisco: Jossey-Bass, 1986. 111 pages.

Lewis, Linda H. (ed.). *Addressing the Needs of Returning Women.* New Directions for Continuing Education, no. 39. San Francisco: Jossey-Bass, 1988. 117 pages.

Liberal Education in a Technical Age. London: Parrish, 1955. 128 pages.

Lifelong Education and University Resources. Paris: Unesco, 1978. 193 pages.

Lifelong Learning During Adulthood. New York: College Entrance Examination Board, 1978. 59 pages.

Lifelong Learning Trends: A Profile of Continuing Higher Education. Washington, D.C.: National University Continuing Education Association, 1990. 54 pages.

Lillard, Lee A., and Tan, Hong W. *Private Sector Training: Who Gets It and What Are Its Effects?* Santa Monica, Calif.: Rand, 1986. 85 pages.

Lindeman, Eduard C. *The Meaning of Adult Education.* Norman: Oklahoma Research Center for Continuing Professional and Higher Education, 1990. (Originally published in 1926.) 143 pages. (*S*)

Lippitt, Gordon, and Lippitt, Ronald. *The Consulting Process in Action.* (2nd ed.) San Diego, Calif.: University Associates, 1986. 213 pages.

Little, Lawrence C. (ed.). *The Future Course of Christian Adult Education.* Pittsburgh, Penn.: University of Pittsburgh Press, 1959. 322 pages.

Little, Lawrence C. (ed.). *Wider Horizons in Christian Adult Education.* Pittsburg, Penn.: University of Pittsburgh Press, 1962. 338 pages.

Liveright, A. A. *Union Leadership Training: A Handbook of Tools and Techniques.* New York: HarperCollins, 1951. 265 pages.

Liveright. A. A. *Strategies of Leadership.* New York: HarperCollins, 1959. 140 pages.

Liveright, A. A. *A Study of Adult Education in the United States.* Brookline, Mass.: Center for the Study of Liberal Education for Adults at Boston University, 1968. 138 pages.

Liveright, A. A., and Haygood, Noreen (eds.). *The Exeter Papers: Report of the First International Conference on the Comparative Study of Adult Education.* Boston: Center for the Study of Liberal Education for Adults, 1968. 141 pages.

Livingstone, Richard. "The Future in Education." In *On Education.* New York: Macmillan, 1944. 127 pages. (*X*)

London, Jack; Wenkert, Robert; and Hagstrom, Warren O. *Adult*

Education and Social Class. Berkeley: Survey Research Center, University of California, 1963. 246 pages.

Long, Huey B. *Are They Ever Too Old to Learn?* Englewood Cliffs, N.J.: Prentice-Hall, 1971. 48 pages.

Long, Huey B. *The Physiology of Aging: How It Affects Learning.* Englewood Cliffs, N.J.: Prentice-Hall, 1972. 48 pages.

Long, Huey B. *Continuing Education of Adults in Colonial America.* Syracuse, N.Y.: Syracuse University Press, 1976. 75 pages.

Long, Huey B. *Adult and Continuing Education: Responding to Change.* New York: Teachers College Press, Columbia University, 1983a. 210 pages.

Long, Huey B. *Adult Learning: Research and Practice.* New York: Cambridge University Press, 1983b. 367 pages (*H, S*)

Long, Huey B. *New Perspectives on the Education of Adults in the United States.* London: Croom Helm, 1987. 263 pages.

Long, Huey B. *Early Innovators in Adult Education.* London: Routledge, 1991. 161 pages.

Long, Huey B.; Apps, Jerold W.; and Hiemstra, Roger. *Philosophical and Other Views on Lifelong Learning.* Athens: Adult Education Department, College of Education, University of Georgia, 1985. 92 pages.

Long, Huey; Hiemstra, Roger; and Associates. *Changing Approaches to Studying Adult Education.* AEA Handbook Series in Adult Education. San Francisco: Jossey-Bass, 1980. 154 pages.

Long, Huey, and Lord, Charles B. (eds). *The Continuing Education Unit: Concept, Issues, and Use.* Athens: University of Georgia Center for Continuing Education, 1978. 140 pages.

Long, Huey B., and others. *Self-Directed Learning: Emerging Theory and Practice.* Norman: Oklahoma Research Center for Continuing and Professional Education of the University of Oklahoma, 1989. 135 pages.

Loomis, Charles P., and others. *Rural Social Systems and Adult Education.* East Lansing: Michigan State College Press, 1953. 392 pages.

Lord, Russell. *The Agrarian Revival: A Study of Agricultural Extension.* Studies in the Social Significance of Adult Education in the United States, no. 17. New York: American Association for Adult Education, 1939. 236 pages.

Lorimer, Frank. *The Making of Adult Minds in a Metropolitan Area.* New York: Macmillan, 1931. 245 pages.

Loughary, John W., and Hopson, Barrie. *Producing Workshops, Seminars, and Short Courses: A Trainer's Handbook.* Chicago: Association Press, Follett, 1979. 202 pages.

Lovell, R. Bernard. *Adult Learning.* New York: Wiley, 1980. 170 pages.

Lovett, Tom. *Adult Education, Community Development, and the Working Class.* London: Lock, 1975. 176 pages.

Lovett, Tom (ed.). *Radical Approaches to Adult Education: A Reader.* New York: Routledge, 1988. 311 pages.

Lovett, Tom; Clarke, Chris; and Kilmurray, Avila. *Adult Education and Community Action: Adult Education and Popular Social Movements.* London: Croom Helm, 1983. 163 pages.

Low, Theodore Lewis. *The Museum as a Social Instrument.* New York: Metropolitan Museum of Art, 1942. 70 pages.

Low, Theodore Lewis. *The Educational Philosophy and Practice of Art Museums in the United States.* Contributions to Education, no. 942. New York: Teachers College Press, Columbia University, 1948. 245 pages.

Lowe, John (ed.). *Adult Education and Nation-Building: A Symposium on Adult Education in Developing Countries.* Edinburgh: Edinburgh University Press, 1970a. 258 pages.

Lowe, John. *Adult Education in England and Wales: A Critical Survey.* London: Michael Joseph, 1970b. 356 pages.

Lowe, John. *The Education of Adults: A World Perspective.* (2nd ed.) Paris: Unesco, 1982. 223 pages. (X)

Lowy, Louis. *Adult Education and Group Work.* New York: Whiteside, Morrow, 1955. 224 pages.

Lowy, Louis, and O'Connor, Darlene. *Why Education in the Later Years?* Lexington, Mass.: Heath, 1986. 268 pages.

Luft, Joseph. *Group Processes: An Introduction to Group Dynamics.* (2nd ed.) Palo Alto, Calif: National Press Books, 1970. 122 pages.

Luke, Robert A. *How to Train Teachers to Train Adults.* Englewood Cliffs, N.J.: Prentice-Hall, 1971. 48 pages.

Lumsden, D. Barry (ed.). *The Older Adult as Learner: Aspects of*

Educational Gerontology. Washington, D.C.: Hemisphere, 1985, 250 pages.

Lumsden, D. Barry, and Sherron, Ronald H. (eds.) *Experimental Studies in Adult Learning and Memory.* New York: Wiley, 1975. 208 pages.

Lusterman, Seymour. *Trends in Corporate Education and Training.* New York: Conference Board, 1985. 23 pages.

Lyman, Helen Huguenor. *Reading and the Adult New Reader.* Chicago: American Library Association, 1976. 259 pages.

Lyman, Helen Huguenor. *Literacy and the Nation's Libraries.* Chicago: American Library Association, 1977. 212 pages.

Lynton, Rolf P., and Pareek, Udai. *Training for Development.* Homewood, Ill.: Irwin, 1967. 408 pages.

Lyon, Margaret Charters. *The Selection of Books for Adult Study Groups.* Contributions to Education, no. 696. New York: Teachers College Press, Columbia University, 1937. 228 pages.

MacCormick, Austin H. *The Education of Adult Prisoners: A Survey and a Program.* New York: National Society of Penal Information, 1931. 456 pages.

McGee, Leo, and Neufeldt, Harvey G. *Education of the Black Adult in the United States.* Westport, Conn.: Greenwood Press, 1985. 108 pages.

McGivney, Veronica, and Sims, David. *Adult Education and the Challenge of Unemployment.* Milton Keynes, England: Open University Press, 1986. 128 pages.

McGlynn, Mary B. *A Comprehensive Study of Continuing Education.* Washington, D.C.: University Press of America, 1977. 152 pages.

McIntosh, Naomi E.; Calder, Judith A.; and Swift, Betty. *A Degree of Difference: The Open University of the United Kingdom.* New York: Praeger, 1977. 320 pages.

Macken, E., and others. *Home-Based Education: Needs and Technological Opportunities.* Washington, D.C.: National Institute of Education, 1976. 130 pages.

McKenzie, Leon. *Adult Education and the Burden of the Future.* Washington, D.C.: University Press of America, 1978. 96 pages.

McKenzie, Leon. *The Religious Education of Adults.* Birmingham, Ala.: Religious Education Press, 1982. 256 pages.

McKenzie, Leon. *Adult Education and Worldview Construction.* Malabar, Fla.: Krieger, 1991. 146 pages.

MacKenzie, Norman; Postgate, Richmond; and Scupham, John. *Open Learning: Systems and Problems in Post-Secondary Education.* Paris: Unesco, 1975. 498 pages.

MacKenzie, Ossian, and Christensen, Edward L. *The Changing World of Correspondence Study: International Readings.* University Park: Pennsylvania State University Press, 1971. 376 pages.

MacKenzie, Ossian; Christensen, Edward L.; and Rigby, Paul H. *Correspondence Instruction in the United States.* New York: McGraw-Hill, 1968. 261 pages.

Mackie, Robert (ed.). *Literacy and Revolution: The Pedagogy of Paulo Freire.* New York: Continuum, 1981. 166 pages.

McLagan, Patricia A. *Helping Others Learn: Designing Programs for Adults.* Reading, Mass.: Addison-Wesley, 1978. 101 pages.

McLagan, Patricia A. *Models for HRD Practice.* (4 vols.) Alexandria, Va.: American Society for Training and Development, 1989. Unsequenced volumes variously paged.

MacLaren, Gay. *Morally We Roll Along.* Boston: Little, Brown, 1938. 308 pages.

McLeish, John A. B. *The Ulyssean Adult: Creativity in the Middle and Later Years.* New York: McGraw-Hill, 1976. 309 pages (X)

MacLellan, Malcolm. *The Catholic Church and Adult Education.* Washington, D.C.: Catholic University of America, 1935. 125 pages.

McMahon, Ernest E. *The Emerging Evening College: A Study of Faculty Organization and Academic Control in Ten Eastern University Evening Colleges.* New York: Teachers College Press, Columbia University, 1960. 163 pages.

Mansbridge, Albert. *An Adventure in Working-Class Education.* White Plains, N.Y.: Longman, 1920. 73 pages.

Mansbridge, Albert. *Fellow Men: A Gallery of England, 1876–1946.* Freeport, N.Y.: Books for Libraries Press, 1970. (Originally published in 1948.) 116 pages.

Maorong, Wang; Weihua, Lin; Sun, Shilu; and Jing, Fang (eds.). *China: Lessons from Practice.* New Directions for Continuing Education, no. 37. San Francisco: Jossey-Bass, 1988. 130 pages.

Marriott, Stuart. *A Backstairs to a Degree: Demands for an Open*

University in Late Victorian England. Leeds, England: Department of Adult Education and Extramural Studies, University of Leeds, 1981. 107 pages.

Marriott, Stuart. *Extramural Empires: Services & Self-Interest in English University Adult Education, 1873–1983.* Nottingham, England: Department of Adult Education, University of Nottingham, 1984. 137 pages.

Marsh, C. S. *Adult Education in a Community: A Survey of the Facilities Existing in the City of Buffalo, New York.* New York: American Association for Adult Education, 1926. 192 pages. (X)

Marshall, Lorraine, and Rowland, Frances. *A Guide to Learning Independently.* Milton Keynes, England: Open University Press, 1983. 224 pages.

Marsick, Victoria J. (ed.). *Learning in the Workplace.* London: Croom Helm, 1987. 217 pages.

Marsick, Victoria J. (ed.). *Enhancing Staff Development in Diverse Settings.* New Directions for Continuing Education, no. 38. San Francisco: Jossey-Bass, 1988. 119 pages.

Marsick, Victoria J., and Watkins, Karen E. *Informal and Incidental Learning in the Workplace.* London: Routledge, 1990. 270 pages.

Martin, G. Currie. *The Adult School Movement: Its Origin and Development.* London: National Adult School Union, 1924. 435 pages.

Masland, John W., and Radway, Laurence I. *Soldiers and Scholars: Military Education and National Policy.* Princeton, N.J.: Princeton University Press, 1957. 530 pages.

Mason, Robin, and Kaye, Anthony (eds.). *Mindweave: Communication, Computers, and Distance Education.* Elmsford, N.Y.: Pergamon Press, 1989, 273 pages.

Matkin, Gary W. *Effective Budgeting in Continuing Education: A Comprehensive Guide to Improving Program Planning and Organizational Performance.* San Francisco: Jossey-Bass, 1985. 447 pages. (X)

Maurice, Frederick Denison. *Learning and Working.* London: Macmillan, 1855. 202 pages.

Mead, Margaret, and Byers, Paul. *The Small Conference.* Paris: Mouton, 1968. 126 pages.

Mearnes, Hughes. *The Creative Adult.* New York: Doubleday, 1940. 300 pages.

Medary, Marjorie. *Each One, Teach One: Frank Laubach, Friend to Millions.* White Plains, N.Y.: Longman, 1954. 228 pages.

Medsker, Leland, and others. *Extending Opportunities for a College Degree: Practices, Problems, and Potentials.* Berkeley: Center for Research and Development in Higher Education, University of California, 1975. 398 pages.

Mee, Graham. *Organization for Adult Education.* White Plains, N.Y.: Longman, 1980. 114 pages.

Mee, Graham, and Wiltshire, Harold. *Structure and Performance in Adult Education.* White Plains, N.Y.: Longman, 1978. 127 pages.

Meland, Bernard E. *The Church and Adult Education.* Studies in the Social Significance of Adult Education in the United States, no. 16. New York: American Association for Adult Education, 1939. 114 pages.

Mendelsohn, Pam. *Happier by Degrees: A College Reentry Guide for Women.* New York: Dutton, 1980. 302 pages.

Menson, Betty (ed.). *Building on Experiences in Adult Development.* New Directions for Experiential Learning, no. 16. San Francisco: Jossey-Bass, 1982. 129 pages.

Merriam, Sharan B. (ed.). *Linking Philosophy and Practice.* New Directions for Continuing Education, no. 15. San Francisco: Jossey-Bass, 1982. 106 pages.

Merriam, Sharan B. (ed.). *Themes of Adulthood through Literature.* New York: Teachers College Press, Columbia University, 1983. 421 pages.

Merriam, Sharan B. (ed.). *Selected Writings on Philosophy and Adult Education.* Malabar, Fla.: Krieger, 1984. 189 pages.

Merriam, Sharan B., and Caffarella, Rosemary S. *Learning in Adulthood: A Comprehensive Guide.* San Francisco: Jossey-Bass, 1991. 376 pages. (X)

Merriam, Sharan B., and Cunningham, Phyllis M. *Handbook of Adult and Continuing Education.* San Francisco: Jossey-Bass, 1989. 718 pages. (X)

Merriam, Sharan B., and Simpson, Edwin L. *A Guide to Research for Education and Trainers and Adults.* Malabar, Fla.: Kreiger, 1989. 200 pages. (S)

Meyer, Peter. *Awarding College Credit for Non-College Learning: A Guide to Current Practices*. San Francisco: Jossey-Bass, 1975. 195 pages.

Mezirow, Jack. *Dynamics of Community Development*. Metuchen, N.J.: Scarecrow Press, 1963. 252 pages.

Mezirow, Jack. *Transformative Dimensions of Adult Learning*. San Francisco: Jossey-Bass, 1991. 247 pages. (X).

Mezirow, Jack, and Berry, Dorothea. *The Literature of Liberal Adult Education, 1945-1957*. Metuchen, N.J.: Scarecrow Press, 1960. 308 pages.

Mezirow, Jack; Darkenwald, Gordon G.; and Knox, Alan B. *Last Gamble on Education: Dynamics of Adult Basic Education*. Washington, D.C.: Adult Education Association, 1975. 206 pages. (O, S)

Mezirow, Jack, and Associates. *Fostering Critical Reflection in Adulthood: A Guide to Transformative and Emancipatory Learning*. San Francisco: Jossey-Bass, 1990. 386 pages.

Michalak, Donald F., and Yager, Edwin G. *Making the Training Process Work*. New York: HarperCollins, 1979. 152 pages.

Miklas, Sebastian (ed.). *Principles and Problems of Catholic Adult Education*. Washington, D.C.: Catholic University of America Press, 1959. 232 pages.

Miles, Matthew B. *Learning to Work in Groups: A Program Guide for Educational Leaders*. New York: Teachers College Press, Columbia University, 1959. 285 pages.

Millar, J.P.M. *The Labour College Movement*. London: N.C.L.C. Publishing Society, 1979. 301 pages.

Miller, Harry G., and Verduin, John R., Jr. *The Adult Educator— A Handbook for Staff Development*. Houston, Tex.: Gulf, 1979. 178 pages.

Miller, Harry L. *Teaching and Learning in Adult Education*. New York: Macmillan, 1964. 340 pages.

Miller, Harry L., and McGuire, Christine H. *Evaluating Liberal Adult Education*. Chicago: Center for the Study of Liberal Education for Adults, 1961. 184 pages.

Miller, Juliet V., and Musgrove, Mary Lynne (eds.). *Issues in Adult Career Counseling*. New Directions for Continuing Education, no. 32. San Francisco: Jossey-Bass, 1986. 105 pages.

Miller, Randolph Crump. *Education for Christian Living.* Englewood Cliffs, N.J.: Prentice-Hall, 1956. 418 pages.

Miller, Valerie. *Between Struggle and Hope: The Nicaraguan Literacy Crusade.* Boulder, Colo.: Westview Press, 1985. 258 pages. (X)

Mills, H. R. *Teaching and Training: A Handbook for Instructors.* (3rd ed.) London: Macmillan, 1977. 274 pages.

Ministry of Reconstruction, Adult Education Committee. *Final Report.* London: His Majesty's Stationery Office, 1919. 409 pages.

Minzey, Jack D., and LeTarte, Clyde. *Community Education: From Program to Process.* Midland, Mich.: Pendell, 1972. 275 pages.

Mire, Joseph. *Labor Education: A Study Report on Needs, Programs, and Approaches.* Madison, Wis.: Inter-university Labor Education Committee, 1956. 200 pages.

Molyneux, Frank; Low, George; and Fowler, Gerry (eds.). *Learning for Life: Politics and Progress in Recurrent Education.* London: Croom Helm. 1988. 320 pages.

Monroe, Margaret E. *Library Adult Education: The Biography of an Idea.* Metuchen, N.J.: Scarecrow Press, 1963. 550 pages.

Moon, Rexford G., Jr., and Hawes, Gene R. (eds.). *Developing New Adult Clienteles by Recognizing Prior Learning.* New Directions for Experiential Learning, no. 7. San Francisco: Jossey-Bass, 1980. 88 pages.

Moore, David Price, and Poppino, Mary A. *Successful Tutoring: A Practical Guide to Adult Learning Processes.* Springfield, Ill.: Thomas, 1983. 164 pages.

Moore, Marti, and Bostaph, Charles. *Crossroads: A Back to School Career Guide for Adults.* Cranston, R.I.: Carroll Press, 1979. 117 pages.

Moore, Michael (ed.). *Contemporary Issues in American Distance Education.* Elmsford, N.Y.: Pergamon Press, 1990a. 419 pages.

Moore, Michael. *The Effects of Distance Learning: A Summary of Literature.* University Park: American Center for the Study of Disance Education, Pennsylvania State University, 1990b. 74 pages.

Moran, Gabriel. *Education Toward Adulthood: Religion and Lifelong Learning.* New York: Paulist Press, 1979. 151 pages.

More, William S. *Emotions and Adult Learning*. Lexington, Mass.: Heath, 1974. 180 pages.

Moreland, Willis D., and Goldenstein, Erwin H. *Pioneers in Adult Education*. Chicago: Nelson-Hall, 1985. 271 pages.

Morgan, Barton; Holmes, Glenn E.; and Bundy, Clarence E. *Methods in Adult Education*. (3rd ed.) Danville, Ill.: Interstate, 1976. 282 pages.

Morin, Lucien (ed.). *On Prison Education*. Ottawa: Canadian Government Publishing Centre, 1981. 332 pages.

Morrison, Theodore. *Chautauqua: A Center for Education, Religion, and the Arts in America*. Chicago: University of Chicago Press, 1974. 351 pages. (*X*)

Morton, John R. *University Extension in the United States*. Birmingham: University of Alabama Press, 1953. 144 pages.

Moss, Robin. *Video: The Educational Challenge*. London: Croom Helm, 1983. 163 pages.

Mouton, Jane Srygley, and Blake, Robert R. *Synergogy*. San Francisco: Jossey-Bass, 1984. 188 pages.

Mueller, A. D. *Principles and Methods in Adult Education*. Englewood Cliffs, N.J.: Prentice-Hall, 1937. 428 pages.

Mugridge, Ian, and Kaufman, David (eds.). *Distance Education in Canada*. London: Croom Helm, 1986. 317 pages.

Munk, Robert J., and Lovett, Marc. *Hospitalwide Education and Training*. Chicago: Hospital Research and Educational Trust, 1977. 67 pages.

Museums for a New Century: A Report of the Commission on Museums for a New Century. Washington, D.C.: American Association of Museums, 1984. 144 pages.

Mushkin, Selma (ed.). *Recurrent Education*. Washington, D.C.: National Institute of Education, U.S. Department of Health, Education and Welfare, 1973. 347 pages.

Nadler, Leonard. *Designing Training Programs: The Critical Events Model*. Reading, Mass.: Addison-Wesley, 1982. 252 pages.

Nadler, Leonard, and Nadler, Zeace. *The Comprehensive Guide to Successful Conferences and Meetings: Detailed Instructions and Step-by-Step Checklists*. San Francisco: Jossey-Bass, 1987. 447 pages.

Nadler, Leonard, and Nadler, Zeace. *Developing Human Resources:*

Concepts and a Model. (3rd ed.) San Francisco: Jossey-Bass, 1989, 298 pages.

Nadler, Leonard, and Nadler, Zeace. *The Handbook of Human Resource Development, Second Edition.* New York: Wiley, 1990. Sections separately paged.

Nadler, Leonard, and Wiggs, Garland D. *Managing Human Resource Development: A Practical Guide.* San Francisco: Jossey-Bass, 1986. 294 pages.

Nakamoto, June, and Verner, Coolie. *Continuing Education in the Health Professions: A Review of the Literature, 1960–1970.* Syracuse, N.Y.: ERIC Clearinghouse on Adult Education, 1973. 329 pages.

Neil, Michael W. (ed.). *Education of Adults at a Distance: A Report of the Open University's Tenth Anniversary International Conference.* London: Kogan Page, 1981. 270 pages.

Nelson, Thomas H. *Ventures in Informal Adult Education.* New York: Association Press, 1933. 120 pages.

New York Adult Education Council. *A Picture of Adult Education in the New York Metropolitan Area.* New York: New York Adult Education Council, 1934. 32 pages.

Newman, Anabel P. *Adult Basic Education: Reading.* Needham Heights, Mass.: Allyn & Bacon, 1980. 235 pages.

Newman, Michael. *The Poor Cousin: A Study of Adult Education.* London: Allen & Unwin, 1979. 249 pages.

Newsom, Barbara Y., and Silver, Adele Z. (eds.). *The Art Museum as Educator: A Collection of Studies as Guides to Practice and Policy.* Berkeley: University of California Press, 1978. 830 pages.

Niebuhr, Herman, Jr. *Revitalizing American Learning: A New Approach That Just Might Work.* Belmont, Calif.: Wadsworth, 1984. 164 pages.

Nielsen, Aage Rosendal. *Lust for Learning.* Thy, Denmark: New Experimental College Press, 1968. 360 pages.

Niemi, John A. (ed.). *Mass Media and Adult Education.* Englewood Cliffs, N.J.: Educational Technology Publications, 1971. 124 pages.

Niemi, John A., and Gooler, Dennis D. (eds.). *Technologies for Learning Outside the Classroom.* New Directions for Continuing Education, no. 34. San Francisco: Jossey-Bass, 1987. 115 pages.

Niemi, John A., and Jessen, Daniel C. *Directory of Resources in Adult Education.* DeKalb, Ill.: ERIC Clearinghouse on Career Education, 1976. 167 pages.

The 1919 Report: The Final and Interim Reports of the Adult Education Committee of the Ministry of Reconstruction, 1918-1919. Nottingham, England: Department of Adult Education, University of Nottingham, 1980. 409 pages. (X)

Noble, Pat. *Resource-Based Learning in Post Compulsory Education.* London: Kogan Page, 1980. 192 pages.

Noffsinger, John S. *Correspondence Schools, Lyceums, Chautauquas.* New York: Macmillan, 1926. 145 pages.

Nowlen, Phillip M. *A New Approach to Continuing Education and the Professions.* New York: National University Continuing Education Association, American Council on Education, and Macmillan, 1988. 244 pages.

Nyquist, Ewald B.; Arbolino, Jack N.; and Hawes, Gene R. *College Learning Anytime, Anywhere.* Orlando, Fla.: Harcourt Brace Jovanovich, 1977. 164 pages.

Ogden, Jean, and Ogden, Jess. *Small Communities in Action.* New York: HarperCollins, 1946. 244 pages.

Ogden, Jean, and Ogden, Jess. *These Things We Tried.* Charlottesville: University of Virginia Extension, 1947. 432 pages.

Ohliger, John. *Listening Groups: Mass Media in Adult Education.* Boston: Center for the Study of Liberal Education for Adults, 1967. 78 pages.

Ohliger, John, and Gueulette, David. *Media and Adult Learning: A Bibliography with Abstracts, Annotations, and Quotations.* New York: Garland, 1975. 486 pages.

O'Keefe, Michael. *The Adult, Education, and Public Policy.* Cambridge, Mass.: Aspen Institute for Humanities Studies, 1977. 63 pages.

Okun, Morris A. (ed.). *Programs for Older Adults.* New Directions for Continuing Education, no. 14. San Francisco: Jossey-Bass, 1982. 103 pages.

Oliver, Leonard P. *Study Circles: Coming Together for Personal*

Growth and Social Change. Washington, D.C.: Seven Locks Press, 1987. 165 pages.

Olsen, Edward G., and Clark, Phillip A. *Life-Centering Education.* Midland, Mich.: Pendell, 1977. 201 pages.

Open University. *Report of the Committee on Continuing Education.* Milton Keynes, England: Open University Press, 1976. 126 pages.

Organisation for Economic Co-operation and Development. *Learning Opportunities for Adults.* Vol. 1: *General Report.* Paris: Organisation for Economic Co-operation and Development, 1977a. 81 pages.

Organisation for Economic Co-operation and Development. *Learning Opportunities for Adults.* Vol. 3: *The Non-Participation Issue.* Paris: Organisation for Economic Co-operation and Development, 1977b. 208 pages.

Organisation for Economic Co-operation and Development. *Learning Opportunities for Adults.* Vol. 4: *Participation in Adult Education.* Paris: Organisation for Economic Co-operation and Development, 1977c. 440 pages.

Organisation for Economic Co-operation and Development. *Learning Opportunities for Adults.* Vol. 2: *New Structures, Programmes, and Methods.* Paris: Organisation for Economic Co-operation and Development, 1979. 204 pages.

Organisation for Economic Co-operation and Development. *Learning Opportunities for Adults.* Vol. 5: *Widening Access for the Disadvantaged.* Paris: Organisation for Economic Co-operation and Development, 1981. 257 pages.

Otto, Wayne, and Ford, David. *Teaching Adults to Read.* Boston: Houghton Mifflin, 1967. 176 pages.

Overstreet, Harry A., and Overstreet, Bonaro W. *Town Meeting Comes to Town.* New York: HarperCollins, 1938. 263 pages.

Overstreet, Harry A., and Overstreet, Bonaro W. *Leaders for Adult Education.* Studies in the Social Significance of Adult Education in the United States, no. 24. New York: American Association for Adult Education, 1941. 202 pages.

Oxford and Working-Class Education. (2nd ed.) Oxford: Clarendon Press, 1909. 190 pages.

Ozanne, Jacques. *Regional Surveys of Adult Education*. New York: American Association for Adult Education, 1934. 48 pages.

Parker, Allen, and Raybould, S. G. (eds.). *University Studies for Adults*. London: Michael Joseph, 1972. 250 pages.

Parkyn, George W. *Towards a Conceptual Model of Life-Long Education*. Paris: Unesco, 1973. 54 pages.

Parry, R. St. John. *Cambridge Essays on Adult Education*. Cambridge, England: Cambridge University Press, 1920. 230 pages.

Paterson, R.W.K. *Values, Education, and the Adult*. New York: Routledge & Kegan Paul, 1979. 306 pages.

Pati, Sura Prasad. *Adult Education*. New Delhi, India: Ashish Publishing House, 8/81 Punjabi Bagh, 110 026, 1989. 327 pages.

Patton, Michael Quinn. *Utilization-Focused Evaluation*. (2nd ed.) Newbury Park, Calif.: Sage, 1986. 368 pages.

Patton, Michael Quinn. *Creative Evaluation*. (2nd ed.) Newbury Park, Calif.: Sage, 1987. 264 pages.

Patton, Michael Quinn. *Qualitative Evaluation and Research Methods*. Newbury Park, Calif.: Sage, 1990. 532 pages.

Paulston, Rolland G. (ed.). *Non-Formal Education: An Annotated International Bibliography*. New York: Praeger, 1972. 333 pages.

Paulston, Rolland G. *Other Dreams, Other Schools: Folk Colleges in Social and Ethnic Movements*. Pittsburgh, Penn.: University Center for International Studies, University of Pittsburgh, 1980. 279 pages. (*X*)

Pear, T. H. *The Maturing Mind*. London: Nelson, 1938. 152 pages.

Peers, Robert. *Adult Education: A Comparative Study*. (3rd ed.) New York: Routledge & Kegan Paul, 1972. 374 pages.

Peffer, Nathaniel. *New Schools for Older Students*. New York: Macmillan, 1926. 250 pages.

Peffer, Nathaniel. *Educational Experiments in Industry*. New York: Macmillan, 1932. 207 pages.

Penland, Patrick R., and Mathai, Aleyamma. *The Library as a Learning Service Center*. New York: Dekker, 1978. 237 pages.

Pennington, Floyd C. (ed.). *Assessing Educational Needs of Adults*. New Directions for Continuing Education, no. 7. San Francisco: Jossey-Bass, 1980. 107 pages.

Permanent Education. Strasbourg, France: Council of Europe, 1970. 512 pages.

Perraton, Hilary (ed.). *Alternative Routes to Formal Education: Distance Teaching for School Equivalency.* Baltimore, Md.: Johns Hopkins University Press, 1982. 329 pages.

Perry, Walter. *The Open University: History and Evaluation of a Dynamic Innovation in Higher Education.* San Francisco: Jossey-Bass, 1977. 298 pages.

Perspectives of Adult Education in the United States and a Perspective for the Future. Washington, D.C.: U.S. Government Printing Office, 1972. 65 pages.

Peters, A. J. *British Further Education: A Critical Textbook.* Elmsford, N.Y.: Pergamon Press, 1967. 368 pages.

Peters, John M., and Associates. *Building an Effective Adult Education Enterprise.* AEA Handbook Series in Adult Education. San Francisco: Jossey-Bass, 1980. 180 pages.

Peters, John M.; Jarvis, Peter; and Associates. *Adult Education: Evolution and Achievements in a Developing Field of Study.* San Francisco: Jossey-Bass, 1991. 491 pages. (X)

Petersen, Renee, and Petersen, William. *University Adult Education: A Guide to Policy.* New York: HarperCollins, 1960. 288 pages.

Peterson, David A. *Facilitating Education for Older Learners.* San Francisco: Jossey-Bass, 1983. 342 pages.

Peterson, David A.; Thornton, James E.; and Birren, James E. *Education and Aging.* Englewood Cliffs, N.J.: Prentice-Hall, 1986. 240 pages.

Peterson, Gilbert A. (ed.). *The Christian Education of Adults.* Chicago: Moody Press, 1984. 302 pages.

Peterson, Richard E., and Associates. *Lifelong Learning in America: An Overview of Current Practices, Available Resources, and Future Prospects.* San Francisco: Jossey-Bass, 1979. 532 pages. (S)

Peterson, Richard E., and others. *Adult Education and Training in Industrialized Countries.* New York: Praeger, 1982. 500 pages.

Phinney, Eleanor. *Library Adult Education in Action.* Chicago: American Library Association. 1956. 182 pages.

Pöggeler, Franz (ed.). *The State and Adult Education: Historical and Systematical Aspects.* Frankfurt, Germany: Verlag Peter Lang, 1990. 487 pages.

Pole, Thomas. *A History of the Origin and Progress of Adult*

Schools. London: Woburn Press, 1967. (Originally published in 1814.) 128 pages.

Popiel, Elda S. (ed.). *Nursing and the Process of Continuing Education.* Saint Louis, Mo.: Mosby, 1973. 248 pages.

Portman, David N. *The Universities and the Public.* Chicago: Nelson-Hall, 1978. 214 pages.

Poston, Richard Waverly. *Small Town Renaissance: A Study of the Montana Study.* New York: HarperCollins, 1950. 231 pages.

Poston, Richard Waverly. *Democracy Is You: A Guide to Citizen Action.* New York: HarperCollins, 1953. 312 pages.

Poston, Richard Waverly. *Democracy Speaks Many Tongues.* New York: HarperCollins, 1962. 206 pages.

Powell, John Walker. *School for Americans: An Essay in Adult Education.* New York: American Association for Adult Education, 1942. 212 pages.

Powell, John Walker. *Education for Maturity.* New York: Hermitage House, 1949. 242 pages.

Powell, John Walker. *Learning Comes of Age.* New York: Association Press, 1956. 235 pages.

Powell, John Walker. *Channels of Learning: The Story of Educational Television.* Washington, D.C.: Public Affairs Press, 1962. 178 pages.

Power and Conflict in Continuing Education: Survival and Prosperity for All? Belmont, Calif.: Wadsworth, 1980. 247 pages.

Prawl, Warren; Medlin, Roger; and Gross, John. *Adult and Continuing Education Through the Cooperative Extension Service.* Columbia: Extension Division, University of Missouri, 1984. 279 pages.

Proctor, William Martin (ed.). *Annotated Bibliography on Adult Education.* Los Angeles: Frank Wiggins Trade School, 1934. 124 pages.

Prosser, C. A., and Bass, M. R. *Adult Education: The Evening Industrial School.* New York: Century, 1930. 390 pages.

Pugni, J. L. (ed.). *Adult Education Through Home Study.* New York: Arco, 1965. 176 pages.

Queeney, Donna S. *An Agenda for Action: Continuing Professional Education Focus Group Reports.* University Park: Office of Continuing Professional Education, Pennsylvania State University, 1990. 81 pages.

Quick, Thomas L. *Training Managers So They Can Really Manage: Confessions of a Frustrated Trainer.* San Francisco: Jossey-Bass, 1991. 190 pages.

Quigley, B. Allan (ed.). *Fulfilling the Promise of Adult and Continuing Education.* New Directions for Adult and Continuing Education, no. 44. San Francisco: Jossey-Bass, 1989. 127 pages.

Ramsey, Grace Fisher. *Educational Work in Museums of the United States: Development, Methods, and Trends.* New York: Wilson, 1938. 289 pages.

Rankin, Sally H., and Duffy, Karen L. *Patient Education: Issues, Principles, and Guidelines.* Philadelphia: Lippincott, 1983. 308 pages.

Rasmussen, Wayne D. *Taking the University to the People: Seventy-Five Years of Cooperative Extension.* Ames: Iowa State University Press, 1989. 300 pages.

Ratcliff, A.J.J. *The Adult Class.* London: Nelson, 1938. 172 pages.

Raybould, S. G. *The English Universities and Adult Education.* London: Workers' Educational Association, 1951. 169 pages.

Raybould, S. G. *Adult Education at a Tropical University.* White Plains, N.Y.: Longman, 1957. 114 pages.

Raybould, S. G. (ed.). *Trends in English Adult Education.* London: Heineman, 1959. 258 pages.

Raybould, S. G. *University Extramural Education in England, 1945–62: A Study in Finance and Policy.* London: Michael Joseph, 1964. 207 pages.

Rayward, W. Boyd (ed.). *The Public Library: Circumstances and Prospects.* Chicago: University of Chicago Press, 1978. 162 pages.

Read, Margaret. *Education and Social Change in Tropical Areas.* London: Nelson, 1955. 130 pages.

Reagan, Michael V., and Stoughton, Donald M. (eds.). *School Behind Bars: A Descriptive Overview of Correctional Education in the American Prison System.* Metuchen, N.J.: Scarecrow Press, 1976. 321 pages.

Recurrent Education: A Strategy for Lifelong Learning. Paris: Organisation for Economic Co-operation and Development, 1973. 91 pages.

Reddy, G. Ram (ed.). *Open Universities: The Ivory Towers Thrown Open.* New Delhi, India: Sterling, 1988. 270 pages.

Redfield, Robert. *The Educational Experience.* Pasadena: Fund for Adult Education, 1955. 61 pages. (*X*)

Redman, Barbara Klug. *The Process of Patient Education.* St. Louis, Mo.: Mosby, 1984. 315 pages.

Ree, Harry. *Educator Extraordinary: The Life and Achievement of Henry Morris.* White Plains, N.Y.: Longman, 1973. 163 pages.

Reeves, Floyd W.; Fansler, Thomas; and Houle, Cyril O. *Adult Education.* New York: McGraw-Hill, 1938. 172 pages.

Reilly, Jane A. *The Public Librarian as Adult Learners' Advisor: An Innovation in Human Services.* Westport, Conn.: Greenwood Press, 1981. 152 pages.

Revans, Reginald W. *The Origins and Growth of Action Learning.* Bromley, England: Chartwell-Bratt, 1982. 846 pages.

Review of Educational Research, 1950, *20* (entire issue 3).

Review of Educational Research, 1953, *23* (entire issue 3).

Review of Educational Research, 1959, *29* (entire issue 3).

Rice, A. K. *Learning for Leadership.* London: Tavistock, 1965. 200 pages.

Richards, Jack C., and Rodgers, Theodore S. *Approaches and Methods in Language Teaching: A Description and Analysis.* Cambridge, England: Cambridge University Press, 1986. 171 pages.

Richards, Robert K. *Continuing Medical Education: Perspectives, Problems, Prognosis.* New Haven, Conn.: Yale University Press, 1978. 214 pages.

Richmond, Rebecca. *Chautauqua: An American Place.* New York: Duell, Sloan, and Pearse, 1943. 180 pages.

Rivera, William M. (ed.). *Planning Adult Learning: Issues, Practices, and Directions.* London: Croom Helm, 1987. 188 pages.

Rivera, William M., and Schram, Susan G. *Agricultural Extension Worldwide: Issues, Practices, and Emerging Priorities.* London: Croom Helm, 1987. 294 pages. (*X*)

Riverin-Simard, Danielle. *Phases of Working Life.* Montreal: Meridian Press, 1988. 241 pages.

Roberts, Hayden. *Community Development: Learning and Action.* Toronto: University of Toronto Press, 1979. 201 pages.

Roberts, Hayden. *Culture and Adult Education: A Study of Alberta and Quebec.* Edmonton, Canada: University of Alberta Press, 1982. 174 pages.

Roberts, Robert. *Imprisoned Tongues.* Manchester, England: Manchester University Press, 1968. 214 pages.

Robinson, Edward Stevens. *The Behavior of the Museum Visitor.* Publications of the American Association of Museums, New Series, no. 5. Washington, D.C.: American Association of Museums, 1928. 72 pages.

Robinson, John. *Learning over the Air: 60 Years of Partnership in Adult Learning.* London: British Broadcasting Corporation, 1982. 256 pages.

Rockhill, Kathleen. *Academic Excellence and Public Service: A History of University Extension in California.* New Brunswick, N.J.: Transaction Books, 1983. 308 pages.

Rogers, Alan (ed.). *The Spirit and the Form: Essays in Adult Education by and in Honor of Professor Harold Wiltshire.* Nottingham, England: Department of Adult Education, University of Nottingham, 1976. 159 pages.

Rogers, Alan. *Teaching Adults.* Milton Keynes, England: Open University Press, 1986. 197 pages.

Rogers, Everett M., and Shoemaker, F. Floyd. *Communication of Innovations: A Cross Cultural Approach.* (2nd ed.) New York: Free Press, 1971. 476 pages.

Rogers, Jennifer (ed.). *Teaching on Equal Terms.* London: British Broadcasting Corporation, 1969. 141 pages.

Rogers, Jennifer. *Adults Learning.* (3rd ed.) Milton Keynes, England: Open University Press, 1989. 199 pages.

Rogers, Jennifer, and Groombridge, Brian. *Right to Learn: The Case for Adult Equality.* London: Arrow Books, 1976. 202 pages.

Rohfeld, Rae Wahl (ed.). *Expanding Access to Knowledge: Continuing Higher Education, NUCEA, 1915–1990.* Washington, D.C.: National University Continuing Education Association, 1990. 265 pages.

Rosenblum,Sandra H. (ed.). *Involving Adults in the Educational Process.* New Directions in Continuing Education, no. 26. San Francisco: Jossey-Bass, 1985. 110 pages.

Rosencranz, Howard A. (ed.). *Pre-Retirement Education: A Manual for Conference Leaders.* Storrs: Program in Gerontology, University of Connecticut, 1975. 140 pages.

Rosentreter, Frederick M. *The Boundaries of the Campus: A History of the University of Wisconsin Extension Division, 1885–1945.* Madison: University of Wisconsin Press, 1957. 210 pages.

Rosow, Jerome M.; Zager, Robert; and Associates. *Training—The Competitive Edge: Introducing New Technology into the Workplace.* San Francisco: Jossey-Bass, 1988. 241 pages.

Ross-Gordon, Jovita M.; Martin, Larry G.; and Briscoe, Diane Buck (eds.). *Serving Culturally Diverse Populations.* New Directions for Adult and Continuing Education, no. 48. San Francisco: Jossey-Bass, 1990. 112 pages.

Rossman, Mark H.; Fisk, Elizabeth C.; and Roehl, Janet E. *Teaching and Learning Basic Skills: A Guide for Adult Basic Education and Developmental Education Programs.* New York: Teachers College Press, 1984. 180 pages.

Rossman, Mark H., and Rossman, Maxine E. (eds.). *Applying Adult Development Strategies.* New Directions for Adult and Continuing Education, no. 45. San Francisco: Jossey-Bass, 1990. 93 pages.

Rosten, Leo. *O K*A*P*L*A*N! M*Y K*A*P*L*A*N!* New York: HarperCollins, 1976. 361 pages.

Rowden, Dorothy (ed.). *Handbook of Adult Education in the United States.* New York: American Association for Adult Education, 1936. 423 pages.

Rowden, Dorothy. *Enlightened Self-Interest: A Study of Educational Programs of Trade Associations.* Studies in the Social Significance of Adult Education in the United States, no. 3. New York: American Association for Adult Education, 1937. 85 pages.

Rowntree, Derek. *Teaching Through Self-Instruction: A Practical Handbook for Course Developers.* London: Kogan Page, 1986. 386 pages.

Rowntree, J. Wilhelm, and Binns, Henry Bryan. *A History of the Adult School Movement.* London: Headley, 1903. 88 pages.

Rumble, Greville, and Harry, Keith (eds.). *The Distance Teaching Universities.* London: Croom Helm, 1982. 256 pages.

Russ-Eft, Darlene; Rubin, David P.; and Holmen, Rachel E. *Issues in Adult Basic Education and Other Adult Education: An Anno-*

tated Bibliography and Guide to Research. New York: Garland, 1981. 180 pages.

Ruud, Josephine B., and Hall, Olive A. *Adult Education for Home and Family Life.* New York: Wiley, 1974. 249 pages.

Sanders, H. C. (ed.). *The Cooperative Extension Service.* Englewood Cliffs, N.J.: Prentice-Hall, 1966. 436 pages.

Sanford, Nevitt. *Learning After College.* Orinda, Calif.: Montaigne, 1980. 280 pages.

Savile, A. H. *Extension in Rural Communities: A Manual for Agricultural and Home Extension Workers.* Oxford, England: Oxford University Press, 1965. 148 pages.

Schechter, Daniel S. *Agenda for Continuing Education: A Challenge to Health Care Institutions.* Chicago: Hospital Research and Educational Trust, 1974. 112 pages.

Scheffknecht, J. J. *The Tutor: Introductory Considerations Concerning Tutor Training.* Strasbourg, France: Council for Cultural Cooperation, Council of Europe, 1975. 52 pages.

Schein, Edgar, and Bennis, Warren G. *Personal and Organizational Change Through Group Methods.* New York: Wiley, 1965. 376 pages.

Schlossberg, Nancy K. *Counseling Adults in Transition: Linking Practice with Theory.* New York: Springer, 1984. 212 pages.

Schlossberg, Nancy K.; Lynch, Ann Q.; and Chickering, Arthur W. *Improving Higher Education Environments for Adults: Responsive Programs and Services from Entry to Departure.* San Francisco: Jossey-Bass, 1989. 281 pages.

Schlossberg, Nancy K.; Troll, Lillian E.; and Leibowitz, Zandy. *Perspectives on Counseling Adults: Issues and Skills.* Pacific Grove, Calif.: Brooks/Cole, 1978. 152 pages. (X)

Schoenfeld, Clarence A. *The University and Its Publics: Approaches to a Public Relations Program for Colleges and Universities.* New York: HarperCollins, 1954. 284 pages.

Schoenfeld, Clarence A., and Zillman, Donald N. *The American University in Summer.* Madison: University of Wisconsin Press, 1967. 225 pages.

The School and Continuing Education: Four Studies. Paris: Unesco, 1972. 256 pages.

Schramm, Wilbur; Lyle, Jack; and Pool, Ithiel de Sola. *The People*

Look at Educational Television. Stanford, Calif.: Stanford University Press, 1963. 209 pages.

Schuller, Tom, and Megarry, Jacquetta (eds.). *Recurrent Education and Lifelong Learning.* World Yearbook of Education, 1979. London: Kogan Page, 1979. 335 pages.

Schuster, Marie. *The Library-Centered Approach to Learning.* Palm Springs, Calif.: ETC Publications, 1977. 112 pages.

Schütze, Hans G., and Istance, David (eds.). *Recurrent Education Revisited: Modes of Participation and Financing.* Stockholm, Sweden: Almqvist & Wiksell, 1987. 162 pages.

Schwartz, Alvin. *Museum: The Story of America's Treasure Houses.* New York: Dutton, 1967. 256 pages.

Schwartz, Bertrand. *Permanent Education: Educating Man for the 21st Century.* Vol. 8, Project 1, of Plan Europe 2000. The Hague, Netherlands: Martinus Nijhoff, 1974. 244 pages. (X)

Schwertman, John B. *I Want Many Lodestars.* Notes and Essays on Education for Adults, no. 21. Chicago: Center for the Study of Liberal Education for Adults, 1958. 111 pages.

Scott, Marian. *Chautauqua Caravan.* East Norwalk, Conn.: Appleton & Lange, 1939. 310 pages.

Scott, Roy V. *The Reluctant Farmer: The Rise of Agricultural Extension to 1914.* Urbana: University of Illinois Press, 1970. 362 pages.

Scottish Education Department. *Adult Education: The Challenge of Change.* Edinburgh: Her Majesty's Stationery Office, 1975. 136 pages.

Screven, C. G. *The Measurement and Facilitation of Learning in the Museum Environment: An Experimental Analysis.* Washington, D.C.: Smithsonian Institution Press, 1974. 91 pages.

Seaman, Don F., and Fellenz, Robert A. *Effective Strategies for Teaching Adults.* Columbus, Ohio: Merrill, 1989. 189 pages.

Seashore, Marjorie, and others. *Prison Education: Project NewGate and Other College Programs.* New York: Praeger, 1976. 329 pages.

Seay, Maurice F. (ed.). *Adult Education: A Part of a Total Educational Program.* Bulletin of the Bureau of School Service, vol. 10, no. 4. Lexington: University of Kentucky, 1938. 192 pages.

Seay, Maurice, and others. *Community Education: A Developing Concept.* Midland, Mich.: Pendell, 1974. 424 pages.

Seekings, David. *How to Organize Effective Conferences and Meetings.* London: Kogan Page, 1981. 208 pages.

Selman, Gordon, and Dampier, Paul. *The Foundations of Adult Education in Canada.* Toronto: Thompson Educational Publishing, 1991. 310 pages. (*X*)

Senior, Barbara, and Naylor, John. *Educational Responses to Adult Unemployment.* London: Croom Helm, 1987. 174 pages.

Sewart, David; Keegan, Desmond; and Holmberg, Borge. *Distance Education: International Perspectives.* London: Croom Helm, 1983. 445 pages.

Seybolt, Robert Francis. *The Evening School in Colonial America.* Urbana: University of Illinois Press, 1925. 68 pages.

Seybolt, Robert Francis. *Source Studies in American Colonial Education: The Private School.* University of Illinois Bulletin, no. 28. Urbana: University of Illinois, 1928. 109 pages.

Seyfert, Warren C. (ed.). *Capitalizing Intelligence: Eight Essays on Adult Education.* Cambridge, Mass.: Graduate School of Education, Harvard University, 1937. 141 pages.

Shannon, Theodore, J., and Schoenfeld, Clarence A. *University Extension.* New York: Center for Applied Research in Education, 1965. 115 pages.

Sharer, Robert E. *There Are No Islands: The Concerns and Potentials of Continuing Education.* North Quincy, Mass.: Christopher, 1969. 127 pages.

Shaw, Nathan C. (ed.). *Administration of Continuing Education.* Washington, D.C.: National Association for Public School Adult Education, 1969. 438 pages.

Shaw, Wilfred B. *Alumni and Adult Education.* New York: American Association for Adult Education, 1929. 117 pages.

Shearman, Harold C. *Adult Education for Democracy.* London: Workers' Educational Association, 1944. 95 pages.

Sheats, Paul H.; Jayne, Clarence D.; and Spence, Ralph B. *Adult Education: The Community Approach.* New York: Dryden, 1953. 530 pages. (*S*)

Shelburne, James C., and Groves, Kenneth J. *Education in the*

Armed Forces. New York: Center for Applied Research in Education, 1965. 118 pages.

Sherron, Ronald H., and Lumsden, D. Barry (eds.). *Introduction to Educational Gerontology.* (3rd ed.) Washington, D.C.: Hemisphere, 1989. 308 pages.

Shields, James J., Jr. *Education in Community Development.* New York: Praeger, 1967. 127 pages.

Shipp, Travis (ed.). *Creative Financing and Budgeting.* New Directions in Continuing Education, no. 16. San Francisco: Jossey-Bass, 1982. 89 pages.

Shor, Ira, and Freire, Paulo. *A Pedagogy for Liberation: Dialogues on Transforming Education.* South Hadley, Mass.: Bergen and Garvey, 1987. 203 pages.

Shute, R. Wayne. *For Adults Only: A Lifetime of Learning.* Salt Lake City, Utah: Deseret, 1968. 206 pages.

Simerly, Robert G. *Planning and Marketing Conferences and Workshops: Tips, Tools, and Techniques.* San Francisco: Jossey-Bass, 1990. 219 pages.

Simerly, Robert G., and Associates. *Strategic Planning and Leadership in Continuing Education: Enhancing Organizational Vitality, Responsiveness, and Identity.* San Francisco: Jossey-Bass, 1987. 247 pages. (X)

Simerly, Robert G., and Associates. *Handbook of Marketing for Continuing Education.* San Francisco: Jossey-Bass, 1989. 521 pages. (X)

Simon, Brian (ed.). *The Search for Enlightenment: The Working Class Education in the Twentieth Century.* London: Lawrence & Wishart, 1990. 334 pages.

Simpson, Edward G., Jr., and Kasworm, Carol E. (eds.). *Revitalizing the Residential Conference Center Environment.* New Directions for Adult and Continuing Education, no. 45. San Francisco: Jossey-Bass, 1990. 105 pages.

Simpson, Edwin L. *Faculty Renewal in Higher Education.* Malabar, Fla.: Krieger, 1990. 159 pages.

Simpson, J. A. *Today and Tomorrow in European Adult Education: A Study of the Present Situation and Future Developments.* Strasbourg, France: Council of Europe, 1972. 223 pages.

Skager, Rodney. *Lifelong Education and Evaluation Practice.* Elmsford, N.Y.: Pergamon Press, 1978. 155 pages.

Skager, Rodney, and Dave, R. H. *Curriculum Evaluation for Lifelong Education.* Elmsford, N.Y.: Pergamon Press, 1977. 140 pages.

Smith, Clarence B., and Wilson, Meredith C. *The Agricultural Extension System of the United States.* New York: Wiley, 1930. 402 pages.

Smith, George Baxter. *Purposes and Conditions Affecting the Nature and Extent of Participation of Adults in Courses in the Home Study Department of Columbia University, 1925–1932.* New York: Teachers College Press, Columbia University, 1935. 86 pages.

Smith, Helen Lyman. *Adult Education Activities in Public Libraries.* Chicago: American Library Association, 1954. 96 pages.

Smith, Peter, and Kelly, Mavis. *Distance Education and the Mainstream: Convergence in Education.* London: Croom Helm, 1987. 207 pages.

Smith, Robert M. *Learning How to Learn: Applied Theory for Adults.* New York: Cambridge University Press, 1982. 201 pages. (*H, S*)

Smith, Robert M. (ed.). *Helping Adults Learn How to Learn.* New Directions for Continuing Education, no. 19. San Francisco: Jossey-Bass, 1983. 109 pages.

Smith, Robert M.; Aker, George F.; and Kidd, J. R. *Handbook of Adult Education.* New York: Macmillan, 1970. 594 pages (*S*)

Smith, Robert M., and Associates. *Learning to Learn Across the Life Span.* San Francisco: Jossey-Bass, 1990. 382 pages. (*X*)

Snow, Robert H. *Community Adult Education.* New York: Putnam, 1955. 170 pages.

Soifer, Rena, and others. *The Complete Theory-to-Practice Handbook of Adult Literacy: Curriculum Design and Teaching Approaches.* New York: Teachers College Press, 1990. 212 pages.

Solinger, Janet W. (ed.). *Museums and Universities: New Paths for Continuing Education.* New York: Macmillan, 1990. 351 pages.

Solmon, Lewis C., and Gordon, Joanne J. *The Characteristics and Needs of Adults in Postsecondary Education.* Lexington, Mass.: Lexington Books, 1981. 155 pages.

Solomon, Daniel (ed.). *The Continuing Learner*. Chicago: Center for the Study of Liberal Education for Adults, 1964. 95 pages.

Solomon, Daniel; Bezdek, William E.; and Rosenberg, Larry. *Teaching Styles and Learning*. Chicago: Center for the Study of Liberal Education for Adults, 1963. 164 pages.

Sommer, Robert F. *Teaching Writing to Adults: Strategies and Concepts for Improving Learner Performance*. San Francisco: Jossey-Bass, 1989. 252 pages.

Sorenson, Herbert. *Adult Abilities: A Study of University Extension Students*. Minneapolis: University of Minnesota Press, 1938. 190 pages.

Sork, Thomas J. (ed.). *Designing and Implementing Effective Workshops*. New Directions in Continuing Education, no. 22. San Francisco: Jossey-Bass, 1984. 96 pages.

Sork, Thomas J. (ed.). *Mistakes Made and Lessons Learned: Overcoming Obstacles to Successful Program Planning*. New Directions for Adult and Continuing Education, no. 49. San Francisco: Jossey-Bass, 1991. 98 pages.

Squires, Geoffrey. *The Curriculum Beyond School*. London: Hodder and Stoughton, 1987. 244 pages.

Squires, Gregory D. *The Learning Exchange: An Alternative in Adult Education*. East Lansing: Institute for Community Development and Services, Michigan State University, 1975. 50 pages.

Squyres, Wendy D. (ed.). *Patient Education: An Inquiry into the State of the Art*. New York: Springer, 1980. 359 pages.

Stacy, William H. *Integration of Adult Education*. New York: Teachers College Press, Columbia University, 1935. 148 pages.

Stanage, Sherman. *Adult Education and Phenomenological Research: New Directions for Theory, Practice, and Research*. Malabar, Fla.: Krieger, 1987. 421 pages.

Stanley, Oliver (ed.). *The Way Out: Essays on the Meaning and Purpose of Adult Education*. Oxford, England: Oxford University Press, 1923. 115 pages.

Staton, Thomas F. *How to Instruct Successfully: Modern Teaching Methods in Adult Education*. New York: McGraw-Hill, 1960. 292 pages.

Stenzel, Anne K., and Feeney, Helen M. *Volunteer Training and*

Development: A Manual for Community Groups. New York: Seabury Press, 1967. 223 pages.

Stephens, Michael D. (ed.). *International Organizations in Education.* London: Routledge, 1988. 165 pages.

Stephens, Michael D., and Roderick, Gordon W. (ed.). *Teaching Techniques in Adult Education.* Newton Abbot, England: David and Charles, 1971. 206 pages.

Stern, Bernard H., and Missall, Ellsworth. *Adult Experience and College Degrees.* Cleveland, Ohio: Press of Western Reserve University, 1960. 249 pages.

Stern, H. H. *Parent Education: An International Survey.* Hull, England: University of Hull, 1960. 163 pages.

Stern, Milton (ed.). *Power and Conflict in Continuing Professional Education.* Belmont, Calif.: Wadsworth, 1983. 276 pages.

Stevenson, Colin. *Challenging Adult Illiteracy: Reading and Writing Disabilities in the British Army.* New York: Teachers College Press, 1985. 213 pages.

Stewart, Cora Wilson. *Moonlight Schools for the Emancipation of Adult Illiterates.* New York: Dutton, 1922. 194 pages.

Stewart, David W. *Adult Learning in America: Eduard Lindeman and His Agenda for Lifelong Learning.* Malabar, Fla.: Krieger, 1987. 289 pages (*O, S*)

Stocks, Mary. *The Workers' Educational Association: The First Fifty Years.* London: Allen & Unwin, 1953. 158 pages (*X*)

Stoikov, Vladimir. *The Economics of Recurrent Education and Training.* Geneva, Switzerland: International Labour Office, 1975. 115 pages.

Stokes, Kenneth (ed.). *Faith Development in the Adult Life Cycle.* New York: Sadlier, 1982. 320 pages.

Stone, C. Walter (ed.). "Current Trends in Adult Education." *Library Trends,* 1959, *8,* 1–122.

Stone, Elizabeth W. "Personnel Development and Continuing Education in Libraries." *Library Trends,* 1971, *20,* 1–183.

Stone, Ferdinand F., and Charters, Jessie A. *Alumni Interest in Continuing Education.* Columbus: Ohio State University Press, 1932. 40 pages.

Storey, David S., and Rohrer, K. Hugh. *The Historical Development of Community Education and the Mott Foundation.* Mt.

Pleasant: Center for Community Education, Central Michigan University, 1979. 64 pages.

Strauss, Bert, and Strauss, Frances. *New Ways to Better Meetings.* New York: Viking Penguin, 1951. 177 pages.

Striner, Herbert. *Continuing Education as a National Capital Investment.* Kalamazoo, Mich.: Upjohn Institute for Employment Research, 1971. 118 pages.

Strother, George B., and Klus, John P. *Administration of Continuing Education.* Belmont, Calif.: Wadsworth, 1982. 304 pages.

Stubblefield, Harold W. (ed.). *Continuing Education for Community Leadership.* New Directions for Continuing Education, no. 11. San Francisco: Jossey-Bass, 1981. 128 pages.

Stubblefield, Harold W. *Towards a History of Adult Education in America.* London: Croom Helm, 1988. 186 pages. (*O, S*)

Studebaker, John W. *The American Way.* New York: McGraw-Hill, 1935. 206 pages.

Styler, W. E. *Adult Education and Political Systems.* Nottingham, England: Department of Adult Education, University of Nottingham, 1984. 227 pages. (*X*)

Taylor, Katharine Whiteside. *Parents and Children Learn Together.* New York: Teachers College Press, 1967. 329 pages.

Taylor, Maurice C., and Draper, James A. (eds.). *Adult Literacy Perspectives.* Toronto: Culture Concepts, 1989. 484 pages.

Taylor, Richard; Rockhill, Kathleen; and Fieldhouse, Roger. *University Adult Education in England and the USA: A Reappraisal of the Liberal Tradition.* London: Croom Helm, 1985. 247 pages.

Teather, David C. B. (ed.). *Towards the Community University: Case Studies of Innovation and Community Service.* New York: Nichols, 1982. 244 pages.

Tennant, Mark. *Psychology and Adult Learning.* New York: Routledge, 1988. 181 pages. (*H*)

Tennant, Mark (ed.). *Adult and Continuing Education in Australia: Issues and Practices.* London: Routledge, 1991. 265 pages.

Thatcher, John H. (ed.). *Public School Adult Education: A Guide for Administrators.* (Rev. ed.) Washington, D.C.: National Association of Public School Adult Education, 1963. 199 pages.

Thelen, Herbert A. *Dynamics of Groups at Work.* Chicago: University of Chicago Press, 1954. 379 pages.

Thomas, Alan M. *Beyond Education: A New Perspective on Society's Management of Learning.* San Francisco: Jossey-Bass, 1991. 201 pages.

Thomas, Alan, and Ploman, Edward W. (eds.). *Learning and Development: A Global Perspective.* Toronto: Ontario Institute for Studies in Education, 1986. 222 pages.

Thomas, J. E. *Radical Adult Education: Theory and Practice.* Nottingham, England: Department of Adult Education, University of Nottingham, 1982. 73 pages.

Thomas, J. E. *Learning Democracy in Japan: The Social Education of Japanese Adults.* Newbury Park, Calif.: Sage, 1985. 153 pages.

Thomas, J. E., and Elsey, Barry (eds.). *International Biography of Adult Education.* Nottingham, England: Department of Adult Education, University of Nottingham, 1985. 709 pages.

Thompson, Clem O. *University Extension in Adult Education.* Bloomington, Ind.: National University Extension Association, 1943. 322 pages.

Thompson, Jane L. (ed.). *Adult Education for a Change.* London: Hutchinson, 1980. 256 pages.

Thomsen, Carl; Sydney, Edward; and Tompkins, Miriam D. *Adult Education Activities for Public Libraries.* Paris: Unesco, 1950. 102 pages.

Thomson, Frances Coombs. *The New York Times Guide to Continuing Education in America.* New York: Quadrangle Books, 1972. 811 pages.

Thorndike, Edward L., and others. *Adult Learning.* New York: Macmillian, 1928. 335 pages. (S)

Thorndike, Edward L., and others. *Adult Interests.* New York: Macmillan, 1935. 265 pages.

Thornton, A. H., and Stephens, M. D. (eds.). *The University and Its Region: The Extra-Mural Contribution.* Nottingham, England: Department of Adult Education, University of Nottingham, 1977. 192 pages.

Thoroman, E. C. *The Vocational Counseling of Adults and Young Adults.* Boston: Houghton Mifflin, 1968. 195 pages.

Titmus, Colin J. *Adult Education in France.* Elmsford, N.Y.: Pergamon Press, 1967. 201 pages.

Titmus, Colin J. *Strategies for Adult Education: Practices in West-*

ern Europe. Milton Keynes, England: Open University Press, 1981. 239 pages.

Titmus, Colin J. (ed.). *Lifelong Education for Adults: An International Handbook.* Elmsford, N.Y.: Pergamon Press, 1989. 590 pages. (*X*)

Titmus, Colin J., and others. *Terminology of Adult Education.* Paris: Unesco, 1979. 154 pages. (*X*)

Tittle, Carol Kehr, and Denker, Eleanor Rubin. *Returning Women Students in Higher Education: Defining Policy Issues.* New York: Praeger, 1980. 213 pages.

Tjerandsen, Carl. *Education for Citizenship: A Foundation's Experience.* Santa Cruz, Calif.: Schwartzhaupt Foundation, 1980. 713 pages.

Todd, Frankie (ed.). *Planning Continuing Professional Development.* London: Croom Helm, 1987. 228 pages.

Torbert, J. Keith. *The Establishment of an Adult School.* New York: Macmillan, 1936. 218 pages.

Torres, Carlos Alberto. *The Politics of Nonformal Education in Latin America.* New York: Praeger, 1990. 181 pages.

Tough, Allen. *The Adult's Learning Projects.* (2nd ed.) Toronto: Ontario Institute for Studies in Education, 1979. 192 pages. (*S*)

Tough, Allen. *Intentional Changes: A Fresh Approach to Helping People Change.* Chicago: Follett, 1982. 192 pages. (*S*)

Townsend Coles, Edwin K. *Adult Education in Developing Countries.* (2nd ed.) Elmsford, N.Y.: Pergamon Press, 1977. 199 pages.

Townsend Coles, Edwin K. *Maverick of the Education Family: Two Essays in Non-Formal Education.* Elmsford, N.Y.: Pergamon Press, 1982. 111 pages.

Tracey, William R. *Managing Training and Development Systems.* New York: American Management Association, 1974. 480 pages.

The Training of Functional Literacy Personnel: A Practical Guide. Paris: Unesco, 1973. 104 pages.

Trenaman, J. M. *Communication and Comprehension.* White Plains, N.Y.: Longman, 1967. 212 pages.

True, Alfred Charles. *A History of Agricultural Extension Work in the United States, 1785–1923.* U.S. Department of Agriculture, miscellaneous publication no. 15. Washington, D.C.: U.S. Government Printing Office, 1928. 220 pages.

Tunstall, Jeremy (ed.). *The Open University Opens.* Amherst: University of Massachusetts Press, 1974. 191 pages.

Ulich, Mary E. *Patterns of Adult Education: A Comparative Study.* New York: Pageant Press, 1965. 205 pages.

Ulmer, Curtis. *Teaching the Disadvantaged Adult.* Washington, D.C.: National Association for Public School Adult Education, 1969. 100 pages.

Unesco. *Second World Conference on Adult Education.* Paris: Unesco, 1962. 48 pages.

Unesco. *It's Never Too Late to Learn.* Paris: Unesco, 1982. 83 pages.

Unesco and the International Association of Universities. *Lifelong Education and University Resources.* Paris: Unesco, 1978. 193 pages.

U.K. Department of Education and Science. *Adult Education: A Plan for Development.* London: Her Majesty's Stationery Office, 1973. 311 pages.

U.K. Ministry of Education. *The Organisation and Finance of Adult Education in England and Wales.* London: Her Majesty's Stationery Office, 1954. 67 pages.

Universities Council for Adult Education. *University Adult Education in the Later Twentieth Century.* Birmingham, England: Department of Extramural Studies, University of Birmingham, 1970. 88 pages.

Universities in Adult Education. Paris: Unesco, 1952. 172 pages.

Urban Extension: A Report on Experimental Programs Assisted by the Ford Foundation. New York: Ford Foundation, 1966. 44 pages.

Usher, Robin, and Bryant, Ian. *Adult Education as Theory, Practice and Research: The Captive Triangle.* London: Routledge, 1989. 212 pages.

Utterback, William E. *Group Thinking and Conference Leadership.* (Rev. ed.). Troy, Mo.: Holt, Rinehart & Winston, 1964. 244 pages.

Van de Wall, Willem. *The Music of the People.* Studies in the Social Significance of Adult Education in the United States, no. 6. New York: American Association for Adult Education, 1938. 128 pages.

Van Hoose, William H., and Worth, Maureen Rousset. *Counseling*

Adults: A Developmental Approach. Pacific Grove, Calif.: Brooks/Cole, 1982. 236 pages.

Verduin, John R., Jr. *Curriculum Building for Adult Learning.* Carbondale: Southern Illinois University Press, 1980. 171 pages.

Verduin, John R., Jr., and Clark, Thomas A. *Distance Education: The Foundations of Effective Practice.* San Francisco: Jossey-Bass, 1991. 279 pages.

Verduin, John R., Jr.; Miller, Harry G.; and Greer, Charles E. *Adults Teaching Adults: Principles and Strategies.* Austin, Tex.: Learning Concepts, 1977. 202 pages.

Vermilye, Dyckman W. (ed.). *Lifelong Learners—A New Clientele for Higher Education.* San Francisco: Jossey-Bass, 1974. 178 pages.

Vermilye, Dyckman W. (ed.). *Relating Work and Education.* San Francisco: Jossey-Bass, 1977. 282 pages.

Verner, Coolie. *Adult Education Theory and Method: A Conceptual Scheme for the Identification and Classification of Processes.* Chicago: Adult Educational Association of the USA., 1962. 34 pages.

Verner, Coolie, and Booth, Alan. *Adult Education.* Washington, D.C.: Center for Applied Research in Education, 1964. 188 pages. (S)

Verner, Coolie, and Davison, Catherine. *Physiological Factors in Adult Learning and Instruction.* Tallahassee, Fla.: Adult Education Research, Information Processing Center, 1971. 26 pages.

Verner, Coolie, and Millard, Frank W. *Adult Education and the Adoption of Innovations by Orchardists in the Okanagan Valley of British Columbia.* Vancouver: Department of Agricultural Economics, University of British Columbia, 1966. 92 pages.

Verner, Coolie, and White, Thurman (eds.). *Participants in Adult Education.* Washington, D.C.: Adult Education Association, 1965. 44 pages.

Vincent, John H. *The Chautauqua Movement.* Boston: Chautauqua Press, 1886. 308 pages.

Vogel, Linda J. *The Religious Education of Older Adults.* Birmingham, Ala.: Religious Education Press, 1984. 217 pages.

Vogel, Linda J. *Teaching and Learning in Communities of Faith: Empowering Adults Through Religious Education.* San Francisco: Jossey-Bass, 1991. 250 pages.

Von Moltke, Konrad, and Schneevoigt, Norbett. *Educational Leaves for Employees: European Experience for American Consideration.* San Francisco: Jossey-Bass, 1977. 269 pages.

Votruba, James C. (ed.). *Strengthening Internal Support for Continuing Education.* New Directions for Continuing Education, no. 9. San Francisco: Jossey-Bass, 1981. 112 pages.

Wade, Louise C. *Graham Taylor: Pioneer for Social Justice, 1851–1938.* Chicago: University of Chicago Press, 1964. 268 pages.

Wagner, Daniel A. (ed.). *The Future of Literacy in a Changing World.* Vol. 1: *Comparative and International Education.* Elmsford, N.Y.: Pergamon Press, 1987. 344 pages. (X)

Wain, Kenneth. *Philosophy of Lifelong Education.* London: Croom Helm, 1987. 259 pages.

Waldron, Mark W., and Moore, George A. B. *Helping Adults Learn: Course Planning for Adult Learners.* Toronto: Thompson Educational Publishing, 1991. 194 pages.

Wallack, Walter M.; Kendall, Glenn M.; and Briggs, Howard L. *Education Within Prison Walls.* New York: Teachers College Press, 1939. 187 pages.

Waller, Ross D. *Learning to Live.* London: Art and Educational Publishers, 1946. 63 pages.

Wallis, John, and Mee, Graham. *Community Schools: Claims and Performances.* Nottingham, England: Department of Adult Education, University of Nottingham, 1983. 81 pages.

Waples, Douglas. *People and Print.* Chicago: University of Chicago Press, 1937. 228 pages.

Waples, Douglas; Berelson, Bernard; and Bradshaw, Franklyn. *What Reading Does to People.* Chicago: University of Chicago Press, 1940. 222 pages.

Waples, Douglas, and Tyler, Ralph W. *What People Want to Read About.* Chicago: University of Chicago Press, 1931. 312 pages.

Ward, Betty Arnett. *Literacy and Basic Elementary Education for Adults.* U.S. Office of Education Bulletin, no. 19. Washington, D.C.: U.S. Government Printing Office, 1961. 126 pages.

Ward, Kevin, and Taylor, Richard (eds.). *Adult Education and the Working Class: Education for the Missing Million.* London: Croom Helm, 1986. 195 pages.

Ware, Caroline F. *Labor Education in Universities.* New York: American Labor Education Service, 1946. 138 pages.

Warner, Paul D., and Christenson, James A. *The Cooperative Extension Service: A National Assessment.* Boulder, Colo.: Westview Press, 1984. 194 pages.

Watson, Charles E. *Management Development Through Training.* Reading, Mass.: Addison-Wesley, 1979. 340 pages.

The WEA Education Year Book 1918. Nottingham, England: Department of Adult Education, University of Nottingham, 1981. 512 pages.

Webster, Thomas G.; Hoffman, Margaret E.; and Lamson, Warren E. (eds.). *Continuing Education: Agent of Change.* Washington, D.C.: U.S. Government Printing Office, 1971. 229 pages.

Wedemeyer, Charles A. *Learning at the Back Door: Reflections on Non-Traditional Learning in the Lifespan.* Madison: University of Wisconsin Press, 1981. 260 pages.

Weeks, Edward. *The Lowells and Their Institute.* Boston: Little, Brown, 1966. 202 pages. (X)

Weil, Dorothy. *Continuing Education.* New York: Rawson, Wade, 1979. 234 pages.

Weingand, Darlene E. (ed.). "Adult Education, Literacy and Libraries." *Library Trends,* 1986, *35*(2), 183–345.

Weinstock, Ruth. *The Graying of the Campus.* New York: Educational Facilities Laboratories, 1978. 160 pages.

Welch, Edwin. *The Peripatetic University: Cambridge Local Lectures, 1873–1973.* Cambridge, England: Cambridge University Press, 1973. 229 pages.

Welford, A. T. *Ageing and Human Skill.* Oxford, England: Oxford University Press, 1958. 300 pages. (X)

Whipple, Caroline A.; Guyton, Mary L.; and Morriss, Elizabeth C. *Manual for Teachers of Adult Elementary Students.* Washington, D.C.: American Association for Adult Education, U.S. Office of Education, 1934. 186 pages.

Whitelock, Derek (ed.). *Adult Education in Australia.* Elmsford, N.Y.: Pergamon Press, 1970. 288 pages.

Whitelock, Derek. *The Great Tradition: A History of Adult Education in Australia.* St. Lucia, Australia: Queensland University Press, 1974. 327 pages.

Williams, Donald B. *Agricultural Extension: Farm Extension Services in Australia, Britain, and the United States of America.* Melbourne, Australia: Melbourne University Press, 1968. 218 pages.

Williams, Gareth. *Towards Lifelong Education: A New Role for Higher Education Institutions.* Paris: Unesco, 1977. 188 pages.

Williams, W. E., and Heath, A. E. *Learn and Live: The Consumer's View of Adult Education.* London: Methuen, 1936. 271 pages. (X)

Willis, Sherry L.; Dubin, Samuel S.; and Associates. *Maintaining Professional Competence: Approaches to Career Enhancement, Vitality, and Success Throughout a Work Life.* San Francisco: Jossey-Bass, 1990. 328 pages.

Wilms, Wellford W. *Public and Proprietary Vocational Training.* Lexington, Mass.: Heath, 1975. 207 pages.

Wilson, John P. (ed.). *Materials for Teaching Adults: Selection, Development, and Use.* New Directions for Continuing Education, no. 17. San Francisco: Jossey-Bass, 1983. 115 pages.

Wilson, Louis R. (ed.). *The Role of the Library in Adult Education.* Chicago: University of Chicago Press, 1937. 321 pages.

Wilson, Meredith C., and Gallup, Gladys. *Extension Teaching Methods and Other Factors That Influence Adoption of Agricultural and Home Economics Practices.* Extension Service Circular no. 495. Washington, D.C.: U.S. Government Printing Office, 1955. 80 pages.

Wirtz, Willard. *The Boundless Resource: A Prospectus for an Education-Work Policy.* Washington, D.C.: New Republic, 1975. 205 pages.

Witkin, Belle Ruth. *Assessing Needs in Educational and Social Programs: Using Information to Make Decisions, Set Priorities, and Allocate Resources.* San Francisco: Jossey-Bass, 1984. 415 pages.

Wittlin, Alma S. *The Museum: Its History and Its Tasks in Education.* New York: Routledge & Kegan Paul, 1949. 297 pages.

Wlodkowski, Raymond J. *Enhancing Adult Motivation to Learn: A Guide to Improving Instruction and Increasing Learner Achievement.* San Francisco: Jossey-Bass, 1985. 314 pages. (S)

Wolfbein, Seymour L. *Education and Training for Full Employment.* New York: Columbia University Press, 1967. 264 pages.

Woodley, Alan, and others. *Choosing to Learn: Adults in Educa-*

tion. Milton Keynes, England: Society for Research into Higher Education and Open University Press, 1987. 202 pages.

Woodyard, Ella. *Culture at a Price.* Studies in the Social Significance of Adult Education in the United States, no. 23. New York: American Association for Adult Education, 1940. 125 pages.

Workers in Adult Education: Their Status, Recruitment, and Professional Training. Strasbourg, France: Council of Europe, 1966. 102 pages.

World Conference on Adult Education, Cambridge, 1929. London: World Association for Adult Education, 1930. 556 pages.

World Education Report, 1991. Paris: Unesco, 1991. 149 pages.

The World of Literacy: Policy, Research, and Action. Ottawa: International Development Research Centre, 1979. 128 pages.

Woytanowitz, George M. *University Extension, 1885–1915: The Early Years in the United States.* Iowa City, Iowa: National University Extension Association, 1974. 171 pages.

Yearbook of Adult and Continuing Education. Chicago: Marquis Academic Media. Issued annually from 1975–76 to 1980–81.

Yeaxlee, Basil A. *Spiritual Values in Adult Education.* 2 vols. Oxford, England: Oxford University Press, 1925. Vol. 1, 320 pages; vol. 2, 455 pages. (*X*)

Yeaxlee, Basil A. *Lifelong Education: A Sketch of the Range and Significance of the Adult Education Movement.* London: Cassell, 1929. 168 pages.

Young, Michael, and others. *Distance Teaching and the Third World: The Lion and the Clockwork Mouse.* New York: Routledge & Kegan Paul, 1980. 249 pages.

Youngman, Frank. *Adult Education and Socialist Pedagogy.* London: Croom Helm, 1986. 273 pages.

Zelko, Harold P. *The Business Conference: Leadership and Participation.* New York: McGraw-Hill, 1969. 290 pages.

Zoll, Allen A. *Dynamic Management Education.* (2nd ed.) Reading, Mass.: Addison-Wesley, 1969. 502 pages.

Name Index

Subject Index

A

Academy for Educational Development, 247

Administration, and program design, 287–288

Adult basic education (ABE), and literacy, 196, 201–202, 205, 208

Adult education: approaches to, 205; as body of knowledge and practice, 70–77; characteristics of, 72; concepts of, 7, 22, 48, 68; impact measures for, 90–91; models of, 74; philosophy of, 60–70; practice of, 265–317; radical, 262–263; residential, 295–299

Adult Education Association (AEA), 43–44

Adult Education Committee (United Kingdom), 17

Adult education councils, and coordination, 83–85

Adult education field: achievements of, 318–321; adult educators in, 59–97; adult learners in, 98–119; and aspects of adult life, 226–228; aspects of literature of, 1–119; bibliographies on, 55–57; biographies in, 30–33; comprehensive works on, 37–58; as ecosystem, 321; essays on, 51–55; establishment of, 15–21; final words on, 35–36, 57–58, 318–321; future of, 321; general histories of, 3–5; general treatments on, 37–42; goals of, 193–264; handbooks on, 42–45; history of, 3–36; internationally, 14, 19–20, 22, 23, 29–30, 31, 41, 42, 45, 49–51, 57; and libraries, 163–172; life-span learning reorientation of, 22–30; precursor institutions in, 5–14; providers in, 121–192; summations of, 33–35; surveys of, 45–51

Adult educators: and adult education as body of knowledge and practice, 70–77; analysis of concerns of, 59–97; background on, 59–60; and comparative education, 91–96; counseling, referral, and promotion by, 81–87; development of, 80–81; and evaluation, 87–91; final word on, 96–97; and leaders and leadership, 77–81; motivations of, 98–99; and philosophy of adult education, 60–70

Adult learners: age and, 114–118, 248–249; aspects of, 98–119; background on, 98–99; demographic characteristics of, 101–103; as educationally disadvantaged, 107–110; final word on, 118–119; goals related to aspects of life of, 226–264; learning skills of, 283–286; motivations of, 104–107; needs and interests of, 110–113; participation rates for, 99–101; teaching methods

Please remember that this is a library book,
and that it belongs only temporarily to each
person who uses it. Be considerate. Do
not write in this, or any, library book.

Date Due

APR 4 '01			
AP 10 '0			
AP 11 '05			

BRODART, CO.   Cat. No. 23-233-003   Printed in U.S.A.